The
World Atlas of
CHEESE

The World Atlas of CHEESE

by Nancy Eekhof-Stork

English-language edition edited by
Adrian Bailey

PADDINGTON
PRESS LTD

THE TWO CONTINENTS
PUBLISHING GROUP

© 1976 Spectrum Amsterdam, for text and illustrations.
© 1976 Paddington Press Ltd., for English-language edition.

Produced by Spectrum Amsterdam International Publishing,
Amsterdam, The Netherlands.

Phototypeset by Tradespools Ltd, Frome, Somerset.
Printed by Smeets Offset, Weert, The Netherlands.

Library of Congress Cataloging in Publication Data

Eekhof-Stork, N   M
   The world atlas of cheese.

   Bibliography : p.
   Includes indexes.
   1. Cheese.   2. Cheese – Varieties.   I. Title.
SF271.E34   1976   641.3'7'3   76-2170
ISBN 0-8467-0133-2

IN THE UNITED STATES
PADDINGTON PRESS LTD
TWO CONTINENTS PUBLISHING GROUP

IN THE UNITED KINGDOM
PADDINGTON PRESS LTD

IN CANADA
distributed by
RANDOM HOUSE OF CANADA LTD

IN AUSTRALIA & NEW ZEALAND
distributed by
ANGUS & ROBERTSON PTY LTD

Contents

Maître Corbeau, sur un arbre perché,
Tenait en son bec un fromage . . .
Jean de la Fontaine, FABLES

Introduction

Cheese – one of our most basic, nourishing and flavorful foods – is found in nearly every part of the world, not only in quantity but in enormous variety: from the reindeer cheese of Lapland and the yak's milk cheese of Nepal to a long list of international favorites such as Cheddar and Brie, Gouda and Gorgonzola, Roquefort, Feta and Parmesan.

Cheese is very much the product of a given land and its people. Indeed, the entire range of the world's cheeses is due not only to man's inventiveness, but to a host of other factors that make up the environment he lives in: climate, soil, vegetation, altitude, the state of the area's economic development, the kind of milk-producing animals available, even national taste and customs.

The making of cheese is a domestic skill that became an art, an art that became an industry. Most of the prominent national cheese types have gradually evolved from traditional farmhouse methods. The successful combination of art and industry has resulted in the manufacture of durable, high-quality cheeses capable of being produced on a large scale and transported over long distances without much loss of original character. Yet there remain hundreds, perhaps thousands of small, rural types that never reach the big markets, cheeses that have been made for centuries in secluded and remote valleys or in high alpine meadows.

Cheese as an everyday item means different things to different people. In Provence, in the south of France, it is probably a small, white, goat's milk cheese wrapped in chestnut leaves, called a Banon – delicious with a glass of rosé. In Somerset, England, it is likely to be a Cheddar, eaten with bread and a glass of beer. In the United States, it may also be Cheddar – but a Cheddar from Wisconsin, to be enjoyed with New York or California wine. In Denmark the choice is Samsø; in Holland, Gouda or Edam; in Mexico, Queso Fresco, flavored perhaps with a sprinkling of chili powder. With the growing number of gourmet cheese shops springing up in many areas, it is possible to sample both staple and gourmet varieties from all over the world.

THE WORLD ATLAS OF CHEESE sets out to explore the world of cheese in its entirety. In the country-by-country survey that forms the major part of this atlas, virtually all cheeses – from the most familiar to the most obscure – are described in their national context: how the climate and geography of an area affects the local dairy industry; how the various national cheeses originated; how they are made, packaged and sold; how they taste, look and smell; how they can be enjoyed. In addition, data panels for most of the countries provide vital information on specific cheeses, their weight, consistency, rind formation, fat content, etc. The text is supplemented by an abundance of drawings and photographs, plus a series of cheese maps and production diagrams detailing the manufacture of several major cheese types (Emmental, Cheddar, Gouda, Camembert and Cottage Cheese).

We have also provided special sections at the beginning and end of the book which deal with the more practical aspects of the world of cheese. Particularly helpful are the sections entitled "Cheese in Your Home" and "Cheese and Wine," where detailed information is given for preparing cheese boards, hosting cheese and wine parties, and selecting complementary cheeses and wines. Cooks should especially enjoy the recipe section, with its more than 45 international cheese dishes; and for the more daring, there's a section entitled "Make Your Own Cheese." A general overview of the history of cheese and cheesemaking from earliest times, of modern milking techniques and milk preparation, and of the nutritional value of cheese can be found in the opening sections.

The popularity of cheese in the world's larder is growing at a remarkable rate. With this in mind, THE WORLD ATLAS OF CHEESE is dedicated to cheeselovers everywhere, in the hopes that it will widen their horizons, whet their appetites, and add to their enjoyment of one of the world's most basic and sumptuous foods.

History of cheese and cheesemaking

The history of cheese only becomes fascinating, and understandable, when viewed against the history of the mammal and its milk: a history reaching back before man. The animals lived wild, multiplied and suckled their young, fighting a battle of life and death with other animals, and with nature itself. Man came and killed them for their meat; later he recognized the advantages of taming and domesticating them and relied on them for many purposes. The domestic animals helped with the heavy work. They produced dung, both a fertilizer and a fuel. When necessary, the animals could be slaughtered and eaten. They bred in captivity. They gave milk. This all happened many thousands of years before the Christian era. Where and when man started milking and making cheese for the first time is a supposition based on archeological discoveries.

Early milking

Up to now the oldest pictorial evidence comes from Mesopotamia (*c.*3500-2800 B.C.). The beautiful relief of Al Ubaid and a stamp seal from the Jemdet Nasr era show how the Sumerians milked their cattle and handled the milk. In Egypt, in the tomb of Horus-aha, second king of the first dynasty (*c.*3000-2800 B.C.), pots were found with what chemical analysis has virtually proved to be the remains of cheese. Cheese is also mentioned in hieroglyphic texts. The

LEFT: A beautiful Assyrian relief from the palace of Sennacherib, showing a man with a herd of cattle.

LEFT: A scene from Homer's *Odyssey*: Odysseus, clinging to a ram, escapes from the cave of the cyclops Polyphemus, the one-eyed shepherd and cheesemaker. Homer also describes how Polyphemus made his cheese, an early type of the popular Greek Feta.

LEFT: Twelfth-century dairy workers, one with a butter churn, another milking two cows and the third a goat. The goat's milk was probably used to make cheese.

Die Landleüt Heluctiæ habēd dreyerley gewerb/etlich den Acker-bauw/ vnd das ist der gröste teil : die anderen bau-wend den weyn : die dritten / deren auch gar vil ist/ vmb alle gebirg erneerend sich allein des vychs/des sy so vil habend / das nit die weyber allein / sonder starcke menner vnd knecht die küy melckend/käß vñ ziger machend. Die werdend genennt Sennen / jre wonungen vnd werckstatt Señhütten/ɾc. Herumb der merteil käß vñ schmaltz zůbereitet werdēd/dar-zů kein frauwen hand kumpt/ɾc.

newest archeological discoveries have been made in Africa. Cave paintings in the Libyan Sahara, very like those in Spain and France, show what appears to be milk processing, and date from the period 5500-2000 B.C. The origin of these Sahara tribes is still an open question. Did they already live here in prehistoric times. Did they tame their animals and learn to use their milk? Or was Asia their original homeland and did they come to Africa as nomad shepherds, bringing with them knowledge of milking? The Sahara was certainly not as arid in those days. There was sufficient pasture for cows, sheep or goats. But, unfortunately, after the period around 2500 B.C. nothing more has been found to shed further light on how these tribes lived. Was their herdsmen's existence no longer possible there? Were they forced to look for new grazing lands? These facts are not known.

The continual movement of tribes looking for better living conditions was usual and often assumed the pro-portions of large-scale migrations. Indo-European peoples probably came from the Asian steppes to the Dnieper valley, and then spread, from about 3000-2000 B.C., further over the Balkans, Northern Europe and Asia.

It is possible that the Indo-Euro-peans introduced their knowledge of cheese to Europe, or that tribes already there knew about it earlier. The Basques, for example, perhaps the only pre-Indo-European race left on the Continent, already had words for cheese and whey. In southeastern Europe indications have been found that seem to strengthen the hypoth-esis that milking in Macedonia and Thessaly first took place in 6500-5000 B.C. Thus is the earliest history of milking and cheesemaking shrouded in unsolved mysteries; the answers may never be revealed.

However this may be, it is certain that the perforated pots dating from the Bronze Age (3000-1000 B.C.) were used for making cheese. The classical writers supply ample evidence of the fact that when the Greek and Roman empires were at the height of their glory, cheese was a very well-known and popular daily food, and certainly nothing new. From these sources we know that throughout the Roman occupied territories the preparation of cheese was being perfected.

ABOVE: Woodcut from *Schweizer Chronik* [Swiss Chronicles] by J. Stumpf, 1548. The text says that many Swiss live from dairying, and "... they have so many cattle that not only the wo-men, but the strong men and servants milk them and make cheese."

Caseus Kß.

LEFT: A market cheese vendor in fifteenth-century Germany. Woodcut from *Hortus Sanitatis*, printed in Mainz, hometown of the famous printer Gutenberg.

As for Asia, it is known that cattle were kept in the Indus Valley, but no pictures have been found of actual milking. The mammals that are repre-sented have small udders and are unlikely to have been milked. The first references to milking date from a period after the arrival of Indo-European settlers on the upper reaches of the Indus, who were accus-tomed to drinking milk and to eating cheese. Later they moved to the Ganges Valley where they influenced tribes who knew nothing about milk-ing. Asia, however, has never become a great dairy region, partly because the Hindu and Buddhist religions con-sider the cow a sacred animal, using milk and dairy produce as offerings. Dairy produce has never been a day-to-day food in this area.

Some like it...

Over the whole world there have re-mained areas where no milking cattle are kept or where no milking is done, for very different reasons. Some peoples have always thought it morally wrong to withhold the milk from the animals' own young. Many had religious objections. Others did not like the smell or taste of milk, refusing to touch it if they could help it. The food value of milk was not always appreciated by those who had other sources of proteins and fat, especially meat. Lastly, in areas worked very intensively for a certain crop, farmers could not afford to keep more cattle than absolutely necessary, and then only as draught animals. The Chinese, for instance, concentrated on rice growing, and regarded milk as nothing but a sickly secretion unfit for human consumption.

Over the centuries, the borders vanished between the areas where milk was used and where it was not. Migra-tions of peoples and foreign influences paved the way for hitherto unknown products like milk and cheese. There was only one large land mass – the Americas – where milk and cheese remained absolutely unknown until the Europeans arrived.

Cheese and cheesemaking

How cheese was prepared cannot be established archeologically, neither can the equipment used, but we may assume that all over the world, wherever milking was discovered, the art of cheesemaking was learned very

9

soon after. Originally, this is likely to have been sour-milk cheese. Everywhere milk will spontaneously turn sour, especially in hot countries and in those with a moderate climate, and the increased acidity will curdle the milk separating it into flocculated proteins, fat and fluid whey. This must have happened countless times, and it is but a small step to pour the thickened mass in plaited baskets, or in perforated pots. The remaining fluid could thus be removed and a sort of fresh acid-curd cheese was achieved. Methods varied from country to country. The rough gourd in which some cheesemakers soured the milk gave it a special flavor, as did the wicker basket that others used; the casks used by the Mongols were never cleaned, so that the remaining bacteria soured the milk quicker.

The discovery of rennet

The curdling of milk with rennet (a curdling agent prepared from the stomachs of animals) must be credited to luck more than to Aristeus, Bacchus or Pan. According to Greek mythology, the gods of Olympus decided to make the lucky mortals a gift of everlasting value by teaching them the making of cheese.

Of course, there is probably some truth in the story of the Arab who passed through the desert with his caravan and found that the milk he was carrying with him, contained in a dried sheep's stomach, had been curdled better and quicker than ever before. Herdsmen always have animal skins handy in which milk can be kept. After slaughtering his young cattle, primitive man may have examined the stomach, and especially the partly digested milk, which led to further experiments. The next step would be to hang a strip of a lamb's stomach, or any other still-sucking animal, in milk, just to see what happened. In some such way, and with a little luck, the curdling power of animal rennet may have been discovered. Even in our days of chemistry and technology, no better substitute for this natural renneting material has been found. Other cheesemakers discovered the curdling properties of certain plants or vegetable juices in the same accidental way.

Removal of most of the moisture made the cheese firmer and improved its keeping qualities, particularly when it was pressed, dried in the sun and

ABOVE: An early Italian delicatessen, selling meat and cheese. Fresco from the castle of Issogne in the Valle d'Aosta, dating from the fifteenth century.

salted. This proved to be a very welcome development for the wandering nomads, as well as for cheese traders.

The great discoveries were now made, although the chemical and physical principles upon which they rested remained unknown. Individual recipes and working methods evolved, invariably on a trial-and-error basis, and their success was determined by many variables: milk, rennet, temperature, acidity, curd quality, degree of salt, pressure, etc. Knowledge was handed down from father to son, mother to daughter, people to people.

RIGHT: A rare Japanese painting, showing the Dutch colony at Decima (Nagasaki). Dairy cows must have been curiosities to the Japanese, who did not know any form of dairying. The Dutch held a trade monopoly from 1609 to 1854, as Japan was closed to all other foreigners.

At the beginning of our era, in the markets of Rome, countless different cheese types were sold: either soft, fresh, or hard cheeses, prepared with milk from cow, sheep or goat. Julius Caesar wrote of the Germans that their food for the greater part consisted of milk, cheese and meat. In numerous European countries cheese was being made, and marketed outside their own borders.

After the fall of the Roman Empire and the decline of civilization, the history and development of cheese suffered a long period of obscurity.

A new beginning

With the spread of Christianity, monasteries were founded throughout the Western world. The monastic orders, apart from their religious mission, set themselves additional tasks. In the early Middle Ages, they were almost the only centers of cultural enterprise. They also cultivated the fields, nursed sick people, lodged pilgrims, looked after cattle and made cheese. It was the monks who gave European cheesemaking a new start by passing their precious experience and knowledge to others. Famous cheese varieties, such as the ancestors of today's Port-Salut, came from their monasteries.

Following the reign of Charlemagne (742-814), when great advances were made in all fields, a new stimulus appeared that greatly influenced the history of cheese.

LEFT: A dairy farmer from the north of Holland in his cheesemaking room. Note the Gouda and Edam shapes. Usually it was the farmer's wife who was responsible for the cheesemaking.

BELOW: An idyllic farm scene, taken from *Herbal*, by the Italian naturalist Pierandrea Mattioli, from the sixteenth century. *Plus ça change . . .*

ABOVE: Still life with cheese, by the Dutch painter Floris Claesz van Dijck. Although painted in 1613, the cheeses are probably similar to those of today. Still-life painting was long and laborious – the cheeses and the bread have begun to deteriorate, dry and crack.

The Viking trade

The Viking expeditions started as trading expeditions, but degenerated too often into plunderings and invasions. Expeditions under Knut the Great (1016) brought the knowledge of Scandinavian cheesemaking to the Baltic countries, to England, Normandy, the area of the Volga and the Black Sea, and to Byzantium. They re-established forgotten trade contacts with northern and southern Europe, founded trading posts in Novgorod and Kiev and demonstrated the advantages of sea trading.

The Crusades (1096-1270) also had their influence. Contact with the superior Byzantine and Arab cultures brought a new outlook. Cheese was among the things affected by the resulting cultural revaluation and the Crusaders had had a taste of interesting foreign varieties. At the same time international trading and exchange were very much strengthened, so that cheese recipes and cheesemaking methods no doubt found their way to foreign regions, thus giving the trade a welcome impetus. In the eleventh century Byzantium reached its height of prosperity, but after its downfall, commerce shifted to Venice. Italian markets became centers of world trade and of the traffic between East and West. Venetian ships carried on the lucrative business; Dutch merchants became ship owners, specializing in freight, which they later completely dominated in the Mediterranean. In all respects life and prosperity of medieval towns depended on foreign trade. German merchants towns founded the Hanseatic league and developed into mighty commercial states, sailing the seas in all directions with their ever bigger and faster merchant ships, armed against pirates and competitors.

World trade spread out over the North Sea, Baltic Sea, the Mediterranean and the Atlantic. The Age of Discovery began and the New World was colonized. Asia, and especially East India, proved a treasure house for the greedy Europeans. People moved from country to country and from continent to continent, and the settling of experienced cheesemakers in other countries meant the introduction of new varieties. Large cities in many countries held regular markets and fairs, which were visited by foreign traders with their products. The guilds came into being with their famous guild-halls in the big trade centers of northern France, England and the Netherlands.

With the growth of the cities, the need for good cheese as a general food increased enormously. Since it was one of the accepted international commercial products, every cheese-producing country aimed at increased production, even if it was not enough to meet home demand. Yet they were spurred on by the possibility of selling abroad, and that foreign varieties might be more attractive than the home variety.

As far as cheese preparation methods are concerned, an important difference sprang up between those countries having good cattle and pastures and also sea and river ports – essential for successful exports – and those countries where production was battling against unfavorable circumstances. The first had to make cheese that was easily transportable – cheese whose quality was not affected by travel, and that would be resistant to changing weather conditions and temperatures. The others stuck to the same old methods, making their

LEFT: In spite of her frequent appearance throughout history in romantic folk song, a milkmaid's life was hard, her contribution to the farm work equal to that of a man. A milkmaid in nineteenth-century Normandy.

ABOVE: The nineteenth century was an age of invention and technical progress. This is an early Danish milking machine, an illustration from the *British Journal of the Royal Agricultural Society* in 1892.

BELOW: A rural aspect of central Paris, when you could buy fresh milk from the goat herd – you stood by while the goats were milked.

attractive but perishable cheeses to be sold in the immediate surroundings.

For Dutch Edam cheese, for instance, in demand all over the world, a cheese cloth was applied early on to form a well-closed rind under the press. The cheeses were treated with extra care and primitive cheese presses were replaced by heavier ones able to apply pressure more evenly, which again improved the quality of the end product. Transportation and storage had to be done according to precise prescriptions. Yet cheeses were not always of satisfactory quality, and the quality variations were great. The adulteration of foodstuffs was commonplace in the days before official regulations and control were instituted. To reach high quality standards, the cheesemaker needed great experience, feeling and love for his craft. Cheesemaking was to remain an art rather than a science or a technical process until the twentieth century.

Sudden modernization
It seems as if cheesemaking, hardly changed during the last eight to ten centuries, tried all at once to make up the leeway and became an ultra-

BELOW: A French butter and cheese factory before the turn of the century. The milk is skimmed and churned, while a steam engine drives all the machinery and heats the milk.

modern industry. A series of exciting discoveries in the bacteriological, chemical and technical fields set off this rapid modernization.

The great German chemist and agriculturalist Justus von Leibig had already determined in 1836 that the fermentation of cheese could be explained in purely scientific terms. Twenty years later Louis Pasteur, working in the brewery town of Lille, discovered how microorganisms brought about the fermentation process in beer. He applied his theories to lactic fermentations, and also the fermentation of wines, showing how heat could destroy the organisms, thus slowing down the biochemical process. In 1876 he published his findings, recommending that milk be heated in order to destroy the harmful bacteria, and at the same time delaying the development of the useful bacteria. Pasteur's research was primarily concerned with the fermentation of beer and wine. His co-worker, the Russian biologist Ilya Metchnikov, occupied himself with milk acid bacteria, their fermentation, and the pasteurization of milk. Soon the pasteurization process became widely adopted.

Pasteur also distinguished two types of bacteria: the anaerobic (those which do not need air for multiplication), and the aerobic bacteria (those which do need air). He showed how certain forms of bacteria can form highly resistant spores, findings that were confirmed by the physicist John

Tyndall, who discovered spores that were almost totally resistant to heat. Following the great advances made in the field of biochemistry, pure starter cultures and standardized rennets were prepared in laboratories. The mysteries of the ripening process and the complex actions of taste and aroma-forming bacteria were gradually unraveled.

These discoveries, and the many others that were bound to follow, gave the dairy industry the scientific backing that it needed. Not only could the production of the well-established cheeses be improved, but uniform quality and excellence were almost guaranteed. Furthermore, the laboratory experiments led to the development of entirely new cheese types.

At the same time, the nineteenth century was the age of industry and invention. Cheesemaking was not the only traditional craft to change almost beyond recognition when influenced by technological progress. The small, cooperative or private enterprises had simple beginnings: they were equipped with a steam engine to provide heat and to drive the machinery; but the basic cheesemaker's skills were unchanged. These early factories have now given way to ultramodern, mammoth industries, where cheese is made from milk in one continuous process, fully automated and controlled not by skilled cheesemakers but by operators. Thanks to the specialized research carried out by scientific institutions and by the industry, the quality of the cheese made in these production units is of uniform and quite high quality, even though it may lack the individual charm of the farmhouse cheese.

The interesting thing is that farmhouse cheese, produced and marketed on a small scale, has not been eradicated by industrialized cheesemaking. Factory cheese was needed to cope with rising demand; farmhouse cheese has remained in existence because its qualities, uniqueness and individuality have always been prized and recognized by gourmets everywhere. Farmhouse cheese has surely profited from research and technological improvements as well, and it is every bit as good, maybe better, than the same cheese produced a hundred years ago. It is bound to keep its own specific place in the cheese assortment of most countries.

ABOVE: Cheese presses became stronger and sturdier. This type in cast iron is an American improvement, patented in 1848.

LEFT: This dog-drawn milk cart was a feature of everyday life in Belgium less than two generations ago.

13

Milking cattle

The working relationship between men and animals stretches far back into prehistory. We cannot say with accuracy where and when the first animals provided milk for man, nor when the first oxen pulled the first load, or which animals provided a pelt to clothe primitive human hunters.

Animals that once lived wild were first tamed and then turned into domestic helpers, into draught animals pulling carts and plows, and some were coaxed to give their surplus milk that had been produced for their young. This was drunk by man, and

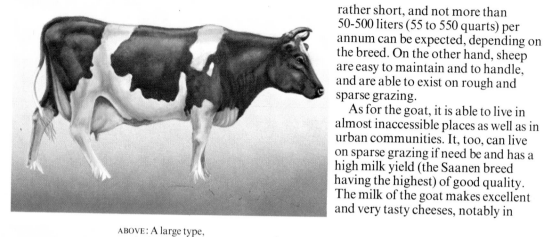

ABOVE: A large type, marked with broad areas of black and white, the Frisian has a very high milk-producing capacity. It is well established in Western Europe, Great Britain, the United States (as the subtype Holstein-Frisian), Canada, Australia, New Zealand and South Africa.

rather short, and not more than 50-500 liters (55 to 550 quarts) per annum can be expected, depending on the breed. On the other hand, sheep are easy to maintain and to handle, and are able to exist on rough and sparse grazing.

As for the goat, it is able to live in almost inaccessible places as well as in urban communities. It, too, can live on sparse grazing if need be and has a high milk yield (the Saanen breed having the highest) of good quality. The milk of the goat makes excellent and very tasty cheeses, notably in

later made into cheese and butter. At a rough guess, the first animals may have been milked in the Pleistocene age, about one million years ago.

It is interesting to speculate whether or not mare's milk cheese was ever produced; certainly at one time horses were milked, but this practice has now ceased. Today, the camel provides many nomad tribes with their milk. No other animals can replace it in the arid, desert climate. It can carry loads up to 150 kg (330 lbs) and can travel at roughly 3-4 km (1.8-2.4 miles) per hour, steadily and indefatigably. It is a big drinker, downing 100 liters (110 quarts) of water in one go, which it can reserve for long periods. The camel gives milk for two years after calving: the first year to the calf and the second year to man.

Sheep, too, are ancient providers of milk and are also valued for their wool and meat. In France, the Balkans, Spain and Italy sheep are milked to make very special cheeses, such as the French Roquefort, made from the milk of the famous Larzac breed, sheep with small, intelligent heads.

The lactation period during which the ewe can be milked is generally

ABOVE: The milk of the fawn or cream-colored Jersey cow is extremely rich in butter fat. The animals are relatively small; milk production is between 2,500-3,500 kg (5,500-7,700 lbs) yearly. Jerseys are often crossbred with native stock to improve the fat content of the latter's milk. It is the most important breed in Australia and New Zealand.

ABOVE: Ayrshire cattle are either red and white or almost pure white, and of relatively small stature, with almost vertical horns. The breed has a wide distribution, particularly in Great Britain, the United States and Canada.

ABOVE: Like the Jersey, the Guernsey cow was originally bred on the Channel Islands. Guernseys are the larger of the two, yet still fairly small. They are found in England and the US.

France and in Italy, and goats are widespread in Africa, India, Turkey and Iran. Like the camel, both sheep and goats provide milk for nomad tribes, who are often obliged to be nomadic to follow their livestock to fresh and distant grazings. The Laplanders are also obliged to travel with their migratory reindeer, which yield a quantity of milk, some of which is made into a rare cheese.

The greater proportion of the world's cheeses are, however, made from cow's milk. In prehistoric times, in the woods of northern Europe, there lived herds of wild, long-haired bovines, probably the ancestors of the domestic cattle of today. Over a long period of time, men gradually discovered the advantages of cross-breeding, and thus introduced many varieties from which modern stocks have descended. But cross-breeding was not the only cause of numerous varieties. Climate, soil, food and drinking water also had their influence. Also, man made use of cattle for purposes other than dairying which influenced their development, so that shape, size and color widely diverged.

The modern cow was originally

BELOW: The Shorthorn is bred in two distinct types: a beef variety (also called the Durham) and a dual-purpose type known as the Dairy or Milking Shorthorn. The latter is kept primarily in Great Britain and the United States. Its importance tends to decrease because of its relatively low milk productivity. To many breeders, the beef and milk combination is their great advantage.

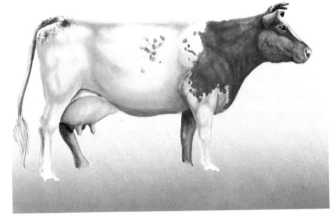

RIGHT: The Swiss Brown (Braunvieh) is one of the most famous cattle breeds. Although mainly a dairy breed, they are sometimes bred as a mixed type for their beef, as they are heavier and fleshier than many other breeds. Originating in Switzerland and characteristic of the Alpine landscape, the Braunvieh has spread to the United States and South American countries.

indigenous to Europe before colonists introduced it to other areas of the world. The colonists and their descendants cross-bred according to the environment and requirements, to produce either a milk type, a meat type, or both. Meat stocks are found mainly on the prairies and pampas of North and South America, where they are maintained in vast herds. The milking cattle of the dairy zones require more attention than do the meat stocks, the best milk producers are selected, and their yield increased by careful breeding and attention to their environment and feed. The composition of the milk from the various breeds differs considerably, and also from the various species, facts that have a decided influence on the preparation of cheese.

Milk production can only be gauged approximately. With the cow, for example, the milk yield is affected by the animal's food, whether the food comes from concentrates – maize, alfalfa, and so on – or from fresh grass and rich soil. Climate is also an influence: during a rainy period the milk yield is higher, while in periods of drought it decreases. The animal's life cycle is also important to the dairyman: towards the end of the milk-giving period the yield falls, but the milk is richer in dry matter. The soil gives the milk certain beneficial flavors – the soil in England's Cheshire meadows has noticeable salt deposits, affecting the flavor and structure of Cheshire cheese. The air contains microorganisms that end up in the milk and act on the cheese during ripening. These factors can be so influential that a really expert taster can often tell you where the cheese has been made, provided that the milk was not pasteurized.

ABOVE: Red and white Normandy cattle are the most common dairy breed in France. In Normandy alone there are more than 2.5 million head of this indigenous stock, each producing some 3,000 kg (6,600 lbs) of milk per year. The breed is thought to be a cross between local cattle and cattle introduced by the Vikings during the Middle Ages.

BELOW: Sheep and goats are very adaptable to areas where there is little or no meadowland, or where the terrain is mountainous. The milking breeds of sheep produce about 500 liters (550 quarts) a year, milk which is remarkably rich in fat and proteins.

BELOW RIGHT: The goat is to be found everywhere in the world, on the steppes and in the deserts, on high mountains and around the towns. It yields approximately 500 to 800 liters (550 to 880 quarts) of milk per year, with a higher fat content than the milk from most cattle.

Other milk-producing bovines include the yak, the zebu and the water buffalo. The yak lives in the high Himalayas, often above 4,000 m (13,200 ft), where it survives the icy cold and snow. For the Tibetans and some Nepalese, the yak is the sole source of milk, but on the lower slopes, where the climate is marginally more temperate, the yak is crossed with the zebu, to form the hybrid chowrie.

The zebu is found mostly in India, East Asia and Africa, in fact in all tropical areas, where they are called "the children of the sun." They can be recognized by the large, fatty hump near the shoulders and the thick folds of skin under the neck. There are many breeds; some are good milkers, others not so productive. Cross-breeding with the best European cows produces a higher milk yield but also destroys, after several generations, many of the zebu's unique qualities.

The water buffalo prefers a cool bath now and then, wallowing about in the thick river mud, yet they too are well adjusted to a hot climate and are important milk providers for India, China, the Philippines, Turkey, Egypt, southern Italy and the Balkans.

The dairy farmer's job

Are they still to be found, those rustic farms, where the milk pails jangle early every morning and the cows are persuaded, by gentle word and experienced hand, to part with their milk? Are there still farms where the farmer rolls up his trousers to "tread" the curd; where glistening, yellow cheese lies on display in cool airy cellars with a cross above the window to keep the evil spirits at bay?

Milk churns can still be seen at intervals on country roads, standing like soldiers in a row, waiting to be picked up and taken to the dairy factory. Donkeys, one churn on each side, still carry milk to some market center. And, way up on the slopes of the Himalayas, Sherpa women are still milking yaks to make butter and cheese.

Yet, change is always just round the corner: for better or for worse depending how you view progress. One thing is certain, all over the world the dairy farming business is changing. Many farms now have hundreds of heads of cattle, farms that are run by a new style of farmer, with the attitudes and abilities of a corporate managing director.

The animal's rights
A long time ago, Hoard, the editor of the American journal *Hoard's Dairyman* used to say: "Treat your cow as you would want to be treated if you were a cow." When the animal becomes merely a means of production,

ABOVE: The dairy farmer's job in biblical times. The print refers to Deuteronomy 32:14: "Butter of kine, and milk of sheep, with fat lambs and rams of the breed of Bashan, and goats with the fat of kidneys of wheat; and thou didst drink the pure blood of the grape."

the striving for profitability can create the risk that the needs of the animal are conveniently forgotten. But they must not be ignored. When a cattle owner interests himself in the behavior of his herd as well as their physical characteristics – he does not have to be an ethologist to do that – he can usually tell if they are both healthy and happy. And he will recognize that high milk yield is not the only barometer of an animal's well-being. Both as an investment and a living creature, the milking animal needs and deserves proper care.

Firstly, she wants a proper "home," a place that is big enough, well ventilated and clean. In some countries the weather is so good that no stables are needed. On the other hand, on modern farms, cattle are not milked outside anymore, but are driven to a special milking shed or milking area where the milking machine is waiting for them. In all cases good housing is important.

All milking animals need a set, regular routine, and a peaceful situation during milking. Noise frightens them and the milk is held back. Yodelling, as the Swiss do, they seem to like. And cows are very keen on a cattle biscuit before milking begins.

Food for thought
Secondly, the animal needs proper food. The modern farmer has come a long way from that comfortable, well-loved figure of the romantic novel. Even when he has the right economic knowledge, he must be sufficiently good as a manager to put a policy into practice. The obvious business objective is to get a high price for his milk. He can only do that if the quality is also high. The right fodder and the right amounts of fodder per animal are of overriding importance. An average cow eats 60-75 kg (132-165 lbs) of grass per day, with enough food value to yield 15-22 liters (33-48.4 quarts) of milk. Some cows produce even more milk and these need additional roughage and concentrates.

ABOVE: A corner of the living room of a farmhouse in Les Landes, France. The women of the household feed the cattle through an opening in the wall between the living room and the cowshed. The picture probably dates from the late nineteenth century.

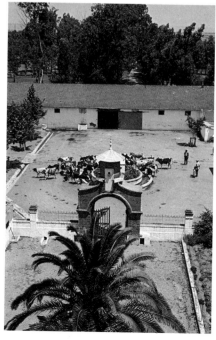

LEFT: A well-organized dairy farm in Algeria. In countries with a hot climate the farmer has to meet different challenges than those in the milking areas of more temperate zones.

Unless this is produced on the farm, it must be bought outside, thus creating cost difficulties. The fodder must provide an exact balance with the animal's needs in relation to milk yield, the lactation period and gestation.

Research into the needs of the milking animal and into the properties of many foodstuffs has helped the farmer to select, from a wide variety of products, a balanced and efficient diet for his cows. This is of particular importance in those cases where he does not have enough pastureland available to turn his cattle out to graze all summer.

Another problem is feeding in winter, when no grass is available in moderate to cold climates. An enormous quantity of good hay, gathered in the summer, dried by the sun and stored in a dry place, has always been essential for the cattle to survive. Storage of fodder in silos, an American invention of the late nineteenth century, was an improvement; fodder stored in hermetically sealed containers underwent a light fermentation process, but kept its good qualities and was liked by the cows. The important thing however was that it improved the milk yield in winter (when milk is scarce because many cows are in their dry period prior to calving); besides it is less labor-intensive than traditional methods. There is, however, the risk of foreign smells in the milk and cheese when silo feeding is not done expertly.

Of course it would be throwing money away to give a cow more fodder

ABOVE: A modern, mobile milk wagon. The cows enter at one end, stand two by two while being milked and leave the wagon at the other end. Note the four tanks of the milking machine in the central passage: two for the animals at the left and, out of the picture, two on the right.

LEFT: A licensed milker at work in India, where all cattle are sacred to the Hindu religion.

than it needed for health and the required milk production. Water, an absolute essential, costs little in the productive dairy-farming countries. In hot and arid lands, water can be a very expensive commodity, affecting the entire cheesemaking process from the choice of cattle fodder right through to the manufacturing stages.

The good economist-farmer keeps a record of every animal's milk yield, fodder intake and other details. He selects the best milk givers for breeding. He may keep a bull for the purpose, or rely on artificial insemination, which means that sperm from a selected bull is introduced into the cow's uterus. Top quality cattle, when they fulfill all qualifications, are recorded in the national herd book.

Finally, it is essential to keep the cattle in good health. Over the centuries, farmers have done a wonderful job, treating their sick animals as best they could, finding practical remedies, and delivering calves without the help of today's specialized veterinary surgeons. But the fight against tuberculosis and other dreaded diseases such as foot and mouth disease can only be successful with the help of modern science. In the poorer countries, science needs to be backed by international aid programs and voluntary professional advice.

The right combination

The dairy farmer's income is dependent on the milk price he obtains, but this is determined mostly by economic factors outside his control. Since he works on small margins anyway, his economic position is a very vulnerable one. Many farmers try to diversify by looking for a supporting activity, e.g., arable, pig, or chicken farming. Making farmhouse cheese, rather than selling the milk to the cheese factory, is another possibility. It may well be more lucrative, farmhouse cheese being very much sought after. But problems of available labor and so on must be considered. Investments must be made, cheesemaking and storage rooms must be available, and the cheesemaker must be sure of the sales possibilities. Would it be worth it? These, and many other questions have to be closely examined before a start is made to enter, successfully, the cheesemaking profession, or to continue this difficult but rewarding craft.

Milk production

The udder of the cow develops under the influence of certain hormones when the animal reaches sexual maturity; but milk formation commences only after the birth of the first calf. Generally speaking, the cow is then two years old. In nature, milk production stops as soon as the young animal can absorb other food; but in cows kept as milking cattle, this lactation period lasts much longer, for approximately three hundred days, during which time the milk yield slowly reduces. This is followed by a dry period of some two months, which the cow certainly deserves.

Three months after the birth of her calf, if the cow has once again been inseminated, her body can concentrate on the development of the new offspring and gather strength for the next lactation period, which will begin with the birth of her next calf. During the first four days, the cow produces the yellowish colostrum, also called beestings or green milk, which contains everything needed to keep the new-born calf alive and to start its development. In some countries beestings is used in cooking. In Holland it was once kept to give a protective coating to Leiden cheeses, but it is otherwise useless for dairy purposes. After the colostrum period comes the "new milk," possessing a higher than average fat and protein content, which slowly reduces. The lactation period ends with the "old milk," when the fat content increases again to far above the average.

The udder
The udder consists of a left and right half, separated by a muscular band fixed to the pelvis and carrying the udder. This division can be seen much more clearly from the outside than the one between the front and rear quarters into which each udder half is divided. There is a complete separation between the four quarters: this has an advantage, for if one of them becomes infected the other three continue to produce milk normally.

Each quarter is provided with a nipple, or teat, with an opening at the end, sealed by a circular (sphincter) muscle; it opens by pressure (hand milking) or intermittent suction (calf or mechanical milker). Above the teat in each quarter there is a wider space, or udder system, acting as a reservoir for the milk produced. This is at the

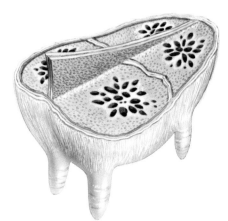

LEFT: Cross-section of a cow's udder. There are four quarters, each with a corresponding teat.

LEFT: Longitudinal section of the udder, showing two quarters with teats, udder system (where there is space for the storage of newly secreted milk) and gland tissue.

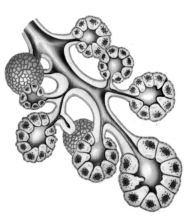

LEFT: Cluster of alveoli, the secretory cells which may be regarded as tiny milk factories. Milk is carried from them, via a system of channels, into the udders.

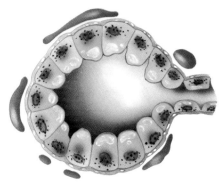

LEFT: Close-up of an alveolus. The glandular epithelium lining consists of secretory cells with the nucleus (dark) and milk constituents being formed (yellow). Probably some cells specialize in producing milk fat, others in milk sugar. The milk constituents are emptied into the central cavity (lumen) and leave via the outlet shown on the right.

receiving end of a number of channels or milk ducts which are fed by numerous narrow milk capillaries in the alveoli. These are arranged in clusters like bunches of grapes and together form the milk-producing gland tissue.

Milk production takes place in the secretory cells with which the inside of each alveolus is lined; the alveolus itself is surrounded by blood capillaries through which some "raw materials" for milk production are transported to the milk cells. Only a few milk components are taken directly from the blood, as most of the main components, such as fat, protein and milk sugar, are produced independently by the alveoli.

Milking
The cow secretes its milk under the influence of certain nerve stimuli, which in nature are mostly caused by the suction of the newborn calf. On the farm, cows are stimulated by artificial methods, such as giving them fodder concentrates, or by rubbing the udders. Here, milk secretion is based for the most part on habit, the so-called conditioned reflex: the process may even be triggered by rattling the milking buckets or starting the engine of the milking machine. The nerve stimuli travel via the central nervous system to the hypophysis, which reacts by adding the hormone oxytocin to the blood, the same substance which in childbirth contracts the muscles around the womb. Oxytocin contracts the muscles around the alveoli in the udder; all milk is pressed out of them and flows into the udder system from which it is milked.

If the cow is not stimulated in this way, milking cannot take place. In other words, the cow must be encouraged to allow the milk to flow. When the animal is uneasy or frightened, or is in pain, however, the milk withdraws. When this happens the effect of the oxytocin is neutralized by another hormone, adrenalin, which activates various body functions and stops milk production when milking is postponed too long. Dairy cows are usually milked twice a day, early in the morning and in the late afternoon, perhaps the two most important and carefully regulated periods in the routine of the dairy farm.

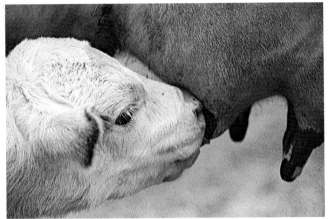

ABOVE: When a calf drinks, it both presses and sucks. In hand milking, a certain pressure by an experienced and sensitive hand is required.

ABOVE: In machine milking, the milk is drawn from the teat by intermittent suction. The cows are tied to a mobile milking machine brought into the pasture twice a day.

BELOW: Anatomy of a milk cow. Only those organs of special importance to milk production are illustrated.

A. Brain
B. Central nervous system
C. Heart

D. Aorta, the chief arterial trunk
E. Mammary artery

F. Intestine
G. Udder
H. Teats

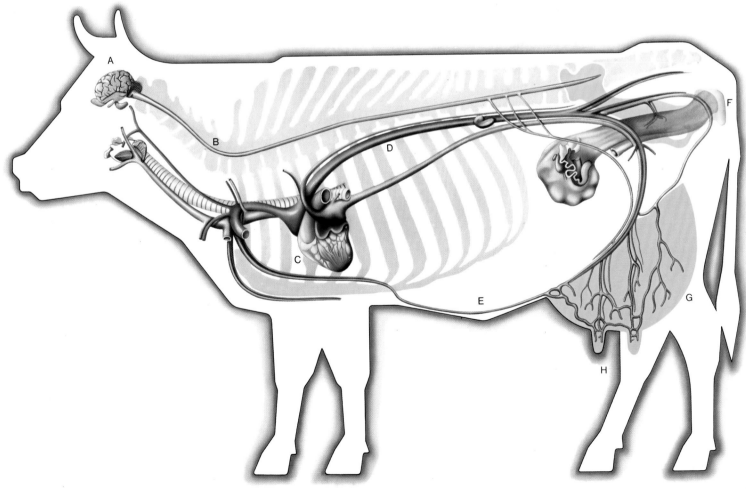

Milking and treatment of milk

Cattle are milked either by hand or by machine. In developed countries, with a steady increase in the size of herds, milking by machine is the more practical method. For farmers owning animals with a short lactation period and small milk yield, like sheep and goats, a milking machine is normally too high an investment, but there are exceptions. For example, the sheep that provide the milk for the famous Roquefort cheese are milked by machine, because automation is an economic advantage for the Roquefort producers.

Milking machines are more practical in the modern dairy, since they are both expedient and hygienic. When cows are milked by hand, each stream of milk that goes into the pail is in contact with the surrounding air in the milking shed and, to a lesser extent, the hands of the milker. With a machine this has little chance of happening.

Most modern dairy farmers have a cooling tank in which to store the milk until the mobile tanker arrives. It is inevitable – and desirable – that microorganisms inhabit the cheese milk, but a high concentration of organisms can mean the risk of a bad quality cheese for both the cheese farmer and the factory. For this reason, the fresh milk must remain at a low temperature, at which microorganisms can only develop slowly.

In recent years the biochemical structure of dairy milk has been the subject of considerable investigation. Antibiotics, such as penicillin, may interfere with the cheesemaking process, as may pesticides, the residues of which may be concentrated in the soil and thus in the grass upon which cattle feed. These investigations have led to increased national and international

LEFT: Hand milking a Frisian cow in a meadow. Milking by hand is an art, which used to be a part of the education of a farm child. With the advent of machine milking, the art is dying out. Hand milking should start slowly. When the cow begins to give well, it should be done vigorously but rhythmically.

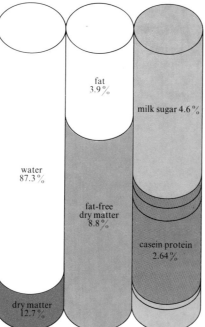

LEFT: This diagram shows the average composition of cow's milk. It tends to vary with breed, climate, the season, grazing conditions and other factors. There are also great individual differences.

fat 3.9%

milk sugar 4.6%

water 87.3%

fat-free dry matter 8.8%

albumen, globulin, other proteins 0.3%

serum protein 0.4%

casein protein 2.64%

citric acid salts 0-.15%

mineral salts 0.7%

dry matter 12.7%

standards governing the purity of milk.

The treatment of cheese milk

For many types of cheese the milk is partly skimmed. The creamy layer of the evening milk is ladled off, and the next day the skimmed milk is mixed with the fresh morning milk. Cheese made with partly skimmed milk has a lower fat content than whole milk cheese.

In the cheese factory the milk is not skimmed by a ladling process, as this is too slow and costly. Instead, a separator is employed which separates the milk into skimmed milk and cream. This skimmed product is then mixed with whole milk until the desired fat content is achieved. The fat content desired depends on a number of factors, but in general these proportions are followed: 1% fat in the milk gives a cheese of 20% fat; 2.25% gives a content of 40%; and 3.2% gives a cheese of 45%.

Bringing the milk to the right fat content is called standardizing. In most modern factories, before the fat content is determined, the milk must be pasteurized. Few cheese types are now made from raw milk, because of the many sources of contamination that exist between the cow and the factory, such as unhygienic milking, long transportation distances, wrong fodder and sick cows. All of these may introduce harmful bacteria into the cheese milk, and this is why milk is usually pasteurized.

The pasteurization process is named after the French chemist Louis Pasteur, who noticed that germs were destroyed in temperatures of 70°C (158°F) and above. Apart from the harmful bacteria, a great number of other microorganisms present in the

LEFT: Milking by hand. The milker takes the two front teats in his full fists. The top of the index finger squeezes and closes the teat cavity (left); the milk is pressed downwards by the subsequent pressure of the other fingers (center) and vigorous jets of milk stream into the pail (right). The rear quarters are the next to be milked.

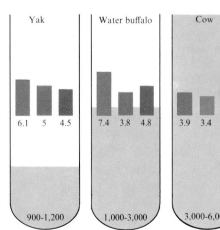

RIGHT: Modern carousel milking unit. The milker stands in the center, while the carousel moves slowly. Eight cows are milked at the same time.

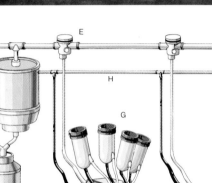

RIGHT: Diagram of a milking machine. The vacuum pump (left) maintains a partial vacuum and creates a sucking action against normal atmospheric pressure. In the teat cups (enlarged) the vacuum sucks the milk from the teats. The milk goes into an airtight vat via a tube or pipe, where air and milk are separated. From there it goes to storage churns, or to a large refrigerated tank to await collection.

A. Vacuum pump
B. Moisture separator
C. Regulator
D. Vacuum gauge
E. Vaccum pipe with connecting cocks
F. Pulsator
G. Teat cups
H. Milk pipe
J. Milk de-aerator
K. Storage vats

milk are also destroyed. Although the risk of turning out a defective cheese is thus largely eliminated, some bacteria are pretty persistent: they may survive the pasteurization treatment or leave spores behind them, the spores of butter acid bacteria, for example. The type of feed may also present a problem, especially when cattle have been fed with silo fodder, for the bacteria may remain in the milk, giving the cheese a rancid taste.

A disadvantage of pasteurization is that useful organisms are decimated, which tends to produce a cheese slightly more bland than one made from raw, unpasteurized milk. On the other hand, if the milk is overheated it loses some of its natural qualities and is also not good for cheesemaking.

In practice, the maximum pasteurization temperature may not exceed 75°C (167°F) and the milk may be held for a maximum of fifteen seconds at this temperature. After pasteurization the milk is cooled to the temperature needed for curdling, and at this stage is said to have been "pre-treated."

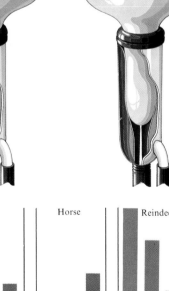

RIGHT: Detail of the teat cups. Because permanent suction would be painful to the cow, the installation includes a pulsator which alternates suction with normal pressure, in a rhythm of 44-46 strokes per minute. In the left-hand diagram, suction has been interrupted, atmospheric pressure enters the cup, the rubber lining folds together, and no milk is sucked from the teat. In the right-hand diagram the suction pipe (right) removes the air, the lining opens, and the vacuum in the milk pipe (center) draws off the milk.

RIGHT: This diagram shows the average composition and production of milk from various mammals.

 Milk fat in %

Proteins in %

Milk sugar in %

 Milk production per head per year in liters (1 liter = 1.1 quarts)

	Camel	Sheep	Goat	Horse	Reindeer	Yak	Water buffalo	Cow
fat/protein/sugar	5.4 3.9 5.1	7.4 5.5 4.8	4.5 2.9 4.1	1.5 2.1 5.7	16.9 11.5 2.8	6.1 5 4.5	7.4 3.8 4.8	3.9 3.4 4.6
production	750	300-500	500-800	2,000	30	900-1,200	1,000-3,000	3,000-6,000

The principles of cheesemaking

The technique of cheesemaking consists of removing the greater part of the water which makes up the bulk of the milk, while retaining the dry matter – proteins, milk fat and milk sugar, minerals, vitamins, and so on. With this process, ten volumes of milk can be reduced to about one volume of (semihard) cheese.

Fresh milk, if left standing long enough, turns sour and thickens by itself, producing a type of cheese that has been made for thousands of years. To make a good-quality cheese which can be kept for long periods of time, a more complex procedure is called for, requiring the use of a curdling agent such as rennet. Rennet curdles the milk, provided that the milk has been previously soured and is at the correct temperature. Souring is now done with a special starter culture.

Rennet is usually obtained from the stomach bag of young calves, and is stimulated by the calcium contained in the milk to convert the protein known as casein into an insoluble compound. In other words, rennet turns the milk into curd, which is the main element of cheese. Curd is a junket-like mass of insoluble dry matter, which before it is drained also contains a large proportion of whey, the name given to the water which has elements of sugar, minerals and fat.

The cheesemaker's task is to separate the whey from the curd particles, perhaps the most delicate part of the cheesemaking process. The curd must be cut very slowly and carefully, especially in the beginning, in order to prevent fat and curd particles escaping into the whey as it is being drained off. The separation between whey and curd is noticeable almost at once. For the fresh and soft types of cheese, the curd is hardly cut at all. For the hard varieties it is first cut into large pieces and then gradually into smaller ones, expelling as much whey as possible. Finally, a fairly solid mass of curd is obtained, which may be dried even further before being collected in molds and then pressed. With most types of cheese this is only half the process: cheeses acquire their proper texture and flavor only after a period of curing and ripening.

No two cheese types are made by exactly the same method: the endless variations are caused by differences in milk, curdling, cutting, draining, stirring and other techniques.

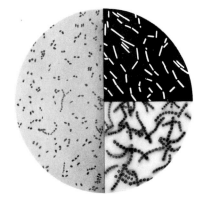

ABOVE: Prior to curdling, the cheese milk is soured by the addition of a starter. This micrograph shows the lactic acid bacteria it contains (left); the enlargements (right) reveal the existence of two distinct types: the rod-shaped (above) and the spherical (below). The bacteria convert the milk sugar into lactic acid and help the milk to coagulate.

BELOW: The curd is regularly cut and stirred. Here, the curd grains can be clearly seen. Depending on the recipe, part or almost all of the whey is run off.

ABOVE: A calculated amount of starter culture is added to the cheese milk. The milk must be brought to the right temperature (slightly different for each cheese type) before curdling.

ABOVE: A small quantity of rennet is added. This curdles the previously soured milk. The curdling time varies widely, according to the rennet strength and milk temperature.

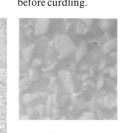

ABOVE: Close-up of the curd particles, showing their white, glossy texture. At this stage they are almost tasteless.

ABOVE: In the cheese vat, the curd is separated from the whey by pushing it to one side of the vat. The whey can then be run off.

RIGHT: The cheesemaker may collect the curd in a cheese cloth and allow more whey to drain away. For many cheese types, the wet curd is wrapped in muslin, put into a mold and pressed.

Cheese ripening

One of the most important phases in the cheese-forming process is the ripening period. When the curd has formed and the whey has drained, the cheese remains as a white mass with little or no flavor, and it is hard then to imagine how it could develop into a delicacy. During ripening, the salt spreads through the cheese, and the cheese also loses some of its moisture, becoming more solid and containing a higher proportion of dry matter with a more decided cheese taste. But at the same time a number of extremely complicated chemical and biological processes have been taking place.

In practice, experienced cheesemakers of the past always knew only too well how they could avoid or encourage certain developments. They knew how, but they didn't know why, and it was not until the twentieth century that a complete picture of the complex, biochemical processes within a ripening cheese became available.

Of the microorganisms present in cheese, the manufacturer needs the useful ones and tries to eliminate those harmful to the character and quality of the cheese. Milk acid bacteria are very useful microorganisms, and milk sugar is their favorite food, which they use and form into milk acid. The acid level that arises eventually makes the cheese more or less sterile, as a result of which the bacteria perish, but leave behind them a protein-consuming enzyme. Casein, the most important protein in cheese, contains no less than

LEFT: Constant attention is needed; here Stiltons are turned one by one to ensure a consistent degree of drying and ripening throughout the whole cheese.

BELOW: In a downstairs room in a Dutch cheese farm, the fine Gouda cheeses, glossy with their plastic coating, are laid out on wooden planks to ripen for a minimum of four weeks. Cheese dealers may let them ripen further.

LEFT: With soft cheeses the degree of ripeness is very easy to determine with certainty when the cheese is cut. When the body has ripened throughout, and no white chalky strip remains in the middle, the cheese is *à point*, as the French say – just right, like these specimens illustrated.

twenty-one amino acids, plus many other elements. As the protein decomposes these acids and elements are liberated throughout the cheese, to influence its taste and aroma. Ammonia may be formed, and its pungent odor is easily detected in some types.

The milk fat is also subjected to chemical processes. A small part of it is split by another enzyme, and the resulting fatty acids further contribute to the final flavor of the cheese. Some bacteria, living on the milk sugar, produce gas, which cannot escape from the paste and so forms holes, such as those characteristic of Emmental.

Apart from this natural ripening process, specific cultures can be added to the cheese, perhaps to encourage the formation of a white mold flora on the rind, as with Camembert. Under moist conditions an orange-red smear of coryne bacteria may grow on the surface, as with Limburger. Surface ripening is usually faster than normal internal ripening, and in contrast to this, it works from the outside toward the center. Another method is to introduce a mold to the interior of the cheese, where it spreads and causes blue-veining, and an often sharp, piquant taste, as in Roquefort. The optimum length of the ripening period depends on the cheese type. As a rule, the harder the cheese the longer it should ripen, and also, the longer a cheese ripens, the harder it gets.

BELOW: With blue cheese, the ripening process is even more spectacular. When fresh, the cheese has a nondescript appearance. Holes are punched in, by hand or by machine, creating air channels in which the blue mold can develop. A mold culture is added to the cheese milk as a rule, the holes being there merely to encourage the mold to grow in the cheese. An open texture of the paste also facilitates the spread of veining throughout the cheese.

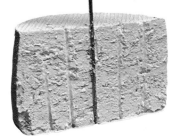

Classification of cheeses

The world of cheese, with its overwhelming variety of types, is almost impossible to classify. Many countries apply their own system, coupled to legal conditions. What goes for one country does not necessarily go for another. A national cheese sometimes has to meet different requirements in another country and gets another classification. This book tries, in a data panel at the end of each of the country chapters, to classify the different aspects of that country's most important cheeses.

A) The *milk* used is a very obvious criterion. Cow's milk is the most common. With a little practice, you can soon recognize other milks by their typical flavor. We indicate the different milks as follows:

ㅁ *Cow's milk*
ㅁ *Goat's milk*
ㅁ *Sheep's milk*
＊ Refers to a note at the foot of the data panel

B) The International Dairy Federation has made a classification which is useful because it appeals to the nontechnical cheese amateur. It is a classi-

ABOVE: This old print, made about a century ago, shows a storage room full of the globe-shaped Edam cheeses – one of the best known representatives of the semihard type, made of cow's milk and with a dry rind.

fication by type of *consistency*. This consistency is determined by the proportion of dry matter (proteins, milk fat, milk sugar, minerals) to moisture. The less moisture the cheese contains, the harder it is. The difficulty is that this ratio is never constant, but changes as a cheese gets older. You could call a mature semihard cheese "hard," and the same cheese when young "soft." Still, it is an easily recognizable characteristic. Look at these examples:
- Sbrinz contains ca. 65% dry matter and 35% moisture.
- Romadur contains ca. 40% dry matter and 60% moisture.
- Speisequark contains ca. 20% dry matter and 80% moisture.

According to consistency, we distinguish four groups:

O *Fresh cheeses* like Fromage Frais, Speisequark, Cream Cheese, which are not or hardly ripened and can be eaten almost immediately.

● *Soft cheeses,* like Camembert, Limburger, Brinzâ which stick to the knife and may be spreadable.

■ *Semihard cheeses,* like Gouda, Stilton, Fontina – firm but smooth and easy to cut.

RIGHT: The gradations of consistency – from soft to hard – can be explained by reference to the fat and moisture content of each cheese. The more cheese results from a given amount of milk of a specified dry matter content, the more moisture it contains and the softer it is. The more fat it contains the richer and smoother (but not necessarily softer) it will be. There are exceptions to this rule – the diagram provides some examples.

Name	Average yield of cheese in kg per 100 liters milk (1 kg = 2.2 lbs; 100 liters = 110 quarts)	Fat content in %			Moisture content in %			
		<30	30–40	40–50	<40	40–50	50–60	>60
Parmigiano	7		●		●			
Emmental	8.1			●	●			
Romadur (20% fat)	9	●					●	
Edam	9.5			●		●		
Fontina	9.5			●				
Gouda	10.5			●				
Cheddar	10.8			●	●			
Romadur (40% fat)	11			●			●	
Valençay	11			●			●	
Romadur (50% fat)	12			●			●	
Kâskaval	17.5			●		●		
Queijo de Serra	18.5			●		●		
Brinzâ	19			●			●	
Queso Rosell	25			●				●

■ *Hard cheeses,* like Emmental, Sbrinz, Parmesan – hard to very hard, sometimes difficult to cut, but ideal to grate.

C) Classification by the exterior of the cheeses, the *rind*, is another method that is easily employed by the non-expert.

Here are the main types:
— *No rind* or hardly any rind: this is the case with, among others, most fresh cheeses.
▢ *Dry rind:* this is the natural crust that develops during ripening under normal conditions.
❀ *White mold flora* on the surface.
❖ *Orange-red smear* of coryne bacteria on the surface ("washed cheese").
⅜ *Blue-veined cheese:* this is the blue or greenish-blue mold spread throughout the interior of the cheese.

D) Another criterion is the *fat content.* This is calculated according to the percentage of fat in the dry matter of the cheese. For example, if the fat content is 50% and the total dry matter 40%, it means that 100 parts of cheese contain 20 parts fat (40 parts dry matter, 60 parts water). The content is expressed as a percentage of the dry matter because a cheese, when it gets older and loses moisture, would otherwise have a continuously changing percentage.

Some countries indicate fat content with the symbol + (e.g., 48+), because the percentage is a minimum requirement and the actual fat content may be higher.

The categories mentioned under A, B, C and D are the easiest and most useful ways to differentiate the many cheeses of the world. These classifications can be found in the data panels.

Cheese however, can also be grouped in other ways.

E) *Preparation* of cheese can vary greatly. There are countless recipes and variations on recipes. We have illustrated in detail the modern factory production of five representative cheese types. Most popular cheeses are made according to one of these main methods.
I. Emmental production (p. 105), representing hard cheese with heated ("cooked") and pressed curd.

LEFT: No one has ever managed to establish exactly how many different types of cheese France produces. It is said that there are as many cheeses as days of the year, and in all imaginable varieties: fresh, soft, hard; with dry, white or red rinds; or blue-veined; or flavored by herbs; and from cow's or goat's or ewe's milk.

II. Cheddar production (pp. 56-57), representing hard cheese with cheddared and pressed curd.
III. Gouda production (pp. 68-69), representing semihard, pressed cheese.
IV. Camembert production (pp. 84-85), representing unpressed cheese with or without rind flora.
V. Cottage Cheese production (p. 155), representing fresh cheese.
Different from these types are:
VI. The plastic curd or kneaded cheeses, for which the curd is immersed in hot water and kneaded (e.g., Caciocavallo).
VII. The whey cheeses, for which whey is boiled down (e.g., Mysost).
VIII. The albumen cheeses, for which the milk proteins are made to flocculate by heating (e.g., Schabzieger).

F) As to the *curdling method,* a division can be made between curdling with the aid of rennet (most cheeses) and curdling without rennet but only with sour milk (e.g., Sauermilchkäse).

G) A division is possible in *ripening* methods (long or short-ripened, under moist or dry conditions, resulting in large, medium, small or no holes, etc.).

H) Finally there is the difference in *shape* and *weight* of the cheese. Although this says little about its qualities, we have included these features in the data panels, as they help in recognizing the cheeses.

Finally, we must mention processed cheese, which is made from a base of natural cheeses, it is manufactured by a very different production method. In this book, the emphasis is very much on the natural cheeses of each country; there is a separate section on processed cheese beginning on p. 227.

RIGHT: An example of the classification methods used in this book: among cow's milk cheeses one can distinguish fresh, soft, semihard and hard types (middle column); in each of these groups further subdivisions are possible on the basis of the exterior: no rind, dry rind, white mold, red bacteria, and finally, blue-veined (right-hand column). The symbols are explained in the text on these pages.

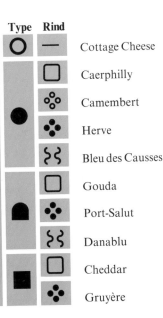

Milk	Type	Rind	
	○	—	Cottage Cheese
	▢	▢	Caerphilly
	●	❀	Camembert
		❖	Herve
		⅜	Bleu des Causses
🐄	▢	▢	Gouda
	◖	❖	Port-Salut
		⅜	Danablu
	◼	▢	Cheddar
		❖	Gruyère

Cheese and the senses

Sight, hearing, smell, taste and touch: the five essentials that give life its real dimensions. When Shakespeare wrote: "The air nimbly and sweetly recommends itself to our gentle senses," he could have been a cheese expert talking about cheese, not a poet writing about castles. The cheese expert needs all his senses about him; but professionals do not have to be the only ones to use their senses to make sound judgments about cheese. As a layman, you too can do a good job if you know what to look for and how to go about it.

Judging cheese

For a start, it is a good idea to take a close look at the cheese. Its appearance often gives it away. The cheese should be well shaped, neither bulging, too flat or too thick. A smooth, well-sealed rind without cracks or cloth creases shows it has been carefully produced. Some cheeses have rind flora and this should be evenly distributed, free of any coloring that is not expected in the particular cheese type. The cheese paste itself should have no mold, unless, of course, it is a blue cheese. It should have a fresh color, varying from white to light cream to ochre-yellow according to variety. The cutting surface should be unbroken; cracks indicate faulty production or storage.

Cheeses, of course, cannot speak. But they can express themselves and the cheese expert listens. He takes a hard or semihard cheese in his hand, holds it to his ear, taps with hand, fist or a special hammer, and listens. A hollow answer indicates an open texture with too many holes; a dead sound, a "blind" body with hardly any eyes, or holes. He can make a judgment about whether it has too few, too many, or just enough holes; whether they are properly distributed over the body; and whether they are too large or too small.

An instrument called a cheese trier or cheese iron is usually pushed into the cheese and the boring tested. Is the trier well filled with cheese? Does the cheese look springy? Are there any holes? These are the sort of questions the expert asks.

Taste and smell

But, it is after the cheese trier is removed or the cheese is cut, that the next sensory experience begins. The

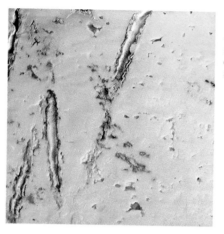

LEFT: The taste of Gorgonzola. The flavor and aroma of this splendid Italian blue cheese is unmistakable.

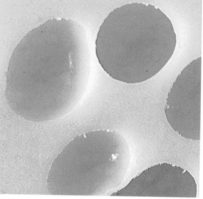

LEFT: The sound of an Emmental. Tapping the rind of a whole cheese tells the expert whether its holes or "eyes" are well distributed and of the correct size.

LEFT: The look of a Sage Derby. The unique pattern of this cheese is not caused by veining, but by the green, ground sage leaves worked into the curd.

LEFT: The feel of a ripe Brie. When at the peak of its condition, the soft, glossy paste almost flows from the rind.

aroma is released. There are six basic aromas: fruity, flowery, resinous, spicy, foul or burned. These rather fancy terms are seldom used by the expert. He has his own jargon. He finds the cheese aroma either good, fresh, sweet or sour. Sometimes, moldy, gassy or tainted with ammonia, none of which means necessarily that the cheese is below standard. It could be a characteristic of the variety. One thing that must be there is the aroma of the particular milk that has been used. Cow, goat, sheep all have their own unique aroma.

The full aroma is not actually released until the cheese has been brought to room temperature. Consequently, the consumer usually gets the full benefit; the expert, who often tests the cheese in cold storage, only gets part of it. He relies on his acutely developed sense of smell and his acquired knowledge to make sound judgments.

Taste invariably follows smell. It is the combination of taste and smell that gives the gustatory sensation. There are four basic flavors: sweet, salt, sour or bitter. When the cheese is finely divided in the mouth, coming into contact with the entire surface of the tongue, the aroma is fully released to the senses. And memory stores the experience, ready for future acceptance or rejection. It has then become a personal matter outside of the practical judgment of experts.

Soft varieties of cheese are often judged in the first place by touch. The resilience of the body is checked by pinching. The shopper can do this before buying, checking whether it is firm or pliant and soft, that is to say, unripe or well-ripened. If the body of a soft cheese can be pressed out of the rind it is of excellent quality.

For the consumer, it is hardly possible to go into a supermarket and carry out all these sensory tests. If it were, no doubt what is now called a private cheese party would get a public counterpart, causing no end of problems both for the storekeepers and those of the public who are less partial to this delicious foodstuff. In a specialized cheese shop, you may find sympathetic staff who will allow you to handle cheeses and will be pleased to discuss them with you. In that case, you are lucky and you should learn what you can.

To make sure that the consumer

gets what he expects, most countries have grading and supervision systems. Cheeses are graded and classified and given a marking that tells the origin, fat content and type. The quality of the cheese is carefully checked.

Cheese is a living thing

Seeing, hearing, smelling, tasting, touching are the sensory perceptions that make life a total experience. Cheese, more than almost any other edible commodity, demands the use of all these senses, if proper judgments are to be made about its qualities and applications. Cheese by its very character – a product produced by organic processes aided by human expertise – demands, like wine, the awareness of the artist coupled to, at least, a rudimentary knowledge, if it is to be adequately assessed and fully appreciated.

To be a professional cheese judge takes years of training and experience. To be a layman with a knowledge of cheese, takes a natural liking for the commodity, plus curiosity, feeling, perhaps a desire for surprises, and five senses that are eager and well developed.

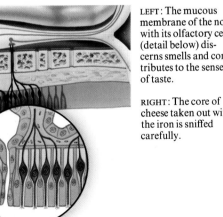

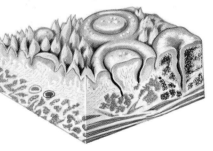

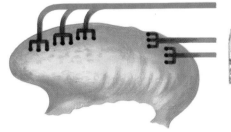

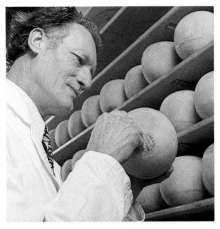

LEFT AND RIGHT, AND BELOW LEFT AND RIGHT: With a cheese iron, or cheese trier, a "boring" is taken out of the cheese and examined. Texture, color, incidence of holes, progress of ripening, etc., are all judged.

LEFT: The mucous membrane of the nose with its olfactory cells (detail below) discerns smells and contributes to the sense of taste.

RIGHT: The core of cheese taken out with the iron is sniffed carefully.

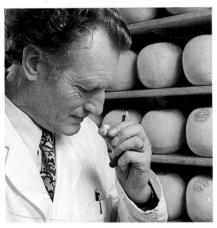

FAR LEFT: The tongue sends taste impulses from various areas to the brain.

LEFT: A detail of the tongue's differently shaped papillae.

RIGHT: Tasting is the final test. The expert has a finely developed sense of taste, and long experience enables him to detect details that would evade the layman.

Quality control

Nearly all countries with an important cheese production have legal regulations and controls. Cheese is defined in precise terms and regulations are laid down for the production of the various types. These regulations can show great differences from country to country.

As far as the milk is concerned, there are usually regulations about what animals may supply the milk for a given cheese; the milk must be hygienically obtained and, of course, be free of germs. Sometimes the maximum acid level is prescribed as well as the last acceptable time that the milk can be delivered to the cheese factory.

Most countries make cheeses with different fat content. Germany even has eight classes of less than 10% to 60%. For many cheeses minimum fat contents have been established that must be observed. The fat content should be stated on the cheese itself or on the package.

As far as the preparation is concerned, most countries restrict themselves to general regulations about the correct fat and moisture contents of their cheeses. However, there are some countries which prescribe special preparation methods.

In every country attention is paid to additives. Starter cultures and rennets must be examined regularly for micro-organisms. Sometimes it is stated that rennet may only be made from calf stomachs; sometimes other rennets, indicated by their names, are allowed. Additions like herbs and spices are often described and it is indicated for what cheeses they may be used. Almost every country states exactly what chemicals may be used and what is the maximum amount allowed. Coverings like wax, paraffin, plastic, and oils are also dealt with. The cheesemaking rooms in most countries must meet special requirements of size, technical installations, cleanliness and so on. Even the staff must meet certain requirements as far as health and hygiene are concerned. The ripening is statutory in various countries: a minimum time is indicated in Canada, for example, and a ripening temperature. For the moment the Netherlands is still the only country with regulations for cheese ripened in foil and France for pre-packed cheese.

Apart from cheese in general, cheese groups also have statutory definition,

ABOVE: Quality tests are carried out in the factory itself. Here, Mr. Italiano inspects some Pecorino cheese at his factory in Melbourne, Australia.

e.g., hard cheese, semihard cheese, soft cheese, fresh cheese. Generally the water content of the fat-free cheese mass is taken as a standard. Specialities like Sauermilchkäse or whey cheese are also bound to statutory regulations.

How supervision of the statutory regulations is to be carried out is also determined by the law makers. The inspectors are either exclusively inspectors by profession or experts, like cheese traders and cheese technicians, commissioned by the controlling authority. There are countries that have a judging system for quality, usually with a point evaluation to determine in what quality class a cheese belongs.

During the Stresa Convention in 1951 (see below), the first international agreements were fixed between nine countries. The names of particular cheeses were protected and their area of origin determined. This made it difficult for imitations to be offered as the real thing. For instance, for Roquefort, the municipalities where it can be made were precisely stated as well as for the Bleu du Haut Jura; the latter cheese must be produced above 800 m (26,400 ft). Comté must be made exclusively in the province of Comté and only from the milk of cows from the breed Pie rouge de l'Est or Montbéliard, whose milk must be delivered after each milking. For Cantal, the pastures must also be located above 800 m (26,400 ft). Parmigiano, of

BELOW: Before a load of Gouda cheese is shipped abroad, a random test is taken by an official inspector.

which the area of preparation is also exactly indicated, may only be made between April 15 and November 11 and must ripen for at least two summers; Pecorino Siciliano may only be made on Sicily from fresh sheep's milk from October to June.

In 1967 a code of quality standards was fixed, thanks to the FAO (Food and Agriculture Organization) and WHO (World Health Organization), for the 5.3 million tons of cheese made yearly by thirty-three countries. There are countries which produce less than 100,000 tons yearly, but seventeen countries supply 87% of the world's production. The aim of the "Code of Principles," set up by these organizations is to forbid the use of misleading names and descriptions of nondairy products, so that these cannot be mistaken for dairy products. It also gives international standards for cheese in general and for a number of specific cheeses. Some of these recommendations have already been accepted by the governments of the countries concerned.

The purpose of all this is to protect the cheese trade and the consumer against dishonesty. Laws and regulations may make a negative impression, but here they show that the authorities are concerned with value for money and with giving the consumer the cheese that he asks for.

The Stresa Convention
At the request of the Netherlands, France, Austria, Belgium, Denmark, Italy, Norway, Sweden and Switzerland, in 1951 an agreement was concluded giving international protection to the names of a number of well-known cheeses. The following groups were established:

GROUP A: The names Roquefort (France) and Pecorino Romano, Gorgonzola, Parmigiano Reggiano (Italy) may only be used for cheese prepared in the original countries according to the regulations applicable. The names cannot be used for any other cheese.

GROUP B: The names Camembert, Brie, St.-Paulin (France); Fontina, Fiore Sardo, Asiago, Provolone, Caciocavallo (Italy); Emmental, Sbrinz, Gruyère (Switzerland); Gudbrandsdalsost, Nökkelost (Norway); Samsø, Maribo, Danbo, Fynbo, Elbo, Tybo, Havarti, Danablu, Marmora (Denmark); Svecia, Herrgardsost (Sweden); Pinzgauer Bergkäse (Austria); Gouda, Edam, Friese and Leiden (Netherlands) may be used for imitations prepared in other countries, on the condition that the country where the cheese is produced is indicated (e.g., Norwegian Gouda).

French cheeses and French law
Finally, it may be useful to name the French cheeses that have their names protected by French law. This means that they may be imitated abroad, but if you buy a French cheese with this name you may be sure that it is original, genuine and made according to the regulations applicable. The most important are: Beaufort, Bleu des Causses, Bleu du Haut Jura, Cantal, Chaource, Gruyère de Comté, Fourme du Cantal, Maroilles, Munster, Neufchâtel, Pont-l'Evêque, Reblochon, Roquefort, Saint-Nectaire.

LEFT: Some of the labels, new and old, employed to distinguish cheese of a controlled quality. The selection includes: the official Belgian inspection mark (far left); the label for Camembert, Pont-l'Evêque and Livarot cheeses from the Pays d'Auge (center left); the stamp of the original French monastery cheese Port-du-Salut – the ancestor of many Port-Salut and St.-Paulin versions (center, bottom row); the casein label for Dutch farmhouse Gouda (upper right-hand corner); and the special label for Normandy Camembert V.C.N. (below right).

The world of cheese

RIGHT: The map shows the cheese countries of the world, classified in four categories according to their national production figures.

A world of surprises, not only in its infinite variety of taste and smell, but in facts and figures too. Just look at the production, export and consumption data on these pages. For example, the United States is the biggest cheese producer of the world, but it hardly exports at all. The Netherlands, small as it is, is the biggest exporter. New Zealand exports almost all of its cheese. Do they keep anything for themselves, one wonders? Others eat their own cheese and export relatively little, e.g. France. The Greek and French have the biggest consumption per head of the population, while Japanese eat no more than 400 g (14 oz) yearly per head. It often looks contradictory, but not when the facts are considered. Size of population, geographical and climatic conditions, and history all have an influence.

There are large areas where little or

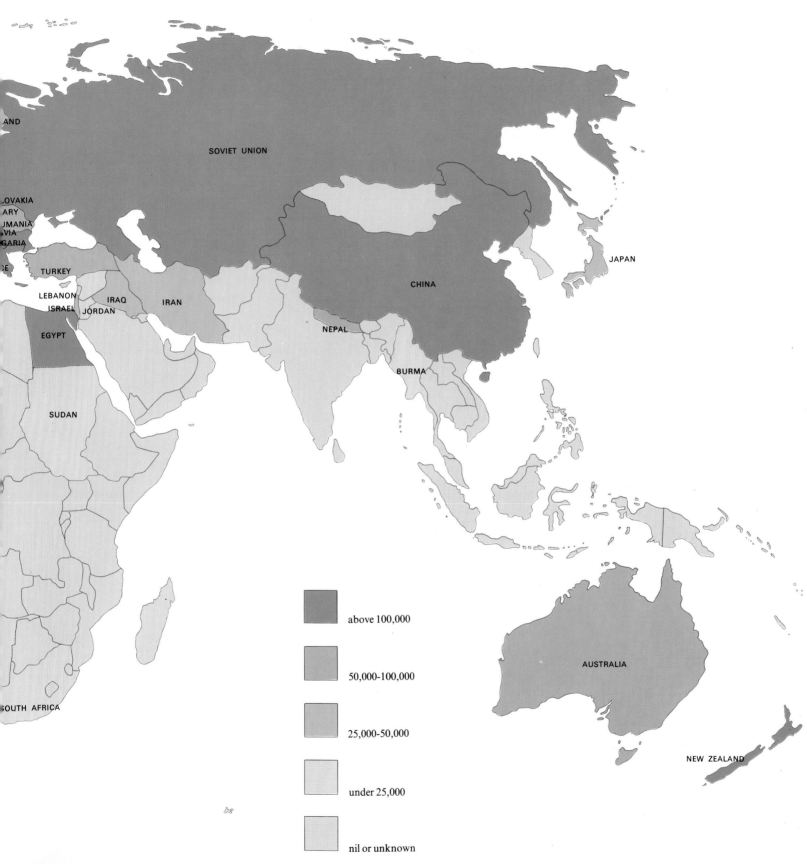

AND

SOVIET UNION

LOVAKIA
ARY
UMANIA
VIA
GARIA

CE

TURKEY

LEBANON

ISRAEL JORDAN

EGYPT

IRAQ

IRAN

CHINA

JAPAN

NEPAL

BURMA

SUDAN

SOUTH AFRICA

above 100,000

50,000-100,000

25,000-50,000

under 25,000

nil or unknown

AUSTRALIA

NEW ZEALAND

31

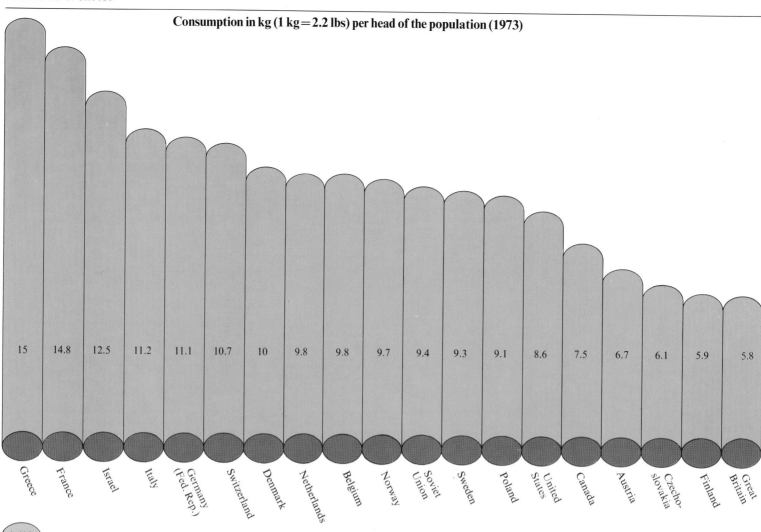

Consumption in kg (1 kg = 2.2 lbs) per head of the population (1973)

Greece	France	Israel	Italy	Germany (Fed.Rep.)	Switzerland	Denmark	Netherlands	Belgium	Norway	Soviet Union	Sweden	Poland	United States	Canada	Austria	Czechoslovakia	Finland	Great Britain
15	14.8	12.5	11.2	11.1	10.7	10	9.8	9.8	9.7	9.4	9.3	9.1	8.6	7.5	6.7	6.1	5.9	5.8

Total production [full column] and export [lower part of column] in thousands of metric tons per country, including fresh cheese (1973)

United States	Soviet Union	France	Germany (Fed.Rep.)	Italy	Netherlands	Poland	Argentina	Great Britain	Egypt	China	Germany (D.D.R.)	Greece	Canada	Denmark	Czechoslovakia	Bulgaria	Yugoslavia	New Zealand
1,410	1,255	899	567	512	335	306	219	199	186	170	161	142	137	127	125	124	110	101
3.2	7.5	160.6	81.9	21.9	206.9	3.4	6.9	6.4	1.0	?	?	1.2	5.4	83.9	8.3	17.2	0.5	90.0

no cheese is made. In the chapter on the history of cheesemaking, we have tried to find the reasons why. It should be remembered, however, that nowadays in many countries some cheese may be made, but not commercially and in such small quantities that it is not yet recorded. We may have some cheese surprises to come.

Now that transportation and storage difficulties can be largely overcome, the cheeses that for so long have only had a regional significance can be carried all over the world, even from land-locked countries that a hundred years ago were unknown as international cheese producers. This can be seen from the rising cheese production and export figures of certain countries. Another indication is the wide variety of cheeses to be found in shops today – a factor which shows both the greater availability and the growing interest in cheese as a food.

EUROPE

ABOVE: Sturdy white-and-black-faced cattle in a lush meadow promise plenty of wholesome milk from which good cheese can be made.

Key to symbols in national maps

In the maps of Great Britain, the Netherlands, France, Switzerland and Italy, the important original cheeses of each country have been marked by means of a symbol representing their shapes, and located in the region where each respective cheese originally came from.

The many different shapes in which cheese is made have been grouped in the following categories.

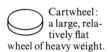

Ball: either a perfect sphere or (mostly) flattened or otherwise distorted.

Cartwheel: a large, relatively flat wheel of heavy weight.

Flat disc: much smaller than the cartwheel and usually weighing under 1 kg (2.2 lbs).

Cylinder: of varying height and diameter, but always taller in relation to its diameter than the cartwheel. In some cases, the two following subtypes have been distinguished.

Low cylinder.

Tall cylinder.

Oval or any similar fancy shape.

Loaf: a large rectangular shape which tends to be higher than its width. The brick shape, the width of which is greater than its height, is also included in this category.

Cube or a similar shape.

Truncated cone, pyramid or similar shape.

Bar.

Rectangular or square. The bigger block form is also included in this category.

Cheese sold in a basket.

Cheese sold in a container, whether this be a bag, sack, pot, jar or plastic cup.

Triangular: this is a rare shape, the triangular portions of cheese usually being cuts of a bigger, cylindrical cheese.

Key to symbols in data panels

Milk

Cow's milk

Goat's milk

Sheep's milk

Refers to a note at the foot of the data panel

A combination of symbols means that more than one kind of milk is used, either alternatively or mixed together. The sequence of the symbols does not indicate any order of importance.

Type

○ Fresh cheese

● Soft cheese

◖ Semihard cheese

■ Hard cheese

Rind

— No rind or hardly any rind

▢ Dry rind

White rind flora

Orange-red rind smear ("washed cheese")

Blue-veined cheese

Form
This is described in the terms explained above, with a few additions for some otherwise unclassifiable cheeses. When a cheese is habitually made in many different shapes, rather than one typical form, the term "varying" is employed.

Weight
The average weights of the usual forms in which the cheese is made are indicated. Where weights vary widely, the term "varying" is employed.

% **Fat content**
The required minimum percentage of fat in the dry matter is given; where no official regulations exist, the average percentage. Where two figures are given, the cheese may be made in a certain number of percentages between and including the percentage mentioned. Where no reliable information is available,

the symbol "?" is used.

Note
For a more detailed explanation of the terms used in this classification, please refer to pp. 24-25.

Please note that cheeses are discussed primarily under the country where they originally came from, even if they are produced on a large scale in other countries. Cheeses selected for inclusion have been chosen for their interest rather than their production figures. The list of cheese types of each country is not exhaustive.

Text and data panels describe the usual and typical form in which each cheese type is made. Individual differences can, and will, occur, since cheese is a living thing, made by many different artisans and factories, each with his own methods and recipes.

National maps:
Great Britain: p. 53
The Netherlands: p. 65
France: p. 77
Switzerland: p. 103
Italy: p. 117

BELOW: The dairy regions of Europe. In southern Europe, there is not always a clear distinction between cattle raised for meat and those raised for dairy farming; the raising of both tends to be less intensive than in western Europe. Also, in southern Europe milk production from sheep and goats may be more important than that from cows.

☐ Dairy farming

FINLAND

Helsinki

Stockholm

SWEDEN

BALTIC SEA

Copenhagen

SOVIET UNION

Moscow

n

ANY
R.)

POLAND

Warsaw

Prague

CZECHOSLOVAKIA

Vienna

Budapest

AUSTRIA

HUNGARY

RUMANIA

CASPIAN SEA

Belgrade

Bucharest

YUGOSLAVIA

BLACK SEA

BULGARIA

Sofia

Tirana

Istanbul

ALBANIA

TURKEY

GREECE

Athens

35

Norway

If Scandinavia were likened to a piece of cheese, then Norway might resemble the rind – a hard, irregular and crumbled crust. The elongated stretch of land consists for the most part of an imposing but inhospitable plateau of barren rock, some 70 % of which is above the tree line. For over a million years the Atlantic ocean has frayed the Norwegian coast. The sea borders the country in all directions save that of the east, driving deep into the fjords and fissures that were first cut by the retreating glaciers during the Ice Age.

From early times the Norwegians have made a virtue out of necessity, turning to the oceans for their livelihood. The sea was full of fish, and the rugged coast formed many a natural harbor for the ships built by a nation of master shipbuilders. Although the fishing industry has played an important part in Norway's economy, only a small proportion of Norway is under cultivation. The country has thus had to rely on foreign trade since the days of the Vikings. Oslo, Bergen, Stavanger and Trondheim were trading centers that were thriving even during the Middle Ages. The Norwegians exported timber and fish, and the holds of the returning ships often contained cheeses brought from other lands. An early cheese type that dates from this period, and is still being made, is the semihard, spiced cheese called *Nøkkelost*, which bears some resemblance to Dutch Leiden cheese. It used to carry the mark of St. Peter's crossed keys, the arms of the city of Leiden; hence its name: *nøkkel* is the Norwegian word for "key."

Early farmhouse cheese

Only some 3 % of Norway can be successfully cultivated, although the warm Gulf Stream influences the climate. Even as far north as the Lofoten region, the weather can be mild and the grass is of excellent quality. Until the beginning of the twentieth century and the introduction of hydroelectric power, Norway was almost entirely agricultural. A source of cheap power, electricity brought about the growth of manufacturing industries, and especially the pulp paper, wood and canning industries.

Norway's pasture land, albeit of limited acreage, provides good grazing for cattle. Consequently, cattle breeding and dairying have made a substantial contribution to the na-

ABOVE: Norway is a sparsely populated country with the majority of people living in the south. This isolated church is situated on the northern coast.

BELOW: Farmhouses on the plateau of Geiranger, between Bergen and Trondheim. Here you might still find farmhouse goat cheese.

tional economy for centuries. The early farmers quickly learned how to make the very best of their dairy product. They found that the skimmed milk, left behind after the butter had been made, could be used to produce a delicious cheese. Cheesemakers used beautifully carved and decorated cheese molds, and for transporting their cheese and butter there was the traditional *tine*, a strikingly shaped, elegant wooden container. The symbol of this container, rendered in the national colors red, white and blue, is today the emblem of the entire Norwegian dairy industry.

Although Norway has many farms, they are among the smallest in Europe, and in past times the cheese production per farming family was not very high. Much of the cheese was made for immediate consumption and eaten fresh. *Pultost*, the nonfat cheese made from sour, skimmed milk, is an early cheese type, produced long before the arrival of manufactured cheeses. This soft cheese is made throughout Norway, and there are seemingly endless varieties with only very slight differences in preparation. Some might contain caraway seeds, others have had cream added to them to make the cheese richer. Pultost is also known as *Ramost* and *Knaost*, according to the locality.

When you consider Norway's mountainous character, it is not surprising that goat's milk was once as popular, if not more so, than cow's milk. The two were frequently mixed to give variety to the taste. This taste for sharp, pungent cheeses remains, and goat cheeses are still made here and there on the farms, as is the whey cheese *Gjetost*.

Farmer to factory

Even now there are several farmers who still make cheese for their own consumption, but the production of cheese for the market has long since moved from the small farms to the factories. The development of the factory industry started as long ago as 1856. The farmers in some of the valleys decided to build a communal farm in the mountains, where the cattle grazed during the summer months. The aim was to process the rich quality summer milk, and the move heralded the first cooperative dairy plant in northern Europe. The initiative was so well received that

dairy factories began to appear everywhere throughout the country. Today there are an impressive two hundred or so cooperative establishments. In keeping with the progressive approach to farming and cheesemaking, an improved road system was planned. Roads were laid to the farms, even those outlying properties in the mountains, so that the transportation of milk from farm to factory is fast and efficient. While the traditional origin of the cheeses formed the basis of their quality, the cooperative effort enabled mass production to get under way. Factories are now not only making Norway's standard cheese types, but new brands as well, including *Norbo*, *Ridder* (a cheese similar to St.-Paulin) and the easy-melting, rindless *Norvegia*, so popular in the kitchen. Also being produced are blue *Normanna*, Norwegian *Gouda*, *Edam*, *Tilsit*, *Port-Salut*, *Camembert*, *Brie*, *Emmental* and the glorious cream cheeses *Crème Château* and *Château Bleu*, to mention but a few. The entire cheese production, its inspection and marketing both at home and abroad, is controlled by the Norske Meierier, which works together with the Ministry of Agriculture.

Cheese for the long winter

In addition to fresh cheeses, the dairy farmers used to make cheeses that could be kept for eating during the long winter months, when milk was not so plentiful. As a rule, the cheeses were prepared during the summer from the milk surplus to be stored for the coming winter. It has been suggested that the unique, brown cheese called *Gammelost* owes its name to its long-keeping properties. *Gammel* is the Norwegian word for "old"; while *ost* simply means "cheese." Another explanation is that Gammelost is a cheese made from a very old recipe. A more likely explanation, however, is that it got its name because of the cheese's appearance – not only did it turn a greenish-brown color, but it developed a mold growth as well. Whatever its origin, the present factory-made Gammelost is ready for consumption within four to five weeks, and is one of Norway's freshest cheese types.

The mold spores that settle on Gammelost endow it with a delicious flavor. In the dark days before the sterilization of cheesemaking equipment, the farm cheeses grew a spontaneous mold culture. When the cheese was made in wooden vessels and molds, there were always traces remaining from the previous batch and mold spores were extremely productive. This is considered unacceptable in the hygienic modern factory, and the result is that spontaneous growth is now completely suppressed. However, the soft and smooth Gammelost would not be Gammelost without its unique, distinctive flavor: sharp and aromatic. For this reason, to maintain its character, the dairies inoculate the cheese with laboratory-grown molds. Once these have settled on the cheese they develop a kind of long, furry texture, the fur is pressed into the paste by hand to spread through the cheese, which slowly turns a brownish color. Gammelost contains less than 3% fat.

ABOVE: A row of Gammelost cheeses in the ripening room. The mold is regularly pressed into the cheeses by hand. With its unique, pungent aroma and taste, Gammelost is a real contribution to the range of world cheeses.

LEFT: A wedge cut from a Jarlsberg cheese. Jarlsberg is a large, full-cream, firm cheese with many regular holes.

Ancient revival

Another true veteran among Norway's cheeses is *Jarlsberg*. Its name derives from an old estate on the west bank of Oslo Fjord in the south, where the Vikings first settled. The farmers of this region made a large, firm, full-cream cheese with holes. The cheese more or less died out when attention shifted to the products of the dairy plants, but it was not totally forgotten. In the laboratories of the University of Agriculture in Ås, experiments were continued until the correct method of preparing the original product was established. As Norwegian taste had not changed over the ages, Jarlsberg once again became a popular cheese, both in Norway as well as abroad. The taste is somewhere between a Gouda and an Emmental: mild and nutty, with a slight hint of sweetness.

Morning begins with Mysost

The most popular Norwegian cheese on the home market is undoubtedly *Mysost*, a cheese made from whey – *Myse* is the Norwegian word for "whey." Without a piece of Mysost on the table, the Norwegian breakfast is incomplete. More than 30% of the total cheese production consists of this brown whey cheese, which is marketed in various forms.

Whey cheeses, like skimmed-milk cheeses, were originally products of expedience, but in Norway and other Scandinavian countries, their status has been considerably elevated. The whey cheese types originated from goat's milk, because cow's milk was made into butter and the whey was consequently deprived of butter fat. Goat's milk, on the other hand, was used only for drinking, or for cheese-making. The whey cheeses were

LEFT: *Landgang* (meaning "gangway"), the Norwegian version of a hero sandwich – a meal in itself. itself.

ABOVE: Warehouses in the old harbor in Trondheim. Situated as it is on a fjord, Trondheim is one of Norway's many natural harbors.

Name	Milk	Type	Rind	Form	Weight	% Fat content
Crème Château	🐐🐄	●	—	flat disc	1.5 kg	60
Gammelost	🐐🐄	■	□	cylinder	2-3 kg	0.5-3
Jarlsberg	🐐🐄	■	□	cylinder	10 kg	45
Mysost	🐐🐄🅰	■	—	loaf	1.5 kg	10-33
Nøkkelost	🐄	■	□	cartwheel	12-15 kg	45
Norbo	🐄	■	□	cylinder	4 kg	45
Norvegia	🐄	■	□	loaf	4.5 kg	45
Pultost	🐄	○	—	container	varies	varies
Ridder	🐄	■	❖	low cylinder	1.5-2 kg	60

Key to symbols on page 34. 1 kg = 2.2 lbs.

known as *Gjetost*, *gjei* being the Norwegian word for "goat."

The manufacture of Mysost starts with either goat's milk or cow's milk, or a mixture of both. When made with pure goat's milk whey, the product is called *Ekte* (genuine) *Gjetost*. The cream is skimmed for butter and the milk goes to make cheese. The remaining whey is heated very slowly until the water has evaporated, and the milk sugar forms a kind of brown, caramelized paste known as *prim*. At this stage milk or cream is often added, which changes the fat content of the

RIGHT: Old label from a Gammelost cheese. The making of this ancient cheese type is a tradition on Norwegian farms. The cheese is said to date back to Viking times.

BELOW: These beautifully decorated and carved wooden dairy utensils were once used for cheese- and buttermaking. In the foreground is a *tine*, used to transport butter and cheese.

ultimate product. However, the brown color, sweetish flavor and firm, tough consistency remain the general characteristics of all Mysost varieties.

Mysost is not, strictly speaking, a cheese, since cheese is, by definition, a product made from pressed curds. Dairy-made Mysost, the commercial variety, is still similar in quality to that originally produced by the mountain farms in former times, and in the distant past it must have been a real champion among the Norwegian cheeses. It is even said that this was the cheese the Vikings carried with them as food when they went on their predatory raids, and from it they got their courage and endurance. Whatever the truth, their present descendants still consider Mysost an essential beginning to a busy day.

Food for hearty appetites
For centuries the Norwegian way of life demanded that the people be independent, especially with regard to the food supply. Foodstuffs had to be preserved during the long winter months, especially in the isolated mountain farm dwellings. For this reason many of Norway's traditional

foods are smoke or salt-cured – salted mutton, salted ham and salt fish. Norway's cuisine can engender some fabulous thirsts, hence the popularity of beer and the powerful aquavit. Today the Norwegian larder is supplemented by a variety of imported foods, but the Norwegian diet continues to remain simple, robust, filling and fresh. With fish as a staple food, the national menu consists of such delights as fish soups, herring, salt fish and pickled fish (salmon is a particular delicacy); there is also an abundance of roast lamb, veal, fine vegetables, crusty flatbreads, potato cakes, fruit, cream, buttermilk and – of course – cheese. Cheese, especially Gjetost or Mysost, is used in sauces and on their famous open sandwiches. An impressive example is a French loaf cut lengthwise, well buttered and decorated with a selection of fish, meat, salad and cheese, according to taste. This arm's-length sandwich is called *landgang*, meaning "gangway," and is best indulged in when preceded by a glass or two of aquavit and accompanied by Norway's favorite drink – beer. Norway's cuisine can engender some fabulous thirsts.

BELOW: The range of Norway's cheeses: on the extreme left is a speckled, half-circle of spicy Nøkkelost. On top of it, next to a Norwegian Edam is a white Gjetost, a goat's whey cheese. In the foreground is a dark-brown, round Gammelost; to the right of this, a half Jarlsberg with its characteristic, large holes. In front is Cheddar, blue Normanna and Port-Salut. At the extreme right an orange Ridderost sandwiched between Gouda and Tilsit. In front are two triangular portions of Crême Château. The cheese with the paprika on top is Norvegia; to the left a Swiss type. A number of foreign cheeses are also included.

Sweden

Sweden's geographical position, with Norway to the west and the Baltic to the east, has by no means isolated her from contact with other nations. In common with her adventurous, sea-faring neighbors, the Swedes were also traders who, according to an ancient runic inscription carved on a stone at the Rännarebanan, "courageously sailed to the gold in the West, and in the East they fed the eagles."

Visby, the oldest Hanseatic League settlement on the Baltic island of Götland, was the junction of overseas trade routes between Russia and the West during the Middle Ages. Even in the country's early history, dairy farmers were making and exporting large quantities of butter, but no cheese, or at least very little, as cheese was imported from other countries – Sweden was one of the principal importers of Dutch cheese until well into the nineteenth century. Yet it is an established fact that cheese was made on both sides of the Vättern Lake over a thousand years ago: *Götaost* (Götland cheese) in Västergötland and goat's milk cheese in Östergötland. The social, cultural and economic life of the Scandinavian peoples has

TOP: Although only 9% of Sweden's land area is suitable for any form of agriculture, the country has over 2.5 million head of cattle. Much of the milk is made into cheese, which has an important place on the national menu.

ABOVE: A wooden church spire at Trono, Ålsingland, a fine example of traditional country architecture.

always been finely interwoven, and since curds and buttermilk were staple foods of the Vikings, there is little doubt that cheese varieties and methods of preparation were exchanged during that period of Scandinavia's history.

The parson's cheese

Cheese was valued as an item of currency in sixteenth-century Protestant Sweden. In areas where pastures were owned by the church, the local vicar exacted rent from the parishioners who farmed the land in the form of quantities of milk and sometimes of fresh cheese. The vicar or his wife would make cheese from the milk, which could then be bartered in exchange for other necessities – meat, perhaps, or butter, eggs and fish. The name *Prästost*, literally "parsonage cheese," is a reminder of this old custom. Such cheeses were often highly valued. *Småland-Prästost*, named after the district of fertile meadows in the south of Sweden, was widely known, far beyond the boundaries of the region where the cheeses were made. It has remained a popular country cheese, but it is now factory-

made from a mixture of fresh and pasteurized milk, the fresh milk giving the cheese an extra aroma and flavor. The cheesecloth in which it is pressed remains around the cheese.

Cheese in a cold climate
Lappernas Renost, made from reindeer milk by the seminomadic Laplanders, can hardly be considered one of Sweden's most popular national cheeses – but it is probably the most northerly cheese in the world. The Laplanders make the cheese in small quantities for their own consumption, sometimes as an accompaniment to coffee, into which the cheese is dipped. Reindeer milk is characterized by its extremely high fat content, but it is a scarce commodity, as one animal can only produce about 25 liters (27.5 quarts) of milk a year. The production of reindeer cheese is thus minimal, its enjoyment limited to the Lapps.

Sweden's sharp and spicy cheeses
Very much in vogue, and one of Sweden's biggest-selling cheeses, is the tall, round *Hushållsost*, or "household cheese." Hushållsost is a traditional farmhouse cheese, which for centuries had been made from whole milk by the farmers of southern Sweden. Now a modern factory product, it can be found in a variety of shapes and with a varying fat content. The name also varies: *Boxholms Gräddost, Lilliput* or *Smålands Gräddost*, the last type being characterized by many small holes. The taste is mild, and the cheese only requires one or two months to ripen.

A much longer ripening period is needed for the extremely popular *Svecia* cheese to reach its ultimate perfection. Svecia is a true Swedish speciality; it has an abundance of irregular eyelets and a smooth consistency. Like the Hushållsost, it is marketed in various types. There are mild Svecias and deliciously piquant ones, with a range of nuances in between. A well-matured Svecia, one that has been ripening for more than twelve months, is a splendid cheese with a pure, fresh and yet definite flavor. One type of Svecia is spiced with cumin seeds and cloves, and is ready to eat after only two months' ripening. Another clove- and cumin-flavored cheese, the *Kryddost*, takes much longer to mature, and after one year it possesses an extremely sharp, spicy taste. It is often recommended as

LEFT: These symbols and runic inscriptions were carved on rock surfaces by the Vikings. Runes played an important part in divination and were thought to have influenced weather, crops and cattle.

an ingredient for lobster dishes, as it is one of the few cheese varieties able to hold its own beside the pronounced flavor of lobster. Kryddost is available in fat contents of 30 and 45%.

Even larger and heavier than Svecia, to which it is comparable, is *Västerbotten* cheese. Originally called Burträsk cheese, it was first made during the middle of the last century, in a cheese dairy in the old village of Burträsk. It became widely copied, however, and changed its name to Västerbotten, and was registered as such. Today only a cheese from the Västerbotten region can carry that name; each is stamped with the letter W following careful inspection to see that regulations have been met. One Västerbotten cheese weighs approximately 20 kg (44 lbs), and usually has a fat content of 50%. After ten to twelve months of ripening, it has a dry and somewhat crumbly texture, and a very pronounced flavor.

Cheeses for the smörgåsbord
During the past twenty years or so, the Swedish cheese industry has not only concentrated on the manufacture of traditional varieties, but has also added to the range of national cheeses. Today local cheeses are being made and foreign cheeses imitated. There are a number of ways by which a cheese manufacturer can increase the selection and the simplest is to produce a specific type of cheese, but with varying fat content. A factory can also

RIGHT: Kryddost cheese, spiced with cumin and cloves. When well matured it is a very tasty, semi-hard cheese with many small eyes.

LEFT: The Swedish Santa Claus features on this old cheese label. At Christmas, the Swedes enjoy the special, festive cheese God Julost.

introduce new shapes and sizes, or it can experiment with various mold cultures and with shorter or longer periods of ripening, which can influence the appearance and taste of a cheese. The atmosphere in the ripening room can significantly affect a cheese's character. If, for example, a cheese is stored in a moist atmosphere, the rind growth will develop much more vigorously. Finally, technical and marketing influences may lead to entirely new innovations, such as the production of prepacked cheese, which ripens inside its foil.

Sweden's weeping cheese

One of the main types of foil-ripened cheese is *Riddarost*, which is sold with a fat content of either 30 % or 45 %, both spiced and plain, and has no visible rind. Some examples of the cheese have a faintly theatrical quality: for special occasions you can order from the factory in Götene, a cheese weighing 500 kg (1,100 lbs), measuring a cubic meter (3⅓ cubic feet). Two representatives from the factory accompany the giant cheese, so that they may cut it in the presence of the customer – always a spectacular event. The large pieces are then divided into loaves of approximately 1 kg (2.2 lbs), from which manageable portions are cut.

Another principal cheese type, also available with fat contents of 30 % and 45 %, is the currently popular

TOP: Supervisors at work in a modern cheese storeroom. They use a special knife to take samples from cheeses selected at random in order to assess their progress and development.

ABOVE: A display of some fine Swedish cheeses. The big wedge with the large eyes is Grevé. A piece of Tilsiter-style cheese sits on top of some Kryddost. The drum-shaped cheese with the slicer is Swedish Cheddar, behind it a portion of Västgö-taost. Far right is a sample of red-waxed Fontina, and far left some Swedish Camembert.

Herrgårdsost. As it matures it acquires a mild, nutty flavor, and if stored for a year or more its eyes, as they say, "start to cry," the holes becoming shiny and moist. It melts easily when heated, and is therefore an ideal cooking cheese. A version of Herrgårdsost is the foil-ripened *Drabant*, very popular at the breakfast table due to its surprising mildness. There is a still mellower version known as *Billinge*.

One of the finest of all Swedish cheeses is *Grevé*, a cheese of the Emmental type, but ripened with a different mold culture which gives it a slightly less dry texture. After some ten months' ripening, the Grevé has the same moist-looking eyes as the Swiss Emmental, with its aroma and flavor similar as well.

Many of the lesser-known Swedish cheese varieties have developed from such regional types as *Västgötaost* from Västergötland, *Hälsingeost* from Hälsingland, and *Buost* and *Vålåloffen* from Jämtland. Decidedly non-fat is the Buost, a long, flat, rectangular cheese, which after its salt bath is kept moist. Hälsingeost is soft and smooth, but somewhat sharp and even slightly bitter to taste; it is made of a mixture of cow's milk and 10 % goat's milk. These last two cheese varieties are not paraffined, but develop a rind growth, as does Vålåloffen, with its pale orange rind like Port-Salut.

Passed by the runes

The farmhouse heritage of certain other varieties is more difficult to establish. *Fontina* and *Scandia* both have a fat content of 45 % and are made in the shape of a wagonwheel with sharp edges; the Fontina is red-paraffined.

Swedish Fontina should not be confused with the famous Italian cheese of the same name, the Fontina d'Aosta, although the shape is vaguely similar.

Any country that has a progressive dairy industry like that of Sweden, and that has a large public demand for foreign cheeses, strives to produce good, competitive imitations. It is thus not surprising that a whole series of Swedish cheeses has been copied or derived from foreign cheese types: *Tilci, Havarti, Ambrosia* (of the Tilsit type), Swedish *Cheddar, Gouda, Edam, Port-Salut, Brie, Camembert, Party* (somewhere between Brie and Camembert), *Stilton, Stockkumla dessertost* (like Stilton, but without the

Name	Milk	Type	Rind	Form	Weight	% Fat content
Getost			—	cube	200-500 g	30
Grevé			□	cartwheel	12-14 kg	30-45
Herrgårdsost			□	cartwheel	12-20 kg	30-45
Hushållsost			□	cylinder	2 kg	45-60
Mesost			—	loaf	1.5 kg	10-30
Prästost			□	cylinder	12-15 kg	50
Riddarost			—	loaf	1 kg	30-45
Svecia			□	cartwheel	12-24 kg	30-55
Västerbotten			□	cartwheel	20 kg	30-50

Key to symbols on page 34. 453 g = 1 lb; 1 kg = 2.2 lbs.

BELOW: Whey cheeses are a real Scandinavian speciality. They are often of firm consistency (Mesost), but can sometimes be spread (Messmör).

characteristic rind), *Ädelost* (Roquefort type, but made from cow's milk instead of sheep's milk), full-cream cheeses such as *Crème Chantilly, Crème Château, Crème Noisette,* and various types of *Färskost* (cottage cheese and curds).

By far the greater part of Swedish cheese production finds its way to the consumer in small packs under the new trademark "Ostmästeren." All cheeses are given an official inspection, and those that are accepted are stamped with a *runmärkt* ("rune brand"). As a rule, the Swedes are expert cheesemakers, and the quality is high. Those cheeses that are pressed and bound in cheesecloth are additionally protected by a paraffin covering; the Swedish cheesemakers prefer this to plastic wrapping because of effects on the ripening process. With paraffining, the curds must be finished dry, and not too much salting can take place. Thus the salt content of most Swedish cheeses is quite low.

Swedish farmhouse cheese
Traditional farmhouse cheesemaking still survives in spite of the newly developed methods and the internationally inspired factory cheeses. In the north of the country, on the summer farms, a quantity of *Getost* is made from raw goat's milk. Production of this cheese has been commenced on a fairly limited scale by small dairies and is based on pasteurized milk. After about one month,

BELOW: A characteristic raised house in Dalarna, central Sweden.

RIGHT: A nomadic Laplander in his tent of reindeer hide. The rare reindeer cheese is stony-hard, flat, and round in form. The Lapps often dunk it in coffee.

Getost is ready to eat. The Swedes like to serve it on tunnbröd (very thinly sliced bread, not unlike a matzo in appearance), often with a slice of brown whey cheese called *Mesost*. Mesost – to the Norwegians, "Mysost" – is a caramel-like substance derived from thickening the whey, which has been separated from the prepared curd. Noteworthy, too, is *Getmesost*, a whey cheese made from goat's milk and formerly prepared in iron pots, from which it obtained a relatively high iron content.

The Swedish table
At its most sophisticated, the famous smörgåsbord is an awe-inspiring selection of dishes, a very extensive buffet with a tempting display of hot and cold meat and fish dishes, salads, sauces, cheeses and breads. The rustic and traditional affair from which it derived is a meal of salt fish, cheese, bread and butter – smörgåsbord means "bread and butter table" – washed down with aquavit. Many Swedes begin their smörgåsbord meal with knäckebröd and paper-thin slices of hard rye bread with *Potkäs*, or Pot cheese – a mixture of grated cheese, butter, brandy and various herbs. Camembert is eaten in Sweden in a manner all on its own. The cheese is cut into sections, then breadcrumbed and fried. A compote is served with it made from *hjortron*, yellow, marble-sized berries from the mountain swamps of north Sweden, with a very delicate, somewhat raspberry-like flavor.

Cheesemaker's cake
One of Sweden's special, sweet delicacies is the traditional and festive *ostkaka*, a cake which is practically made in the manner of a cheese. It differs from other cheesecakes in that cheese is not one of the added ingredients. The cake calls for a large quantity of milk mixed with cream. This is curdled with rennet before the remaining ingredients are added: eggs, sugar, flour and flavorings. The mixture is then poured into a copper mold, and baked. As is happening in many countries today, people are forgetting how to prepare these dishes, now that they are commercially available.

Finland

A land of a thousand lakes and numerous islands, Finland is breathtakingly beautiful, but little suited to large-scale agriculture. The north of Finland stretches well above the Arctic Circle and consists mainly of treeless tundra; even the central part of the country is unable to support much cattle. It is understandable, then, that the main population lives in the more fertile south, where the arable land, especially around the coast, is encouraged by the warm Gulf Stream. Yet even here, in some places the granite spurs of the rocky lake plateau extend right to the sea and defy the plow. As the southernmost part of Finland is on the same latitude as the Shetland Islands, summers are short and winter nights long.

The climate is so severe that the ground is covered by snow for at least five months of the year. Winter usually arrives in November, freezing up the extensive system of waterways until April or May. Finland's lakes and canals, and most of her ports, are thus ice bound, prohibiting transportation and communications. Add to this the fact that only about 10% of the land is under cultivation, and you might begin to wonder how Finland manages to export considerable quantities of dairy produce as well as grow cereal crops and fruit.

Perhaps it is the crisp, cold, hygienic quality of the air and the well-scrubbed, healthy appearance of the people that gives other nations such confidence in Scandinavia's butter, cheese and other milk products. Whatever the reason, there is a ready market, and plenty of incentive for Finland's farmers.

Keeping the cows warm

In competition with the more modern, attractive ways of making a living, farming in Finland is on the decline as a profession. In the past, however, Finnish farmers achieved great accomplishments, and those that remain still do. As far as important agricultural products are concerned, Finland is able to meet its own milk needs, even though most farms are extremely small. Given the scarcity of arable land, the average farm can only support half a dozen cows. These must be wintered indoors, and thus a large proportion of the crops is allocated for their winter feed. The cows are extremely important to the farmer, for more than half of his income must

come from milk.

Over the last decades, the Finnish cattle have increased their milk yield, which is now sufficient to meet the demands of a population very fond of milk. There is even enough for the home cheese market and for the ever-increasing cheese export market, which accounts for about 50% of the total production, most of which goes to the United States.

Farmhouse cheese

Until more than a century ago, Finnish farmers made cheese for their own consumption. A small quantity of farmhouse cheese is still made now and then, preserving the sometimes extraordinary methods of preparation. In *Ilves* cheese, for example, an egg is added to the fresh curds. The surface of *Juustoleipä*, a speciality of central Finland, is grilled above an open fire,

LEFT: Most of Finland's beautiful country is lakeland or pine forest. There are bears in the forests, and the lakes abound with crayfish.

BELOW: The short summers and the long, bitterly cold winters are not exactly ideal for dairy farming. Only 13% of Finland is arable, the southern coastal areas being the warmest and the most fertile.

RIGHT: An old print showing how Juustoleipä cheese was roasted by an open fire in the farm kitchen.

or in the oven, then set aside to ripen; in a few days it is ready to eat. Such farmhouse cheeses are difficult to find, even in their locality; Juustoleipä, however, can be bought in Sotkamo, which boasts a cheese factory. You might be lucky enough to come across some *Kutunjuusto* if you happen to be near Tampere, in the west of the country; these little cheeses continue to be made on scattered farms, and are the only Finnish cheeses to be made from goat's milk. The delicious, soft and creamy *Turunmaa*, which originated in the southwest, is now almost entirely factory-made, both here and in other parts of the country.

The Swiss influence

Halfway through the last century, the Finnish cheese industry acquired a more professional and expert touch. A landowner of considerable foresight engaged a Swiss cheesemaker, Rudolf Kloessner, to produce a quantity of *Emmental* on his estate. So great was the success of the experiment that the demand for Swiss expertise attracted a number of Swiss cheesemakers to Finland.

The arrival of the Swiss heralded the period of cooperative cheese production. Begun on a limited scale, by the early years of the twentieth century it had enlarged considerably. The major development of the Finnish cheese industry, however, dates from after the Second World War. In 1952 the country had paid off its war debts and begun its economic recovery. Stimulated by Valio, the Finnish dairy cooperative society, the cheese factories became ultramodern establishments, technically equal to many larger cheese producers in other countries. Today quality control is strict, and each cheese for home consumption bears a label stating its fat content, the price range and the factory where it was made.

A flair for imitation

Finland produces a number of cheeses which are either imitations of foreign cheeses, or inspired by their example: *Kartano* (Gouda type), *Kesti* and *Kreivi* (Tilsit type), *Juhla* (Cheddar type), *Luostari* (Port-Salut type), *Kappeli* (Remoudou type) and *Aura* (a blue-veined cheese). On the home market, Finnish *Edam* remains the top favorite. Its flavor is very similar to the famous spherical Dutch cheese, but its

ABOVE: The cheese kettle monument in honor of Rudolf Kloessner, the Swiss cheesemaker who introduced Finnish Emmental in 1856. The cheese now constitutes an important part of Finland's cheese production.

ABOVE: An Ilves cheese, wrapped and labeled. Ilves is one of the small, farmhouse cheeses, now also factory-made.

shape is either round or oblong.

By far the most important cheese for export is Finnish Emmental, even though its preparation is now vastly different from the method taught by Rudolf Kloessner. Pasteurized milk, instead of the traditional raw milk, is used in enormous stainless steel vats. One vat can produce twelve Emmental cheeses at a time, each cheese weighing 80 kg (17.6 lbs). Manual labor is no longer employed: the cheeses are turned, washed and packed automatically. The consistency is a little less dry and sweet than the original Emmental, but the quality of the cheeses has not suffered.

Between 1920 and 1972, the annual per capita consumption of Finnish cheese rose from .5 kg to 5.9 kg (1.1 lbs to 13 lbs). The Finns use cheese as a dessert, and in the preparation of several dishes, one of which is *Lihamurekepiiras*, a meatloaf encrusted with pastry. Favorite accompaniments are buttered white bread, brown and rye bread, knäckebröd and paper-thin crispbread.

Name	Milk	Type	Rind	Form	Weight	% Fat content
Ilves	⌂	○	—	flat disc	1 kg	40
Juustoleipä	⌂	○	—	rectangular	250 g	40
Kutunjuusto	⌂	○	—	rectangular	200 g	30
Turunmaa	⌂	●	◻	cylinder	6.5 kg	50

Key to symbols on page 34. 453 g = 1 lb; 1 kg = 2.2 lbs.

Denmark

To produce cheese in quantity, quality and variety you need large herds of dairy cattle; these in turn demand wide acres of lush pastures encouraged by a temperate climate. This is why Denmark, of all the Scandinavian countries, is by far the most important as a producer of cheese. Unlike Norway and Sweden, it has no rough, mountainous countryside. The highest point is only 170 meters (1.3 miles) above sea level, and nearly everywhere there are green fields and fertile soil. The bitter winter can suddenly turn into a mild spring with sunshine and gentle rain – a more favorable climate for farming and cattle raising is hard to imagine.

Denmark's agricultural policies came about as a result of two main factors. To begin with, an intensive reclaiming of sandy heathlands and marshes eventually provided large areas of fertile grazing, and this compensated for unpromising mineral wealth and lack of industrial raw materials. The second factor is that Denmark occupies a very advantageous position between the North Sea and the Baltic and lies on the path of several important trade routes. Today, about 95% of the land area is cultivated, and there is a well-organized system of cooperative farming. Denmark has become one of the world's great producers of bacon, butter, cereals and meat – and, of course, cheese.

The Danish food industry has also benefited by the fact that the Danes are people with hearty appetites. Their average daily diet is the richest of all Scandinavian countries. Anxious to promote Danish dairy products, the Danes have developed a very high standard of hygiene and controls, with the result that Denmark has inspired great confidence among her many cheese-importing customers.

The cheeses of prehistory

Some of the earliest settlers on the Danish mainland were primitive tribes from Finland and Lapland, who arrived more than four thousand years ago. Archeological finds show that they kept goats, sheep and cows, and doubtless cheese formed a part of the daily menu. The Danes became skilled in the art of cheesemaking, learning from other countries special techniques of preparation, skills which they generously shared and spread

LEFT: The wealth of Denmark. A rich land of pastures, well-fed cows and dairy farms, some of the important aspects of the national economy. Perhaps this is why the windmill in the background is featured on the Danish 10-kronen banknote.

BELOW: A beautiful old farmhouse with decorative copper-work windows. The windows are curved to give the occupants a wider angle of vision than would plain, flat ones.

abroad through the agency of the Vikings. Denmark was the real homeland of these fierce sea warriors, and it is likely that the inhabitants of the regions in which Vikings permanently settled became familiar with Danish cheeses, perhaps also with cheeses from elsewhere in Europe which the Vikings, like modern tourists, brought home in their ships.

The next important influence on Danish cheese came from the Cistercian monks of the Middle Ages, who developed new methods of manufacture, which they passed on to the farmers and landowners in districts adjacent to their monasteries. It is not strange that the first simple cheese dairies were found particularly in these monasteries. The Cistercians were forbidden to eat meat, and experimented to find a nutritious replacement.

Avoiding the use of rennet as a starter, they found that the leaves of certain insectivorous plants, probably of the genus *Drosera* (e.g., the Venus' flytrap and the Sundew), could be used instead. The juice released by these plants to dissolve trapped insects contains the same enzymes as rennet.

The monks probably taught the farmers the art of maturing cheeses in addition to making fresh ones. Gradually the goat's milk and sheep's milk were replaced by cow's milk.

Smoked cheese, status cheese

The Scandinavians developed a taste for certain smoked foods, following the need to preserve, and thus smoke, their fish. It was but a short step to the smoking of cheese. In Finland fresh cheeses were smoked over a straw or hay fire in the open air. Such a cheese is *Fynskt Rygeost*. Traditionally a farm cheese, it is now mainly produced in factories, where the curds are conveyed in aluminum containers through a smoke chamber. Afterwards, cumin seed can be added, either sprinkled on the curds or mixed with them. The cheese does not mature and can only be kept for a few days.

Originally farmers made cheese for their own consumption, and for use as currency, to pay the taxes levied by the church. It is likely that many European churches were built, as it were, on a foundation of cheese.

As towns began to grow, the demand for cheese increased and pro-

LEFT: Seascape with cows. The view is from one of the Faeröes, the Danish islands in the Atlantic Ocean, between Britain and Iceland.

BOTTOM: Havarti is a semihard cheese of the Tilsit type. The cheese is named after the farm of one of Denmark's greatest cheese pioneers, Hanne Nielsen. In the nineteenth century she experimented with foreign and local cheeses, and produced much cheese of excellent quality.

BELOW: The harbor of Århus, Denmark's second largest city and home of the Danish Cheese Export Board.

duction kept pace. Among those considered to be very experienced cheesemakers were the inhabitants of the island of Samsø (which would one day make Danish cheese world-renowned). The annual production of Danish butter and cheese during the first half of the thirteenth century reached nearly 60,000 kg (132,000 lbs). In the province of Thy in North Jylland, from which *Tybo* cheese takes its name, cheese became a status symbol: the larger the cheeses, the greater the professional skill of the makers, and on this skill the prosperity of the region depended. Some cheeses reached such colossal dimensions that several men could hardly lift them.

Royalties from cheese

During the reign of King Christian II at the beginning of the sixteenth century, religious observance held that it was forbidden to eat cheese during Lent. Christian's position was somewhat ambivalent: he was the upholder of the faith, but also a champion of Danish cheese, and those Danes who took the trouble could obtain from the king a special letter of dispensation (for a suitable fee, of course) by which cheese and religious observance became reconciled.

Christian was responsible for considerable improvements in the quality of Danish cheese and other dairy products. Deciding that the industry needed foreign expertise, he sent for some Dutch farmers, cheesemakers from near Edam, who settled on the island of Amager near Copenhagen. In the same manner which the Finns absorbed some of Switzerland's cheese culture, the traces of Dutch influence in the Danish cheese industry can be clearly found today.

The first export market

The Dutch cheesemakers' example had an inspiring effect on the Danish cheese industry. Many landowners, who were previously only interested in horses, became involved in dairy farming. On the estates and the large farms, cellars were turned into cheese

LEFT: The production of factory-made Cheddar cheese for export.

dairies, where an even temperature was maintained throughout the year. Production demanded a greater work force, and the ripened cheeses piled up in the cellars in such quantities that the supply outstripped the demand, however great the latter was. New markets had to be found. *Tybo* cheese was an early export, finding its way to Britain before the nineteenth century, where its highly flavored aroma was much appreciated. *Ejdersted* and *Tyrstrup* were exported from Schleswig-Holstein (then a part of Denmark), albeit in small quantities only. The Danish cheeses of this period differed from region to region: there were both firm and soft cheeses, spicy and simple. As often happens in the course of progress, many have disappeared forever.

The cheese pioneers

In keeping with the practice of many European cheesemakers, experiments were started in an attempt to produce foreign types of cheese for the home market. Around 1800 Constantin Bruun, owner of the Antvorskov estate, invited Swiss cheesemakers to make Emmental from the entire milk yield of his dairy cows. Although production was successful, Danish Emmental gradually developed into a smaller cheese with a character all its own – the present *Samsø*.

On his Bekkeskov estate, Baron Selby adopted British methods of cheese preparation. He did not press his cheese underneath stones, as was the normal practice, but used a screw press. The young engineer Jørgenson of Knabstrup also became famous as a cheesemaker, with his fine examples of Dutch, Parmesan, Swiss and Cheddar cheeses. He startled the Danish cheese world by publishing his manufacturing secrets with a frankness unknown since the days of the medieval monks.

Of all the great cheese pioneers, the most important was Hanne Nielsen. Born in 1829, Nielsen was a countrywoman who was interested in farm produce – so interested that she purchased a farm, named Havarthi, from her husband and decided to make cheese. Undaunted by her lack of foreign languages, she traveled abroad to study cheesemaking. Returning to Havarthi, she started to experiment with Norwegian goat's milk cheese, English Cheddar, Dutch Edam and Gouda, French Camembert and Roquefort, East Prussian Tilsit

LEFT: Newly cut portions of curd receiving a liberal dose of salt.

ABOVE: Factory workers packing the famous blue-veined cheeses. The triangular wedges of cheese are packed into round containers, and each portion receives a label. The label below is of a similar type of Danish Blue to those being assembled above.

and Swiss Emmental. Her farm, which gave its name to the modern *Havarti* cheese, was soon producing enormous quantities of cheese, some of which was sold to the Royal Court. In Denmark her influence was far reaching, and she found time to give lessons in cheesemaking to farmers' wives, who in turn taught others, so that the constantly increasing home industry became a chapter in the country's agrarian history.

The foundation of cooperatives

Around the year 1880, Denmark had three types of dairy establishment in existence: the small farms; the estates where local milk was made into butter and cheese; and the small cheese factories which processed the milk of associated farms. Originally the best cheese came from the estates. Most farmers felt more secure concentrating on crops rather than dairy farming, and many grew wheat for export. But towards the end of the nineteenth century, grain prices fell by 40%, due to the enormous export activity of the now superproductive wheatlands of the world – North America, Australia and Argentina. The Danish farms could only survive this crisis by shifting to dairy and meat production; but to achieve a competitive price for their dairy products they would have to work through close cooperation.

In 1882 the first cooperative dairy factory was opened in Hjedding, in southwest Jutland. Six years later 215 of them had been established throughout the country. While some operated as private concerns, most maintained the cooperative system. A further stimulant to trade was the invention of the centrifugal cream separator, among other technical improvements, which enabled butter to be made on a much larger scale. These kind of improvements also helped the cheesemakers to improve their product.

Denmark's world exports

Even before the nineteenth century, Denmark was a dairy country of world repute, but it was her butter rather than her cheese that attracted foreign buyers. Relatively little attention was paid to cheese production, which could only just satisfy the home market; cheese was available in variety, but not in quantity. This state of affairs persisted until after the Second World War. Then, owing to

LEFT: Cattle breeding in Denmark is far more important than crop farming, which usually serves the cattle industry. Frisians are particularly suitable for both breeding and milk production.

land consolidation, progress in combating cattle disease, and the establishment of cooperative stables which could hold over four hundred cows, milk production greatly increased, despite the decreasing number of farmers. Those farmers that remained concentrated on raising cattle that provided both meat and milk, especially the black and white Frisians, a fine milk and breeding stock, and to a lesser extent the Jersey cow, with its high-fat milk so suitable for buttermaking. The Jersey is also very economic, as it is relatively small and requires little food. Today cheese factories have completely taken over production from the farmers, the milk from the farms being collected by modern refrigerated tankers. Denmark has grown in importance and become the third largest cheese exporter in the world, after Holland and New Zealand.

Pride of place
Foreign influences can still be found in the Danish cheese varieties. The establishment of the national range was originally based on cheeses from foreign countries, mainly from

BELOW: Large, round Samsø cheeses in the brine bath. The label on the left was one used for exported cheese.

Europe, yet these eventually took on a genuine Danish character, due to the properties of Danish milk. Samsø began its career as Emmental, but it later became unmistakably Danish.

As a further step towards establishing the origin of Danish cheeses, the authorities decided to change the names of many types, especially those with foreign origins and those that might be confused with other Scandinavian cheeses. Thus Danish Emmental was renamed Samsø, after the island in the Kattegat. Port-du-Salut became Esrom, after the town where it is made. All the members of the Samsø family, which were made in different towns or districts, such as Mols, Thy and Fyn, were given the possessive suffix "bo" so that Fynbo means "from the island of Fyn." (Fyn or Fünen, incidentally, was the home of Hans Christian Andersen.) To these we can add Molbo, Elbo and Tybo; also Maribo, which is named after the town on the island of Lolland. Most Danish cheeses, therefore, have rightfully been given their own names, which were officially recognized at the Convention of Stresa in 1951.

Cut and come again
Samsø, the Danish cheese with Swiss origins, is round like a cartwheel with sharp edges, and weighs approximately 14 kg (30.8 lbs). It is a full-cream cheese: the paste is firm but not hard, the color is pale yellow. It has shiny holes or "eyes" the size of cherries, and a fine nutty flavor that varies from sweet to strong, depending on the duration of ripening. Some prefer to eat it soon after it has been made, when sweet and very mild, while others maintain that age improves the flavor. A six-month-old Samsø cut into generous portions has a full, rich flavor of such distinction that it really encourages the old European saying, "Cut and come again."

The Samsø family
Samsø became established as the grandfather of all Danish cheese types. It is typically Scandinavian in spite of its Swiss origins. While it may not be counted among the really great cheeses, it is extremely versatile, lending its characteristics to a number of descendants. *Danbo* differs from Samsø in shape, being square instead of round, and sometimes contains

caraway seeds. Well-ripened (up to two years) spiced Danbo is called *Gammelost* and considered a speciality. *Fynbo* is round like Samsø, but smaller and without the sharp edges. It is a product of the island of Fyn and has eyes which are somewhat smaller than the original Samsø. The mild, aromatic *Elbo*, with its very firm paste, is made in a loaf shape and has fewer holes. *Tybo*, the most solid-looking member of the family, is half the size of Elbo. *Molbo* is the last member of the clan, a round cheese with a red rind. The distinct, nutty aroma is immediately apparent on cutting. Highly flavored, and widely exported, Molbo has a firmer consistency than the other Samsøs. Most of these cheeses are made in varying fat contents, usually between 20 and 45%. All the varieties of Samsø lend themselves well to cooking, and are therefore useful in the kitchen.

Esrom and other semihard types

The Samsøs are not the only semihard cheeses found in Denmark. The Gouda-like *Maribo* is either flat and round, or square in shape, and full of very small holes due to the curd's being crumbled, kneaded and then salted. Maribo has a red-paraffined rind and is made with fat contents of 20, 30 and 45%. Its paste is yellow to reddish-yellow in color, and it possesses a distinctive flavor, with a characteristic, quite pronounced aftertaste. *Havarti*, one of the most heavily exported of all Danish cheeses, is loaf or cylindrical in shape, and rather like Tilsit. The rind of Havarti can be left dry or washed. As the cheese ages, the washed rind makes the taste of this cheese, originally fresh and slightly sour, somewhat sharp.

In the monastery town of Esrom, the monks used to make an excellent cheese, which was later forgotten. The monastery is now in ruins, but the Danish Dairy Research Institute has rediscovered Esrom. This full-cream cheese, probably finer and richer than the original, has a deliciously sweet taste, its paste is golden yellow and with small holes. The washed rind gives the cheese so much flavor that lovers of Esrom will advise you not to cut it away, but to eat it with the cheese.

ABOVE: A picturesque old dairy farm on the island of Fyn. The house is half-timbered, and the ridge of the thatched roof is strengthened with wood.

ABOVE: A salute to Danish mythology in the square at Fáborg on the island of Fyn. The statue is called Ymerbrønden, and stands over a well. According to myth, the Scandinavian giant Ymir and the cow that fed him were the first beings to be created. Ymir, also called the Rime Giant, was the embodiment of primeval chaos; he was eventually slain by Odin, who created the world from Ymir's body. The sculpture was made by Kai Nielsen in 1913, and cast in bronze in 1964.

Blue-veined specialities

Denmark makes a selection of blue-veined cheeses, whose origins were greatly influenced by the examples of Roquefort and Gorgonzola. The most famous is the Danish Blue or *Danablu*, which is an excellent cheese and has achieved world-wide fame with the help of very skillful marketing. The consumption of Danish Blue in England far exceeds that of Stilton or Blue Cheshire.

Danablu was first produced before World War I, when Danish cheesemakers were experimenting with various types of mold cultures. Realizing that the mold in cheese is similar to that which grows on stale bread, a cheesemaker by the name of Marius Boel introduced a bread mold culture onto a high-fat cheese made with homogenized milk. He thus invented Danish Blue, and judging by its enormous success, he, too, deserves a statue in his honor.

Danablu come in several types: cylindrical, rectangular or square, with fat contents of 50 or 60%. The paste ripens swiftly and looks milk-white, with a delicate network of blue-green veins. Danablu cuts easier than one would normally expect from such a soft cheese, even though it is sometimes rather crumbly. Its flavor is very pronounced, often distinctly sharp. If you find it too salty, it can be improved by crumbling and mixing with butter or cream. In this form it spreads easily on sandwiches; it is also a favorite Danish accompaniment to meat.

Mycella is a larger cheese, milder in taste, more yellow in color, with a veining nearer green than blue. This is a different mold than that of Danablu. It is called *mycelium*, which gives the cheese its name, and has characteristics in common with Gorgonzola. Apart from the production of national cheese types, Denmark continues to make imitations of foreign varieties, such as *Camembert, Brie, Emmental, Saint-Paulin, Mozzarella*, various whey cheeses, *Hytteost* (cottage cheese) and *Flödeost* (cream cheese).

Smørrebród

The Danes are champion cheese eaters. On average, they consume some 10 kg (22 lbs) per person a year, mainly on open sandwiches – the famous smørrebród.

Smørrebród and the Swedish smörgåsbord are vaguely related. The first means "buttered bread," while the other means "bread and butter table." Both are ways of presenting a variety of foods – fish, meat, eggs and cheese – all at the same time and in as attractive a fashion as possible. The origins of the smørrebród are obscure, but are said to date back to the sixteenth century, and probably earlier; it may simply have been a way of displaying wealth, abundance and hospitality, for the smørrebród was almost certainly confined to the merchant class and the nobility. It should also be remembered that separate courses as such were unknown in the sixteenth century, as were forks and table napkins. Perhaps the Scandinavians were among the more civilized of nations when it came to table manners. This may be why the famous open sandwiches are today tackled with a knife and fork.

Cheese, of course, is a very popular ingredient on these open sandwiches, and may be combined with other foodstuffs, such as chopped egg, mushrooms, bacon slivers, shrimp and smoked fish. These are tastefully arranged with practiced skill on thickly buttered bread, usually rye bread and white bread.

A Danish ambassador

The consumption of cheese has increased to such an extent that a large proportion is marketed pre-packed. For this purpose the cheese is

BELOW: Danish smørrebród is justly famous. In addition to the impressive array of meat, fish and salad choices that go into the preparation of these high-rise, open sandwiches, a selection of cheeses is never omitted.

ABOVE: A large poster advertising the benefits of milk – "Milk is Healthy." The message is not lost on the average Dane, who consumes 123 liters (28 gallons) of milk a year and 10 kg (22 lbs) of cheese.

Name	Milk	Type	Rind	Form	Weight	% Fat content
Danablu	⊿	■	✂	cylinder	2.7-3.2 kg	50-60
Danbo	⊿	■	□	rectangular	6 kg	10-45
Elbo	⊿	■	□	loaf	5-6 kg	20-45
Esrom	⊿	■	❖	loaf	0.5-1.5 kg	45-60
Fynbo	⊿	■	□	cartwheel	7-8 kg	30-45
Fynsk Rygeost	⊿	○	—	container	100-600 g	5-45
Havarti	⊿	■	□ ❖	loaf, cylinder	4-5 kg	30-60
Maribo	⊿	■	□	cartwheel, rectangular	13-15 kg	20-45
Molbo	⊿	■	□	ball	1-3 kg	40-45
Mycella	⊿	■	✂	cylinder	5-9 kg	50
Samsø	⊿	■	□	cartwheel	14 kg	30-45
Tybo	⊿	■	□	loaf	2 kg	20-45

Key to symbols on page 34. 453 g = 1 lb; 1 kg = 2.2 lbs.

made slightly drier than normal, and then is allowed to ripen in the packaging, which prevents a rind from forming; the remaining moisture is retained, but the gases are able to escape.

All cheeses for export must be provided with the *lur* mark, denoting that it has been passed by state quality control. The mark shows four interwoven horns, or *lurs*, which, in the Bronze Age, formed a wind instrument used only on ceremonial occasions. It is applied on a casein disc, which in addition records the fat content and the coded production date; the label grows to form a part of the rind. Before a definite export license is granted, the cheese is once again inspected, this time at the border. A Danish cheese, after all, is as important as an ambassador.

Iceland

The northernmost point of Iceland just touches the Arctic Circle, above which day and night last half a year each and the dark winter seas are covered with drift ice. The island is a volcanic plateau with over a hundred volcanoes, many perpetually capped with snow. Much of the island is covered with solidified lava and huge glaciers; turbulent rivers create spectacular waterfalls and hot volcanic geysers spew rocks high into the air.

For centuries, the inhabitants of Iceland, a country owned successively by Norway and Denmark, were left to their own devices. They fished, they practiced agriculture and they raised cattle. During the 120 to 130 frost-free days of the year, both food for the islanders and fodder for the cattle were coaxed from the most fertile acres of land. In winter the small communities were completely isolated, and each family depended on its own herd of sheep, which have always been better equipped than cattle to endure harsh conditions. The sheep provided meat, milk and wool, ideal stock for the farming family that had to supply its own needs; even today there is hardly a farm without them.

The Icelanders have proved that despite the barren, rocky wastes and the northern climate, the land can be worked to yield adequate and even abundant food – but it has taken centuries of hard labor. The latest development is the growing of vegetables, flowers and even subtropical fruits in glasshouses heated by the thermal springs.

Early accounts of Icelandic cheese appear in the old sagas, where we find mention of *Skyr*, a fresh sheep's milk cheese which was made on farms all over the island. In later centuries farmers learned to improve the keeping qualities of their cheeses with the aid of rennet. Whey cheese – the Norwegian *Mysost* – remains one of the standard varieties, both farm- and factory-produced.

Skyr is usually made from the skimmed milk left over from butter-making. The tepid milk is curdled, or "started," with Skyr from the previous day. It is then quickly cut and set aside for an hour or so, while the whey can be drained off. The following day the residue of the whey is removed, and the soft, fresh, curd-like Skyr is ready to serve. Whipped up with milk and thickly sprinkled with sugar, Skyr is

ABOVE: These primitive Icelandic farm dwellings literally form a part of the landscape – the roof is nothing more than a layer of turf.

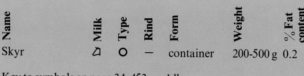

Name	Milk	Type	Rind	Form	Weight	% Fat content
Skyr	⌂	O	–	container	200-500 g	0.2

Key to symbols on page 34. 453 g = 1 lb.

eaten in vast quantities – children love it.

Nowadays, since dairy foods have become an industry, the main production of Skyr takes place in factories. The first farmers' cooperatives date from as far back as 1882, and modern Iceland boasts nineteen dairy factories, processing milk from the island's highly productive herds. Since the nineteenth century Danish cattle have been grazing the scarce pastures, and Norwegian cows were introduced even earlier. Small, rough and hardy, the present cattle have now adjusted perfectly to Icelandic conditions and provide excellent milk.

The island's dairy plants produce various cheese types, including *Tilsit, Gouda, Maribo, Odalsost,* ("baby Swiss"), *Gradaost* (blue cheese), *Camembert, Port-Salut* and *Mysingur* (soft brown cheese). Their quality is high, in keeping with the up-to-date factory equipment and the fact that Iceland's cheesemakers have profited by foreign experience. But as far as the world of cheese is concerned, the simple, traditional Skyr still remains the island's most important contribution.

LEFT: The fresh curd cheese with a tradition stretching over a thousand years – the Icelandic Skyr.

ABOVE: The only arable land is found in a small area between the coast and the mountains. Sea fishing is a more important means of existence than agriculture or cattle breeding.

Great Britain

For the succession of British poets, there have never been enough words to describe the English landscape, which can change not only from county to county, but from mile to mile. In the east, where the land is flat as a table, the soil is black, and the roads of the fen country run straight and true, there commences a gradual confusion of hills and forests, meadowland, villages and towns. Ignore the big cities and follow the rolling, twisting roads. They will take you to the mountains and valleys of Wales, or they will skirt the Pennine chain of hills – the spine of England – to take you north into the rocky, wild Scottish Highlands. Here, the coast-line is indented by deep and narrow estuaries, called firths, in contrast to the wide, placid rivers of England. From the sea ports along the coast, seafarers and explorers swarmed over the globe, and wherever they went they left a small corner of Britain in every foreign field – and possibly a cheese recipe or two.

Britain is steeped in traditions, and its institutions, from parliamentary democracy to fish and chips, have become known all over the world. But the British have often been among the first to start important new developments. Chief among these was the Industrial Revolution, begun here in the eighteenth century when farm workers, hoping to escape rural poverty, sought work in the cities – and found urban poverty instead. They left the farms by the thousands, and the cities began to expand. Yet in spite of the ensuing urbanization and industrialization, a great deal of Britain remains rural and agricultural. The country is rich in cattle and sheep, and has a true maritime climate: mild winters and cool summers, the perfect conditions for dairy farming. It is not surprising, then, that Great Britain has several unique cheese varieties of superb quality. Yet because the British drink a large quantity of milk, they are obliged to supplement their equally heavy cheese consumption by importing cheese from abroad. Over 130,000 tons of cheese are brought in each year, in addition to the 199,000 tons produced at home, of which only 3% is exported. Everybody in England, regardless of class, eats cheese, for along with bread, bacon and beer, it has been a staple for well over a thousand years.

Blue Vinny 1
Caerphilly 3
Cheddar 2
Cheshire 8
Derby 7
Dunlop 11
Gloucester, Double 4
Lancashire 9
Leicester 5
Stilton 6
Wensleydale 10

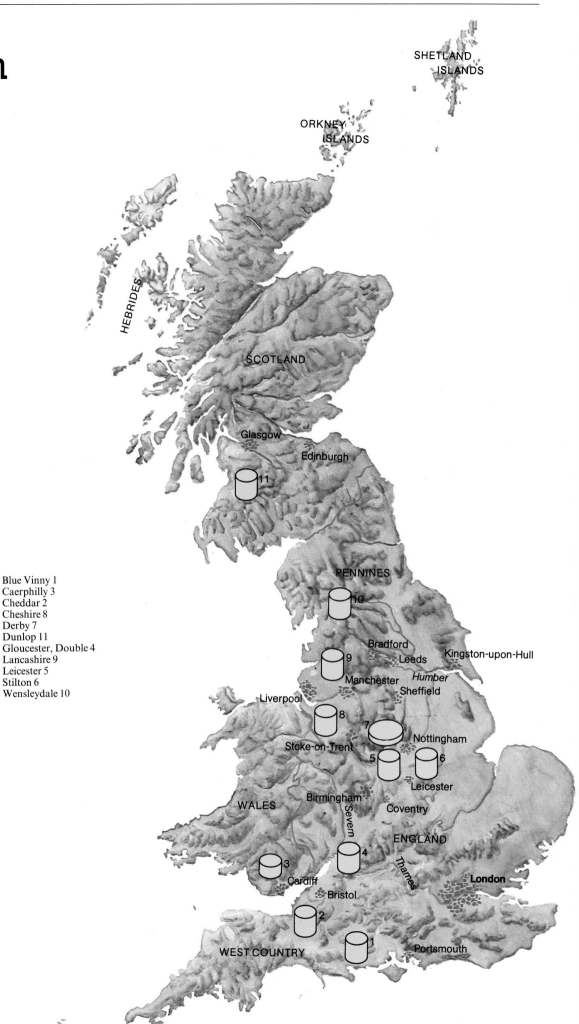

Of the English cheeses that have survived the passing of time to take their places among the great cheeses of the world, there are less than a dozen. The most popular and widely-consumed British cheese is unquestionably the great *Cheddar*, from the county of Somerset in the West Country. Here is a region where for centuries cows have grazed and cheese has been made. Somerset, together with its southern neighbor Dorset, supply well over a quarter of all the cheeses produced in England and Wales. The lovely landscape of Somerset rises abruptly in the northeast to scale the Mendip Hills, where the stalactite caves and the winding, narrow cleft known as Cheddar Gorge leads to the small village of Cheddar. The village with its souvenir shops for tourists is not particularly memorable, yet this is the cradle of a world-famous cheese, once made locally on numerous farms, as well as in some adjoining parishes.

The history of English cheese
In the Middle Ages, a farmer and his family were almost entirely self-supporting, living mainly on the produce of the farm, which included buttermilk, butter, whey and cheese. Whether they made Cheddar as we know it today is an open question, but Cheddar cheese was already in demand in the Elizabethan period, when it was described as an excellent cheese of delicate taste. Cheese was then made from both sheep's milk and cow's milk, but by the seventeenth century the preference for cow's milk was thoroughly established. Traditionally, the farmer or laborer made "common cheese" for his own consumption, a low-fat, skimmed-milk cheese which turned very hard and crumbly. But there were others who

ABOVE: Although England has densely populated industrial centers, there remain large areas of beautiful, remote countryside. Some rural villages, and habits too, have hardly altered since the eighteenth century. From this past, several great cheeses have survived.

RIGHT: In the carefree, rustic days of cheese-making, when a hefty dairymaid would use her ample weight to squeeze the whey from the curd, cheese was pressed with a heavy stone. Later versions of the cheese press employed a screw device or a pulley, so that greater pressure was exerted. Iron cheese presses, which also employ the screw system, date back to the early nineteenth century and are still in use on a few farms.

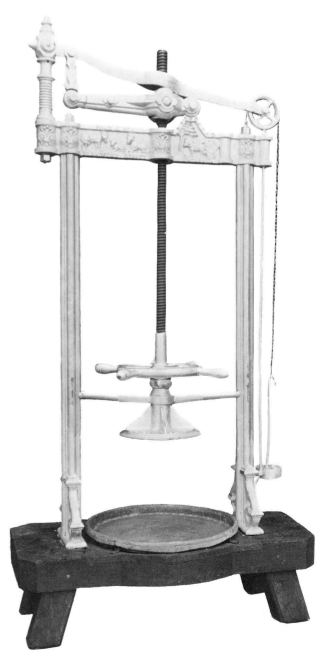

ABOVE: Traditional milk cans. Most British cheese is now made in factories. The milk is transported daily from the surrounding area, usually in large tankers.

made whole-milk cheeses, called "rich cheese," a luxurious, golden-yellow variety sold to the local gentry in the manor house, or in the nearby market town. It was made from full, fresh, morning milk, mixed with skimmed cream from the previous evening. No wonder that this "new milk," or "morning cheese," was described as long ago as 1655 as the best in England.

Not unnaturally, attempts were made to copy it on a cheaper scale. Farmers and merchants began coloring their simple skimmed-milk cheeses to give them the appearance of a richer variety. In some parts of the West Country, cheeses were dyed with saffron, long cultivated there as a food flavoring and as a dye for home-spun yarn. In the eighteenth century it was found that an extract from the fruit of a West Indian tree, *Bixa orellana*, was cheaper to use than saffron and more permanent than carrot juice. This dye, called anatta or anatto, is still the most satisfactory way of coloring cheese; the most notable examples are the bright orange *Leicester* and certain makes of *Scottish Cheddar*.

"The bigger the maid, the better the cheese"

In the good old, hit-or-miss days of cheesemaking, when Britain was entirely agricultural, most cheeses were made by a traditionally buxom, rosy-cheeked dairymaid. There were milkmaids too, and equally endowed, who feature often in English folk songs. In fact, their lives were hard and their work tedious. When no milkmaid was available, the dairy-maid had to milk the cows herself, every morning and evening. She was responsible for the upkeep of the dairy

TOP: In the heart of the Cheddar cheese country is the cathe-dral city of Wells, where cheeses are graded.

ABOVE: The birthplace of Cheddar cheese. According to legend, the caves that are a feature of Cheddar Gorge, Somerset, were once used to mature the cheeses.

LEFT: Milkmaid with a yoke. The old rhyme, "Where are you going to, my pretty maid? / I'm going a-milking, sir, she said," ignores the fact that prettiness in itself was no virtue – brawn and stamina were what was re-quired. A story tells of one village where girls were asked to lift – with one hand – the exceptionally heavy lid of an old chest. Those that failed for-feited their chance of marrying a farmer, for farmers demanded a partner who could pull her weight in the business.

and its equipment – such as there was – and she was required to have perfect knowledge of the cheesemaker's art: how to treat the milk, prepare the curd and press the cheese. Before pressing could begin it was of the greatest im-portance to have the vessels firmly filled. This the dairymaid achieved by climbing onto the lid of the cheese vessel, then pressing down on the curds with her hands, using her full weight, until most of the whey had oozed out. This pre-pressing was essential, because the primitive cheese presses of the day were unable to cope with moist curd. As the old saying goes: "The bigger the dairymaid, the better the cheese."

In the little spare time remaining, the dairymaid had to prepare rennet from the stomachs of calves, churn the butter and attend to the ripening of the cheese. Owing to this intense work program, mishaps did occur with the ripening process. The rule then was, "Save what can be saved." Because cheesemakers were ignorant of critical temperatures, acid percentages and moisture content, cheese had to be saved as often as made.

As far back as the seventeenth century, when the production on farms increased, the neighboring farmers of the Cheddar district began to work on a more or less cooperative basis. Their collective milk output was taken to a cooperative dairy, and from it cheeses of 20 to 120 pounds were made. According to their size they could be kept between two and five years. Towards the end of the seven-teenth century a lively cheese trade had developed across the country and abroad, to the considerable profit of the cheese districts.

Cheese as a family secret

Apart from the cooperative cheeses, the majority of Cheddars were farmhouse cheeses. The quality varied greatly, as did the recipes for making them – recipes that were closely-guarded family secrets passed down from mother to daughter. In the second half of the nineteenth century, a widespread reform was heralded by Joseph Harding who showed the cheesemakers a more enlightened system of production. His slogan was: "Cheese is not made in the field, nor in the byre, nor even in the cow – it is made in the dairy."

What Harding taught became known as the "cheddaring" process. The curd is cut into pieces in the normal manner. When most of the whey has been expelled, the curds are stacked in the vessel to form thick blocks, or parcels. These are turned about and folded, releasing as much moisture as possible. The temperature required during this process is approximately 37°C (98.5°F). The thick pieces, in the meantime, become very firm but "tender like the breast of a chicken." Now the moment of milling has arrived. Formerly, the dairymaid tore the curd by hand into small pieces. At the end of the eighteenth century a curd mill was invented, making the task somewhat lighter. The milled curd is placed back in the vessel, stirred and salted, and finally pressed into a mold. After maturing, the cheese should have a close, but not hard, texture without eyes. Nowadays, the farms that make their own Cheddar are few and far between; the ones that sell it are even fewer. Important customers, such as the Court, restaurants, special establishments and London clubs have a regular order for Cheddars.

Cheddar, the great traveler

The traditional farmhouse Cheddar used to be made between April 1 and November 1, but is now made throughout the year. It is usually produced from the milk of a specific breed of British cow, the Shorthorn. The cheese should have a firm, elastic consistency and a slightly nutty flavor; it must be neither too sweet nor too sour. It should ripen for at least six, but preferably twelve months or longer. The real connoisseur eats mature Cheddar with fresh bread, brown or white, or crackers; butter; sweet pickle

BELOW: A sample of milk is examined in the laboratory. For all cheese products pure milk, hygienically processed and transported, is the first requirement.

BELOW: The blades of this mechanical cutter stir and cut the curd in large troughs.

BELOW: Milling the firm, drained mass of curd. This series of photographs shows the so-called horizontal system in which the curd is processed in long, usually open, cheese tubs or troughs. The most up-to-date system is shown in the drawing below, where a vertical tower is employed.

A. The cheese-making tank. The pasteurized cheese milk (yellow) is pumped into this vat, which has a mechanical stirring and cutting device to handle the curd. The temperature of the curd-whey mixture in the tank is controlled by steam circulating between the double walls of the tank. The milk enters at a temperature of about 30°C (86°F).

B. From the starter tank a calculated amount of starter culture (gray) is added to the cheese milk.

C. Rennet (red) is also added, which causes the cheese milk to coagulate and to separate into curd and whey.

D. The curd is successively cut, stirred and heated to 35–40°C (95–104°F); some of the whey is then drawn off by suction. When these processes have been completed – which may take some 2½ hours – the mixture of curd and whey is pumped to the cheddar tower.

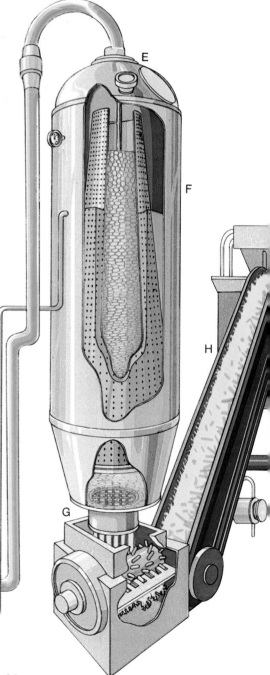

G. At the foot of the cheddar tower, the curd mass is cut into long strips and milled into finger-size pieces.

BELOW: Salt is added to the milled curd, either by hand as here, or automatically as part of a continuous production line.

BELOW: Filling the molds. In times gone by, the dairymaid had to "dress" the cheese with a "skirt" and "cap" of fine muslin cloth. Cheeses are now bound by machine and emerge from the molds in finished form.

BELOW: Cheddars are made both in the characteristic drum shape and in blocks to simplify cutting and prepacking.

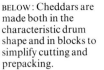

total production
British cheese
199,000 tons p.a. (100 %)

production Cheddar
118,000 tons p.a. (60 %)

of which exported
2,360 tons p.a. (2 %)

E. The cheddar tower. Cheddaring is a decisive step in the making of Cheddar cheese. The manual method consists of piling and repiling blocks of warm curd, so that the curd particles fuse together and form a fibrous mass. At the same time, moisture is expelled and the acidity of the curd increases. In the cheddar tower, this process has been successfully mechanized;

the curd is cheddared, so to speak, by its own weight.

F. In the tower, the curd moves slowly downward, reaching the correct fibrous texture by the end of its path. Whey (blue) separates from the curd through the perforated lining and is partially drawn off. Temperature in the tower is maintained at 32–38°C (90–100°F).

M. In a modern production line like this, cheesemaking can proceed virtually automatically, with a very high output, and in a continuous flow. The end product is uniform, usually of good quality, but lacks individuality. It has been estimated that the cheddar tower alone replaces the equivalent of five skilled cheesemakers, and that labor costs can be cut by more than half; on the other hand, the investments are considerable. This is another factor that forces cheese factories to become larger and larger.

or gherkins; crisp lettuce or celery; and a glass or two of hard cider. Cheddar is also an excellent companion to English draught beer, or a good Burgundy. But then, what isn't!

Since the middle of the last century, Cheddar has been made in cheese factories, also known as "creameries." Today there are more than thirty, spread right across Britain. Factory Cheddar is usually eaten at a somewhat less mature stage than the farmhouse variety, from six to eight months old. It has a very pleasant, mild flavor – milder and less sharp than the tasty farm-made cheese. It melts easily, and is therefore popular as one of the varieties used in Welsh rarebit, where cheese is cooked with beer to make a thickish sauce which is then poured onto buttered toast and browned under the grill. Of all British cheeses, Cheddar has the biggest production, sales and consumption figures. Its fame has reached far beyond the British Isles, traveling with emigrants to parts of the world where the cheddaring process could be established. Thus we have New Zealand and Australian Cheddar, New York State Cheddar and even, it is whispered, *French* Cheddar: *quel triomphe!* The cheese further owes its foreign success to the fact that it travels well and keeps its excellent quality for a long time.

Britain's Gruyère

Yet another reason for Cheddar's popularity is its application to processing. Many varieties of processed cheese use Cheddar as a base, owing to its great stability and wide appeal, qualities which it shares with Gruyère, another favorite of the processers.

Cheddar has always been a cheese demanding much time and investment, if only because of its long ripening period. It is evident that, like so many other "difficult" regional cheeses, Cheddar might have vanished forever, a victim of technical progress and economic efficiency, had it not been for a providential occurrence: the doomed Cheddar found a benefactor, a fresh cheese from Wales – Caerphilly.

H. A conveyor belt feeds the milled curd into a rotating drum, where it is thoroughly mixed with the correct dosage of dry salt.

J. The curd is poured into hoops or molds. Automatic weighing apparatus ensures the correct filling of each mold.

K. The molds move on conveyor belts to the filling machine and from there to the presses. Each mold has a piece of cheesecloth folded into it.

L. A cheese press of the horizontal type, in which the cheeses in their molds are heavily pressed for 12 to 24 hours. After pressing,

they go to airconditioned ripening rooms, while the molds are cleaned and returned to the production line.

A hundred years ago, fresh and snow-white *Caerphilly* cheese was made twice daily on nearly every farm. Contrary to the usual practice, the morning and evening milk were never mixed in making the cheese, most of it was eaten on the farm; the rest was sold in and around Cardiff. Caerphilly was very popular with the miners, because it was easily digested in the confined, cramped conditions, and being very fresh did not dry out at all.

How Caerphilly rescued Cheddar
Compared to most other British cheeses, Caerphilly is quite modern, perhaps no more than 160 years old. It was named after the village of Caerphilly where it was first made. The cheese rapidly became so popular that Welsh farmers, finding it impossible to cope with the demand, turned for help in the late nineteenth century to their neighbors across the Bristol Channel – the Cheddar makers. So it came to be that two very different types of cheese were produced on many farms in Somerset: the traditional Cheddar, a cheese that demanded considerable labor and long periods of ripening; and also Caerphilly, requiring less milk (a Cheddar requires 10 times its weight in milk; a Caerphilly only 1.1 times its weight), and offering a fairly rapid turnover – a Caerphilly could be sold after five to ten days. The Cheddar makers could thus wait patiently for their Cheddars to ripen.

Caerphilly is a soft, fresh cheese, with a mild, slightly sour flavor reminiscent of buttermilk. It is easy to cut into slices and goes well with summer salads, with bread, butter and celery.

The Single and Double Gloucester
Along the Vale of Gloucester and the Vale of Berkeley is the land of the Gloucester cheese. It is likely that cheese has been made here for over a thousand years. The cheeses were known as either Gloucester or Berkeley cheeses, probably according to the district in which they were made. They came in two sizes, the generous, well-matured *Double Gloucester* and the thinner, milder *Single Gloucester*. Of the two, only the Double has remained, perhaps because the cheesemakers, keeping an eye on export markets, appreciated its large proportions and good keeping qualities. Also, a Double Gloucester never becomes sharp, in spite of its long

ABOVE: Caerphilly Castle, in the county of Glamorgan, Wales, lies in the middle of the region where fresh, white Caerphilly cheese is made.

ABOVE: Double Gloucester cheeses. The factory-made cheese on the left is smaller than the traditional size, and is called a "truckle" cheese. On the right is a mature farmhouse cheese.

ripening period of six to twelve months.

Although Gloucesters are ancient cheeses, they were only established as a popular type at the beginning of the eighteenth century, owing to the treatment of the rind. The floor of the curing room was regularly rubbed with bean and potato stalks, leaving a wet, black deposit. The Gloucesters were placed on this and turned twice weekly, which made the rind tough as leather and improved the keeping properties of the cheese. Then came the widespread practice of coloring cheeses with carrot juice, by which it was hoped to convince buyers that the rosier the cheese, the richer was the content of milk. Still later the cheesemakers decided to enhance their product further by painting the rinds with red ochre, instead of the traditional black treatment, sometimes mixing the pigment with beer. Today the cheeses are usually found with a natural, uncolored rind.

The handsome, red cheeses featured in festivals to mark the beginning of spring. They were decorated with flowers and carried through the streets of the small village of Randwick which in old Anglo-Saxon means "the dairy farm on the hill," an additional testimony to the lineage of Gloucester cheese. A similar folklore event is still celebrated on Coopers Hill near Gloucester City on Whit Monday, when cheese wheels are rolled down the hill among great festivities.

RIGHT: Customary cheese rolling on Coopers Hill, near Gloucester city. The figure wearing the white coat and tall hat is the master of ceremonies. The decorated cheese bounces downhill, pursued by a crowd of children. This ancient custom used to be held on Midsummer Day, but has now been changed to Whit Monday.

Cheshire cheese is Cheddar's great rival. Many declare it to be the oldest of all England's cheeses. That it was also a famous cheese is evident by the fact that Cheshire was mentioned in the Domesday Book, by which time it was well established. The Roman soldiers of the 20th Legion, garrisoned in the town of Chester, possibly enjoyed the taste of this salty, crumbly cheese, made from the milk of cows that were gradually superseding the shaggy goats that had grazed here for centuries.

Cheshire cheese is named after the county, although the French, who have appreciated Cheshire for a long time, call it *Chester* after the capital, perhaps because the city was a large cheese market where cheeses were sold for export. The particular appeal and flavor of Cheshire cheese is due not only to the preparation and ripening techniques, but to the quality of the region's soil. Local farmers declare that the Cheshire meadows are the finest in England, and perhaps the most unique, due to salt deposits found in the lands below Nantwich and Middlewich, dating from a period when prehistoric seas covered the area.

Cattle that graze in Cheshire pastures are noted for the high salt content of their milk, which then endows the cheese with such a characteristic flavor that it is impossible to imitate outside Cheshire. The cheese ripens slowly and possesses a fat content of 48%.

LEFT: A fine farmhouse Cheshire cheese. Until well into the nineteenth century, farmers paid their rent in Cheshire cheeses.

LEFT: Making cheese in Wensleydale, Yorkshire. It is important that the curd and whey are well separated, and that the curd is thoroughly drained.

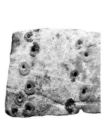

ABOVE: Excellent, rare and expensive – a blue Cheshire cheese. Note the holes where the cheese has been skewered, the mold may then develop in the channels thus formed, a matter of luck and judgment.

Until the Second World War, the cheese was mainly farm produced. There are still some twenty farms making their own cheese, and fortunately it looks as if their number may be increasing. Cheshire is made in three varieties – red, white and blue – and is thus said to endear itself to Union Jack patriots. White Cheshire is a quick-ripening product which uses a larger quantity of rennet as a starter; it is pale cream in color and mild in flavor. Its keeping properties, however, are poor, and it turns acid and bitter in flavor. The red, semimature cheese is made from May to October, has a mild, nutty flavor and is ready for sale after about six weeks. Anatto dye is used to create the orange color of the cheese.

Blue Cheshire is an almost totally different cheese, and one of the greatest "blues" in the world. The invasion of the blue mold is always accidental, although slightly encouraged. The cheesemaker never adds special doses of mold culture, but with an expert eye selects those cheeses which seem to have the propensity for turning blue. He then places these cheeses in a very humid cellar, skewering them occasionally with the hope that the blue may develop in the air channels. His satisfaction when the mold takes is considerable, because this splendid cheese, quite the equal of Stilton, has become rather rare and fetches high prices.

A blue Cheshire cheese is distinctive in appearance, being orange with blue veining. It has turned from the crumbly texture of the ordinary cheese to a soft, buttery one with a unique taste. There are no better accompaniments than crusty, fresh bread, farmhouse butter and ale, or fruity Burgundy, or – it's up to you.

The good cheese of Mrs. Paulet
Fortunately for the devotees of blue cheese, there is plenty of *Stilton* to supplement the lack of blue Cheshire. This almost sounds as if blue Cheshire would naturally be the first choice, but to the majority of Englishmen, Stilton is *the* blue cheese, and has been aristocracy's companion to Port wine for over three hundred years. Stilton is made in tall, cylindrical shapes weighing either seven or fourteen pounds. Together with Cheddar and Cheshire, it is among the most famous of English cheeses, dating back to the seventeenth

century. Some have suggested that Stilton may have derived from goat's or sheep's milk cheeses which "blued" like Roquefort and were made in the Vale of Belvoir in the Middle Ages.

Popular legend has it that Stilton was first made at Quenby Hall, Leicestershire, the country seat of Lady Beaumont. Her housekeeper, a Mrs. Paulet, had a brother-in-law who was landlord of the Bell Inn in the small village of Stilton. She supplied him with the home-made cheese which was surplus to the household requirements. The Bell was a coaching stop on the Great North road, and the cheese soon became famous as "Mrs. Paulet's cheese." The writer Daniel Defoe, however, reports having enjoyed Stilton cheese at the Bell in the year 1720, some ten years before the arrival of Mrs. Paulet's cheese. Furthermore, there were others who claim to have invented Stilton, notably a Mrs. Orton of Little Dalby near Melton Mowbray. The origin of Stilton remains a mystery, but Mrs. Paulet's complicated recipe was still being used even in this century, until Stilton became a factory cheese.

It is made of the richest whole milk. After curdling, cutting and stirring, the whey is separated from the curds, which are then salted and placed in deep, wooden hoops. The curd is regularly turned so that adequate drainage can take place. Stilton is not pressed. After about one week the curd is removed from the hoop, bound in calico, and left in a cool, moist atmosphere for another week. During this period the characteristic brown rind begins to form, and the cheese gradually becomes firm enough to keep its shape without the cheese cloth.

A fresh, white Stilton is also made. It is very crumbly, with a strong smell and a flavor that is mild and gentle, yet sourish. Only in the cool, humid ripening cellars does the blue mold develop. Fine, steel skewers or needles are driven into the cheese, and the blue mold develops in the resulting channels to spread throughout. Stilton needs four to six months to mature properly; unfortunately, it is often sold when too fresh, when it is hard, white, chalky and acidic in flavor.

Just as the firm of Hutchinson in Whitchurch, Shropshire, store and age their own blue Cheshires, so the world-famous cheese department of Fortnum & Mason in London stores its Stilton.

RIGHT: A small Double Gloucester cheese next to a pot of Fortnum & Mason's best blue Stilton. In the background is a white Stilton.

In the cellars beneath the premises, assistants turn the cheeses daily and regularly brush the rind clean to avoid fungi and mites.

In the seventeenth and eighteenth centuries no such care was taken. Cheeses tended to be stored in damp and dirty cellars, and, interestingly enough, many connoisseurs did not consider a cheese fully matured unless it was swarming with mites. When you consider the prevailing lack of attention to hygiene – even in the dairy – it was not surprising that many cheeses turned blue, and it was the blue cheeses in particular that received the attentions of mites. Today Stilton and other English blue cheeses are made with fine-quality milk and ripened in a carefully controlled environment.

Ripe Stilton should have a well-crinkled, brown rind and a pale, slightly flaky texture. The flavor is smooth and mellow, much milder than other blue cheeses. The blue-green mold should be evenly distributed, although it is often inclined to concentrate towards the center. When the edges are brown the cheese is fully ripe, and although Stilton is available all the year round, it is at its best from November to April, and is especially enjoyed at the Christmas table.

The best way to cut a Stilton is in horizontal slices across the top. The alternate method – that of scooping out the center with a spoon – causes the cheese to go dry and crumbly. This is sometimes remedied by pouring

LEFT: A perfect example of a well-matured, royal Stilton cheese. Fruit and nuts are by no means essential accompaniments. All that is required is a biscuit or a slice of crusty bread, plus a glass or two of Port or Burgundy. Stilton may be purchased almost everywhere throughout the year, but is held to be at its best during the Christmas season.

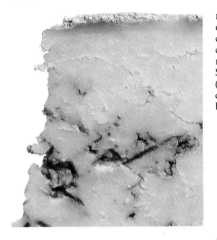

LEFT: A motorway now by-passes the historic Bell Inn at Stilton, Leicestershire. The inn, which is now closed, was where Stilton cheese was sold in the seventeenth century.

LEFT: Blue Wensleydale, the Yorkshire cheese which can compete with the more famous Stilton. Some people claim (Yorkshire folk, no doubt) that Stilton is but a variation of the original, blue Wensleydale. White Wensleydale is said to be *the* cheese to eat with apple pie.

Port wine into the cavity, but this does little to improve matters. Better to cut a modest piece and enjoy it with a few dry biscuits and a stick of celery, and perhaps a glass or two of Port or Burgundy.

Apple pie and cheese

There is another fine British blue, made like Stilton in both white and blue varieties. This is *Wensleydale*, a Yorkshire cheese of more ancient lineage. It is said that Wensleydale was made by the Cistercian monks of the now-ruined Jervaulx and Fountains abbeys, from an original Norman recipe. This would imply that blue Wensleydale is perhaps an ancestor of the Norman Bleu de Bresse, but in many ways it is a closer relative of Roquefort – or rather, it used to be, as the cheese was originally made from sheep's milk (as is the great French cheese), or occasionally from goat's milk, whichever happened to be available.

For centuries the monks had upheld their traditions of agriculture, cattle breeding and dairying, and after the dissolution of the monasteries by Henry VIII in the sixteenth century, they taught their cheesemaking methods to the local farmers' wives.

It was sometime during the seventeenth century that most farms turned to whole cow's milk. In those days, blue Wensleydale would have been eaten on the dale farms, along with the famous York ham and pieces of the oatbread called havercake, alas now extinct. A local rival to the Wensleydale cheese was called Cotherstone, and was made in the village of that name in Teesdale. It was also known as "Yorkshire Stilton," and if it is still being made it's a well-kept secret.

The term "blue" Wensleydale

BELOW: Hebden Bridge in the Pennines, close by the industrial heart of Yorkshire. Britain's largest county has wild moorland, alternating with good pastures and industrial areas.

implies that there is a white one. This is indeed the case, and it is a much bigger seller. White Wensleydale is often sold when very young. It has a slightly sour, buttermilk flavor not unlike Caerphilly.

Making Wensleydale cheese requires careful attention. The great secret is that the curd must not turn sour, and this depends on the freshness and sweetness of the milk, the quantity of rennet and the slow drainage of the curd. Slices of curd, wrapped in calico, are placed on drainage receptacles and turned every twenty minutes. When the whey has been expelled, the curd is salted and put into vessels, where it remains overnight without pressing. The next morning it is bound with calico and pressed for just a few hours; the impression of this calico band can clearly be seen on the cheese afterwards.

During ripening, the cheese, which is still very soft, is turned every day for the first few weeks, and later every other day. It is ripe after some months, and velvety in texture. The majority of Wensleydale cheeses on the market are the white, unripened sort. Blue-veined Wensleydale is fairly rare: it can be spread like butter and has a mild, creamy flavor. A daunting rival of Stilton, it has practically the same shape and weight, but differs in having a gray-white rind.

In the north of England, apple pie and white Wensleydale cheese are a favorite combination. The saying goes in Yorkshire: "Apple pie without cheese is like a kiss without a squeeze." Another well-known verse concurs: "But I, when I undress me / Each night, upon my knees / Will ask the Lord to bless me / With apple pie and cheese."

BELOW: The rugged landscape of Skye in the Hebrides. Although the islands are noted for their whiskey, some still produce their own cheeses.

Centuries ago, when most farms made their own cheese, English cheeses were found in great variety. They say that the railways put an end to the variety, for milk could be transported in bulk to dairies, and cheeses became regional. While it remains true that the odd farm still makes its own cheese, such local specialities as Bath cheese, Oxford, Suffolk (said to be the world's hardest), Essex, the blue Cottenham from Cambridge, the Daventry and the Lincoln have disappeared forever; only the great ones have survived.

The quality of *Leicester* has always been protected, as witness the town crier of Leicester who used to call out a list of fines and punishments for spoiling or adulterating the cheese. In its crumbly structure it resembles Cheshire cheese, but it receives a much greater dose of anatto coloring to give it the familiar, deep orange hue. On the cheese board it contrasts pleasantly with others. Leicester is one of the finest and mildest of English cheeses, and it reaches the peak of perfection after about six to nine months. As it melts easily, it is useful in cooking, especially for Welsh rarebit.

In the kitchens of the scattered farmhouses on the lonely hills of Lancashire, white *Lancashire* cheese is still made, as of old, from a mixture of two days' curd. The curd is kept for a fortnight, during which time the acid develops that is responsible for the whiteness of the cheese. After passing through the curd mill, Lancashire is salted and pressed. At present, a total of about 150 cheeses are made every week on the farms, the rest coming from the creameries. Lancashire is ripe after two to three months and should then be eaten at once, which means that practically the entire production is consumed in the immediate vicinity. A soft cheese, after three months it can still be spread like butter, but it is by no means as mild, having developed a strong aroma and a more pronounced flavor than either Cheddar or Cheshire. Like Leicester, the cheese melts easily, and for this reason used to be called "the Leigh toaster," after the town of Leigh, near Manchester.

The popularity of *Derby* cheese suffers from the fact that it closely resembles Cheddar and, quite simply, most people prefer Cheddar. Production is on a fairly limited scale, and the cheese is not subject to the rigorous grading scrutiny of Cheddars. Derby

ABOVE: Dunlop cheese under the press in an old cheese factory still operating today. Dunlop is often compared with Double Gloucester, which it somewhat resembles, and with Cheddar is the biggest selling cheese in Scotland.

LEFT: There's a lot to be said for a piece of Lancashire cheese and a good glass of ale.

is a mild, pleasant cheese, a solid, hard-pressed type with a fairly high moisture content. It is sold from six weeks old, when it is rather unripe, but the ripening defects from which it once suffered have been eliminated, and a mature Derby – like any good cheese – is worth waiting for.

There is a flavored variety known as *Sage Derby*, which has undergone several changes in its history. Originally, it was flavored with finely chopped, fresh sage leaves, which were mixed with the curd. The next development was to grind the leaves and add spinach juice, which gave the cheese a bright, green streak through its center, like a sandwich. Then the makers created a marbling effect, which is the current fashion. The original type is once more available in limited quantities, however, especially at Christmas time.

The three counties where farmhouse cheese is still made have united to form the "Golden Cheese Hoard of Farmhouse Cheddar, Cheshire and Lancashire." The Milk Marketing Board organizes its production and, with the English Country Cheese Council, promotes both farmhouse and factory cheese produced in England and Wales.

A few other varieties are made, which are of importance in their own region, and are sometimes to be found in the shops of big cities, where they are appreciated as special cheeses.

Regional specialities

More of a curiosity than a speciality is the *Dorset Blue*, otherwise known as *Blue Vinney*. The word *Vinney* is thought to derive from the Old English *fyniz*, meaning "mold." It is a hard, blue-veined cheese that was once produced on nearly every farm in

RIGHT: A fine display of British cheeses, photographed at Wells Stores, Streatley. Next to the Stilton, on the left of the top shelf, is a blue Wensleydale and three Leicesters. Below is a small Double Gloucester perched on two Cheddars; between these and the half of a full-size Gloucester are some baby Cheshires. On the lower shelf is a white Lancashire (far left) next to a white Wensleydale, and various Scottish cheeses (the small round ones at the back are from Islay and the Orkneys). In the front is a large Derby cheese, two Gloucesters and a piece of Sage Derby.

LEFT: The label from a Caithness cheese, made in the far north of Scotland.

Dorset from milk that had been skimmed by hand. Consequently it was fat-deprived, and its chalky, loose consistency caused air pockets favorable for mold development. There were other factors too. In former times, the milk was often contaminated and dairy conditions unhygienic; cheeses would be stored in a shed together with leather horse harnesses and wet boots – conditions ideal for mold development. Blue veining will occur much more readily in a full-fat cheese, with more enjoyable results, and so the spontaneous growth in a Dorset cheese was a rare event – even then, the cheese required eighteen months to mature. It was said to be so hard that the people of Dorset used it to make locomotive wheels.

Blue Vinney is now almost extinct, and attempts to revive it have been unsuccessful. It is possible to find a shop that sells a cheese purporting to be "Blue Vinney," but it is more likely to be a second- or third-grade Stilton.

In recent times a number of new cheeses – some good, some bad – have appeared on the market. There is the upstart *Red Windsor* (a Cheddar impregnated with wine) and a Stilton encrusted with walnuts, not really to be taken seriously. A very pleasant newcomer is *Caboc*, a full-cream, cylindrical cheese covered in oatmeal, and made in Scotland; its taste is sometimes slightly sourish, and nutty due to the oatmeal. There are also several small, soft cheeses from the north of Scotland: *Caithness* cheese, *Orkney* cheese, and *Islay* from the Hebridean island of that name. The most famous of the Scottish clan is certainly the *Dunlop* from Ayrshire. During the lactation period, Ayrshire cows provide an amazing 11,600 kg of milk – nearly 40 liters (48.4 quarts)

per day. Dunlop is said to owe its existence to an Irish refugee of the late seventeenth century, one Barbara Gilmour, who arrived in Ayr and made her cheeses according to an Irish recipe. It is not unlike Cheddar, but light of color and rather bland and moister, even when well-matured. Dunlop is usually eaten quite young, when only a few months old; it goes well with buttered oatcakes and Scotch ale.

The modern, younger generation of Scot seems to prefer the anatto-dyed *Scottish Cheddar*, while the older generation still enjoys such rough-hewn country cheeses as the nameless "farm cheese" flavored with caraway seeds, found in Aberdeenshire. Then there's *Crowdie*, a full-cream, fresh cheese made in country farms by adding rennet to tepid milk straight from the cow. As soon as the curd is formed, it is put into a colander with a cheese cloth and left to drain. After some hours the curd is placed in a basin and mixed with cream and a pinch of salt.

It would be a mistake to suppose that British farmers' wives throughout the country make *cottage cheese* and *pot cheese* to any extent or variety. A few do, here and there, especially in summer when milk tends to sour, but the majority go to the local supermarket and buy processed Cheddar – it's one of the sad facts of our advanced civilization.

The British tend to be resistant to changes in their daily diet. Although they have embraced hamburgers and spaghetti (they even manufacture their own spaghetti and, it is rumored, export it to Italy), only the indigenous cheeses are made in the United Kingdom; one does not find in the range of cheeses any of a clearly foreign origin. In this sense all cheeses made in Great Britain are British originals, stemming mostly from an ancient tradition which has inspired a degree of pride and prejudice: the British seem to prefer their own cheeses to anyone else's.

Name	Milk	Type	Rind	Form	Weight	% Fat content
Blue Vinny	⟋	■	✂	cylinder	6-7 kg	15-45
Caerphilly	⟋	●	☐	low cylinder	3.6 kg	48
Cheddar	⟋	■	☐	cylinder, cube	18-27 kg	48
Cheshire	⟋	■	☐✂	cylinder	22 kg	48
Derby	⟋	■	☐	cartwheel	13-14 kg	48
Dunlop	⟋	■	☐	cylinder	27 kg	48
Gloucester, Double	⟋	■	☐	cylinder	28 kg	48
Lancashire	⟋	●	☐	cylinder, loaf	22.5 kg, 4.5-5.5 kg	48
Leicester	⟋	■	☐	cylinder	13-18 kg	48
Stilton	⟋	■	✂	cylinder	6.4-8.2 kg	48
Wensleydale	⟋	■	☐✂	cylinder	4.5-5.5 kg	48

Key to symbols on page 34. 1 kg = 2.2 lbs.

Ireland

To the Irish, a gentle curtain of soft rain is part of their natural heritage, as are mild winters. The basin-shaped island is badly drained, and there are many rivers, lakes and marshes alternating with wet grassland. The "Emerald Isle" is green indeed, but better suited to cattle raising than agriculture, all the more so as cattle can remain outside throughout the year. The cattle of Cork are famous; so too are the sheep of Galway, Cork and Tipperary.

The Irish shores along the Atlantic Ocean were long thought to be the boundary of the inhabitable world, and for many peoples in their westward expansion the island of Ireland was the end of the trail. The Iron Age Celts populated Ireland, and their culture remains today a strong influence. Much later came the preachers of Christianity – the Roman legions having ignored Ireland – then the Viking invaders, and finally the English, who would remain for many centuries.

All these foreign influences, particularly that of the English, left their mark on traditional Irish culture. This race of people, although they lived on the furthest edge of the European continental shelf must have adopted certain foods and eating habits of other nations. Cheese must have been made since time immemorial, and as elsewhere in the world, it would have been fresh cheese. The Scandinavian invaders who had settled in Ireland taught the Irish how to make cheese which could be preserved.

Following the fall of the Roman Empire, and the successive waves of barbarians across Europe, civilization almost disappeared. In Ireland, however, it had been preserved. When the storm subsided, the island had proved a safe refuge for the culture that had been destroyed elsewhere. From numerous monasteries, the monks dispersed back to the continent to preach the Gospel, and to teach improved agricultural and dairying methods.

A companion to Guinness

It would appear that the Celts are rather indifferent to cheese, and that there is no special Irish cheese type. The average Irishman enjoys a fairly simple but wholesome diet of milk, butter, poultry, bread, potatoes, meat occasionally and fish more frequently (because of the Catholic influence),

TOP LEFT: In the remote corners of southwestern Ireland, as here on the Ring of Kerry, you might still hear the Gaelic language.

TOP RIGHT: Much of Ireland's fine produce is exported, especially lobsters, oysters and a large variety of cheeses. Only in Ireland are you likely to find the indigenous Blarney cheese. Its ideal companions are draught stout, soda bread and Irish butter.

LEFT: The cattle market at Ballymote, Sligo. The Irish are famous for their appraisal of livestock, and especially of horses.

although most of Ireland's famous lobsters and shellfish are exported abroad. Precious little is left of the old Irish cheese specialities. As an indigenous companion to Guinness stout, only *Blarney* may be mentioned: a semihard and whole-fat cheese of 48% with small round holes and a mild flavor, somewhat resembling the Danish Samsø.

The complete disappearance of many original Irish cheeses does not mean that cheese is no longer made in Ireland. On the contrary, production in the dairy industry is increasing by leaps and bounds: at least tenfold during the last decade. The factories produce over thirty thousand tons of cheese a year. Most of these are English cheeses, which is understandable considering the British influence. The most important among these is *Cheddar*, 90% of which is exported; another Cheddar-like cheese is *Killarney*, specially made for export to Canada. Additionally, the range includes versions of *Cheshire, Wensleydale, Caerphilly, Leicester, Double Gloucester, Wexford* (a Cheshire variety, which was first produced in 1964), *Blue, Gouda, Edam, Emmental, Gruyère, Brie, Camembert, Port-Salut, Pont-l'Evêque, Cottage cheese* and other fresh cheeses and cheese spreads. They will even tell you, over a glass of stout, that Irish Camembert is exported to France!

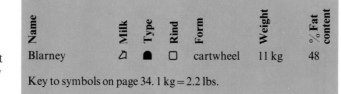

Name	Milk	Type	Rind	Form	Weight	% Fat content
Blarney	⌓	■	□	cartwheel	11 kg	48

Key to symbols on page 34. 1 kg = 2.2 lbs.

Netherlands

The sea would claim much of Holland if it could: the northern and western provinces of the Netherlands are below sea level, and their very existence is the outcome of an age-old struggle between the Dutch and the invading ocean. Because the country is flat – save for the tiny, hilly area south of the province of Limburg – the landscape gives the impression of a vast spaciousness, where land, sea and sky become fused together.

Even before the dykes were built to protect the inhabitants from the sea, there were more than enough fertile, green acres to make the Netherlands a prominent dairy country: round, brick containers with perforated bottoms, apparently cheese molds, have been discovered in ancient Frankish dwellings of the fourth century A.D. We learn from ninth-century records, that the Frisians made butter and cheese for the court of Charlemagne. During the Middle Ages, the collective efforts of farmers from all over Holland led to a prosperous period, with the rise of dairy markets and the *kaaswaag* (cheese weigh-house) where cow's, goat's and sheep's milk cheeses were inspected for quality and weight. Haarlem already had a dairy trade center in 1266, Leiden in 1303, and Leeuwarden in Friesland got its town weigh-house in 1386. At the same time, the export of cheese developed, first overland and via the Rhine to Germany (still the biggest importer of Dutch cheese) and later, when the Dutch became the "freight carriers of Europe," by sea to the farthest corners of the Baltic and Mediterranean.

Looking at the bills of lading of the Dutch trading vessels during that time, it seems incredible that such enormous quantities of cheese could be produced since the milk yield was considerably lower than that of today, the farmer-cheesemakers were ill-equipped, and transport was slow.

Cattle now graze on reclaimed land that was once the sea's dominion – the elegant, piebald Frisians and the robust Groningens with their black-and-white faces. Further inland, along the winding rivers and waterways, Maas, Rhine and IJssel cattle are herded to the spotless dairies. More than a third of the land here is used for cattle breeding and milk production so that the Netherlands is now the biggest cheese exporter in the world.

ABOVE: A special postmark of 1918. It states: "Gouda cheese and pig market; market day on Thursday." The cheese market is still held on Thursday, throughout the year, in the triangular market-place.

Edam 3
Friese Nagelkaas 1
Gouda 5
Kernhem 2
Leiden 4

LEFT: Milking time in a Dutch polder near Volendam. In the summer the farmer goes to the meadow twice a day, but during the winter the cattle are stabled and are milked under cover.

TOP LEFT: The old cheese weigh-house in Gouda, the Kaaswaag, designed and built in 1668 by P. Post. Above the entrance is a fine relief which shows how cheeses were weighed.

TOP RIGHT: A between-the-wars photograph of the famous cheese market in Gouda. This was before the automobile took over, and farmers came to market by horse and cart, bringing their consignment of cheeses. Although most of Holland's Gouda is now made in factories, true farmhouse Gouda is still obtainable everywhere.

BELOW: A typical Dutch farmhouse near Haastrecht. The cheesemaking room lies in the extension of the rear of the house, visible on the far left.

ABOVE: A stack of *Boerenkaas* Goudas (*Boeren* means "farmer"). Only factory cheese carries the name "Gouda" stamped on the rind.

The urban areas that include Amsterdam, The Hague, Rotterdam and Utrecht are grouped to form the modern, industrial heart of the Netherlands – the *Randstad* Holland – and between them, nestling in the green countryside, is Gouda, the birthplace of *Gouda* cheese. Even today there are about a thousand Gouda cheese farms in the provinces of South Holland and Utrecht. Legend claims that the first Gouda cheese was made in the nearby village of Stolwijk; the name Stolwijk is still a guarantee of an extremely tasty type of Gouda.

Traditionally, the area was not only known for the production of excellent milk and cheese, but also for trade and freight: Gouda stands at the junction of two rivers, the Gouwe and the Hollandse IJssel, where shipbuilders once put the resources of the wooded countryside to profitable use. In early times, Gouda was one of the five principal Dutch trading centers, with a flourishing industry in textiles, brewing, leather, pottery and dairy produce. In the thirteenth century there was a thriving cattle market, and also a city market held every six months, where English and Scottish merchants came to buy and sell cheese. According to accounts in old publications, Gouda cheese was compared to England's Derby cheese in freshness and density, and experiments were carried out on the farms with Derby mold cultures.

A good deal in Goudas

Between the famous Gouda Town Hall and the Kaaswaag, which dates from 1668 and sports a marble relief depicting the old weighing trade over the entrance, farmers continue to sell their cheeses according to ancient custom. Each Thursday morning, buyers inspect wagons of cheeses covered with tarpaulins and make their offers – or rather, the buyer suggests a price and the farmer automatically declines. The buyer later returns with a second offer – it's all part of the game – and the farmer suggests a higher figure. Again the buyer walks away, but the third time they will, no doubt, agree. The deal is completed with a slap of hands, and the farmer drives his wagon to the weigh-house.

The number of cheese farms has decreased over the years, so that the

LEFT: Making cheese on the farm. After the curd has been curdled, cut and ripened, it is transferred to a wooden container.

contradictory increase in production can be put down to the improved market value of Gouda farm cheese, and also to the modern methods of manufacture. Since the installation of a cooling system, there is no need to process the fresh milk yield twice daily, as had long been the case. Now "day cheese" is made from fresh morning milk and warmed evening milk from the previous day.

Modern farmhouse ways

The showpiece of modern, hygienic farmhouse cheesemaking is the teak cheese vat, with its stainless steel liner behind which either hot or cold water can circulate. The vat is equipped with an electric mechanism for cutting and stirring the curd, and has a capacity of 1,500 liters (1,650 quarts). An average herd of thirty cows may produce, at the height of the season, about 600 liters (660 quarts) of milk per milking, and for every kilo (2.2 lbs) of cheese about 10 liters (11 quarts) of milk is required.

The making of Gouda cheese is mainly done by women, usually the farmer's wife, assisted by a daughter, and they start at six o'clock in the morning. Long experience has taught them exactly how much rennet and starter to add to a given quantity of milk in the vat, and at what temperature this must be done. Cheese molds are prepared according to the yield of milk: for example, where 400 liters (440 quarts) of milk are used, four 10 kg (22 lbs) molds or five 8 kg (17.6 lbs) molds are needed. The curdled milk is stirred, left for a while, brought to a higher temperature, and then stirred again. When the women have determined with their expert skill that the curd pieces are of the right size and consistency, they fill the molds.

The filling is done in one of two ways: either by dividing the curd into large blocks, and putting a block into each mold, or by crumbling the curd into the mold. This "crumbling" cheese later reveals many small, irregular holes, because of the air incorporated during the process; the so-called "one-piece" shows only a few large and regular holes.

A cheese of great character

After the molds have been filled, the cheese is pressed, stamped with the government mark for farmhouse

LEFT: The curd is then gathered in a cheese cloth.

LEFT: The cloth containing the curd is suspended to allow whey to drain off after which the curd is put into a cheese mold lined with a cloth, well-distributed and firmly pressed.

BELOW: The mold is sealed with a lid, which fits inside its inner rim. The cheeses are then pressed before being given a brine bath.

cheese, wrapped in a clean cloth and pressed again. A period in a tiled, brine bath, with a salt solution of the correct strength, completes the main preparation. During ripening, the Gouda cheese develops its characteristic smell and taste: a farmhouse cheese made from whole, raw milk has a delicious aroma, immediately evident as soon as the cheese is cut. Evident also is the promise of the slightly sweet, full and often somewhat pronounced flavor that surprises the tongue again and again. The cheese remains smooth, even as it gets older. Expert cheese tasters are able to recognize the region – and even the farm – that a particular Gouda cheese comes from. Even those with an untrained palate will at once recognize the subtle transformation that has occurred between an adolescent Gouda and a really mature example, one that has reached, say, the ripe old age of twelve to fourteen months. The rind can become so hard that it needs cutting with a saw before you can proceed with a cheesewire or knife. The paste becomes very firm, rather like Gruyère, and the flavor is slightly salty but full. It has taken on, as wine tasters would say, "a character of great breeding."

Kaasdoop, the Dutch fondu

A small quantity of farmhouse Gouda is retained by the farmer for use in the kitchen. Generous slices are cut for sandwiches, and the rind may be fried with potatoes or added to mashed potatoes or stews. A traditional, simple, utilitarian dish, particularly convenient in the past when the busy farm schedule left little time for elaborate preparation, is the Gouda Kaasdoop, in which cheese is cooked with milk and eaten in the manner of a Swiss fondu, but with brown bread or boiled potatoes. A rather rustic, country dish, it was later taken up by city dwellers who served it in a more elegant fashion with French bread and fondu forks, dipping the bread into the Kaasdoop contained in a fireproof dish over a small flame. The farmers, contemptuous of the Kaasdoop's newly acquired sophistication, eaten in a communal fashion that they considered unhygienic, dropped it from their menu.

LEFT: The official label for Gouda factory-made cheese. The codes refer to the production date and producer.

BELOW: Arrival of milk in a modern cheese factory. An operator controls the fully mechanized process.

total production Dutch cheese 335,000 tons p.a. (100%)

production Gouda 202,300 tons p.a. (60%)

of which exported 103,500 tons p.a. (51%)

The unique and typical qualities of farmhouse Goudas are notably absent from the factory product. This isn't to say that factory Gouda is robbed of a marked degree of excellence. On the contrary, it is widely exported and enjoyed throughout the world. The factory cheese, however, lacks the subtle, distinct character of the farmhouse variety; for the connoisseur the surprise element is gone.

A safe and sure product

Since factory Gouda is made over a wide area and not restricted to a certain region; since the preparation of the curd often demands production on a massive scale, utilizing 10,000 liters (11,000 quarts) of milk, this loss of individuality is hardly surprising. Furthermore, the milk may come from a considerable distance and may be the product of a number of different farms. For these reasons the milk is pasteurized. so that possible bacteria which might cause defects in the cheese are destroyed, as are, inevitably, the microorganisms that create the farmhouse character. In one respect the factory cheese has the advantage of being standardized: the shopper knows in advance what the cheese will taste like. There are three different kinds from which to choose, according to preference: very mild, young Gouda; a more matured and aromatic variety; and the fully matured, old and piquant type. The *Lunchkaas*, or *Baby Gouda*, is a small, model Gouda, always eaten while young and fresh. *Amsterdam* cheese is a Gouda variety with an increased moisture content and a very smooth, full flavor. There is also a spiced Gouda, flavored with cumin seeds, which is eaten when young. It has a spicy, creamy taste that is best appreciated on a slice of brown bread or on toast.

Gouda in the kitchen
Because its firm consistency varies with age, Gouda has many applications in the kitchen. Irrespective of whether the cheese comes from farm

A. In the cheese-making tank, starter and rennet are mixed into the pasteurized cheese milk (yellow), which coagulates within approximately 20-30 minutes. The curd is cut and stirred automatically according to a preselected program. Part of the whey is run off. The temperature during this 1½-2 hours' treatment is increased from 30°C (86°F) to 35°C (95°F).

B. When the curd is ready, it is transferred to a buffer tank. More whey may be run off from the curd-whey mixture.

C. The wet curd is pumped into a filling apparatus. The precise weight of curd is poured into the molds (nowadays made of steel or plastic rather than teakwood), which arrive on a conveyor belt. Immediately after filling, a circular press descends into the mold where it expels more whey from the curd.

D. The filled cheese molds travel to the press.

E. They are pressed for 1-8 hours under a large hydraulic press. There is now a tendency to use higher pressures for a shorter period of time, since this makes possible a continuous flow of production.

F. After pressing, the cheeses – still in their molds – move slowly up and finally down a high stack of cheeses. This "waiting period" between being pressed and salted improves the quality of the cheese.

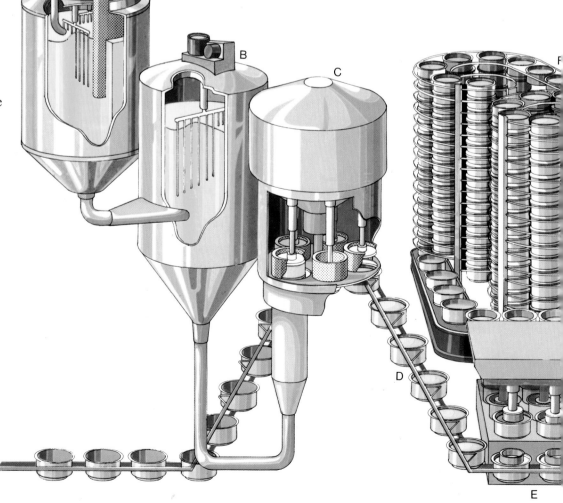

BELOW: Racks of
cheeses are lowered
into the brine bath
and lifted out again
by machine.

BELOW: Each finished
cheese is given a wax
or plastic coating.
This minimizes the
need to wipe and clean
the cheeses during
storage and gives
additional protection
during transport.

or factory, the versatile Gouda is
excellent with many types of bread.
For cooking, choose a young Gouda
when you require a melting cheese; a
mature Gouda when the cheese is to
be served whole, or remain visible in
the dish, as with cheese ragout, cooked
dishes with diced cheese, or baked
cheese schnitzels; and an old cheese
when you need to grate it.

Gouda can be used for a number of
recipes calling for a firm cheese or a
grating cheese, a quality it shares with
Gruyère and Cheddar. It may be used
as a basis for such sauces as Mornay
Sauce; in certain soups such as onion
soup or Dutch cheese soup (see recipe
section); in soufflés; in fish dishes
where a slice of cheese is melted on the
fish. It may also be served in savory
omelettes and in the form of a fondu,
like the previously mentioned
Kaasdoop.

Besides the traditional cartwheel
shape, Gouda is made in square or
loaf-shaped forms, as is the case with
Edam cheese, although the latter is
normally globe-shaped. You can spot
the difference by looking at the official
label: 48% indicates the full-fat
Gouda, while 40% refers to Edam,
with its lower fat content.

G. They are taken out
of their molds – and
are quite firm. The
cheeses have de-
veloped a rind and
have lost most of the
excess moisture. They
are now ready for a
brine bath.

H. Big containers
loaded with cheeses
are lowered into the
brine bath and taken
out again after 1-2
days.

J. This salt bath
serves many
functions: it improves
the flavor and the
structure of the
cheese; it acts as a pre-
servative; and it pro-
motes the formation
of a hard, dry rind.

K. Finally, the
cheeses are transferred
to the ripening rooms.
Often the newly made
cheeses are bought by
wholesalers. Gouda is
marketed in various
degrees of maturity:
"young" Gouda
cheese has been
ripened for at least 3
weeks, "semimature"
Gouda for 2-7 months,
while the very piquant,
crumbly "old" Gouda
has matured for no
less than 10-12
months.

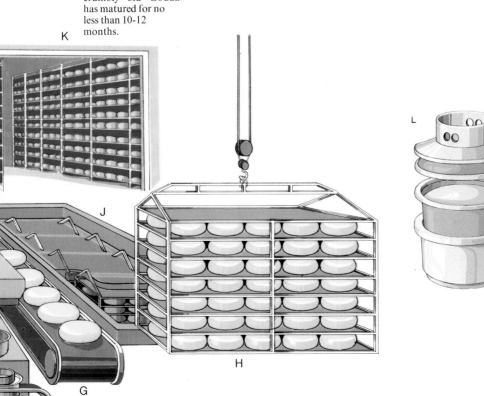

L. Close-up of a
modern polyethylene
cheese mold. From
top to bottom:
follower, inner lid,
perforated lining (re-
placing cheese cloth)
which contains the
curd, bottom. Plastic
molds have proved
much better than
stainless steel ones,
which allow the curd
to cool too quickly.
Traditional wooden
molds are still the
best: taste and flavor
develop better during
the ripening period,
but the difference is
only marginal. In an
automated factory,
wooden molds are too
heavy and clumsy to
handle, and are being
replaced.

Edam cheese is named after the old harbor on the Ysselmeer, north of Amsterdam, in the center of the province of North Holland, where Frisian Edam cheese was first marketed and exported abroad. Edam, with its fat content of 40%, is a little less smooth and less creamy than Gouda, and has a slightly sourish taste when young. In fact this is one of the marketing problems associated with Edam – it is often sold before the magnificent, mature flavor has had time to develop. The lower fat content of Edam is due to its being partly made with skimmed milk; Gouda, with more fat, is made from whole cow's milk.

All the world recognizes the familiar, bright red, or yellow, ball of cheese with its waxy coating, yet Edam is seldom waxed for the home market. The process is reserved for export cheeses, which are colored before leaving the warehouse; the treatment gives the cheeses added protection.

The focal point of the cheese industry is not the town of Edam, however, but that of Alkmaar. Here, on a Friday morning, the cheese market becomes an international tourist attraction. Members of the cheese bearers' guild – the last of the medieval guilds – dress in white suits and hats of different colors to identify the various warehouses they represent. The golden balls of Edam cheese, or the flat wheels of Gouda, are piled high upon wooden sleds of a decidedly Japanese-looking design; the sleds are pulled by cheese porters over the gray brick surface of the marketplace.

Edam cheese has always been a profitable product – there has been a weigh-house in the market since the thirteenth century – and Amsterdam merchants acknowledged this by helping to finance the reclaiming of land from the Ysselmeer, to provide more pastures. The original, whole-milk Edam cheese was prepared in more or less the same way as farmhouse Gouda. Its globe-shaped, easy-

RIGHT: The small, ancient town of Edam with its fifteenth-century bell tower. Edam gave its name to the most famous of all Dutch cheeses. In the foreground is a typical drawbridge, over one of the countless, narrow canals.

to-transport form, not unlike a large grapefruit, came from the Edam cheese mold known as the *kaaskop*. This *kaaskop*, meaning "cheese head," was often used as a helmet during riots, which is said to be why the Dutch are known in many countries by this nickname. Edam's spherical shape is almost unique among cheeses, and is achieved by the tendency of the curd to become firm very readily at an early stage in preparation.

The explorer's cheese
Since the nineteenth century, both on farms and in small factories, Edam cheese has been made from a mixture of whole morning milk and the skimmed evening milk of the previous day. In modern factories the old, wooden cheese molds, the *kaaskop* forms, have been replaced by plastic molds; cheese cloth is no longer used.

Unlike Gouda, farmhouse Edam is no longer made. The smallest variety today is the *Baby Edam* cheese weighing about 1 kg (2.2 lbs), a cheese that is eaten young and is less tasty than the larger type, which weighs 1.7 kg (3.7 lbs). *Commissekaas* (in France called *Mimolette* and for marketing reasons is colored orange with anatto dye) is even heavier, while *Middelbare* is the largest Edam of all. In a different form there is the handsome *Broodkaas*, less salty than the regular Edam, and mainly for use in hotels. Some Edam cheeses are spiced with cumin.

The keeping properties of Edam have been known to be remarkable: in 1956 an expedition to the South Pole found a tin of raw-milk Edam cheese, left behind by the Scott Expedition in 1912. The natural protein and fat disintegration had been at work for forty-four years: the cheese was sharp, but not spoiled.

RIGHT: Sorting cheeses at the Alkmaar cheese market. Those in front are Goudas, at the rear are Edams. Edam cheeses are colored red or yellow for export, but not usually for home use.

Leiden cheese is made on a number of large farms along the Old Rhine in the dune region near Leiden. It is a spicy, piquant cheese of partly skimmed milk and buttermilk. In the past, the fresh milk was poured into oval vats that stood in cold, running water, and left for the cream to rise. Today the milk is left for skimming after cooling in the same tub in which the cheese is made. In 12 to 24 hours, the cream is skimmed off, left for a day to sour, then churned into a fairly assertive farm butter. The cheesemaker, in the meantime, warms up a portion of the skimmed, pre-ripened milk, using it to bring the remainder of the milk to curdling temperature. Then buttermilk and rennet are added, the curd is stirred and cut, and the whey is drawn off. A quantity of the curd is now separated from the rest, into which cumin seed is kneaded, a treatment which to a large extent dries the curd.

The traditional way of kneading, where the farmer would clean his feet in whey and afterwards tread the curd, is now considered unhygienic; this is rather a pity, since the very special structure that was characteristic of Leiden cheese no longer develops. The

BELOW: The old method of kneading Leiden cheese. It has never been established which suffered most – the farmer's feet or the cheese! The modern method still demands an intensive working of the curd.

spiced, kneaded curd is sandwiched between two layers of the remaining, unspiced curd, bound in a cheese cloth and placed in a mold. The cheese is pressed for 20 to 24 hours before receiving a second pressing with mold and cloth removed. The sides of the cheese develop their spherical shape, and a special cheese mark is applied, consisting of the two crossed keys of the city of Leiden, the name *Boerenleidse* and a fat content figure of 30 + (more than 30%).

Punishment by the beestings

Leiden farmhouse cheese requires a long period of ripening. In the final stages of ripening, the rind is colored by an application of anatto dye, which is well rubbed in. This treatment has largely replaced the old-fashioned method of rubbing the cheese rind with a mixture of coloring matter and beestings. Beestings is the first milk given by a cow after calving; it is much thicker and richer than ordinary milk and contains an unusual amount of protein. This was mixed with anatto to be applied to the rind, which acquired a fine, glossy, mahogany-colored protective layer. This is not dissimilar to the technique used by the makers of the old English Gloucester cheese, which used to be rubbed with a substance obtained from decomposing vegetable matter. Beestings used to be stored in a pot, since it was not always available, and after several weeks it began to smell rather repulsive, to say the least. Some farmers used to punish their children by forcing them to sit by the beestings pot – a corrective measure that doubtless did very little to increase the consumption and appeal of Leiden cheeses on the farms.

Irrespective of the beestings treatment, a well-ripened Leiden cheese is very piquant and almost sharp of taste, with a dry but elastic structure. The fat content varies from 32 to 36%. The indication of 20 + on the government cheese mark is, in fact, too low, although legally prescribed. The farmers ignore this and put their own additional mark of 30 + on their cheeses. Factory-made Leiden cheese is allowed a 20% and a 40% type: the first is eaten young, the second when more mature. This factory cheese has a piquant taste, but is less sharp than the farmhouse variety.

LEFT: The milk is poured into the metal containers seen in the foreground. The machine at the rear pumps cold water to thoroughly chill the milk. In this way a natural creaming process takes place: the cream floats to the surface and can then be skimmed off; it is usually made into butter. The remaining skimmed milk is made into farmhouse Leiden cheese, which can have a varying fat content.

ABOVE: The drained curd is well mixed with cumin seed, a particular feature of Leiden cheese. Other cheeses also contain cumin, but lack the unique taste of Leiden, which is fairly sharp and dry.

The beautiful, black-and-white Frisian cattle are one of the finest dairy breeds in the world. In spite of this indigenous stock, Friesland is not noted for its cheeses, because the manufacture of butter has always had top priority. The lean, skimmed milk *Friese Kanterkaas* and *Friese Nagelkaas* had a hard time competing with farmhouse Leiden and *Delft* cheese, and even the Delft fell out of favor and is now extinct. The Frisians, however, survived. The quantity of starter is all-important to the making of Frisian cheese. So is the addition of fresh buttermilk, the milling of the curd and the hot water bath. The cheeses also are subject to long pressing and covered ripening; the process is not unlike the one used for English Cheddar.

Cumin and caraway seeds are wonderful additions to rye bread, which was made in northern Europe during Roman times. They are also used to flavor several Scandinavian and Dutch cheeses. Perhaps the ancient breadmakers, who also made cheese, decided to try to spice their cheeses as they did their bread – and thus a taste for spiced cheeses developed.

Nagelkaas is a spiced cheese, flavored with cumin and cloves, hence the name – *nagel* means "nail" and refers to the shape of the clove; the cheese is said to go well with a glass of Gewürztraminer. The unspiced *Kanterkaas* is a product of the processed cheese industry. The cumin-spiced Kanter is so like Leiden factory cheese that it shares the same classification. After about six months' ripening, the aroma and flavor are fully developed. Both cheeses have a 40% and 20% variety, the latter possessing a higher moisture content, which makes it smooth in spite of the low percentage of fat.

The accident that led to Kernhem
During wet winters before the days of improved storage conditions, Edam cheeses in the warehouses of the tenant farmers sometimes collapsed into strong-smelling, flat discs with an orange-colored rind flora of coryne bacteria, and when cut the cheese stuck to the knife. The farmers found, however, that this "knife sticker" was a delicacy. The Netherlands Institute for Dairy Research experimented with this accidental cheese, and from it

LEFT: Three lovely old cheese labels: respectively, a Rembrandt self-portrait; a Dutch landscape scene (intended for export); and a label combining two well-known Dutch products – cheese and tulips.

BELOW: A nineteenth-century print showing an old cheesemaking room. The cheese press stands on the left; to the right is the curd mill. In the center, wet curd is pre-pressed under a stone.

developed *Kernhem* cheese, a totally new type with a creamy flavor.

Since 1906, strict controls regulate the high standard of Dutch cheeses, and those that pass the inspection receive the government mark which indicates the country of origin (Holland), the producer and production date in code and, in most cases, the name of the cheese and the fat content. Export cheese is even more thoroughly inspected and, as we have mentioned, the Dutch are the biggest cheese exporters in the world. Even so, it is odd that cheese fails to play a more important role in the Dutch kitchen. Cheese is used for sandwiches and snacks, but is rarely used in dishes apart from a few homely applications of Gouda, the fondu-style Kaasdoop, and Houtsnip (white bread with a slice of cheese topped with a piece of rye bread, and cut into small pieces). Over the last few years, however, foreign influence has brought about certain changes, and Dutch cheese features in many imported, international recipes.

ABOVE: Leiden cheese is colored by rubbing the rind with anatto dye, and sometimes with beestings, the first milk obtained after a cow has calved.

Name	Milk	Type	Rind	Form	Weight	% Fat content
Edam	⚲	●	□	ball	1-6.5 kg	40
Friese Nagelkaas	⚲	●	□	cartwheel	7-8 kg	20-40
Gouda	⚲	●	□	cartwheel	2.5-20 kg	48
Kernhem	⚲	●	❖	flat disc	1.8 kg	60
Leiden	⚲	●	□	cartwheel	7-8 kg	20-40

Key to symbols on page 34. 1 kg = 2.2 lbs.

Belgium and Luxembourg

In the Middle Ages, the southern Netherlands occupied most of the area which is now Belgium, and was a major center of trade and commerce. Most international routes over land or sea met in Bruges, but towards the close of the fourteenth century, Antwerp began to overtake Bruges. The city became a great trading port for Spanish and English wool, French wine, Portuguese spices, Dutch butter and cheese, Sandinavian wood and fish, and flax from the surrounding districts.

No dairy produce of any consequence was produced in the southern provinces of the lowlands bordering the North Sea, even though the ground was fertile enough. There was more money to be made from arable farming, for those traders who supported and propped up the country's living standards. Neither was the cow highly thought of as a producer of milk, unlike the sheep or the goat; the farmer used his cattle for pulling the plow, and as a source of manure, rather than milk or cheese – as with everything in farming, it's a matter of carefully judged economics.

Cheese from a crisis
Serious problems affected agriculture at the end of the nineteenth century, forcing drastic changes on Belgian farming, especially in the wheatlands, following the fall in grain prices. Farmers turned to cattle breeding, and the economic value of meat, milk and other dairy produce soon rose; the cows quickly left the sheep and goats well behind. Although Belgian farmers maintained their agrarian traditions, they began to pay careful attention to cattle breeding; this combined with good feeding soon increased the milk yield. Before 1900, the first dairy factories had been established, mainly for the processing of butter; after the Second World War, more factories were built and cheese began to be produced. New cheese factories were constructed to meet the growing demand, and existing plants were modernized.

Until the mid-1960s, Belgium's main production was centered on the semihard cheeses of the Gouda and Saint-Paulin variety, but a change in the national preference led to the rehabilitation of original Belgian soft cheeses.

ABOVE: Cows grazing in a meadow in the Belgian Ardennes. Frisian cattle, together with this white or blue-spotted breed, are found all over central and southern Belgium; the white breed represents about half the cattle stock of the country.

ABOVE: A philatelic rarity: a Belgian postage stamp dating before the Second World War, joined to a Dutch official cheese control stamp.

The return of the farmhouse cheese
The most famous of all Belgian cheeses is, or rather was, the *Limburger* – famous if only for its persistent, omnipotent aroma. It was made in the Liege region, and sold in Limburg, but it has now been almost totally superseded by the *Herve* cheeses, Limburger itself having been adopted by the Germans, who make it in considerable quantity.

Although Limburger failed to make a comeback, the renaissance of farmhouse cheeses is well established. Among them are such types as *Remoudou, Brusselsekaas, Fromage en panier* and *Plattekaas* (curd cheese). Herve comes from the grazing area of that name, in the north of the province of Liège, a rolling stretch of country between the Vesdre and the Meuse. Herve is the generic name of a number of different types, of which Remoudou is the most valued. The name comes from the Walloon word *remoud* or, roughly, "after-milk." It is made from the milk that a cow gives at the end of the lactation period, when the milk is very rich in fat. With the introduction of artificial insemination, the cows are continuously productive, and are never dry all at the same time.

The stinking cheese
The preparation of Herve begins with the pouring of warm, raw milk into a metal cheese vat, called a *tine* (a word found both in Dutch and Norwegian) where, with the aid of a little rennet, it thickens within $1\frac{1}{2}$ hours. After a rest period, a perforated pot or colander is placed on the curd; the pot fills with whey, and 40 to 50% is ladled off. The next stage introduces the traditional *spantafel*, a large draining board with a rim about 6 inches high, divided lengthwise by planks to form gutters, down which the whey runs to be drained through apertures. The entire contraption – made by local craftsmen – is built on a stand so that it slopes to allow drainage.

The cheesemaker pours the wet curd from a pan quickly and evenly along the gutters, until they are completely filled. The whey is drained off, the longitudinal strips of curd are then turned through 90°, with a practiced, deft movement of the cheesemaker's arms, and the curds rest while further whey is strained off. This process is repeated three times. The strips are

then cut into cubes, placed back onto the *spantafel*, between planks now arranged to form rectangular divisions, and each cheese is turned regularly by hand for the next 48 hours. Air currents in the room must be avoided, as they would spoil the newly made cheeses.

In the old days, the cheesemaker would then place the cheeses next to one another on a cheese board, where they were treated by dusting with salt, but today a special salting table is used. The unripe cheeses are collected by so-called *affineurs*, who take them from the farm to their establishments, where the cheeses are washed and again treated with salt and lukewarm brine. Due to this process, and also the damp air in the processing room, the initially hard, chalk-white cheese becomes soft and smooth, while the ripening bacteria present on the reddish-brown rind imparts an outstanding aroma and penetrating flavor, especially with Remoudou, which has earned the dubious nickname of "the stinking cheese."

The final packing shape is a cube, measuring 6 × 6 cm (about 2.5 × 2.5 in). Factory-made Remoudou,

ABOVE: This drawing shows the traditional method of making farmhouse Remoudou cheese. The girl on the left is cutting the curd by hand, with the aid of a curd knife. In the center is a metal container called a *tine*, and filled with curd on top of which a small, perforated colander rests. The colander fills with whey, which is then scooped out. When most of the whey has been strained off, the curd

is poured onto the long table (behind the girl on the left) called a *spantafel*, a draining board fitted with longitudinal planks. The man turns the long strips of curd which form between the planks. When the strips have drained and are firm, they are cut into cubes and placed on another, similar table (right). Here the cheesemaker turns them regularly for a period of 48 hours. The cheeses are

then salted by hand on the salting table (far right), then left to dry. During the maturation time of about six weeks, the cheeses are regularly turned and washed with lukewarm brine, as the woman on the right is doing. The washing technique encourages the growth of a reddish, bacterial flora, which gives the cheese its unusual, piquant taste and sharp aroma.

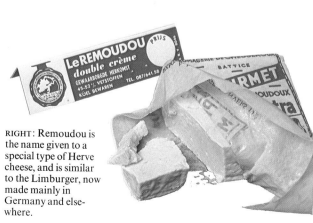

RIGHT: Remoudou is the name given to a special type of Herve cheese, and is similar to the Limburger, now made mainly in Germany and elsewhere.

like so many mass-produced cheeses, uses pasteurized instead of raw milk, and the refining process takes place either in the factory, or on the premises of the *affineurs*.

The methods of manufacture, as used by traditional craftsmen, can be seen in the Musée du Remoudou, a museum devoted to cheese and established by the Seigneurerie Folklorique du Remoudou. The premises are the ripening cellars of an old cheese factory in Battice, close by the town of Herve to the east of Liège. The Seigneurerie keeps the rightful fame of real, old Remoudou alive in more than one sense, for the odor of the famous "stinking cheese" is impregnated in the stones of the museum.

Cheeses of Flanders and the south
A variety of the washed cheeses is the *Plateau* cheese, with a consistency that is somewhere between soft and semihard; during ripening the rind is kept moist by regularly dampening it with fresh water. In Flanders, *Plattekaas* (fresh curd cheese) is a type that includes many fresh, unripened varieties, cheeses with different fat

LEFT: Once a cheese dairy in the village of Battice, now a small museum devoted to the history of Remoudou.

contents according to the amount of cream added. Skimmed-milk cheese has less than 20% fat; the semifat variety has 20% to 35%; the full-fat cheese, from 35% to 45%; cream cheese has more than 45% fat in dry matter.

The French-speaking part of the country has its own fresh cheeses: *Fromage en panier* and *Fromage en cassette*. These are still made in limited amounts in southern Belgium, from either buttermilk, skimmed milk or whole milk, and sold in small baskets covered with walnut leaves. Often, the curd is flavored with pepper. The Belgians enjoy eating this cheese on toast, with a layer of butter on the cheese – a local delicacy.

In fact, the Belgians are great eaters who have invented some classic – and filling – soups and stews, and dishes that include cheese. Excuses for festivals and communal feasts are not exactly numerous, but when they do arise the quantities of food that appear are prodigious: plates are overfilled with cold cuts of assorted meats, sausages, selections of cheeses, bread, wine and beer – especially beer.

A scene straight out of a Brueghel

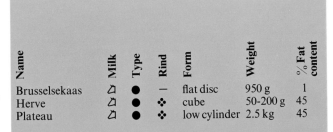

Name	Milk	Type	Rind	Form	Weight	% Fat content
Brusselsekaas	△	●	—	flat disc	950 g	1
Herve	△	●	❖	cube	50-200 g	45
Plateau	△	●	❖	low cylinder	2.5 kg	45

Key to symbols on page 34. 453 g = 1 lb; 1 kg = 2.2 lbs.

LEFT: In the monastery of Lesse, cheese is sold by the monks. It is a Saint-Paulin type which has been prepared in the cloisters since ancient times.

ABOVE: The wrapping for the cheese produced by the monastery of Lesse, near Dinant.

LEFT: A dairy-worker monk, using the cheese press at Lesse.

painting is enacted every three years in the town of Wynghene south of Bruges. The local residents honor the painter by dressing in the costume of the period, and members of several guilds – bakers, butchers, brewers and cheesemakers – present their products to the general enjoyment of all.

Other cheeses from Belgium and Luxembourg

The most typically Belgian cheese is the *Brusselsekaas* (Brussels cheese), or *Hettekaas*, and it is made in two phases from pasteurized, skimmed milk. The coagulated mass is cut into small blocks, and in the 12-hour rest period that follows, they contract, acidify and release whey. Afterwards this fresh curd is put into sacks and placed on a grid to drain. The curd is then ground, salted and molded to shape with metal hoops. The cheeses must first be laid out on planks to drain further, and then on rush matting to dry. The second phase in the complicated process allows the cheeses to ripen for two months in a humid ripening room. Every eight days they are dipped and turned in lukewarm water and then finally in a brine bath. The cheese is then cut into pieces and packed in cellophane and, after yet another bathing and draining treatment, is packed in boxes or plastic containers. The end product is very moist and salty, and very much to the national taste.

Finally, Belgium produces many imitations of foreign cheeses, including *Gouda, Edam, Emmental,* and, for the export market, large quantities of *Cheddar, Camembert, Brie* and *Saint-Paulin.*

In Luxembourg, the cheese industry concentrates mainly on the fresh types, like the skimmed-milk *Fromage blanc, Cottage cheese,* and *Kachke's Fromage cuit,* a cheese that can be favorably compared to the Concaillotte from Franche Comté.

The quality of the Belgian, hard-cheese types is guaranteed by regular official inspection. Two favorable judgments out of three inspections allows the cheese to carry a mark denoting quality, stamped in purple ink on the rind, plus the Belgian emblem of origin – a Breughelian picture of two porters bearing a pile of various cheeses on a plank.

France

The cheeses of France are renowned for their excellence and astonishing variety – no other country has so many different types, and many of them are copied all over the world. Second only to the Greeks in their consumption of cheese, the French eat a yearly average of 14.8 kg (32.6 lbs) per person. Like the wines they so perfectly accompany, French cheeses – unique and delicious – are the pride of both their region of origin and France herself. They vary considerably in flavor and appearance: some are wrapped in straw, others in paper, or in leaves. Some are coated with grape seeds, coarsely crushed peppercorns, herbs or halved walnuts. They may be round, square, lozenge or heart-shaped, in a roll or a pyramid; soft and tender, hard as a rock, blue-veined, snow-white, red, black or speckled. Dozens of once rare local cheeses now enjoy a wide reputation, though many others are still found only in remote places where family cheesemakers have been producing them for hundreds of years.

As General de Gaulle once said, comparing the pastoral and political character of France, "How can one possibly govern a country that produces over 370 different cheeses?" We cannot, in this book attempt to list them all. Let us instead make a tour of France, to sample not only the humble village cheeses, but those aristocrats of the French table, the Gruyères, Camemberts, Bries and Roqueforts, which many people maintain are the finest cheeses in the world.

The flavor and fragrance of Provence
The Mediterranean climate has made Provence one of the most attractive areas of France. Stretching from the Italian border to beyond the wild Camargue, the landscape can be both arid and harsh, soft and abundant. The mountains, gorges and valleys produce a glorious profusion of sub-tropical fruits and flowers. The cuisine matches the varied character of the land and its people; it is rich, spicy, oily and pungent. How odd, then, that Provence boasts no great regional cheese, but only small, unpretentious ones made for local consumption. You have to search for them: *Cachat*, for example, a sheep's milk cheese, eaten either fresh or in a marinade of brandy, vinegar, local herbs and spices. Then there's *Banon* with a

ABOVE: A fine display of French regional cheeses. Nowhere in the world can such variety be found as in France.

BELOW: Château-renard near Avignon, a typical southern French town in lovely surroundings.

striking aroma and a powerful, nutty flavor, covered with savory and wrapped in chestnut leaves. Banon is fortified with brandy or white wine, and subjected to five weeks of mysterious fermentation in a sealed earthenware pot. *Poivre d'Ane* is a simple *chèvre* (goat's milk cheese) sprinkled with savory and rosemary, giving it the fragrance of the Provençal countryside.

To the north of the area, local specialties are easier to find – *Picardon* in the Drôme region and *Pelardon* across the Rhône are tiny, goat's milk cheeses, white and fresh, with a lovely full flavor. *Saint-Marcellin* from the Isère is a dairy milk cheese to be eaten fresh (usually mixed with herbs) or ripened in chestnut leaves. Further into the mountains, at the foot of Mont Blanc, is the original home of *Bossons Macérés*, a special *chèvre*, ripened with alcohol, olive oil and fragrant herbs, to give the cheese a very strong, tangy flavor. It is here, in the French Alps, that we meet the first of our great French cheeses – the Gruyères.

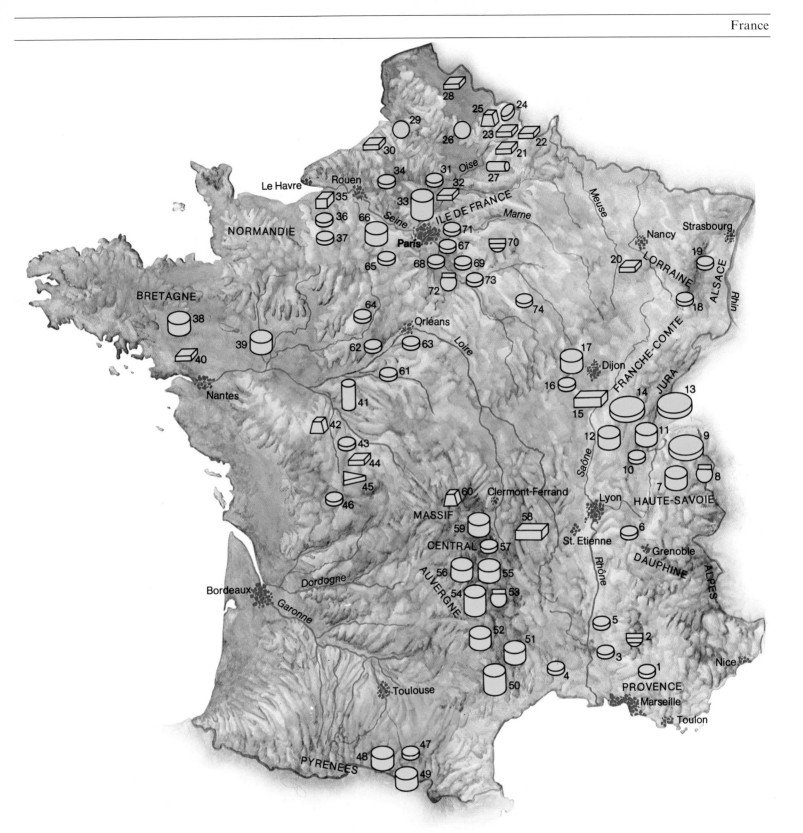

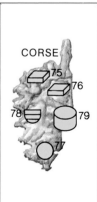

BELOW: Saint-Claude in the French Jura, where alpine pastures produce many excellent cheeses.

The birthplace of *Gruyère* cheese stretches across the French-Swiss border. On the French side it encompasses the Haute Savoie and the region of Franche-Comté; on the Swiss side the cantons of Fribourg, Vaud and Neuchatel. Here, language and landscape are shared alike, but the exclusive right to use the name "Gruyère" was long a bone of contention between France and Switzerland – it was granted to both countries by the Convention of Stresa in 1951.

The French border country has high mountains and deep valleys with many springs and rivers. The climate is often harsh, with marked seasonal changes. The rural character of the land and people is such that, even today, many farmers live far from the market centers and transport is difficult. For this reason, the medieval farmers decided to make a cheese which could be kept for the longest possible time, and so Gruyère was born. The trouble with Gruyère, however, is that one cheese demands from 500 to 1,000 liters (550 to 1,100 quarts) of milk – too much for one farm to produce. Thus the farmers began to form cooperatives. Cheese was made from the communal milk in small huts called *fruitières*, as these produced the fruits of communal effort. The first *fruitières* were already in existence in the Middle Ages. In 1267, the farmers of a small Jura village were making a cheese called *Vachelin*, an ancestor of the Gruyère. Also recorded in early historical documents were small goat's milk cheeses called *Chevrets*.

Fine art of cheese

Today, the main types of French Gruyère cheese are *Comté*, *Beaufort* and *Emmental*. Nowadays many experts regard Emmental as a cheese apart from Gruyère; the two others are still considered subvarieties of Gruyère.

Both Gruyère and Emmental have achieved great stature in the world of cheese, because they fulfill so many requirements with such success. From very simple beginnings they have evolved to become fine works of art: Emmental with its wide-eyed honeycomb texture and bold, wagon-wheel proportions; Gruyère, the smaller of the two – in size, but not in character. Yet they have much in common, although confusion may arise over the appearance of the paste. Emmental

LEFT: Saint-Véran in the French Alps, the highest inhabited village in Europe.

has big holes while many varieties of Gruyère have a closed body with a few cracks here and there. On the other hand, there are Gruyères with holes. Gruyère de Comté, for example, has large, elliptical holes in the paste, as can be seen in the picture on the opposite page; the princely Beaufort may have a few small holes or none at all.

These cheeses are splendid additions to the range of table cheeses. In the kitchen their uses are legion: few cheese types are more adaptable to the repertoire of French cooking, a fact that is recognized by great chefs and ordinary housewives alike.

Comté – the choice of the French

Like champagne, France is its own biggest customer for *Gruyère de Comté*. The cheese has a slightly moist and crumbly rind: the consistency is firm, with a bit of give, and the holes – or "eyes" – are as big as nuts. Owing to the molds that form on the rind, the taste and smell of the cheese have a more pronounced character than that of Emmental. Comté is made from evening milk, set aside in wooden or metal dishes for ripening and creaming up. When the cream has been skimmed off, it is mixed with morning milk, processed raw, and not subjected to the heat treatment of the Swiss Gruyère. This influences the slow ripening process: it requires at least six months at a temperature of 18° to 20°C (64° to 68°F), and needs continuous attention to encourage the development of the rind mold. This is why the cheese is not brushed, as Beaufort is, but wiped with a brine-soaked cloth. The cellars of the cheese huts are too small to store the cheeses for the required six months while production continues, so the nonripened *Comté Blanc* cheeses are sold to *affineurs*, who let the cheeses ripen in their spacious storage cellars before sending them to market. Farmers, cheesemakers and *affineurs* have together formed the *Syndicat du Véritable Gruyère de Comté*, which has set up strict regulations governing production to protect the quality of the cheese.

Beaufort, the prince of Gruyères

Compared to Comté, the *Beaufort (de Montagne)* is almost "blind," as the experts say: it is not allowed to form eyes, or holes. It has a smooth and creamy consistency, with an excellent fruity aroma and taste. The shape of a Beaufort is somewhere between the straight-sided Comté, and the convex-sided Emmental and the cheese usually weighs from 30 to 60 kg (66 to 132 lbs). The French author Brillat-Savarin, one of the most famous gourmets of the early nineteenth century, called Beaufort "the prince of Gruyères."

Its fame is due mainly to the use of extremely rich milk, collected in the valleys of Tatentaise and Maurienne, 1,500 to 2,500 meters (about 20,000 to 32,000 feet) above sea level, luscious alpine meadows affording excellent summer grazing. The milk is made into cheese according to methods passed down by generations of farmers over the centuries. The cheeses ripen in the cooperative Cave de Gruyère de Beaufort at a temperature of 10° to

LEFT: Here in the Haute Savoie is the original home of the great French Gruyères: Comté, Beaufort and Emmental.

12° C (50° to 54° F). For the first two months they are salted in the morning, brushed in the afternoon and turned the next day; later, this treatment is carried out every third day. The production of Beaufort de Montagne is relatively small, however, though in the valleys some *Beaufort d'Hiver*, or *Laitier*, is additionally made in the winter.

Emmental, a labor-saving giant
Emmental is descended from the famous Swiss cheese of the region around Berne, but in France it is considered one of the original types of French Gruyère. Today Emmental is equal to them both, and is the pride of the Haute Savoie, Haute Marn Haute Saône and Côte d'Or. Nowhere in the world is so much Emmental cheese made as in France; the nation produces more than its greatest competitors: the United States, Germany, Austria, Finland and even Switzerland itself. In spite of this, the French decline to make the cheese for export. Almost all French Emmental is eaten by the French, who have created such a demand that they themselves are believed to import it from Switzerland, the country of origin. In any event, Swiss Emmental doesn't have far to travel, since the area around Lake Geneva is really one great cheese-producing region.

Normally a meter (39.37 inches) in diameter, French Emmental is a huge cartwheel of a cheese, which might weigh anywhere from 60 to 130 kg (132 to 286 lbs); it can be recognized by the red mark signifying its origin. The mild, somewhat sweet taste is reminiscent of fresh nuts; the consistency is softer than that of Gruyère, and it has many large holes. During ripening, the hard rind turns a dark yellow or light brown. One of the most remarkable things about this giant among cheeses is that it is entirely produced by mechanical means, in large dairy factories. Even the brushing, polishing and turning are done by machine. So well developed is the process of automation, that a modern Emmental factory requires a very small labor force.

LEFT: The characteristic large-holed texture of a fine Gruyère. Nearly all the Gruyère produced is consumed in France itself.

BELOW: A Gruyère cheese factory at the end of the nineteenth century. Although the process may now seem primitive, it was the start of mass production. In the center stands the great cheese kettle. The curd hangs above in a cloth. The man on the right tends to the fire, which is necessary, among other things, for rewarming the cheese. A double press is seen in the foreground.

BELOW: Alsace is famous for cheeses as well as wines – the two are splendid partners. Here is the famous wine town of Riquewihr, with its picturesque houses and steep main street.

In addition to the hard Gruyères and Emmental, the mountain slopes along the Swiss border yield several kinds of soft cheese. In Savoie these are generally called *Tommes*, the *Tomme de Savoie* being one of the more familiar varieties. When made according to the ancient farmhouse methods, they are ripened in natural caves; they may be treated with brandy and brushed, or sometimes, in the variety known as *Tomme au raisin*, they are coated with grape pulp. After each turning, the cheesemaker presses the mold into the rind by hand; the crust which forms gradually develops gray, white, yellow and red spots, and becomes very dry. Modern production procedures demand that they be prepared in a more simplified manner, to develop a natural rind. The ivory to yellow-colored cheese, which has a fat content varying between 10 and 30%, has a fresh and particular taste, which is occasionally slightly bitter or sourish. *Reblochon* is another mountain cheese, ripened like the Tommes in caves. It is a semihard cheese, with a dark, yellow-washed rind. The rich, unskimmed milk that makes the cheese is processed immediately after milking, when it is still warm. This, it seems, gives Reblochon its characteristic flavor – mild, creamy and fragrant.

In the Haute Jura, in Gex and Septmoncel, we find two fine blue cheeses, both of which are entitled to use the name *Bleu du Haute Jura*; individually they are identified as *Bleu de Gex* and *Bleu de Septmoncel*. Like the Tommes, they are an ancient variety, once made in huts high on the mountain slopes, but today production takes place in small, central cheese dairies. Twice a week, even during the cold weather, milk is brought down the winding, narrow roads to the two dairies, which handle more than 2,000 liters (2,100 quarts) a day. From the curds comes a firm, white cheese, evenly blue-veined after maturing, with a fresh though modest flavor. Like certain wines, these cheeses do not seem to travel well, which is why most are consumed in the region where they are made; small quantities can be found, however, in Lyon, St. Etienne and Grenoble.

Cheese with a fortified flavor
A far more stable and hardy blue

LEFT: Grape skins and pips from the wine press cover the rind of a Fondu au Raisin.

BELOW: Cheeses in the cellar of a well-stocked cheese shop. Top left is Langres, below is Carré de l'Est. At the bottom are heart-shaped Rollots, right are cream cheeses.

cheese is the popular *Bleu de Bresse*, which comes from the rich meadow country between the Saône and the Jura. Although small in size, the cheeses share certain characteristics with Gorgonzola, except that they are much milder. *Cancoillotte* (or *Cancaillotte*) is an unripened curd cheese, mostly a home-made product from the vicinity of Besançon. The curds are placed in a warm part of the kitchen to ferment, and to develop a strong, unique flavor. They are then heated with milk, or butter and white wine, according to the family recipe. The melted cheese, a *fromage fondu*, is then poured into a dish, and left to form a thick paste, to be used in combination with various dishes: in a savory pastry, with potatoes and fried eggs, and so on. As a snack, hot Cancoillotte is eaten with fresh bread or toast.

Quite a number of these regional, farmhouse cheeses are specially prepared, in order to enhance or increase their flavor. Herbs may be added, or the cheeses may be soaked in wine, brandy or even coffee, as is a cheese called *Laumes*.

In the Burgundy country of the Côte d'Or, a little further to the west past Dijon, is the small village of Epoisses, where *Fromage d'Epoisses* is made from well-chilled evening milk mixed with fresh morning milk. As soon as the mold forms, the cheeses are soaked in water and an *eau de vie* made from grape pulp, called *Marc de Bourgogne*. Just before they are sold, they are again soaked in the *Marc*, which has been fortified by a good, white Burgundy. Cheeses thus treated are called *Epoisses confits au vin blanc*, or *confits au Marc*. A variety of the *Tomme au Raisin* is the *Tomme au Marc de Raisin*, which is coated with grape pulp and left to form a hard crust of pips; *Fondu au Marc de Raisin* is similar, but is made from pasteurized milk. A challenge to strong teeth and robust digestions, the pips in both varieties are best left on the plate, even if the manufacturers do suggest otherwise!

An inheritance from Ireland
Where France meets the German border to the northeast, the rolling fertile meadows merge into the wooded Vosges, a land of mineral springs and spas, of light and delicate wines, of dialects blending French and

ABOVE AND RIGHT:
Munster cheese
labels. There are only
a few farms remaining
where traditional
farmhouse Munster is
still made. You can
find them along the
Route de Fromage,
along the top of the
Vosges, west of the
small town of
Munster.

Also from Vosges and other provinces of the northeast comes the square-shaped *Carré de l'Est*, with its spotlessly white mold. *Carré* ripens on screens, and its paste is homogeneous, with a fat content of 40 to 60%. The cheese is slightly salted, and its flavor resembles that of Camembert, the famous Normandy cheese to which Carré de l'Est has become a forceful competitor.

A royal favorite

The extreme northwest of France, along the Belgian border, is rich pasture land. The cheeses produced there are strong and full-flavored, the most famous of which is named after the town of Maroilles. *Maroilles* is the great speciality of the region, which has been making similar cheeses for over a thousand years; by the sixteenth century the fame of the cheeses was so widespread that they found their way to the court of Spain. Sometimes the cheese was made by order: in the twelfth century on the feast of St. Jean-Baptiste (June 24) certain villages were required to make their milk into cheese for the abbey of Maroilles, where St. John was the patron saint. The cheeses are allowed to mature for several months, during which time they are carefully washed with water and then turned. Maroilles is a square cheese with a reddish rind, the paste being pale, soft and slightly salted; its flavor is delicious, strong and full, without being sharp. Each weighs approximately 800 g (1.8 lbs). A smaller version, *Sorbais*, weighs only 600 g (1.3 lbs); the even smaller *Mignon* 400 g (.9 lb), and the very smallest – the *Quart* – only 200 g (.4 lb). Other Maroilles-type varieties include *Manicamp* and *Monceau*; the French loaf-shaped *Baguette* and the twice-salted *Maroilles Gris* or *Vieux Lille*, with its grayish rind. The latter matures for five or six months in very moist cellars, by which time the *Vieux Lille* has become liquid and might be considered over-ripe. It has a very pronounced flavor, and the aroma is distinguished by a definite smell of ammonia. A large proportion of various Maroilles types continues to be made on farms.

German, of sausages and beer and farmhouse cheeses. The cheeses are eaten with finely chopped onions, caraway seeds and crisp bread, together with beer or, better still, the spicy, white Gewürztraminer wine. This is the area of France known as Alsace-Lorraine, and its greatest cheese is *Munster*.

It is said that the cheese was first made by Irish monks who settled in Vosges in the seventh century. Munster is a round cheese with an orange-red rind, a yellow and very soft consistency, and a quite distinct, tangy flavor. Real farmhouse Munster is becoming very rare, and consequently more and more expensive; the few farms still making it can be recognized by the new small Munsters left outside to dry; the cheeses remain outdoors for a week before being stored in the cellars. Here they ripen for two months on beds of rye straw alongside the now mature cheeses, from which they acquire the rind flora. Factories in Vosges, as well as elsewhere in France and abroad, have adopted this method; they also manufacture a large Munster called *Géromé*, nicknamed the "red head," which was originally made in the mountain huts of Gerardmer, on the east slopes.

LEFT: "Good cheese from Maroilles, who wants my good Maroilles," cried the street vendor. From a print by Carle Vernet, 1815.

According to legend, Louis XIV and the Crown Prince, the Dauphin, when visiting the north of France, were served nonripened Maroilles that had been flavored with garden

81

MAROILLES MIGNON 45%
Tradition et Qualité
LESIRE et ROGER
Laiterie de Mondrepuis
02 - FRANCE
MATIÈRE GRASSE
BUTTERFAT Fett. i. Tr.

LEFT: A label from a small Maroilles cheese weighing 300 g (10.5 oz). This cheese is made in Thiérache in northern France, primarily from the milk of Pie Noir cattle.

herbs, specially chosen for the occasion. The cheese was so greatly appreciated that it was allowed to be called *Dauphin* from that day onwards, or so the story goes. The name is still given to a herb-and-cloves white Maroilles, which is ripened in molds for three to four months. The taste resembles that of *Boulette d'Avesnes*, a small farmhouse cheese from Avesnes and surroundings, which is made of buttermilk curds to which finely chopped herbs have been added. After three months' ripening the flattened cones have a reddish-yellow surface and a crumbly consistency, and one must be prepared for the first, sharp taste. Neither should the taste of *Rollot* be taken lightly; this is a treacherously innocent-looking, full-cream cheese from Picardy, small and flat, with a round or sometimes heart-shaped form. Another local Boulette comes from Cambrai, the *Boulette de Cambrai*; it is flavored with herbs and spices and eaten fresh.

By no means are all of these northern cheeses sharp and strong flavored. *Mimolette* is a pleasant, mild cheese weighing about 3 kg (6.6 lbs), and is orange-colored with a gray rind. It bears such a close resemblance to the Dutch cheese Commissie, a large type of Edam, that the Dutch call their export version Mimolette, while the French cheese has been nicknamed "Vieux Hollande." The Mimolette is also made in other parts of France, particularly in Brittany.

BELOW: The heavily-salted Maroilles Gris, or Vieux Lille. It is matured for a particularly long period and acquires a gray crust.

The Swiss secret of a French cheese
In the 1850s a farmer named Héroult had a farm in the *département* of the Oise, to the north of Paris. Nearly every day his wife sent her fresh cheeses to the Halles market in Paris. A Swiss cowherd, living on the farm, suggested that she should add some fresh cream to the curds, as was sometimes done in his home country. The result was so successful that Madame Héroult soon had trouble meeting the increased demand, and so it was that *Petit-Suisse* was born. Together with a partner, Charles Gervais, she started the Gervais cheese factory, which is now one of the largest in France. Because of its creamy, very soft consistency, Petit-Suisse is packed in small plastic or paper containers. It has a 60% fat content, and the taste is very fresh, slightly sourish and nutty. Petit-Suisse is popular with both adults and children as a dessert served with fruit, or alone, with a little sugar. So too is the closely related semisalted *Demi-sel*.

An ancient Christmas delicacy
Where the river Epte runs before and beyond the town of Gournay, some of the finest dairy country between Paris and the sea is to be found. This fine butter and cream area is known as the Pays de Bray, and its most famous cheese is *Neufchatel*. As long ago as the fifteenth century, English merchants arrived via Dieppe and, along with other goods purchased in the region, they took back some of these cheeses for the Christmas market at home – the cheeses were probably much the same as now: small, weighing about 100 g (3½ oz) each. When purchased fresh, the white flora can just be seen, but it is sometimes left to ripen further. Neufchatels have a soft paste, which is lightly salted and has a pure and refreshing flavor. They come in various shapes which determine their names: the best known is the cylindrical *Bonde or Bondon*; there is also the square-shaped *Carré*, the rectangular *Briquette* and the heart-shaped *Coeur*.

LEFT: The rich pasture-lands of Normandy here reach the sea at Etretat, near Le Havre. The region to the south produces some famous cheeses: Pont-l'Evêque, Livarot, Camembert.

Camembert cheese takes its name from the Normandy village of Camembert in the *département* of the Orne. Legend says that the cheese was first made in 1791 by Marie Harel, who eventually passed the recipe on to her daughter, also called Marie. She and her husband, Victor Paynel, sold the cheese at the local markets, and it became so famous that a statue was erected to the elder Marie at nearby Vimoutiers.

Like many legends, Camembert's exists on fancy rather than fact. Marie Harel did not invent Camembert cheese – she didn't even live in Camembert. The cheese had already been described in a seventeenth-century dictionary as a splendid cheese which, like the excellent *Livarot*, was for sale in the market at Vimoutiers. It is likely that cheeses of the Camembert type were enjoyed by William the Conqueror, when they were known as *Augelot*, now a local name for the famous cheese *Pont-l'Evêque*. Augelot cheese came from the Pays d'Auge, where Camembert, Livarot and Pont-l'Evêque have been made for centuries.

In the old days, the ripening of Camembert was left to nature. At one time it had a red rind; later it became blue-crusted because the cheese was very sensitive to the formation of undesired molds. Marie Harel was the first cheesemaker to establish a regular mold flora and, in this respect, was the inventor of *modern* Camembert.

Factory production commenced towards the end of the last century, and has been improved since the introduction of *Penicillium candidum*, a white inoculated mold, in 1910. Unfortunately, the cheese is sometimes oversalted, which interferes with its true characteristics.

A real Camembert has a fine, supple consistency, a taste reminiscent of mushrooms and a strong aroma; a Camembert cheese inspired the Surrealist poet Léon-Paul Fargue to call it "les pieds de Dieu" – "the feet of the Lord." When the first Camembert factories were established outside Normandy, the Syndicat des Fabricants du Véritable Camembert de Normandie was founded, in order to identify and protect the cheese of the region. Special regulations also exist concerning *Gournay*, the smaller Camembert, and other similar types.

LEFT: The familiar, chipwood box for Camembert superseded the straw packaging. Patented in the 1890s, the box helped preserve the cheese and improved exports.

BELOW: Norman farmers have made butter, cream, cheese and cider for well over a thousand years. The products have greatly influenced Normandy's regional cooking.

LEFT: An estate in Normandy. The region has abundant orchards in addition to its pastures. Cider and Calvados, the Norman brandy, are made from the apples.

BELOW: The idyllic river valley of the Risle, one of the small rivers which meanders through Camembert country to the Seine estuary.

BELOW: The cheese-making room of the Coopérative Laitière at Vicq, France. In the foreground are a number of cheese-making vats, considerably smaller than those in the large drawing below. To the right, workers remove the distributor plates and stack the trays of molds.

BELOW: The correct quantity of wet curd is discharged onto the distributor plates. It is important that each mold be evenly filled.

LEFT: The trays of molds are continuously stacked and turned. Note the wet curd in the tall molds; it will eventually settle into the familiar, round cheese we associate with Camembert.

A. This buffer tank contains pasteurized cheese milk. After addition of starter, the milk is pumped into one or more of the cheesemaking vats. Its temperature should be 31-32°C (88-90°F).

B. The cheesemaking vats are large, open vats, similar to the traditional type. Rennet is added, and in very modern production lines (as the one shown here), the Camembert mold culture is also added directly to the cheese milk. It takes about an hour for the milk in the vat to coagulate. From right to left, the successive stages are shown: the first vat is filled with milk; in the second vat milk is curdling; in the third vat milk coagulates to form curd; from the fourth vat the curd is poured into the molds; the last vat is empty and ready to be filled with prepared milk.

E. The molds stand on trays; on top of them sits a distributor plate with openings that channel the right amount of wet curd into the molds.

C. This apparatus, which is anything but traditional, is a stirring device. Lowered into any of the vats, its slow rotation mixes and gently stirs the curd. This phase is preceded by careful cutting of the coagulum, which may be done mechanically or by hand; the curd layer should measure about 1.5-3 cm ($\frac{1}{2}$-$1\frac{1}{4}$ in). In the meantime, some whey can be run off.

D. When the curd is ready, this feeder screw is lowered into the vat, into which it fits closely. It rotates, expelling the curd-whey mixture through the opening in the end of the vat and into the molds. One full turn of the screw displaces enough curd to fill one tray of molds.

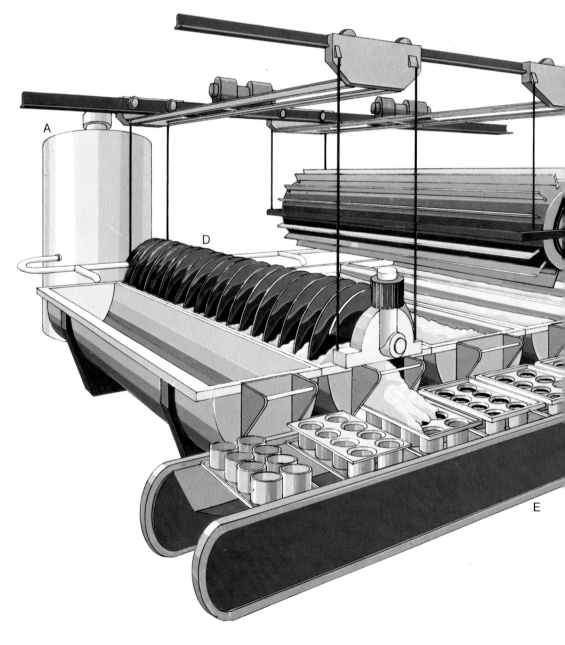

LEFT: Originally, the white mold grew spontaneously, and slowly, on the cheeses. Modern manufacturers encourage the action by spraying the cheeses with *Penicillium candidum,* while in the drying and ripening rooms.

LEFT: Fresh Camemberts in the ripening room. On some of them the white mold is beginning to appear.

total production French cheese 898,800 tons p.a. (100 %)

production Camembert 186,000 tons p.a. (20.7 %)

export soft cheeses 57,100 tons p.a.

F. At the end of the conveyor belt, the trays of molds are stacked. A considerable amount of whey is drained off, the cheeses being pressed, so to speak, by their own weight. Workers turn the trays a few times during the draining process. As the excess moisture is expelled, the volume of the curd diminishes.

G. After about twenty-four hours the cheeses are taken from their molds and salted, usually by means of a brine bath. Large containers, filled with the young cheeses, are immersed in a salty solution.

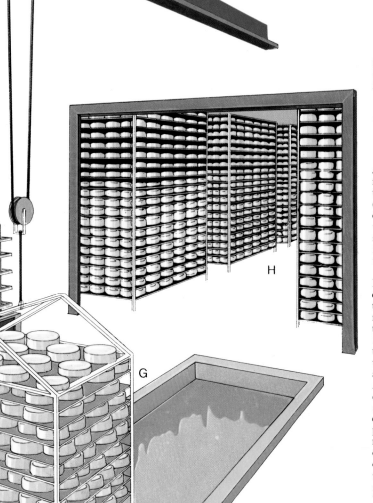

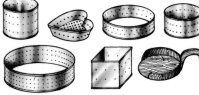

ABOVE: Camembert is made in the traditional tall, narrow molds (top left); other soft cheeses are made in a wide variety of mold shapes. Note the perforations that allows the whey to drain. For the same purpose, some molds have no bottom at all.

H. The cheeses are dried and transferred to the high-humidity ripening room. At a temperature of 13-15°C (55-59°F), the characteristic white mold begins to appear on the surface. After 7-12 days the cheeses are packed and distributed. The cheese has an even, pure white growth of mold, but the ripening of the interior has only just begun, and will require further maturing before it is "*à point,*" as the French say. During transport, and in the shop, the ripening process slowly continues.
  Many soft cheeses, with or without surface molds, are prepared along these lines, among them Brie and Carré de l'Est. Camembert, however, represents no less than two-thirds of all soft cheese produced in France.

With Camembert, Pont-l'Evêque and Livarot are the three world-famous cheeses of the Pays d'Auge, and guaranteed as original by the mark of the Syndicat de la Marque d'Origine Pays d'Auge. Like most widely marketed cheeses, Pont-l'Evêque is mainly factory produced, made from very fresh milk, and then cured for four to five weeks. The small cheeses are then washed, causing the rind to turn yellow and the flavor and aroma to become stronger. If the cheeses are not washed, the rind becomes gray instead, and slightly cracked. The consistency of the pale-yellow cheese is soft and supple. Other varieties of Pont-l'Evêque are *Trouville* and the much larger *Pavé de Moyaux*.

Livarot – there is also a local variety sold as *Lisieux* – was once a skimmed-milk cheese, but it is now made from the skimmed evening milk of the previous day, mixed with the full-cream morning milk. The cheeses do not ripen on the farm but are sold on the market in Livarot or Vimou-tiers as *Livarot Blanc* to *affineurs,* who in Normandy are called *cavistes*.

However, the farmer-cheesemakers, and with them the professional *cavistes*, are being replaced by factories, where the fresh cheeses are placed in a drying room in order to develop the bacteriological flora on the rind. After some weeks they are transferred to caves possessing a strong, ammoniac atmosphere, where they remain for two months. Because a maturing Livarot cheese is inclined to dip in the center, each cheese is bound with five strips of cattail leaf or paper; the stripes left by this corset have earned Livarot the nickname of "the Colonel." The consistency is soft, with small eyes, the flavor is mild and fresh, and the aroma quite strong. If the cheese is found to have a chalk-white center, it indicates that the whey has not been adequately drained during the manufacture.

"The cheeses have arrived"
Toward the south, where the river Mayenne idly threads its way through the Normandy countryside in the direction of the Loire, stands Entrammes with its abbey of Notre Dame de Port-du-Salut, built in 1233. After Napoleon's reign, Trappist monks returned from exile, bringing with them a dozen dairy cows; they settled here and began producing a

LEFT: No fewer than twenty-two gold medals testify the high standards of craftsmanship that have gone into the making of this brand of Pont-l'Evêque.

LEFT: One of the three great cheeses from the Pays d'Auge – Livarot. The cheese has a supple consistency with small holes, the taste is fresh and mild, the aroma surprisingly strong.

LEFT: This Trappist monk is washing the small Port-Salut cheeses, made by him and his fellow monks at the Abbey of Notre Dame de Port-du-Salut in Entrammes.

BELOW: The small, delicate goat's milk cheeses (*chevres*) called Sainte-Maure are recognized by the straw or stick which pierces the length of each cheese. Some maintain that without it the Sainte-Maure would fall apart! It is an unusually fine and tasty cheese from Touraine, "the garden of France." The Sainte-Maure is locally very popular, especially when accompanied with a cool, dry Loire wine, such as Muscadet.

LEFT: A great deal of goat's milk cheese is made on the island of Corsica. The cheeses are notoriously strong and, like the Corsicans themselves, highly individual.

splendid cheese for their own consumption. Increased production followed a decision to use milk supplied by local farmers, and *Port-du-Salut* cheese soon reached the street markets of Paris. A cheese factor named Mouquet, who sold cheese in the capital over a hundred years ago, would put out a notice board proclaiming the arrival of a new supply – "*Arrivage des fromages*" – and within the hour his entire supply would be sold. Production, still done according to the ancient recipe, now amounts to some 200,000 cheeses a year. Port-du-Salut is a flat and cylindrical cheese with a pale yellow rind. It is semihard, has good keeping properties and a mild flavor.

Other Trappist monasteries soon followed with a cheese "*façon de Port-du-Salut*"; in 1878, however, the name of the original abbey cheese was placed under legal protection. In 1909 the monks from Entrammes helped to establish, far from the abbey, a then ultramodern, commercially run factory where cheese was made under the name of *Port-Salut*. The cheese called *Saint Paulin*, made in all parts of France, can be considered a close relative, although it is prepared somewhat differently.

Rare and spicy cheeses of the southeast
Between Tours and Poitiers is a land watered by tributaries of the Loire, a land so abundant that it is called the "garden of France" – Touraine; in Tours, they say, the very best French is spoken. The farmers of Touraine make a flamboyant and popular goat's milk cheese, *Sainte-Maure*, which is influenced by the Camembert in the way it is made and ripened.

East of Touraine, on the Atlantic Ocean, is the *département* of Vendée. Here we can taste *Fromage Nantais*, also called *Fromage de Curé*, a small, square cheese first made in 1890 by a local parish priest. In those days the cheese was known as *Petit Breton*. Production increased sharply after the arrival of a Belgian cheesemaker, who added a professional touch and modified the recipe a little, to suit the taste of his own country. It now slightly resembles Remoudou. Fromage de Curé is also made in Brittany. If we journey south and southeast of Vendée, to Vienne, Deux-Sèvres and Charente, we come to a country where farmers are prolific in the making of

BELOW: In the Pyrenées, a region of spicy, Spanish-style cheeses, much of the milk from sheep is made into fresh cheese and sent to Roquefort. Once there, it ripens in the famous caves where it develops the inimitable, blue-green mold.

dozens of different cheeses, mostly unripened dairy cheeses, and an ever increasing number of *chèvres* – goat's milk cheeses, which ripen only for a short time and are hardly ever seen outside the district of origin. There is *Fromage ae la Mothe*, for example, which is left to dry for about fifteen days between vine or plane tree leaves; the *Chabichou*, the *Carré de Saint-Cyr* and the *Fromage de Ruffec*. Finally, an extremely rare collector's item: a small triangular cheese made of sheep's milk, called *l'Aunis*.

Perhaps the individuality and the rarity of these small cheeses is intended to compensate the cheese explorer for the scarcity that exists in Bordeaux, to the south. No indigenous cheese is found in claret country – the vineyards leave precious little room for meadows. Beyond the *département of* Landes, the foothills of the Pyrenées yield good grazing land for dairy cattle. Influenced by Spanish cookery, the mountain herdsmen make their own fresh cheeses, strongly spiced with pepper and pimento, especially in the Basque country. Such are the cheeses *Orrys* and *Castillon*. In wintertime, when the cattle are kept in stables, *Bethmale* cheese (also known as *Aulus* or *Oustet*) is made, a hard spicy cheese, very suitable for grating. Some cheeses from this area of the Pyrenées are made from the milk of ewes, and they are sent uncured to ripen in the unique caves of Roquefort, home of the famous blue cheese.

The rural cheeses of Corsica
The rugged, mountainous Corsican landscape of pine forest, tumbling, icy streams, ravines and precipitous tracks is strictly sheep and goat country. Mountain herdsmen make cheese from both kinds of milk, sometimes mixed together. From the north and center of the island comes the square and creamy *Niolo* and the slightly more salted *Venaco*, which is ripened for three months. In the south, *Sartenais* is made, and then there is *Bruccio*, a fresh cheese which is sometimes salted and preserved for the winter. Most of Corsica's cheeses are powerful, rough and "goaty" as you might expect. The island also produces a blue-veined cheese, *Bleu de Corse*, which resembles Roquefort; most of the sheep's milk, however, is processed to "white" Roquefort and sent "home" to ripen in the Roquefort caves.

Lovers of cheese may become ecstatic when presented with a *Roquefort*. They describe it as a fine, noble cheese, delicately veined and marbled with a bluish-green mold. Some would say that Roquefort is peerless, the greatest cheese in the world.

Roquefort cheese comes from an area south of the Massif Central and east of the beautiful Gorges du Tarn, an area of poor pasture land. The village of Roquefort-sur-Soulzon stands on the remains of a mountain, Combalou. In prehistoric times, rainwater drained through the porous limestone strata to form a gigantic underground water basin, so weakening the foundations of Combalou that one day the entire mountain collapsed.

Due to the collapse and subsequent displacements, cracks formed called *fleurines*, which serve as natural chimneys and air filters. In the underground caves there is a continuous circulation of fresh air, which distributes the moisture evenly over the entire mountain. Combalou breathes. Condensation and evaporation balance each other, air pressure and temperature are in equilibrium, and the micro-climate is of unequalled purity. Here, the *Penicillium roqueforti* developed, mold families that grow on organic substances.

The poor soil of the arid *causses* made all but the most primitive agriculture impossible, and although grass could hardly grow, the sheep thrived. Their milk was made into a cheese that

LEFT: Roquefort cheese. The legend of Roquefort tells of a herdsman who left a loaf of bread and some fresh curd cheese in the caves of Roquefort. He returned to discover that the cheese had turned moldy, but it was so tasty that the local farmers decided to mature all their cheeses by the same method.

RIGHT: The tall, round forms are filled with curd.

ABOVE: Samples of cheese and cultures of mold are continuously tested and examined in the modern laboratories.

RIGHT: The cheeses mature slowly in the cool cellars, where there is always a gentle flow of air to distribute the spores of *Penicillium glaucum* var. *Roqueforti* to all parts of the caves. These conditions give Roquefort cheese its unique character.

brought fame and prosperity to the *causses* in general, and Roquefort in particular. There is nothing special about the milk of these Lacaune sheep; it is only when a cheese is ripened in the center of Combalou that it acquires from the *Penicillium roqueforti* its greenish veins and unique flavor.

A blessing of blue

The inhabitants of the *causses* protect their prosperity by the Confederation Générale des Producteurs de Lait de Brebis et des Industriels de Roquefort. Its members are the sheep breeders, who twice daily bring their sheep from the *causses* to the hygienic stables, where they are mechanically milked. Also members are the hundreds of manufacturers of "white" Roquefort, both here, on Corsica and in the Pyrenées, and the producers in the caves of Combalou.

A Roquefort cheese receives its blessing of blue by being covered in a thin layer of salt, brushed and pricked, and then stored in the caves in such a way that the moist air can easily reach it. After some weeks it is wrapped in foil, where it continues to ripen. A Roquefort cheese weighs approximately 2.7 kg (5.9 lbs) and is cylindrical in shape. It is also marketed in smaller, pre-packed portions. Its paste is white with blue-green veins and is somewhat crumbly. The smell and taste of this great ewe cheese, the only sheep's cheese in the world to gain such renown, is highly flavored, but nobly so. The cheese is provided with a guarantee label for export purposes.

Roquefort has a long export history. Monastery chronicles of the eighth century mention the transport of Roquefort across the Alps, by which time it was well established: the Romans were acquainted with it, Charlemagne enjoyed it, and by the eleventh century we find it recorded on customs' lists. For hundreds of years, Roquefort cheese has been praised by authors, including Casanova, who had it served with ice-cold ham.

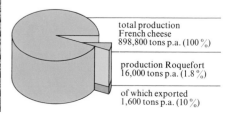

total production French cheese 898,800 tons p.a. (100%)

production Roquefort 16,000 tons p.a. (1.8%)

of which exported 1,600 tons p.a. (10%)

A volcanic, mountainous area of mineral springs, of towns and villages built upon rocky outcrops, of herbal pastures and high passes, the *département* of Cantal gave its name to a mighty cheese that was probably being made during antiquity. Pliny the Elder describes a cheese from near Lozère and Gévaudan, which in many respects resembles the present Cantal. In the second half of the eighteenth century we meet the cheese in the encyclopedia of d'Alembert and Diderot, with an illustration of all the equipment needed for the preparation of a *Fourme du Cantal*. These enormous, drum-shaped cheeses have been sold in the Haute Auvergne and Cantal for centuries, and *Cantal Fermier* is still prepared according to the following, ancient tradition:

Between the middle of May and the beginning of October, the herdsmen tend their cattle in the upland pastures; each herd consists of fifty or sixty cows, usually the mahogany-colored Salers or the smaller Aubracs, a hardy mountain stock. The herdsmen make cheese from the milk, in their old, dilapidated stone huts, using a very laborious process. After being pressed for an hour, the curds are cut into strips and pressed again, a process which is repeated six to ten times. The curds are then left in the cheese press for twenty-four to thirty-six hours, during which time they begin to ripen. They are pressed again and turned at intervals. The turning procedure continues every other day for three months, and at each turning the rind is polished. Twice during the season the herdsmen undertake the journey down the mountain roads to deliver their cheeses, some specimens weighing as much as 45 kg (99 lbs).

ABOVE: The breed of cattle, as much as the pasture land, determines the quality and the character of French dairy cheeses.

Popular breeds are Normandy, Jersey, Saler and Aubrac, the latter being particularly suited to mountain grazing.

ABOVE: Tall, drum-shaped Cantal cheeses – *Fourmes de Cantal* – maturing in a cellar. The Cantal is a beautiful cheese from the Massif Central.

Sometimes called "the French cheddar," it has a smooth texture and a fragrant aroma of the Auvergne meadows.

Modern preparation techniques

Initially, the rind of a Cantal shows golden-colored spots, which vanish as the cheese matures. Gradually, the rind turns darker, nearly black. Later it becomes almost red, and finally grayish white. The full-cream, smooth consistency retains the herbal flavor of the mountain meadows. The climate, the altitude, the type of cattle and especially the condition of the soil make something very special of Cantal Fermier. For this reason, great care has been taken to locate other places where identical natural conditions exist, and where this regional cheese can be produced as original Cantal. The places are: the entire *département* of Cantal itself, eight municipalities of Aveyron, twenty-five of Puy-de-Dôme and one of Haute-Loire. The heaviest cheeses are those from the region of Salers. If a Cantal is made at an altitude of at least 850 meters (33,500 feet), it is entitled to bear the additional label of "Haute-Montagne."

In the cheese dairies of the valleys, away from the pure mountain air but with the help of modern equipment, *Cantal Laitier* is made from pasteurized milk. The method of preparation is the same as that of the Fermier, but the cheese ripens for a maximum of two months, and has a less pronounced taste. These factories also produce smaller Cantals of 8 to 10 kg (17.6 to 22 lbs), called *Cantalets*. Cantal cheese is also permitted in a rectangular shape, provided that it ripens for not less than two months. Finally, there are several partially cured Cantals, such as *Tomme d'Aligot* or *Tomme Fraîche*, which are used a great deal in the preparation of regional dishes.

ABOVE: The process of manufacturing Cantal cheeses. The curd is first prepared in metal tubs.

ABOVE: From the tubs, the curd is cut into blocks to be laid out on a bench or table for pressing.

RIGHT: After a short time the curd is cut into strips and pressed again.

Bleu d'Auvergne

Mountain country seems to go hand in hand with blue cheese. Several prime examples are found in the Massif Central, not the least of which is the *Bleu d'Auvergne*, a dairy cheese that comes from more or less the same area as Cantal. The cheese is flat and cylindrical, and weighs between 2 and 2.5 kg (4.4 to 5.5 lbs); it has a refined taste and a very special bouquet. It is said to stimulate the appetite and be good for the digestion.

As the cheese is rather small, not a great deal of milk is required, which is just as well, considering the scarcity of pasture. In places the landscape is rough, with deep valleys and ravines, and a few winding, narrow roads. From early times, the small farms of the region, which often keep no more than ten to fifteen cows, have made their own cheeses. Since 1870 the farmers have been inoculating their curds with *Penicillium glaucum*, in the manner of the makers of Roquefort. The major part of production has been taken over by cheese dairies, but there are still a few farmers around Thiézac who make their own blue cheese, called *Bleu de Thiézac Fermier*. Twice weekly the farmer must take his cheeses (until recently by donkey or mule) to the *affineur*, who then sets them to ripen in the valleys.

Only carefully collected, high-quality milk is suitable for *Bleu d'Auvergne*, as it is made into cheese when raw. The deep-cooled evening milk of the previous day is warmed shortly before the processing and added to the fresh morning milk. The mold culture, again *Penicillium glaucum*, may be added to the milk, but it is usually sprinkled on the curd after it has been transferred to the molds. After three or four days of washing and turning, the cheeses are taken to the salt rooms, which are kept at a temperature of 10°C (50°F). Here they are rubbed with dry salt and pricked with needles, which enables the air to penetrate and encourages the formation of mold. This process is completed within three to four weeks in a humid room at 8° to 10°C; by then the rind has discolored from yellowish-red to white with reddish spots. As soon as the green veins become visible, the small cheeses are packed in metal foil; they are then stored for another few weeks at a temperature of 2°C (about 36°F).

LEFT: Landscape in the Auvergne mountains, in the *département* of Puy-de-Dôme.

BELOW LEFT: Blue d'Auvergne is one of France's most popular blue-veined cheeses. It is believed to stimulate the appetite and aid the digestion – greatly to be desired in the land of Grande Cuisine.

From moldy bread to monument

Owing to the inherent expertise of the makers, the various blue cheeses of the Massif Central are the best in France. Some are named after their place of origin, such as *Bleu d'Aveyron, Bleu de Thiézac* (which has an entirely different flavor because it is salted when warm) and *Bleu de Laqueuille*. The latter, from the Laqueuille district of Puy-de-Dôme, has a somewhat drier rind and a less distinct flavor than the others mentioned, but it possesses an attractive veining, introduced by Antoine Roussel in 1850. Roussel dipped a piece of moldy bread from his home kitchen into the curds, and subsequently produced a blue cheese that, like Marie Harel, was to earn him a monument.

Finally, we must mention *Bleu de Causses*, which ripens in natural caves in the manner of Roquefort, and is found everywhere in the Auvergne. Its taste greatly depends on grazing conditions, including the composition of the local soil and the hours of sunshine during the summer.

The tender touch

In addition to the illustrious Roquefort and the much-decorated Bleu d'Auvergne, *Saint-Nectaire* cheese deserves to be mentioned. Made in Puy-de-Dôme in the immediate environment of Mont Dore, the cheese was already well known during the reign of Louis XIV. It's a fragile little cheese, prepared from the carefully collected milk of Salers cows and sold by the farmers once every fortnight to private or cooperative *affineurs*. Cylindrical in shape, the cheeses are left to ripen on straw in damp cellars, often the old cellars in Clermont-Ferrand, once used for storing wine. After three months the rind is spotted yellow to ochre-red. After six months the taste of the cheese is at its best: it is then supple and mild, and as they say in France, "*à ta tendre pression il répond*." The major part of the produce is consumed in the region itself. The farmhouse cheese is recognizable by an oval casein disc

ABOVE: This nineteenth-century farmer from the Auvergene is manually pressing the cheese curd. The whey runs into a wooden tub on the left.

bearing a green guarantee imprint; the factory-made cheese has a rectangular label.

A traditional Christmas soup is made with St. Nectaire, where slices of the cheese are mixed into a broth made of water, stale bread and salt. A few spoonfuls of whipped cream may be added before serving.

There is hardly a cheese-producing area of France that cannot boast a *chèvre* or two, and the Massif Central is no exception. It sports a number of these small, characteristic goat's cheeses. Perhaps the best known is *Chèvreton d'Ambert*, or *Brique de Forez*, which is sometimes partially made of cow's milk giving the cheese a less pungent taste and aroma. Mostly, though, only goat's milk is used. A maturation period of fifteen days on rye straw makes the *Chèvreton* a creamy, smooth cheese with a firm texture. Another local cheese is *Chevrotin*, nearly always eaten while fresh, often with double cream and sugar, or with salt and garlic. When left to ripen, these cheeses are placed in dovecot-like cages mounted on high poles, so that the wind may circulate about them. They must be protected

ABOVE: Built on a rocky outcrop, La Roque-Sainte-Marguerite in the district of Aveyron, where a variety of Bleu d'Auvergne is produced.

LEFT: A family lunch *en plein air* in the garden of the Château de Montmelas, Beaujeu. On such occasions local cheeses and wines may be enjoyed at the peak of their perfection.

by the shade of trees, for they quickly ferment and rise if the sun reaches them, spoiling the *Chevrotin's* particular flavor.

All roads lead to Paris
In Paris and the surrounding countryside our tour through the cheese areas of France comes to an end. For many centuries Paris has been the political, administrative and cultural center of the country. It is here that the great traditions of *Haute Cuisine* were established. In the old days, the regional produce of the land, including many varieties of cheese, reached Les Halles, the Paris market. Here the cheeses became nationally known and would gradually achieve world fame. Let us turn then to Brie cheese, the "Roi de Fromages," which is so closely associated with the capital city.

BELOW RIGHT: Brie de Meaux Fermier is not only the "Brie of Bries," but has been honored as the "Roi de Fromages."

LEFT: A wedge of a delicious and noble cheese – Brie de Melun. Ripe Brie has a soft, golden-yellow consistency, should not develop a white core in the paste, and should be slightly runny.

Paris lies in a basin in the earth's crust; it is as if nature had pressed down a pile of dishes until the edges remain slightly above the surroundings, gently sloping inwards, steep to the outside. The hollow in the center forms the Île de France – the area immediately east of the capital – and Champagne, fertile districts with lush pastures. Here is the home of the large *Brie* cheese, known as the "jewel of the Île de France."

Brie became world-famous overnight. At the Vienna Congress in 1814 and 1815, when statesmen of Europe were laying the foundations for the post-Napoleonic period, there were great celebrations, banquets and dinners between negotiations. During one such occasion an argument arose as to which country produced the best cheeses – or so the story goes. Always the diplomat, the Frenchman Talleyrand proposed that the different national cheeses be allowed to compete with one another at a large banquet. But Talleyrand was a gourmet and a cook as well as a diplomat: it is probable that he never doubted the outcome of the competition. *Brie de Meaux* emerged as the very best of some sixty cheeses – unanimously it was crowned "*Roi de Fromages.*" Indeed, Brie was both the king of cheeses and the cheese of kings and king's consorts: Louis XII and Henry IV enjoyed the cheese, as did the wife of Louis XV, Maria Leszczynska, who included Brie in her favorite patties, *bouchées à la reine*; then there was the writer Alexander Dumas who provided his Three Musketeers with meals that always ended with Brie sprinkled with Burgundy.

The first mention of this cheese can be found in the records of the Court of Champagne, dating from 1217. Its name comes from the province of La Brie in the *département* of Seine-et-Marne. Until the middle of the last century, Brie was exclusively made on the farms, often with a red rind flora. Since it now has become almost entirely a factory-made cheese, produced under rigidly controlled hygienic conditions, the desirable red flora only occurs along the edges of the cheese. Preripened evening milk of the previous day is used, mixed with fresh morning milk. The art lies in spooning the curds in six successive layers into a formerly wooden, but now stainless steel, ring, and then removing the whey with the aid of a perforated spoon. The cheese is turned, and on each turning clean reed mats are placed on top and underside. After six or seven days, it is sprinkled with powdered *Penicillium candidum* and then allowed to ripen for four weeks at a temperature of 11-12°C (52-54°F). Should the temperature either rise or fall, immediate changes in shape, color and taste result. A correctly prepared Brie should have an evenly distributed mold layer, a cream-colored soft paste without holes, and a flavor – depend-

NOS SPÉCIALITÉS

Chester en Crème
Chester Français
Tome de Savoie
Cantal Extra
Fourme d'Ambert
Boursault
Munster
Parmesan
Sbrintz
Brie de Meaux
MORBIER du JURA

Name	Milk	Type	Rind	Form	Weight	% Fat content
Aunis		●	☐	triangular	250-300 g	45
Baguette		●	❖	bar	500 g	45
Banon		●	—	flat disc	100-150 g	45-50
Beaufort		■	☐	cartwheel	14-70 kg	50
Bethmale		■	☐	low cylinder	5-7 kg	45
Bleu d'Auvergne,		●	⁘	low cylinder	2-2.5 kg	40
- d'Aveyron		●	⁘	low cylinder	2-2.5 kg	45
- de Laqueuille		●	⁘	low cylinder	2-2.5 kg	45
- des Causses		●	⁘	low cylinder	2-2.5 kg	45
- de Thiézac		●	⁘	low cylinder	2-2.5 kg	45
- de Bresse		■	⁘	low cylinder	0.1-2 kg	50
- de Corse		●	⁘	low cylinder	2 kg	45
- de Gex		●	⁘	low cylinder	5.5-6.5 kg	45
- de Septmoncel		●	⁘	low cylinder	5.5-6.5 kg	45
- du Haut Jura		●	⁘	low cylinder	5.5-6.5 kg	45
Boulette d'Avesnes		●	❖	truncated cone	200-300 g	50
- de Cambrai		○	—	ball	250-300 g	45
Bossons Macérés		●	—	container	varying	45
Boursin		○	—	low cylinder	100 g	70
Brie de Coulommiers		●	❖	flat disc	0.4-3 kg	40-50

ABOVE: The Rue de Mouffetard in Paris, a happy memory for anyone with an appetite who has ever been there. The shop windows display a wonderful variety of foodstuffs and wines: fresh vegetables from all corners of the earth, fresh fish from the Atlantic and Mediterranean, meat, poultry and cheese. Every cheese shop has its own specialities (right).

ing on the variety – which ranges over all nuances, from mild to very strong. After ripening, the cheeses are wrapped in waxed paper, packed in chipwood boxes and provided with a label that guarantees their origin.

Formerly, Brie often carried the name of the place of origin, and varieties still exist with a unique, local character. *Brie de Coulommiers*, for example (also called *Petit Brie*, as it weighs only 450 g [1 lb]) is prepared with fresh or pasteurized milk; it is frequently eaten unripened, at the first appearance of mold, and has a

BELOW: Market porters enjoy a drink in a café bar. Outside, a stack of cheeses stands on the pavement.

very mild and delicate flavor. If the ripening process is allowed to continue, however, the taste becomes more pronounced, resembling that of Camembert; the influence of the air on the rind makes it a very special little cheese. A correct amount of air in the ripening room is a decisive factor for quality. *Fromage "à la Pie"* is always eaten practically fresh. *Brie de Melun*, on the contrary, is well-ripened; unlike other Brie varieties, the mold formation in this cheese takes place spontaneously, and no *Penicillium candidum* is added. After ripening, the cheese has a homogeneous structure, a reddish or blue-white layer of mold, and a nutty flavor, which is not less powerful than the aroma. Varieties of Brie de Melun are *Brie de Montereau* or *Ville Saint-Jacques*. *Cendré de Brie* is coated with ash, and has a gray-black rind. *Fromage de Dreux*, a cousin of Brie, used to be wrapped in chestnut leaves.

Apart from Brie, the surroundings of Paris offer quite a number of cheese varieties, many of them little known outside their place of origin. *Olivet* is a farmhouse cheese from Orleans, wrapped in leaves and preserved in the ashes of vine stalks. The factory version is a rather sharp, white mold cheese, sometimes packed in hay *(au Foin)* or in ashes *(Cendré)*. There is also an *Olivet Bleu*. *Vendôme* and *Villebarou* are both interesting cheeses, difficult to find but worth searching for. Much better known is the fresh cream cheese *Boursin*, widely exported in cardboard boxes. Its light taste is often strengthened by the addition of garlic and herbs, or with a coating of crushed peppercorns. *Selles-sur-Cher* is a very savory *chèvre*, covered with salt and charcoal. *Fontainebleau* rivals Petit Suisse; it is a very light, creamy

Name	Milk	Type	Rind	Form	Weight	% Fat content
- de Meaux	♫	●	✿	flat disc	0.4-3 kg	40-50
- de Melun	♫	●	✿	flat disc	0.4-3 kg	40-50
- de Montereau	♫	●	✿	flat disc	0.4-3 kg	40-50
Bruccio	♫♫	○●	—✿	basket	500 g	45
Cachat	♫	○	—	basket	100 g	45-50
Camembert	♫	●	✿	flat disc	200-300 g	45-55
Cantal	♫	■	☐	cylinder	35-45 kg	45-50
Carré de l'Est	♫	●	✿	rectangular	100-200 g	40-60
Carré de Saint-Cyr	♫	●	☐	rectangular	varying	45
Castillon	♫	■	☐	flat disc	0.5-1 kg	45
Cendré de Brie	♫	●	☐	flat disc	250 g	40-50
Chabichou	♫	●	☐	truncated cone	100 g	45
Chaource	♫	●	✿	flat disc	500 g	45-50
Chèvreton d'Ambert	♫	●	☐	loaf	400 g	40-45
Chevrotin	♫	○	☐	truncated cone	100 g	45
Dauphin	♫	●	❖	oval, bar	200-500 g	50
Demisel	♫	○	—	rectangular	75-100 g	40
Emmental	♫	■	☐	cartwheel	60-130 kg	45
Fontainebleau	♫	○	—	container	varying	60
Fromage "à la Pie"	♫	○	—	basket	600-800 g	40-50
- de Dreux	♫	●	✿	flat disc	150-500 g	30-40
- d'Epoisses	♫	●	✿	low cylinder	250 g	45
- de la Mothe	♫	●	✿	flat disc	250 g	45
- de Ruffec	♫	●	☐	flat disc	250 g	45
- Nantais	♫	●	❖	rectangular	300 g	40
Géromé	♫	●	✿	flat disc	0.3-4.5 kg	40
Gournay	♫	●	✿	flat disc	100 g	45
Gruyère de Comté	♫	■	✿	cartwheel	20-55 kg	45
Laumes	♫	●	✿	loaf	0.6-1 kg	45
Livarot	♫	●	✿	flat disc	300-500 g	40-45
Manicamp	♫	●	✿	rectangular	200 g	40-45
Maroilles	♫	●	✿	rectangular	200-800 g	40-50
- Gris	♫	●	✿	rectangular	200-800 g	40-50
Mimolette	♫	■	☐	ball	2.5-4 kg	40
Monceau	♫	●	✿	rectangular	600 g	45
Munster	♫	●	✿	flat disc	0.3-1.5 kg	40
Neufchatel	♫	●	✿	varying	100 g	40-45
Niolo	♫	○	—	rectangular/basket	500 g	45
Olivet	♫	●	✿	flat disc	300 g	45-50
Orrys	♫	■	☐	low cylinder	10 kg	45
Pelardon	♫	○	—	flat disc	80-100 g	45
Petit Suisse	♫	○	—	small cylinder	30 g	60-75
Picardon	♫	○	—	flat disc	75-100 g	45
Poivre d'Ane	♫♫○	○	—	flat disc	75-200 g	45
Pont-l'Evêque	♫	●	✿	cube	300 g	50
Port-du-Salut	♫	■	✿	low cylinder	1.3-2 kg	45-50
Reblochon	♫	●	✿	flat disc	600 g	45
Rollot	♫	●	✿	flat disc	200-300 g	45
Roquefort	♫	■	❖❖	cylinder	2.7 kg	50-60
Sainte-Maure	♫	●	✿	tall cylinder	300 g	45
Saint-Marcellin	♫	●	✿	flat disc	75 g	40-60
Saint-Nectaire	♫	●	✿	flat disc	1.7 kg	45
Saint-Paulin	♫	■	✿	low cylinder	1.3-2 kg	45-50
Sartenais	♫♫	■	☐	ball	0.5-1 kg	45
Selles-sur-Cher	♫	●	☐	flat disc	150 g	45
Tomme au Marc de Raisin	♫	●	☐	flat disc	1.5-2 kg	20-40
- d'Aligot	♫	○	—	container	varying	45
- de Savoie	♫	■	☐❖	low cylinder	2-3 kg	10-30
Venaco	♫♫	●	☐	rectangular	500 g	45
Vendôme	♫	●	☐	flat disc	250 g	50
Villebarou	♫	●	✿	flat disc	450 g	45

Key to symbols on p. 34. 453 g = 1 lb; 1 kg = 2.2 lbs.

BELOW: An attractive display of cheeses in the window of a *fromagerie*. Top row from left to right: Livarot, Epoisses, Fromage Nantais, heart-shaped Rollot and Bleu de Bresse;

below, left: Brie Coulommiers, Fromage de Dreux, Dauphin, and a number of soft, white-mold cheeses.

and spongy cheese, excellent for a sweet dessert, and is sold as such in the famous Paris café *La Coupole*. Finally, *Chaource* is a wonderful, soft, white-mold cheese, milky to fruity in taste and possibly a touch sour, with a very fine but penetrating aroma.

Many foreign cheeses are produced in France, including *Cheddar, Gouda, Edam, Gorgonzola* as well as cheese spreads. There is a market for these cheeses, but they have a hard time competing with the genuine, natural cheeses that France has to offer.

Paris and French cuisine

Paris became the gastronomic center of the western world because of at least three factors: the imagination and skill for improvisation of ordinary people in the preparation of their food; the importance of elegant, refined cuisine at the royal court; and the radiating influence of French politics and diplomacy. None of these factors should be ignored – least of all the first one. The brilliance of the court life at Versailles, so close to the densely populated and hard-working capital contrasted with, and supplemented, the solid traditions of French country cooking.

The essence of French cuisine is not in complicated, sumptuous recipes, but in excellent ingredients and well-tried methods of preparation. It is not for nothing that the food in even the smallest Paris restaurants is unsurpassed. And so it is with cheese. Every Frenchman knows how cheese should be eaten; the experience of centuries has enhanced his knowledge of the specific quality and character of the many varieties. No meal in France is complete without cheese, eaten with crisp French bread and its ideal companion – wine.

Germany (Federal Republic)

A mighty, lowland plain dominates that stretch of Europe south of the Baltic Sea. From the Soviet Union, it sweeps through Poland, East Germany and the northern territories of West Germany, to reach the Netherlands and the border of Denmark. Along the North Sea, the polders and dykes join up in the west with the Dutch lowlands. For centuries during the Middle Ages this vast area west and north of Danzig was a great trading center. For one thing, there were many well-placed seaports: Lübeck on the Baltic, and Hamburg and Bremen on the Elbe and Weser rivers, which feed into the North Sea.

Together these cities formed the powerful trade federation known as the Hanseatic League. Since the league monopolized most of the produce of northern Europe, it follows that a considerable variety of cheese found its way to and from the transit ports. Furthermore, this was good dairy country. Ostfriesland, Schleswig-Holstein and Niedersachsen – where, unlike Bavaria with its big landowners, farmers owned their own property – are among the most important cattle-breeding regions. This is the natural homeland of the black-patched Frisian-Holsteiner cows. Further to the south the fertile lowlands deteriorate into the desolate Lüneburg Heath, which affords scant opportunity for dairy farmers.

West Germany, in fact, has greatly contrasting landscapes. In the central German highlands, from the Rhineland across to the Bayrischer Wald, rivers run between beautiful hills, which are clad with vineyards and surmounted by castles – the fairyland of the brothers Grimm. Cheese, a traditional fairy food, is made here, although most farms have fewer cattle than those in the north.

Further to the southeast, the central plateau climbs up to the heights of Swabia and Bavaria, where Lake Constance – the Boden See – straddles the Swiss-German border. In the Allgäu Alps east of the Boden See, an area outstanding for cattle breeding and dairy production, the well-known cheese town of Kempten is found. The Allgäu is a truly Alpine landscape of dark pine forests, where the springtime meadows are carpeted with mountain flowers, and the herds of brown cattle are located by the flat, metallic ringing of the cow bells. The Allgäu has now

ABOVE: Drachenstein, a small village surrounded by woods and meadows, in the Baden-Württemburg region, the home of a fresh cheese called Topfen.

LEFT: The brown Allgäu cattle of southern Germany on their way to the fresh, alpine meadows.

superseded the north as a cheese-producing region.

Monasteries, merchants and cheesemakers

Homemade, nonrenneted cheeses were made by the northern Germans over a thousand years ago, and they probably bore close resemblance to the present Sauermilch cheese.

When people learned the skill of making good rennet, a more stable product was established, and cheese-making spread from Schleswig-Holstein all over East and West Prussia. In the castles of the Teutonic knights, founded by the Baltic Germans, cheeses were made: *Herrenkäse* for the nobility and lower quality *Gesindekäse* for the commoners. The village of Lieben-werder, a well-known trade and export center, was even renamed in 1341 as Käsemarkt ("cheese market"); about the same time the cooperative Holsteiner-Meierei system was established, whereby farmers communally processed their milk.

Even so, cheese production far from met home requirements, and in the centuries that followed, cheese was imported from Holland via Hamburg, Bremen and Emden. Northern German merchants visited the weekly markets of Amsterdam and other Dutch cities, while Rotterdam and Dordrecht supplied German provinces via the Rhine. Dutch Edam cheese, colored red since the thirteenth century, was so appreciated by the Germans that the foreign makers of other cheese types began coloring their cheeses red, to be sold as Edam.

Many of Germany's most popular cheese types are copies of, or variations of, foreign originals. The Allgäu has a centuries-old tradition of making *Emmental*, but the quality varied considerably, in spite of the efforts of one Josef Stadler, who in 1821 sent for two experts from Switzerland to try to control the fat content, temperature and ripening. Yet methods remained primitive: the cheese kettle still hung over the open fire; temperature was judged with the elbow; rennet was imperfect; and pressing was done with stones. Drastic improvements came about with the introduction of the *gärkellers* in the 1870s, places established to facilitate the ripening of cheese. The Allgäu Emmental is now a quality product.

LEFT: The massive, thatched roof of a typical farmhouse in the Black Forest, designed to bear the heavy winter snows.

Although Germany produces a great variety of cheeses, with a wide range of flavors, shapes and sizes, plus a remarkable number of fresh- and sour-milk types, there seems to be a particular affection for those pungent, strong cheeses which in some examples have the power to fell trees. It is not really known why these cheeses are so admired – perhaps it is the traditional love of the heroic; possibly Siegfried was raised on a diet of black bread, beer and Handkäse, those archetypal, hand-molded farmhouse cheeses whose modern descendants so readily betray their whereabouts.

Not content with the indigenous types, the Germans looked around for inspiration and finally borrowed, later to naturalize, Limburger and Romadur – the famous "stinking cheese" of Belgium – to which they added the lively Munster cheese from Alsace. The Belgians, at any rate, seem fairly unconcerned that their Limburger has moved several hundred miles downwind.

Another suggestion is that Germany's assertive cheeses compliment the national taste for highly flavored, gamey meats, such as boar, pheasant, hare and venison – or that a strong cheese needs to be washed down by copious draughts of German beer.

Emmental was not the only cheese to make the Allgäu a famous dairy region. From 1830 Karl Hirnbein, advised by the Belgian Herve cheese specialist Grosjean, manufactured

BELOW: Niedersachsen is one of Germany's most important cattle-raising and milk-producing areas; the Frisian-Holstein cattle are the most important breed. Here, the black-and-white cows are milked by machine.

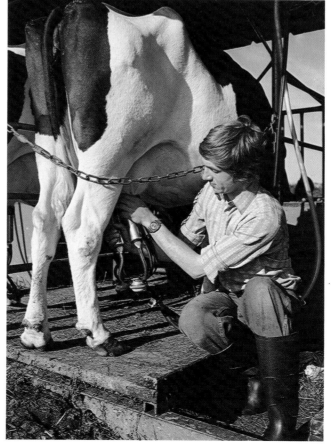

soft Allgäu *Limburger* and *Romadur* cheese. Hirnbein's Limburger was such a success that it is now one of Germany's most important cheeses, in spite of a period of falling interest, which may have brought about a change in consistency – modern Limburger is more solid. There are loaf and block-shaped Limburgers of different weights. The required fat content and names of the cheeses are precisely specified: *Halbfettstufe* (20–30 %), *Dreiviertelfettstufe* (30–40 %), *Fettstufe* (40–45 %), *Voll-fettstufe* (45–50 %) and *Rahmstufe* (above 50 %). The Romadur cheese has an additional type, 60 %, and finally there is a *Doppelrahmstufe* with a fat content up to 85 %. The quantity of the dry matter is also regulated.

Limburger is difficult to make, because this piquant cheese with its reddish bacteria flora is extremely sensitive to both temperature and moisture degree in preparing and ripening. This original Belgian cheese has been almost wholly adopted by Germany, and is manufactured on a large scale. The dry salting by hand has now been replaced by the brine bath: 24 hours for the big Limburger cheeses, 7–12 hours for the small, and 2–4 hours for Romadur, according to fat content. During the first stages of ripening, the cheeses are placed close together; they are separated as soon as the flora appears. The cheeses are then given a mechanical wash with coryne bacteria, from four to eight

ABOVE: A small Münster cheese, the German version of the original French cheese of the Vosges mountains.

ABOVE: Both the farmer and his cow are of sturdy German stock – only the farming methods have changed.

times depending on the size of the cheese. To prevent the flora from being washed away, the wash is kept and used again.

After three or four weeks of ripening the cheeses should show a yellow-brown rindless surface, without cracks but with a somewhat sticky flora. They have a white to yellow-colored paste, which is crumbly, and a pliant, soft core. Consistency varies with the fat content – lower fat Limburgers are firmer, and in the fourth week of ripening the flavor changes from spicy to piquant; Romadur cheese is softer and milder, and is ripe after two weeks.

The *Frühstückkäse* ("breakfast cheese") is a small, round Limburger that ripens in its packing and can be eaten almost fresh, or only a little ripened. Also from the Allgäu is a variety of Limburger called *Weiss-lacker Bierkäse* – excellent with beer – with a white, waxy flora. Although a small cheese of only 60 g (2 oz), it has a prolonged brine bath of 2–3 days, and consequently is a slow ripener, taking some 5-6 months, but can be stored for over a year. The cheese is semihard with a very sharp, piquant flavor, reminiscent of bacon.

The *Allgäuer Gaiskäsle* is made in two types, the orange and the white. The former is prepared from a mixture of 60-80% raw goat's milk and 20-40% pasteurized cow's milk. It develops a thin, yellow to red-brown rind with a coryne flora; the paste is light yellow

ABOVE: Limburger is similar to the Belgian Herve cheese. It originates from around Liége, Belgium, but most is now made in Germany.

ABOVE: Karwendel is a soft cheese with a fat content of 50%. It is made in the Allgäu, an alpine region in southern Germany, and a great cheese area.

and smooth, with a strong, spicy aroma. This cheese is like Romadur, becoming ripe after two or three weeks, and the longer it ripens the more pronounced is the goaty aroma. For the white type a similar quantity of goat's milk is used, between 60 and 70%, but after the brine bath the cheeses are dipped in a solution of whey and Camembert culture; it is ripe after eleven days, and then packed in foil. The cheese bears the white rind flora of Camembert, and has a lighter consistency than orange Gaiskäsle. It develops some holes, has a milder flavor, and a mushroom aroma which becomes more piquant and goaty as ripening progresses.

Other regions, other countries
Another German cheese of foreign ancestry, originating in the French Vosges, is *Münster*, with its soft to semihard paste and red rind flora. It sounds German enough anyway, for an umlaut has been added to the original name, Munster, to avoid any confusion. The cheese comes in weights of 125, 500, 600 or 1,000 g (5 oz to 2 lb 5 oz). It is fine, mild and close-textured, and has a white to yellow color, with a thin skin instead of a rind.

Weinkäse ("wine cheese") is named for its affinity with the fruity Rhine and Moselle wines. The cheese has a white to yellow color; a glossy, delicate paste; and develops a thin skin in the manner of the Münster. It is a flat, round little cheese weighing about 75 g (2.6 oz), with an orange surface flora and fat contents of 30, 40, 45 or 50%. *Butterkäse* has a yellow-brown or red rind, but sometimes develops no rind at all. It was once a soft cheese type, but it is now made slightly more firm – a good Butterkäse should be elastic and easy to cut. The flat round type weighs .5 to 1.5 kg (1.1 to 3.3 lbs), and the sausage-shaped variety weighs 2 kg (4.4 lbs). A similar cheese is *Schnittkäse*: the mild and somewhat sour-tasting paste should never be pappy, chalky or contain holes, faults that do occur with this type of cheese.

The well-known *Tilsit* cheese was first made by Dutchmen living in Tilsit, East Prussia (now Sovetsk, USSR). Today it is also made in West Germany, as is the less strong variant *Ansgar*. From the border region of the Marsch, behind the sea dikes of Schleswig-Holstein comes a cheese

that shares several characteristics with the Tilsit. This is the *Wilster Marschkäse*, a loaf-shaped, semihard cheese and one that is easy to cut, with irregular little holes and a light, somewhat sourish flavor; it is also a very quick ripener. The French cheese Port-du-Salut, first introduced by Trappist monks, is one of the most popular of all cheese types. Several countries make a version, and in Germany it is known simply as *Trappistenkäse,* made according to the French recipe either as a 1.5 kg (3.3 lbs) round, or 2.7 kg (5.9 lbs) loaf-shaped cheese, with a 45 % fat content.

If you cannot identify a cheese by its appearance, you may confirm your suspicions merely by tasting it. No two comparable cheese types are exactly similar, even though they may share similar names. *Edelschimmelkäse* and *Edelpilzkäse* are names that can refer equally to blue-veined cheeses or to cheeses with a Camembert-like white rind flora, but their flavors are sharply distinctive. The latter cheese is made with pasteurized milk (mostly cow's milk, but sometimes mixed with ewe's milk) to which is added a starter and a culture of

ABOVE: View of a modern cheese factory in Waging. Curd from the cheese vats on the upper floor flows via the chute, which can turn a full circle, down to the filling apparatus on the lower floor. Here the molds are filled with cheese.

LEFT: Farmhouse Handkäse, a cheese molded by hand, here flavored with caraway seeds.

LEFT: Another type of Handkäse, the Mainzer Roller, with its typical round shape.

LEFT: The small Weinkäse ("wine cheese") goes well with a glass or two of Rhine or Moselle wine, hence the name.

Penicillium roqueforti – the cheese might have been called Roquefortkäse, but the name Roquefort was protected. The mold veins are evenly spread, and the texture of this fine cheese is smooth, with a slight tendency to crumble. The color is light yellow, the taste piquant to sharp, and the fat content usually higher than the required minimum of 45 %. Also belonging to this group of cheeses is *St. Mauritius*, a small cylindrical-shaped cheese, mildly aromatic with a rind on which a combination of white and red mold can develop. In its unripe stage it is white to cream-yellow with a porous texture, becoming smoother as it ripens and reddening towards the rind.

Three very popular German cheeses are: the *Caramkäse*, shaped either as a sausage, or in blocks of 1 to 2 kg (2.2 to 4.4 lbs), with a smooth rind enclosing a supple, close-textured paste, more aromatic in the smoked version; the bar-shaped *Tapi* cheese, with its butter-yellow color, elastic consistency and fresh, sour taste; and the mild, though slightly more piquant *Parmesello*, a hard, low-fat cartwheel, used for grating.

Fresh, unripened cheeses are of prime importance in the German cheese range. Fresh cheese – in German, *Frischkäse* – is subdivided into the following main types: *Speisequark, Rahmfrischkäse, Doppelrahm-frischkäse* and *Schichtkäse*, according to the cream or fat content. Regional names for Frischkäse tend to vary, however, so that in the Allgäu it's *Zieger*, but in Niederhein it's called *Klatschkäs*, while in Württemberg and Matte in central Germany, it's either *Topfen* or *Luckeleskäs*. Frischkäse must be made from pasteurized milk, or in special cases from a high-quality, soluble milk powder.

The preparation of Frischkäse requires more starter than other cheeses, also less rennet, a low curdling temperature and a longer curdling time. Sometimes herbs or spices are worked in. All varieties have an even, soft consistency, no rind and a fresh, light, sour taste. As most are very soft they are packed in plastic cups or tubs. Their color varies from milk-white to cream-yellow, depending on the fat content: less than 10 % (*Mager*), 10-20 % (*Viertelfett*), 20-30 % (*Halbfett*), 30-40 % (*Dreiviertelfett*), 40-45 % (*Fett*), 45-50 % (*Vollfett*), 50-60 % (*Rahm*) and 60-85 % (*Doppel-rahm*).

Cream cheese sandwich
Low-fat curd cheese is known as Quark, the fat having been removed by skimming. When a certain quantity of the skimmed fat is replaced and mixed with the lean curd, the cheese takes the name *Speisequark*. Cheese factories skim their milk with a centrifuge, which can handle large quantities, and produces a better-quality product. The soured warm or cold milk is thickened, and then enriched by adding the calculated amount of cream; low fat Speisequark is very popular with dieters. Popular too is Quark mixed with fruit pulp, a thinner, moister product because of the fruit, which constitutes 19-22 % of the bulk. *Labquark* or *Labfrischkäse* is prepared by using mainly rennet (*Lab*) for curdling; sometimes the curd is lightly pressed. It is white and somewhat crumbly, with a neutral flavor. As we shall see, Labquark is sometimes used in making Sauermilchkäse.

Rahmfrischkäse is made by adding cream to Speisequark until the desired fat content is reached. The mixture is

ABOVE: A landscape characteristic of Holland: a polder mill in the dairy country of Schleswig-Holstein.

ABOVE: The "Shepherd's Dance" maintains the rural, rustic traditions, and is held every year in the medieval town of Rothenburg.

not completely homogeneous since the curd is pressed before the cream is added (thus the fat is not blended with the whey), and the cheese has a creamier taste. The disadvantage, however, is that fat is more exposed to air due to the incomplete casein enclosure, and the flavor is therefore inconsistent. Rahmfrischkäse is sold in foil-wrapped cubes of 50 or 62.5 g (1.8 or 2.2 oz), in wooden boxes of six.

Schichtkäse is made in layers. It was formerly made by putting a layer of lean Frischkäse into the cheese mold and adding, half an hour later, a layer of fat Rahmfrischkäse, and after a while a top layer of Frischkäse. Today all layers have an identical fat content. After 24 hours in the mold, the Schichtkäse possesses a firm, smooth texture with very few holes and a fresh, sour taste. It comes in packs of 250 and 500 g (9 oz and 1 lb 2 oz). *Fromgap* is a flat, round, fresh product weighing 160–190 g (5-6 oz). It is a white to cream-yellow cheese, sometimes spiced, and is spreadable and freshly aromatic.

Sauermilchkäse
Sauermilchkäse deserves a special place. As *Handkäse* (hand-made cheese), it has been prepared for centuries on farms dotted all over the German countryside. There are still many *Sauermilchkäsereien* in central Germany, Niedersachsen and Hessen. The raw material is *Sauermilchquark*, which unlike Speisequark uses only a starter and no rennet. In the past, the skimmed milk was allowed to sour spontaneously, but today the milk is pasteurized and a culture of lactic acid bacteria is added. Sometimes the mass is lightly pressed and then vacuum packed or deep frozen – in the past it was stamped firmly into barrels for storage and transport.

Home-made Sauermilchquark used to be called *Zieger* (it still is in the Allgäu), which included a ripened version, but the name now applies to albumen cheese. Heating whey causes the albumen protein contained therein to coagulate, producing a type of curd that can be mixed with milk. The protein in Sauermilchquark, as in most cheeses, is casein, while the protein of Zieger is entirely albumen unless, of course, milk is added.

Sauermilchkäse, prepared from ordinary Sauermilchquark, and occasionally in combination with

Labquark, was first made in the late eighteenth century by a Swiss family living in the Harz mountains. A century later production was taken up by factories around Hildesheim and Mainz, and improved by the invention of grinding and molding machines. Two types of Sauermilchkäse were developed, both with a surface flora; the varieties of these cheeses depended on color or shape, or both. In Mainz they made *Gelbschmierekäse* or *Rotschmierekäse*, and their variations were *Harzer, Mainzer, Handkäse, Korbkäse, Spitzkäse* and *Strangenkäse*. They came flat and round, or in a bar or cube. The surface of these cheeses varies from yellow-gold to reddish-brown. The surface is moist; the paste smooth and close-textured; the taste piquant to sharp; and some varieties contain spices.

The names Hand-, Korb, Spitz and Strangen also prefix the second type of Sauermilchkäse, the *Schimmelkäse*, made in the Harz and other mountain areas. These are treated with *Penicillium camemberti* or *Penicillium candidum* according to region. The cheese itself is light yellow in color, the mold either blue-gray or white, depending on the culture used. The paste is smooth and firm, and has a mild, aromatic taste. Rich in protein and low in fat, it is a good diet cheese.

Buttermilk, skimmed-milk and beestings cheeses

Buttermilchquark belongs to the

ABOVE: A farming custom shared with the Swiss: cattle are garlanded with flowers when they move from the valleys to the upland pastures in the spring.

LEFT: A chef makes the sandwiches – with cheese as an indispensable ingredient – for an appetizing *Brotzeit*.

Frischkäse group. Usually made from a mixture of (sour) buttermilk and skimmed milk, it curdles at 38°C (101°F) without rennet. Although production is small, it provides a means of using up the superfluous buttermilk.

The farmers of Paderborn and Nieheim in the Westfalen area make a cheese according to an old recipe, leaving the skimmed milk to thicken spontaneously. They then warm it, drain off the whey and lightly press the curd. The cheese is left to ripen in wooden vats, after which salt and kummel are added by kneading. The cheeses are hand-shaped and stored in boxes lined with hop leaves, which transmit their special flavor. This *Nieheimer Hopfenkäse* is so dry that it must be grated. The cheese is also made in factories, the Sauermilchquark being obtained from suppliers. This factory cheese is ground, pre-ripened, mixed with salt and kummel, molded mechanically and packed – alas, not always with hop leaves – in boxes of 1.5-2 kg (3.3-4.4 lbs). It dries much quicker and is less hard than the farmhouse cheese.

Biestkäse, or *Kolostrumkäse*, hardly rates as a cheese. Beestings is the name given to the first milk obtained from a cow after calving. It has a quite different composition from ordinary milk, being more viscous, saltier and darker in color, and it solidifies when heated to 60°C (140°F); moreover, the albumen and globin content is con-

with salt, pepper, chopped chives and chopped onion; or with hot, boiled potatoes in their skins, an appetizing delicacy. Fresh cheese is also very good with fruit, jelly or syrup. Quark comes into its own in main courses like Quark Haluschka (creamy macaroni, Quark and baked bacon), or in the form of Quarkschnitten (slices of Quark baked in fritter batter), Quarkkartoffeln, Quarkknödel and Quarkpfannkuchen. Rightly famous is the German Quark pastry, from the simple Quarkapfelkuchen (apple pie and Quark) via the refined Quark-auflauf (Quark soufflé) to the delicious Quarksahnetorte (Quark and cream tart).

The amount of Quark eaten by the Germans is enormous. The nation's annual per capita cheese consumption averages more than 11 kg (24.2 lbs), 5 kg (11 lbs) of which is Quark, and the latest figures show an increase. Soon it may be Quark *über alles*!

The German daily schedule allows the people plenty of opportunity to enjoy their vast range of cheeses. In common with the breakfasts of the Low Countries, *Frühstück* might include a selection of cheeses and cold meats, and this meal is followed several hours later by *Zweites Frühstück*, the second breakfast which can be either a hearty repast or merely a couple of cheese sandwiches.

Cheese could well complete the lunchtime *Mittagessen*, and will almost certainly make its appearance at the end of the day when *Abendbrot* is served. It is even possible for the dedicated cheese lover to squeeze in a slice or two during *Kaffee*, the after-noon break when people go to the *Konditorei* for coffee and cakes.

siderably higher. In farm kitchens a kind of porridge is made by warming the beestings and stirring until it thickens. In the Allgäu it is often salted and placed in the oven in a wide plate until the heat cautes the milk fat to rise to the surface.

All Frischkäse varieties attract microorganisms and are sensitive to heat, light, dust and other influences. For this reason, severe quality regula-tions exist in Germany, and cool storage and fast, refrigerated transport is essential.

Cheese in German cookery

Cheese occupies a very important place in German homes. In the big cities, food shops offer a wide variety. The delicatessen store of Dallmayer in Munich, for example, with its marble pillars and fountains, has a display of 130 different types of sausage – and 180 varieties of cheese! Cheese is not only eaten on brown bread or on pumpernickel, but often accompanies ham in veal cutlets (schnitzel): super-schnitzels are filled with ham and cheese and covered with bacon or ragout. All German fresh cheese varieties are extremely popular mixed

Name	Milk	Type	Rind	Form	Weight	% Fat content
Allgäuer Gaiskäsle	⌂ ⌂	▲ ●	❖ ❖	flat disc, cube	62.5-125 g	50
Butterkäse	⌂	▲	❖			
Caramkäse	⌂	▲	☐	flat disc, bar	½-2 kg	45-60
Frischkäse (includes Speisequark Rahmfrischkäse Doppelrahmfrischkäse Schichtkäse)	⌂	○	—	bar, loaf container	½-2 kg 62.5-500 g	45 1-85
Limburger	⌂	▲	❖	cube, loaf	180-1000 g	20-50
Münster	⌂	●	❖	flat disc	125-1000 g	45-50
Nieheimer Hopfenkäse	⌂	■	—	ball	115 g	40
Romadur	⌂	●	❖	loaf	80-180 g	20-60
St. Mauritius	⌂	●	❖	bar	125 g	30
Sauermilchkäse (includes Gelbschmierekäse Rotschmierekäse Harzer Mainzer Handkäse Korbkäse Spitzkäse Stangenkäse)	⌂	■	❖	varying	100-250 g	1½-10
Tilsiter	⌂	■	❖	cartwheel	1.5-20 kg	30-50
Trappistenkäse	⌂	■	❖	low cylinder, loaf	1.5-2.7 kg	45
Weinkäse	⌂	●	❖	flat disc	75 g	30-50
Weisslacker Bierkäse	⌂	■	❖	cube	60 g	40
Wilster Marschkäse	⌂	■	❖	loaf	6 kg	45-50

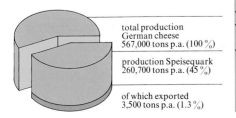

total production German cheese 567,000 tons p.a. (100 %)

production Speisequark 260,700 tons p.a. (45 %)

of which exported 3,500 tons p.a. (1.3 %)

Switzerland

There is an almost unique, fresh, invigorating atmosphere in the Swiss landscape, an appealing, rural, well-ordered neatness, too, that makes so much of the country memorable to the visitor. For a large proportion of the population, however, Switzerland is a modern, forward-looking, industrial nation. Nevertheless, it is also a country of romantic and picturesque views. In some areas there are castles, monasteries and medieval towns. Rivers flow gently through beautiful valleys, but in the mountains they tumble wildly through deep ravines and form countless waterfalls.

The landscape is overpowered by the Alps. The contorted, double-folded and pleated rocks have fractured, exposing their old crystalline cores. Above the forests and grasslands tower the mostly white-shrouded, massive peaks, sometimes sharply etched against the vivid blue sky, other times hidden in clouds or wreathed in mist. It is usually with astonishment that the visitor finds palm trees, camelias and orange groves growing in a mild climate on the protected southern slopes.

But then Switzerland has over 40,000 square kilometers (14,400 square miles) of varying contrasts. It isn't all Edelweiss, cuckoo clocks, cheese, clinical counting houses and flourishing winter sport centers for tourists. There exist many intimate, secluded mountain villages, where strangers are never seen. Whereas the large cities developed into focal points of industry, commerce and international diplomacy, the inhabitants of those isolated valleys remained faithful to their age-old manners and colorful regional dress. On the mountain slopes people work for their bread and cheese with a persistence and ingenuity which helped to make their country one of the richest in the world.

The Swiss Confederation consists of twenty-two independent cantons, and has a republican and federal constitution. Each canton is ruled by its inhabitants according to their needs and circumstances, and most people speak at least two languages. The traditional Swiss neutrality does not mean that the country keeps itself apart from world events. Proof to the contrary is that a modified version of its flag has become the symbol of the Red Cross, a symbol of altruism and

ABOVE: For centuries these alpine pastures have supported the fine dairy herds responsible for some of the world's great cheeses.

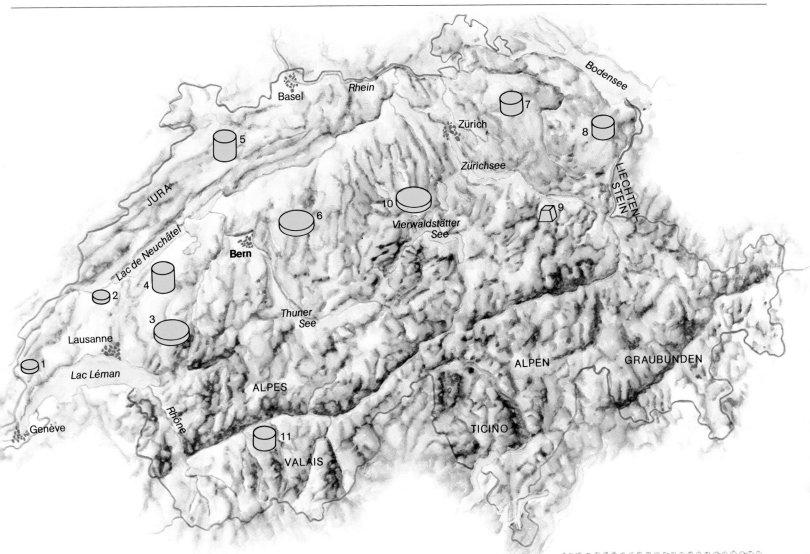

Appenzell 8
Emmental 6
Glarner Schabzieger 9
Gruyère 3
Raclette cheeses 11
Royalp 7

Sbrinz 10
Tête de Moine 5
Tomme Vaudoise 2
Vacherin
 Fribourgeois 4
Vacherin Mont d'Or 1

BELOW: Herding cattle at the end of summer from the mountain pastures to the valleys – and vice-versa in the spring – is an occasion that

demands traditional costume for the herds-men and garlands for the cattle. A scene near Appenzell, south of Lake Constance.

RIGHT: That cheese is an important part of Swiss life and culture is evident from this postage stamp, show-ing milk being poured into the cheese vats.

humanitarian ideals.

From a military point of view, Switzerland has gigantic, natural lines of defense which have always dis-suaded conquerors, but since early history a lively trade route developed through the difficult mountain passes. Even the Romans knew where to find the entrance gates, and they were the first to discover the Alps as a holiday resort. Additionally, they were in search of Helvetian cheese, which at that time was already renowned for its fine quality – the Romans were cheese connoisseurs par excellence.

Switzerland gradually improved its reputation and eventually perfected some of the world's great cheeses – as we shall see. To most Swiss farmers, dairy culture is more important than agriculture. They raise first-grade cattle, and maintain their traditions of craftsmanship and expertise; each

individual district has its own cheese specialities. The success of Swiss cheese has produced a host of foreign imitations; many such copies, how-ever, bear little resemblance to the true product. No wonder that the Swiss are careful to guard their reputation: genuine Swiss cheeses carry the name "Switzerland" in addition to the cheese type. Thus the name "Emmental Switzerland" is the guarantee of origin to look for.

BELOW: Two famous cheeses – Gruyère and Emmental. The Gruyère above has hardly any holes, and is smaller than the "big wheel" Emmental, with its many large holes. The red stamp "Switzerland" is a guarantee of authenticity.

This famous Swiss cheese owes its name to the Emmental valley in the canton of Bern. Cheese has been made here for hundreds of years by the Sennen, cowherds who stayed the entire summer in the high alpine meadows, using their remote mountain huts as dairies. These men were excellent cattle breeders, who milked and tended their cattle; the cheeses they made had good keeping properties. Loading their cheeses on donkeys, they traveled to the markets in the valleys, and even to Basel and Strasbourg to sell these cheeses to the public. They purchased the best meadows and doubtless owned the finest cattle. In those days their cheeses did not have the enormous dimensions of today's Emmental, "the king of cheese." A cheese then weighed a modest 4 to 12 kg (8.8 to 26.4 lbs). Only in the sixteenth century did the Sennen discover how to make larger cheeses which could be kept even longer.

With the expansion of the cities, and the improvement of roads and other means of transport, the demand grew for a cheese that could travel well. The St. Gotthard Pass, constructed in the thirteenth century, had opened up Italy as a market. But it was mainly during the Thirty Years' War in Germany, during the first half of the seventeenth century, that Swiss cheese production grew rapidly. Emmental cheeses were transported in Rhine barges to Rotterdam in Holland, and other ports, where they were sold for ships' stores.

The resources of the Sennen were unable to cope with the increased demand for their cheese, and increasing their herds meant finding bigger pastures. Accordingly, they began to produce cheese on the *Gemeinalpen*, communal meadowland which was more or less in public ownership. Communities that owned these meadows, as well as private landowners, hired cheesemakers to tend the cows and sell the cheese which they had made with their own equipment.

New ideas and experiments in dairy farming during the eighteenth century uprooted the conviction that good cheese could only be made high on the alpine meadows. The first small cheese dairies were soon established in the valleys, using milk from cows that were sometimes stabled throughout

LEFT: No other country can make a Gruyère or Emmental with the skill of the Swiss; traditional craftsmanship can't be copied. The picture shows Emmental curd being drained of whey in a cheese cloth.

ABOVE: The curd is placed in the press. After pressing, drying and maturing, a fine cheese of about 100 kg (220 lbs), with a diameter of about 1 meter (3.3 feet) is produced.

RIGHT: A Senn from Rosenlauital in the Bernese Oberland cleans the milking utensils in front of her farmhouse. Note the collection of cowbells above the door.

the year. These were fed on a balanced diet of hay, clover and concentrated food.

The number of village dairies rose dramatically when it became apparent that no dealer could distinguish the difference between alpine and valley cheese. Practically every village has now got its own small cheese dairy, where the master cheesemaker, assisted by two or three workers, makes three or four Emmental cheeses a day. Genuine Swiss Emmental is produced far beyond the original boundaries of the Bern canton, and a weekly output of about two dozen cheeses per dairy is the national average. Three cheeses a day might not seem much of an output until you consider the fact that an Emmental is by no means a small cheese. An Emmental weighing 80 kg (176 lbs) will require 1,000 liters (1,100 quarts) of milk, the yield of some eighty cows. As the average farm has only ten to fifteen head of cattle, milk must be brought in twice daily from several farms.

Careful steps to a great cheese
Emmental cheese is one of the few cheeses to be made from raw milk only, and as the risk of defects in the cheese is great, considerable skill is required in its manufacturing. The traditional preparation methods have been officially proclaimed, and the observance of the regulations is closely supervised. Not only could mistakes

A. Genuine Swiss Emmental is produced in relatively small village dairies. The atmosphere is quite different from the large, automated, stainless steel production lines seen else-where. Fresh raw milk is brought in each morning from the surrounding farms.

B. The milk is heated to approximately 33°C (91°F), starter and rennet are added, and the milk curdles in 30 minutes. The cheesemaker cuts the curd, the watery whey separates and finally the curd particles are the size of grains.

C. The curd is after-heated or "cooked": it is brought to 53°C (127°F) in 30 minutes' time and stirred for 45 minutes. This makes the curd drier and more solid. When it is judged ready by the cheesemaker, he lifts the curd from the whey.

D. In order to do this, he passes a cheese cloth, fixed to a flex-ible frame, under the curd mass in the cheese vat. He re-moves the frame, and with a helper he ties the cloth into a knot. All the curd is in the cloth, most of the whey remains in the vat.

E. As the mass is hoisted out, more whey leaks away.

F. The mass is lowered into the wooden mold, still in its cloth, and pressed.

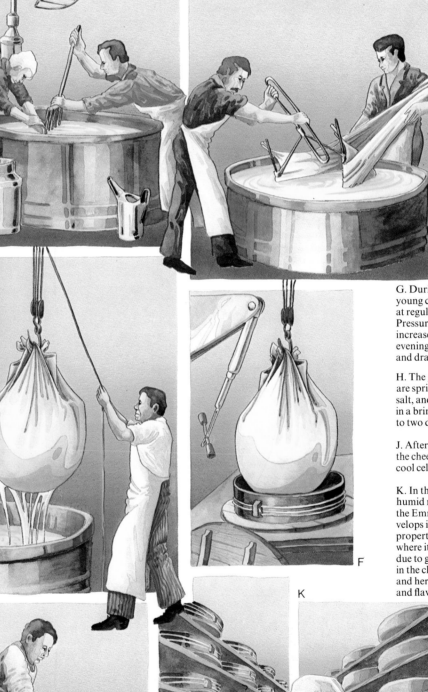

G. During the day, the young cheese is turned at regular intervals. Pressure is gradually increased. In the evening it is quite dry and drained of whey.

H. The great wheels are sprinkled with dry salt, and then floated in a brine bath for one to two days.

J. After the salt bath, the cheeses rest in a cool cellar.

K. In the warm and humid ripening rooms the Emmental de-velops its unique properties. This is where it gets its holes, due to gas formation in the cheese paste, and here the aroma and flavor develop.

occur with the feeding of the cows, the condition of the stable, the milking and quality of the milk, but also in the preparation of rennet or the cheesemaking itself. Moreover, the ripening process in the warm curing room must proceed in a regular fashion, for it is here, and here only, that previous mistakes are revealed, and the whole cheese might have to be thrown away.

A well-made Emmental reaches perfection in the curing room. Under the influence of the correct bacteria cultures, the cheese acquires its sweet-dry flavor, its hazelnut aroma and its shining, cherry-sized holes, caused by the carbonic acid gas which cannot escape from the paste. The rind of Emmental is dry and hard, and colored from golden-yellow to brown. Once or twice a week the cheeses are turned and rubbed with a moist cloth. Turning is now done mainly by machine, but in the old days the cheesemaker had to turn the heavy-weight cheeses by hand.

An officially-approved Emmental bears the legend "Switzerland" plus an indication of the fat content. Exported cheese must have the stamp "Switzerland" printed in red, and radiating out from the center like the spokes of a wheel. After a ripening period of four to five months the taste is still mild, and it takes seven to ten months of maturing before the flavor becomes more pronounced, when a "tear" (a drop of brine) might be spotted in the eyes. Emmental is a perfect cheese for sandwiches, hardened as it is by after-heating during its preparation, and it is also as such excellent for cutting and grating. In hot dishes it is inclined to draw threads, but in rice dishes or in savory pastry it is unsurpassed.

ABOVE: Along the Alpine chain, huge glaciers and moraines spill into the valleys, and from the water-shed countless rivers are formed carrying pure mountain water to the lowland pastures; such natural gifts are important factors in the making of fine Swiss cheese.

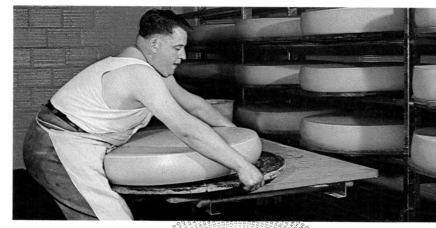

LEFT: The heavy Emmental cheeses must be turned from time to time in the storage cellars, a task requiring strength and long practice – and a diet that includes cheese.

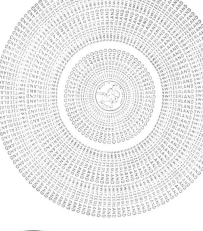

RIGHT: Guarantees of origin protect the product, and the customer, from the many imitations that fail to match the unique character of Swiss cheese.

ABOVE: The export stamp, in red, is printed on the rind of the cheese with this franking machine.

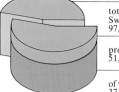

total production Swiss cheese 97,000 tons p.a. (100%)

production Emmental 51,100 tons p.a. (55%)

of which exported 37,600 tons p.a. (73%)

Gruyère, or *Greyerzer*, cheese is the smaller, but equally famous relative of Emmental; it shares with Emmental the red "Switzerland" stamp on the rind, and, in addition, bears an alpenhorn symbol. Gruyère cheese originated in the region of Gruyère, in the canton of Fribourg, where the Swiss black-and-white cattle are found. In 1115, the first Count of Gruyère founded the Abbey of Rougemont and levied a church tax which included payment in cheese from the region. Five centuries later the same type of cheese could be found in the market in Turin, Italy, where it was transported by road, and in the French city of Lyon, which could be reached from Switzerland via the Rhone. Today Gruyère is made in the entire western, French-speaking part of Switzerland.

The weight of a Gruyère cheese varies from 30 to 40 kg (66 to 88 lbs), half that of the average Emmental; it is also ripened differently – in cooler and more humid rooms, causing practically no gas formation to occur. This is apparent from the miniscule cracks when the cheese is cut; only a few small holes occur, none larger than a pea. During the curing period the rind is kept moist, and a red-brown rind deposit forms, giving the cheese its distinguished flavor. To bring the cheese to full maturity requires a curing period of at least ten to twelve months. Five-month-old Gruyère is also marketed, but it is much milder and still elastic in consistency.

The classic fondue
The paste of a well-ripened Gruyère cheese is moister than that of Emmental. When heated it hardly draws any threads, and is therefore excellent for use in hot dishes. When

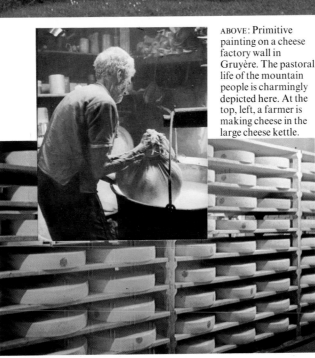

ABOVE: Primitive painting on a cheese factory wall in Gruyère. The pastoral life of the mountain people is charmingly depicted here. At the top, left, a farmer is making cheese in the large cheese kettle.

TOP LEFT: Cheese-making in a *Sennhütte* high on the Hinter-fallenalp in the Toggenburg in northeastern Switzerland. The Senn has knotted a cloth around the curd and is lifting it out of the whey, which remains behind in the kettle.

LEFT: A bank of Gruyère cheeses in the maturing room.

BELOW LEFT: The old town of Gruyère that gave its name to the cheese. It used to be the capital of the Gruyère region in the canton of Fribourg. A great deal of chocolate, as well as cheese, is made in this area.

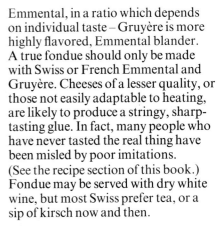

grated and cooked as a topping it gives a beautiful, even, and not too dry crust. The matured variety, which melts easily, is especially suitable for cheese fondue. Fondue, like the Dutch Kaasdoop, was originally a dish of expedience and utility, employing scraps of cheese and stale bread. It eventually acquired sophistication, with wine, kirsch and garlic being added to the melted cheese mixture. It came from the mountains via the cities, and has been adopted by the rest of the world. The Swiss make it with a combination of Gruyère and

Emmental, in a ratio which depends on individual taste – Gruyère is more highly flavored, Emmental blander. A true fondue should only be made with Swiss or French Emmental and Gruyère. Cheeses of a lesser quality, or those not easily adaptable to heating, are likely to produce a stringy, sharp-tasting glue. In fact, many people who have never tasted the real thing have been misled by poor imitations. (See the recipe section of this book.) Fondue may be served with dry white wine, but most Swiss prefer tea, or a sip of kirsch now and then.

The relative hardness of Emmental or Gruyère depends largely on the after-heating of the curd, a process that usually leads to a cheese's being called a "cooked cheese," which is a rather misleading term. *Sbrinz* is Switzerland's third variety of hard cheese, where the finely cut curd is heated to an even higher temperature than Emmental or Gruyère. It is made in the center of Switzerland, where a sturdy race of brown cows graze the high mountain pastures. The cylindrical cheeses weigh from 25 to 40 kg (55 to 88 lbs), and during the fifteenth century were being exported via the St. Gotthard Pass to the south – a considerable proportion of the production still goes to Italy.

The curing period of Sbrinz cheeses is impressively long. After their brine bath they go to an *Abschwitzraum* ("sweating room"), where the temperature is 20°C (68°F). Here they sweat fat and water, and the rind is regularly wiped. After a minimum of four months, the cheeses are placed upright in racks, so that air can circulate around them: they must then mature for eighteen months to two years.

The long curing period makes Sbrinz a very aromatic and full-flavored cheese and, owing to the decomposition of the casein, one that is easy to digest. Another Sbrinz variety is sold as *Spalen*, or *Spalenschnittkäse*, named after the vats in which they used to be packed. It also goes under the name *Innerschweizer*.

A good judge of cheese

The Swiss enjoy the hard, sharp-tasting Sbrinz in many ways. Not cut, but broken off and crumbled on freshly-buttered bread, it is considered a delicacy. It lends itself well to grating, draws no threads when heated, and is excellent for use in soups, sauces and cooked dishes such as cheese soufflé, where one-third of Sbrinz may be substituted for Emmental or Gruyère. Despite the hardness of the cheese, Sbrinz, when cut into thin slices with a cheese or cucumber slicer, melts on the tongue. It is thus sold in delicatessen shops in Saanenland under the name of *Hobelkäse*.

The rigorous inspection accorded to Emmental and Gruyère is also granted to Sbrinz. Farmers, cheesemakers and dealers have formed their own organization, the Schweizerische

ABOVE: Sbrinz cheese, ancestor of Gruyère and Emmental, is a hard, well-matured cheese that is cut into fine slices with a sharp slicer. Thus prepared, it is sold in delicatessens as Hobelkäse. Sbrinz cheeses are here being prepared in Saanenland.

Käseunion, which controls the entire production of Emmental, Gruyère and Sbrinz and supervises the marketing both at home and abroad. Experts assess the cheeses for their consistency, color, aroma, taste and appearance, and points are awarded. A high award provides an extra premium to farmers as well as cheesemakers.

Cheese folklore

Food plays an important part in the symbolism of folklore, and cheese in particular. In Valais and the Bernese Oberland, the dead used to be buried with bread and cheese to nourish them in the long journey to wherever they were bound. In some districts, the Sennen still distribute cheese among the poor. An ancient custom that is still observed is the procession to and from the high alpine meadows in the spring and autumn seasons. One of the Sennen heads the procession, dressed in his most colorful costume, accompanying the *Meisterkuh* or *Herrkuh*, the "master cow," who carries a milking stool between its garlanded horns. In Valais and Graubünden everybody eagerly awaits the annual cow fight, a very innocent and simple version compared to the Spanish spectacular; here the cows merely try to push each other over, and the winner is given the title *la reine*, "the queen," or *vacca pugnèra*, "fighting cow."

ABOVE: Even the smallest rural villages contribute to Switzerland's dairy industry. The terrain of the country is better suited to cattle than to crops.

In addition to its hard cheeses, Switzerland has many semihard varieties with a higher moisture content; they ripen earlier and do not keep as long. Appenzell cheese derives its name from the East Swiss canton of Appenzell where it was originally made, but today it is also manufactured in the cantons of St. Gallen, Thurgau and Zürich. In the Middle Ages, the cheese was so popular, especially in neighboring countries, that there was an ever-increasing shortage on the home market. This was why, from 1571 onwards, the cheese merchants were only allowed to export butter and cheese that exceeded the cantons' requirements.

Soon after preparation, the cheeses are delivered to the cheese merchants, who attend to their ripening, a process that varies from three to six months. In the beginning they are turned daily, then twice weekly, and washed in a mixture of water, white wine, salt, pepper and herbs. The correct composition of this mixture used to be kept secret, but today the cheesemakers exchange recipes and information.

Washing is an important factor in the development of the particular

LEFT: Cheese scraped from the melted surface of a cheese set before an open fire and piled on a plate, is a national Swiss favorite called *raclette*.

BELOW: *Käseteilet* in the Justistal, in the Bernese Oberland. The cheeses made and stored in the mountain huts during the summer are solemnly divided among the cattle owners.

flavor and aroma of Appenzell cheese. A good sized piece of well-ripened Appenzell lends a cheese fondue a full-flavored, very fine aftertaste.

An Appenzell speciality is *Rasskäse* ("sharp cheese"), which is washed the same way, but which has a much lower fat content; it is pale in color with a pungent flavor.

The specialities of Valais

Where the river Rhône flows through the canton of Valais on its way to Lake Geneva you will find the semihard cheeses such as *Gomser*, *Bagnes* and *Orsières*, usually referred to by the collective name of *Raclette* cheeses. *Racler* is a French word meaning "to scrape," and in the region of origin Raclette cheese is used in the preparation of a very popular melted-cheese dish. The cut surface of the cheese is melted before an open fire, or an electric element, and scraped onto a plate, where it is joined by potatoes baked in their jackets, onions and gherkins. The dish takes the name of the cheese, and to be suitable for *raclette*, the cheese must melt evenly and easily, must have a fruity but not too dominating flavor, and must be creamy but not too chewy when served.

As with fondue, raclette should be served with either tea or kirsch, and never with wine, although for the non-Swiss this is, of course, a matter of personal taste.

The remarkably spicy yet not overpowering taste of Raclette cheese is due to the special quality of the milk from the alpine meadows of Valais. The cheesemakers in this region still use raw milk, mostly from Eringer cattle, a breed which varies from red to dark brown in color, or sometimes a splendid black. Because the canton is unable to meet the total demand for such milk, Swiss cheesemakers in other localities have started to produce Raclette cheese using a standardized, usually pasteurized, milk of a specific fat content.

A Raclette cheese, with its reddish rind and weight of 5 to 7 kg (11 to 15.4 lbs), is considered ripe after four to six months. Cheeses of seven months' maturity are preferred by some connoisseurs because of the more mature taste and the greater ease of melting.

BELOW: Derelict *Sennhütten* built in 1607. The buildings were used as primitive alpine dairies.

Less renowned than the great Swiss cheeses, but nationally as popular, are those known as *Bergkäse* ("mountain cheese"), which often have individual names, such as *Justistal, Brienzer Mutschli* or *Nidwaldner Bratkäse*. Despite the arrival of small dairies in the valleys, cheesemaking is still an alpine speciality in the high *Sennhütten*, and the cheeses are usually transported to a nearby village, and left in a *Salzer* or *Gäumer* – places where they may ripen. Nearly every small alpine meadow has its own special cheese. They are usually of a hard type with few holes and washed rinds, and are eaten in the region of production. Of exclusive local importance are the small, cylindrical goat's milk cheeses with rind molds, such as *Formaggini* or *Agrini* from Ticino, the canton whose southernmost point touches Como, Italy. These are made in some areas from milk given by goats who graze the sparsely vegetated, rough mountain slopes.

Poor Folk's Cheese

Green cheese, called *Glarner Schabzieger* or *Sapsago*, is a semihard, fatless cheese made from cow's skimmed milk, and not from goat's milk as is sometimes suggested. Lactic acid is added to the milk, which is then heated to nearly boiling point to coagulate both the casein and albumen, and then ripened under pressure at 20°C (68°F). This causes milk and butter acid fermentation; the lactic acid is a preserving agent. The cheese's green color is due to the addition of a herbal mixture, which includes a clover variety grown exclusively for this cheese. Schabzieger has been made in the canton of Glarus for over a thousand years, first by monks, who used the cheese as food for the monastery community, and also as a medicine for stomach ailments, although the monks' cheese did not contain herbs.

Today the herbs are added after the cheese has ripened for a few weeks, at which point it is ground finely and mixed with the herbs before being pressed into the shape of small cones (*Stöckli*) and sold, or dried. The dried variety, which can be kept almost indefinitely, is finally rubbed to a fine powder and packed in small cartons, each equipped with a sprinkler lid. As the taste of the cheese is so spicy and

BELOW: A consignment of milk arrives at a cheese factory. The milk is weighed immediately on arrival, before being processed. Other particulars regarding the milk, origin, type and quality are carefully noted.

strong, only a little is needed to flavor a slice of bread, which is why it has been called the "poor folk's cheese." Mixed with butter or cream, Schabzieger is eaten on toast, or added to salads, soups and various other dishes. Owing to its low fat and high protein content, it can be highly useful in a restricted fat diet.

A slice of monk's head

Tête de Moine or *Bellelay* cheese used to be made by monks at the Abbey of Bellelay, near Moutier in the Bernese Jura, but was later produced by the local farmers and delivered to the abbey as a church tax. It is made with rich milk from the summer meadows, ripened from three to five months, and marketed from September to March as a winter speciality. The cheese has an exceptionally delicate flavor and taste; it is smooth and creamy, cylindrical in

LEFT: *In memoriam.* Here in Mals in the principality of Liechtenstein, and in certain other places, it is the custom to nail these wooden symbols to the stable when the *Herrkuh,* the leader of the herd, dies. This series of plaques represents quite a few generations.

RIGHT: Symbolism again, in the form of ancient cheese stamps. They were designed as personal insignia by the Sennen and cheese merchants to identify origin or ownership of cheeses.

shape, and weighs 1 or 2 kg (2.2 or 4.4 lbs).

The name "monk's head" originates from its appearance when it reaches the table. It is preferably served whole, and cut by slicing across the top; this top piece is usually replaced as a lid and gives the cheese a patch, rather like a monk's tonsure. The Tête de Moine may also be cut crosswise, in two halves. Experts, after having cut away the edge a few centimeters from the top, will preferably pare the cheese with a knife, and eat the piece on bread sprinkled with pepper and cumin. A fresh white wine should be served with it – the same wine that is used for wetting the cloth in which the remaining cheese is stored.

The Vacherin cheeses

The west of Switzerland produces two types of Vacherin cheese of which the first, *Vacherin Fribourgeois*, has two varieties: *Vacherin à la Main* and *Vacherin à Fondue.* Vacherin Fribourgeois can be traced back in official accounts of banquets held in Fribourg during the fifteenth century. The rind of these cheeses is a brownish yellow, and the Vacherin à la Main has a strong flavor, maturing after three to four months – earlier it is somewhat sourish. Vacherin à Fondue tends to be runny, and is therefore wrapped in a cloth and packed in chip boxes. It is especially good when used to make fondue. For example, Fondue Moitié-Moitié is made of half Gruyère

BELOW: Young cheeses, made in the alpine huts of the Sennen, are kept in these wooden storage houses for further ripening. Cheeses made and stored in the mountains have a fresh aroma of alpine herbs.

and half Vacherin. The ability of Vacherin to dissolve completely in water, before it reaches boiling point, is a solution to those fondue specialists who prefer not to use wine in the preparation of the dish; fondue thus prepared is very appetizing.

Cheese of the forests

The second type of Vacherin, the *Vacherin Mont d'Or,* is protected and inspected by the Centrale du Vacherin Mont d'Or, named after the mountain in southwestern Jura, near the French border. The French cheesemakers produce small, soft cheeses of goat's milk (*chevrotins*) which inspired the farmers in the Swiss region to make something similar, but with the creamy milk from their sturdy, red-white Simmentaler cows. Towards the winter their milk yield was insufficient to produce large cheeses. Furthermore, it had an extremely high fat content, which caused the cheeses to remain unusually soft when emerging from the mold; they had to be prevented from collapsing by encasing each cheese in a container of pine bark. Consequently, Vacherin Mont d'Or has a particular, resinous aroma unique to the cheese, donated by the forests of its birthplace. It is only made during the last four and a half months of the year. The marketing period ends with the beginning of warmer weather, for the cheese's delicate constitution could not stand the summer heat.

When this new product was sold for

the first time in Lausanne in 1880, it became so popular that cheese dairies were soon obliged to assist with production; today sixty such dairies make the cheese. The drained curds are collected by *affineurs*, who ripen them on pine shelves in the special cellars of the Vallée de Joux. The shelves absorb large amounts of moisture from the cheeses, and they are constantly changed and dried; the workshop of the *affineur* can be recognized by the hundreds of boards, placed outside under cover.

After the tenth day of ripening, the rind has developed its reddish-brown coloring, but the cheeses continue to be cured for up to four weeks, after which they are packed in pine boxes. Maturation depends on expert ripening and curing processes, plus accurate judgment: a too fresh cheese has an undeveloped flavor; a too mature cheese loses its quality and reveals short and sharp-edged wrinkles on the surface. A correctly matured Vacherin Mont d'Or has a reddish glaze, and the taste is mild and creamy. It may also have some very small holes, and the rind a surface with several long, flowing folds. The cheese is served in its box. The people of the Jura prefer the Vacherin served with potatoes and cumin seed, accompanied by a dry, white wine (a red wine would overpower its special flavor).

The Swiss Tomme

There is another speciality of the Swiss Jura – *Tomme Vaudoise*, called after the canton where we also find the soft Vacherin. Tomme is more than of just local importance, unlike certain varieties of the French Tomme. The flat and round cheeses, weighing approximately 100 g (3½ oz) each, are ripe after seven to ten days. Their sealed, soft, almost liquid consistency is enveloped by a rind which has a faint white deposit, in between which long rows of red spots occur during longer maturing. The taste is very mild, the aroma modest. If the cheese is less than whole-fat, it is stated on the packing. Tommes are also made elsewhere in Switzerland, formerly by dairy merchants, who sold these *Rahmkäsli* to their customers. They are now made in cheese dairies, using pasteurized milk.

Swiss Tilsit

Towards the end of the last century, a

ABOVE: Cheese fondue is not only an enjoyable dish – it's a national pastime, where the Swiss gather round a communal bowl of melted cheese, mixed with either milk or wine, depending on the recipe. Tea is a frequent accompaniment to fondue – or a glass of kirsch.

BELOW: An ancient type of Swiss cheese, colored green with herbs, is this Schabzieger, sold either in the cone shape, or grated in cartons. The picture shows two old-style labels.

young cheesemaker from the East Swiss cantons made a journey to East Prussia and returned with the recipe for *Tilsit*. The first experimental production caused quite a stir – this semihard cheese was quite different from the much harder varieties with which the Swiss were familiar. Once successfully copied, it needed one hundred cheese dairies to meet the demand. Swiss Tilsit developed rapidly from an imitation to a real Swiss cheese, which became entitled to bear the national quality mark and a new name, *Royalp*; it cannot even be entirely compared with Tilsit made in other countries. Most Royalp cheese is prepared from raw milk instead of the more usual pasteurized milk. Moreover, the Swiss leave the curds floating in the whey, and afterwards the cheese is lightly pressed.

The red rind of Royalp is similar to that of other Tilsits. The fat content may differ: usually it is 45 % but can be lower, which makes the mild flavor a little stronger. Cream Tilsit is particularly fine and delicate. When made from pasteurized milk, it has a less interesting taste, but is preferred by those who dislike such a distinctive flavor and aroma to their cheese. In any case, all Tilsits are mild in flavor if their maturing period does not exceed two or three months, but to be in peak form the cheese should mature for at least four to five months, and not be eaten older than seven months. It is excellent for use in certain salads, and makes a delicious combination with fruit and nuts.

A few foreigners

Besides the original Swiss cheeses, Switzerland also produces a number of foreign varieties such as *Brie, Camembert, Romadur, Limburger, Munster* and *Reblochon*, each of these being soft cheeses; there are also fresh varieties such as *Petit Suisse, Double Crème Carré* (a little firmer than Petit Suisse), *Cottage Cheese* and *Curds*. Owing perhaps to the influence of tourism, they appear more and more in shops and stores. The average Swiss consumes 10.7 kg (23.5 lbs) of cheese per year – and he does it in style. Petit Suisse, for example, is served on a platter with an assortment of garden herbs, and a different flavor can be chosen to dress each mouthful.

Distribution of mountain cheeses

In places where cheese is still being made on the alpine meadows, such as in the Justis valley, the distribution of cheeses amongst the owners of cows, in proportion to the milk yield, is cause for celebration. The event is called *Käseteilet*. One of the most beautiful places in Switzerland is chosen for the occasion, at the entrance to the Justis valley, some five hundred meters (16,500 feet) above the Thunersee. In a meadow with an exquisite view overlooking the forests and mountain ridges, stand three fine old warehouses, and it is here that the cheeses made during the long summer by the Sennen are stored.

The festivities start as soon as the sun has dispelled the morning chill of the high mountains. For once, the peaceful silence is broken by the approach of cars and motorcycles; the rapidly increasing crowd of cattle farmers and other dwellers have arrived to take part in the *Käseteilet*. The warehouses are officially opened, the cheeses taken from the dark rooms, passed from hand to hand, and end up in piles of five on wooden benches, a total weight of about 70 kg (154 lbs) to a pile. This is the average yield of one cow per summer. The *Meistersenn* or *Bergvogt* then places plaques bearing the initials of the cattle owner on each of the piles. Everyone then knows what he is entitled to, and no disputes are expected to arise, except for the good-natured, competitive exchanges during the ensuing eating, drinking and merriment – such as who has the finest cows, the lushest meadow and, of course, the best cheese!

The end of the beginning

As the fall approaches, and before the arrival of snow and ice and tourists in pursuit of winter sports, the mountain herdsmen bring their cows down from the high alpine meadows, for the cattle must be sheltered during the long, cold months until the return of spring.

This event is more than just a manifestation of colorful folklore; it is an essential part of the agricultural year. In the Bernese Oberland, the men light bonfires in the upland pastures, set fire to logs and roll them, crackling and blazing, down the mountain slopes to announce the herd's descent. Perhaps this is a similar ritual to the cheese-

ABOVE: *Alpabfahrt* in the Bernese Oberland. The cows are crowned with a bouquet of flowers and herbs as they descend the mountain slopes on their way to winter stables in the valley. They have spent the summer in the alpine meadows, often above the tree line. *Transhumance* is the name given to this herding of cattle from the mountains to the valleys.

rolling ceremonies practiced in Britain, notably in Gloucestershire, where large cheeses are rolled down Cooper's Hill.

As it winds down from the mountains, the procession announces itself by the distant tinkle of cowbells – the leader of the herd has the largest and most sonorous bell – and eventually you see the men and animals approaching in the distance. The journey takes many hours before it is completed; it is hard work for the herdsmen, for the cows keep breaking formation to forge on ahead, attracted by a kind of bovine nostalgia for the warmth and comfort of their stables, perhaps dimly recollected from the previous winter. As they return, the entire village rushes out to meet the procession, and to celebrate their safe return before the arrival of the dark months ahead.

These celebrations are a very ancient and well-established part of alpine farming life, and one that might seem rather at odds with the highly mechanized and progressive dairy industry for which Switzerland is famous. Such traditions, however, serve to remind the people in the cities that cheese is a national, and essentially *natural*, product, made from fresh grass that becomes wholesome milk – cheese is cut off from its origins when processed by the factory.

Name	Milk	Type	Rind	Form	Weight	% Fat content
Appenzell				low cylinder	6-8 kg	50
Emmental				cartwheel	80-100 kg	45-48
Glarner Schabzieger				truncated cone	45-100 g	1
Gruyère				cartwheel	30-40 kg	45-48
Raclette cheeses				low cylinder	5-8 kg	52
Royalp				varying	4-5 kg	15-55
Sbrinz				cartwheel	25-40 kg	45-48
Tête de Moine				cylinder	1-2 kg	52
Tomme Vaudoise				flat disc	100 g	25-45
Vacherin Fribourgeois				cylinder	7-12 kg	45-50
- Mont d'Or				flat disc	0.3-3 kg	45-55

Key to symbols on page 34. 453 g = 1 lb; 1 kg = 2.2 lbs.

Austria

The landscape of Austria is almost entirely mountainous, an often snow-capped, forested, beautiful country which, like neighboring Switzerland, is covered by the Alps. They run to the east as far as the Vienna Woods and to the hilly country north of the Danube.

It is not an easy country to farm, yet every available and arable piece of ground is cultivated, and the land supports sheep, goats and no fewer than eighteen different types of cattle. The cattle are, of course, suited to the alpine climate and rough terrain, especially the Fleckvieh.

When the Austrians began to copy the successful Swiss cheese industry, Swiss cattle were imported across the border, where they flourished due to the similarity of soil and climate. The Austrians learned the art of cheese-making from the Swiss experts called Sennen, and they were such successful pupils that their *Emmental*, prepared in mountain huts with the aid of copper cheese kettles, soon compared very favorably with the Swiss original. The kettles were supplied to the farmers by the monasteries and the big landowners, who also established the *schwaigen* – large, specialized cattle farms. In Steiermark alone, an area to the east of Tirol, there were over 600. The Benedictine monastery at Admont received about 30,000 cheeses annually from the surrounding districts (at that time the cheeses weighed only $\frac{1}{2}$ to $1\frac{1}{2}$ kg, or 1.1 to 3.3 lbs). For a while, butter production threatened the cheese industry, mainly in the seventeenth and early eighteenth century, but the threat was short-lived.

Today, Austrian Emmental accounts for half the national cheese production, and most of it goes to Italy. There are several similar if less well-known hard cheeses: *Murbodner*, for example, a semihard cheese ripened in aluminium foil; the delicious, mildly aromatic *Bergkäse*, having the wagon-wheel shape of the Emmental, and weighing about 30 kg (66 lbs), but minus the characteristic large holes; and *Groyer*, a sort of Gruyère from the small, valley cheesemakers. There is also the piquant, fresh-tasting *Tiroler Alpkäse*, a type of mountain cheese with a smooth, ivory-colored paste; ripened in a cold, damp atmosphere, it has but few holes, and a mostly dried-up, red rind flora.

RIGHT: The Tyroleans are proud of their traditions – and their local cheeses. His favorite is probably the Tiroler Graukäse.

BELOW: Label of the Trappistenkäse, a widely popular monastery cheese, reminiscent of the original Port-du-Salut from the French Trappist monastery in Entrammes.

The sharp-flavored cheeses
In contrast to their Swiss neighbors, Austrian farmers have traditionally made soft cheeses, either with or without rind flora. Because of the difficulties of transport, these typically regional cheeses are little known outside their places of origin. For centuries the loaf-shaped or flat cylindrical *Tiroler Graukäse* has been made from low-fat curd cheese (Quark), pressed in stacked molds one above the other and left to ripen at around 22°C (72°F). When treated with *Penicillium glaucum* or *roqueforti*, the gray-green mold invades the cheese, sometimes leaving an incompletely ripened white core. The taste is smooth, piquant, but often rather sour, owing to insufficient draining of the whey.

The Austrians are fond of sharp flavor, a characteristic that occurs with very moist or washed cheeses that are allowed to develop a red rind flora. Even Austrian copies of certain foreign cheeses are ripened in moist conditions, or treated with bacteria cultures. *Mondseer*, with its soft consistency and irregular holes, is an Austrian original, even though it is

BELOW: The beautiful, pastoral countryside at Gries near Innsbruck. High in the mountains, farming is very hard work and not very rewarding; Austrian mountain farmers are subsidized by the state.

RIGHT: This type of platform is found in rural areas all across Europe, and as far west as Ireland.

ABOVE: A Tyrolean farmer herding his cattle to fresh pastures.

reminiscent of German Munster. The rind flora is removed and the rind dried before packing; it was previously packed in chipwood boxes, and used to be called *Schachtelkäse*. *Mischlingkäse* is an aromatic, piquant, semihard cheese with few holes. It comes in cartwheels of between 8 to 30 kg (17.6 to 66 lbs), its rind is a uniform orange color due to its dried flora, and it has a varying fat content. The flat, round *Schlosskäse* is a foil-packed, very soft cheese, similar though milder than the German Romadur. *Pinzgauer Bierkäse*, literally "beer cheese," is, as the name implies, a good companion to beer. It's a very piquant cheese that has been a Salzburg speciality since 1650.

Considering the mountainous character of Austria, it isn't surprising that in earlier times goat's milk was used fairly extensively on the farms. Today cheesemakers use only raw, partly-skimmed cow's milk.

A Roman heritage
The Austrians share with the Germans a fondness for fresh cheeses: *Topfen*, for example, is a fresh curd cheese of the Quark type, made from skimmed milk, whole milk or buttermilk, or from a mixture. It is made mostly in creameries, although some is made on the farms of the Ober Österreich region. Topfen is allowed to ripen at a temperature of 20°C (68°F) and after four days it is flavored with a little salt, mixed with butter (the farmhouse variety includes eggs and spices), packed under heat, and sold as a fresh, sourish, sandwich spread. The mellow, piquant and fragrant *Sauerkäse*, with its orange rind and white paste, comes from the Vorarlberg bordering on Switzerland, and it is probably as old as the Romans. In Austria it is a favorite accompaniment to new potatoes. *Quargel* consists of round pieces of *Sauermilchkäse* (prepared as described in the chapter on the Federal Republic of Germany), wrapped in cellophane. *Glundnerkäse* is prepared in the Kärnten region by putting a thin layer of Quark on a dish, covering it with a cloth, and leaving it at room temperature, turning it every day until it becomes waxy and begins to smell. A little kummel and pepper is mixed in, and to finish, fresh crumbled Quark is stirred with it.

To make *Kugelkäse*, richly spiced, dry Quark is put for months by the fire to ripen: then in goes salt, kummel or paprika, and the mass is kneaded into balls. They harden in about eight weeks, but will keep for years, to be grated onto bread. Sheep's milk *Liptauer*, or its cow's milk equivalent, is found in all countries along the Danube. It is often home-made, from Quark mixed with paprika, mustard and spices. The best type can be found in good delicatessen shops, a delicate mixture of Mondseer or other suitable cheese, with butter, sardelle paste, kummel, capers, onions, mustard, paprika and salt, mixed to a solid whole. In restaurants this is often served stirred in beer.

Foreign cheeses are also manufactured, and include *Edam, Gouda, Parmesan, Brie, Camembert, Trappisten, Tilsiter, Romadur, Stangekäse, Rahmfrischkäse* and *Butterkäse*. The majority of Austrian cheeses can be purchased almost everywhere in the country, and particularly in Vienna, the gastronomic capital of Central Europe, where people enjoy the fine Käsetorte, Cordon Bleu schnitzels with Emmental and ham, and Parma schnitzels with parmesan cheese and cream.

Name	Milk	Type	Rind	Form	Weight	% Fat content
Bergkäse	⌂	■	□	cartwheel	30 kg	45
Mischlingkäse	⌂	■	❖	cartwheel	8-30 kg	15-35
Mondseer	⌂	●	❖	flat disc	1 kg	45
Pinzgauer Bierkäse	⌂	◼	❖	cartwheel, loaf	4-30 kg	15
Schlosskäse	⌂	●	❖	flat disc	45 g	35-45
Tiroler Alpkäse	⌂	◼	❖	cartwheel, loaf	20 kg	45
Tiroler Graukäse	⌂	●	✂	low cylinder, loaf	varying	45
Topfen	⌂	○	—	container	varying	10-50

Key to symbols on page 34. 453 g = 1 lb; 1 kg = 2.2 lb.

Italy

Few countries are easier to subdivide at a glance into various large, consolidated land masses than Italy, the boot that ever threatens to prod Sicily in the direction of Spain. In the north the plain of the river Po is girdled by the mighty Alps; southward runs the backbone of the peninsula – the Apennines, stretching from the northwest all the way to the southern-most point; across the Strait of Messina we find Sicily, and above is Sardinia and the smaller Italian islands.

The rivers running down from the Alps supply the lovely Italian lakes, which in their turn flow out into numerous tributaries of the Po, the fountain of life for the Lombardy Plain. This extensive basin, situated between the Alps and the northern Apennines, forms the largest plain of lowland Italy, much larger than the sunny Campagna di Roma and the even sunnier and more southern Campagna Felice near Naples. In Lombardy the summers are hot, but the winters chilly and misty. On both sides of the Po and its widely branched delta on the Adriatic Sea, early farming communities found a land that promised rich cultivation, where the kind of crops that were later established – rye and corn, sugar beet and rice – can often be harvested twice yearly.

The plain and the mountain slopes are no less important for cattle raising and dairy farming: the excellent cattle types yield milk for the preparation of cheeses that are famous throughout the world. This same area is also Italy's most industrialized region: many thousands are employed in the large factories of Turin, Milan and Verona, which has helped to make the northern Italians more affluent and progressive than their countrymen in the south.

South of Lombardy the soil conditions and the climate begin to show a marked change. Below Naples the volcanic ridge of the Apennines slopes sharply into the sea on either side. The flanks of the mountains in Roman times were covered with silver-gray olive orchards and dark cypress woods, that were later stripped bare to provide timber for Italy's mighty merchant and war fleets. Then erosion took a hand, and the soil dried out and the ground silted up after heavy rainfall. For centuries efforts have been

RIGHT: An attractive display of cheeses, hams and salami, some of the basic ingredients of a great national cuisine.

ABOVE: The Tuscan landscape was featured in the paintings of the Italian Renaissance, and has changed but little over the centuries. This town is San Gimignano, to the southwest of Florence.

Asiago 13
Bel Paese 5
Caprino 15
Fiore Sardo 20
Fontina 1
Gorgonzola 6
Grana Padano 9
Mascarpone 8
Mozzarella 14
Pannarone 12
Parmigiano
   Reggiano 11
Pecorino Romano 16
Pecorino
   Siciliano 18
Pressato 10
Provolone 17
Ricotta 19
Robiola 2
Robiolino 3
Stracchino
   Crescenza 4
Taleggio 7

made to make these barren regions fertile again by irrigation and drainage, often with significant results, but this is by no means true for all of the peninsula.

The vegetation displays great local variations, according to the soil and climate, which is in turn affected by the mountains and the sea. Along the coast the summers are hot and increasingly more arid as one moves south. On the islands too one finds diverse conditions: there is a softer, Mediterranean climate on the smaller islands and along the shores of the larger ones.

All over the mainland of Italy agriculture is the primary means of existence. Farming in most areas is characterized by wine production, olive cultivation and the growing of semitropical fruits. Because of the lack of sweet pastureland, there are few cows. Sheep and goats are the most important producers of milk; furthermore, they are cheaper to maintain and are more resistant to harsh conditions. An animal that has long thrived in central Italy is the buffalo, which is kept not only for its good quality milk, but as a draught animal, being more powerful than the ox and more able to withstand hot and dry seasons.

LEFT: A scene of ancient mythology in a mural from the Vattii house in Pompeii.

The traditions of Italian cheese and its importance in everyday life go back to before the Christian era. Virgil, the pastoral poet, tells us that, "Milk gathered in the early morning light is curdled at night; but that of twilight the herdsman puts in wooden vats and brings to the city, or is made into cheese for the winter, having been slightly salted." In antiquity, sheep's and goat's milk were both preferred for making cheese. Not only the large farms, such as those excavated near Pompeii, but also the city households had a separate cheese kitchen, or *caseale*, as well as rooms in which the cheeses could mature. Usually, cheesemaking took place in the spring or early summer. Cheeses were made in considerable variety: there were salted and unsalted ones, hard and soft cheeses in the form of loaves, millstones, flattened cones or bricks, some unspiced, some spiced or with other additions.

Milk and honey
Various Roman authors wrote fairly comprehensive studies of cattle breeding and dairy farming. In his book *De Agricultura,* the oldest extant work in Latin, Cato gives instructions for the summer and winter feeding and stabling of herds. He also gives a number of recipes, including one for a cheese pastry which seems to be a Roman invention. At least two sorts of pastry, Libum and Placenta, could be purchased ready-made – they were served in the home, but also featured in religious devotions. Honey was used as a sweetener, as sugar was unknown. Cato did not indicate exactly which cheese was used, but he did say that it was to be rubbed until fine, so perhaps it was a kind of Ricotta. He sounds surprisingly modern when he stresses again and again the need for strict hygiene in cooking.

In *Rerum Rusticarum,* the writer Varro enumerates the various qualities of sheep, giving detailed instructions about care in sickness and in health, and also discusses many other aspects of farming. Virgil also had decided opinions about livestock: "Goats require attention and no less care than sheep, and are quite as profitable; goats deliver more young, sheep are excellent milk producers." An animal's reaction to the correct sensory stimulus when being milked was not unknown to him either: "The

BELOW: Gioconda – "a delicious table cheese" – and an obvious choice for the label: Leonardo's famous painting of the Mona Lisa, La Gioconda.

BELOW: Milking a goat, from a Roman relief dating from the third century A.D.

more the pail foams while milking, the more richly the milk will flow from the udders."

The cheesemakers of Rome
In the middle of the first century A.D., the agricultural writer Columella gave a very complete and unusually detailed account of everything concerned with farming in *De Re Rustica*. He cites the preparation of cheese as particularly important in isolated regions, where there may be a surplus of milk which cannot be easily disposed of. He suggests using a vegetable starter – such as thistle flower, safflower seed or the juice of green fig bark – for the curdling process, instead of rennet from animals. He also refers to the pressing, salting, rinsing and ripening of cheese, and states that cheese undergoing these processes is especially suitable for export: "It does not then acquire any holes, nor does it become too salty or too dry; the first mistake shows up when the cheese has been insufficiently pressed, the second if it has been salted too much and the third if it has been dried in the sun." In Columella's day, the predecessor of the modern Caciocavallo cheese was already very popular. The curdled milk which had thickened in a warm container was suffused with boiling water, kneaded and formed by hand, or pressed into beechwood containers. A brine bath might then follow, which would harden the cheese, prior to its being smoked above a fire of straw or apple wood; in the big cities this was done in special smokeries. The cheese was made in the form of braids, bottles, or the heads of horses and deer. It seems that it was a particular favorite of the Emperor Augustus who, being a patron of the arts, knew quality when he saw it.

Tricks of the trade
The Augustan age of cheesemaking has been well-documented, and detailed recipes remain, such as this one for cream cheese: "Take a new bowl, with a hole and a plug just beneath the rim; fill it with fresh

LEFT: Pecorino, the famous Italian cheese made from sheep's milk. Pecorino has been made since before Roman times, and Pliny is among those authors who mention it. Legend says that Romulus, the founder of Rome, made this cheese from both sheep and goat's milk.

sheep's milk and add a bouquet of garden herbs, such as marjoram, mint, onion and coriander, suspended upside down so that the stalks and roots are clear of the milk. After five days remove the plug and allow the whey to run off. Close the hole as soon as the milk begins to flow out. After three more days, separate the whey in the same fashion, take out the herbs and discard them. Sprinkle dried thyme and marjoram into the curd, and chives if you wish, then mix thoroughly, and after two more days separate the whey again. Now add finely rubbed salt, and stir. Close the bowl tightly with a lid, and open it only when you are going to eat the cheese."

There were many tricks of the trade, as Columella describes, and they must have evolved over centuries of empirical cheesemaking. Putting fresh pine seeds in the pail beneath the goat helps to curdle the milk. Adding pulverized seeds or herbs to the milk or the curd makes for many varieties in flavor. Fresh cheese can be eaten after a few days by putting it directly from the basket or mold into a brine bath and then allowing it to dry a little in the sun. Dry sheep's cheese can be given an after-treatment in the springtime by soaking large pieces in good grape must in a vat sealed with pitch; the vat is sealed for twenty days, and herbs are added before eating. "But," says Columella, "even without herbs, it isn't bad at all." Cows are described as being more sensitive to heat, cold, soil conditions or altitude than are goats and sheep. He also differentiates four Italian and six foreign breeds according to size, vigor and temperament. Such types include the large, white Umbrian cattle (to this day the most numerous in Italy) and the productive and hard-working Alpine breed, probably the ancestors of the famous, brown Swiss cattle.

Cheshire – the Roman's favorite

During the era of the Roman emperors, the cheese regions were extremely productive, especially with new kinds of cheese. At the *velabrium*, the dairy market in Rome, cheeses were imported from conquered lands under Roman occupation. There were cheeses from the alpine meadows of Helvetia; Gallic cheeses from the Massif Central, Nîmes and Toulouse; Greek ones from the Peloponnesos;

ABOVE: A shepherd near the Temple of Juno, Agrigento, Sicily. Traditions are deeply rooted in the peasant communities of southern Italy.

cheese from the Middle East; and even cheese from Britain. Legend maintains that the Romans were so fond of Cheshire cheese that they built a wall around the city of Chester to ensure the continued progress of its production!

Conversely, vast quantities of Italian cheese left Italy, including the hard cheeses which could survive the long journeys and were popular with the Roman legions. Eventually, the collapse of the Roman Empire put an end to the cheese culture of antiquity. Nothing more is known about cheese production in Italy until the tenth century. It is certain, however, that some aspects of Rome's cultural knowledge were preserved in Christian monasteries, including the techniques of wine production, farming and cheesemaking. When the time came the monks spread their knowledge abroad, hand in hand with the preaching of religion.

RIGHT: Medieval monasteries were cultural centers where, amongst other things, domestic knowledge was carefully preserved. Quite a few monastery cookery books remain, and include recipes for making cheese.

Parmesan, the hard, grainy, drum-shaped cheese, is the queen of the Italian cheeses. Because of the very long and slow maturation, and the low moisture content, the cheese is particularly hard and the crust extremely tough and thick. For these reasons it can survive long transportation and extremes of climate, becoming, with age, richer in taste and aroma, rather than deteriorating. Parmesan is certainly the most famous of that group of cheeses known as *grana*, because of their grainy texture, or more precisely *Formaggio di Grana*.

The grana is a very ancient cheese type that originated in the Po valley. Homer, in the eighth century B.C., knew of a tasty, long-keeping kind of cheese which was transported over vast distances, a very hard product that had to be ground with an iron grater. The Spanish poet Martialis, living in Rome in the first century A.D., mentions a hard, moon-shaped cheese, first made by the early Etruscans of northern Italy. These records suggest that grana cheese was well established long before the Roman Empire came into power. After the fall of Rome, however, the plains of the Po were allowed to deteriorate into an infertile, swamp-like area. Only gradually was it brought into cultivation again, by various monastic orders, who also revitalized the cheese industry.

A mountain of cheese

With perseverance, and over a period of five hundred years, the old traditions found new roots. Parmesan evolved from the old Etruscan recipe, and was made in the tenth or eleventh century. Its birthplace was the town of Bibbiano near Piacenza, an area which in those days belonged to the province of Parma, from which the cheese took its name. Records show that the city of Parma supported a lively trade in *Parmigiano Reggiano* cheese as early as 1364, and the production region south of the Po soon extended as far as Bologna. In Florence, on the other side of the Apennines, Parmigiano Reggiano was already in considerable demand, as is apparent from Boccaccio's description of a land of plenty in his *Decameron*: "There was a mountain made entirely of grated Parmesan cheese, and on top of it people were making nothing but macaroni and

LEFT: The label from a small package of Parmesan cheese.

ABOVE: A stack of fine, drum-shaped Parmesan cheeses, the color of gold and almost as expensive. The cheeses are stamped with their official denomination.

BELOW: Notice the very dark rind of this Parmesan cheese, made from earth mixed to a paste with oil. The picture is an old promotion hand-out from a cheese manufacturer.

noodles, which they boiled in capon broth and threw downhill...."

Meanwhile, north of the Po, the cheesemakers produced *Grana Padano* in more or less the same way, following the example and the success of Parmesan. The centuries-old issue over the birthright of both types ended in 1955 with the legal protection of their names, and the precise determination of the regions of production, following a decree by the Italian government.

Parmigiano Reggiano

Parmesan cheese is produced between the middle of April and the middle of November in modern creameries, which continue to maintain some elements of traditional craftsmanship. The cream, for example, is allowed to rise naturally in 100-liter (110-quart) vats, without the use of a centrifuge. The following morning, this skimmed evening milk together with fresh morning milk is poured into double-walled tanks to settle. After the milk has soured and curdled, the curd is carefully cut so that no fat escapes into the whey. It is then stirred vigorously with a large rod until it

becomes very fine; meanwhile, the steam between the double walls of the vats brings the temperature up to 54°-58°C (129°-137°F). The mass then cools for a quarter of an hour, as the cheesemaker continually monitors the consistency of the curd particles and the acidity of the whey. The curd is gathered in a cloth, which hangs in the whey for a short while, before being put under the press in a wooden hoop and lid, where it is turned every hour. The salting time takes up to three weeks, depending on the weight; the curing time, two or three years. The cheeses are turned and brushed every other day to begin with, later twice a week and finally once a week. After a year they may be provided with a protective coating made of dark, fine earth mixed with oil. The crust of a mature Parmesan is practically bullet-proof, and the cheese-maker is obliged to test its quality by hitting the cheese with a small hammer – the characteristic ring of truth is pleasing to the trained ear.

Guarantee of excellence

Under its impressive crust, a mature Parmigiano Reggiano hides a straw-yellow, very hard, dry paste without any holes; it is very crumbly and melts on the tongue. The taste is deliciously spicy, but not piquant and certainly not sharp, and despite the low fat content it is rich and full. Parmesan is best known as a grating cheese, and very few dishes of pasta or rice are complete without a liberal sprinkling of grana cheese.

Parmesan is categorized according to maturity as *vecchio* (old); *stravecchio* (very or extra old); *tipico* (four to five years old); and *giovane* (young, table cheese).

The Consorzio del Formaggio Parmigiano Reggiano guarantees the origin and quality of the cheese, inspecting and labeling export cheese with extra care. Both the milk supplier and the cheesemaker are subjected to the strict control of the Consorzio, as are the cattle and pastures.

Grana Padano

While Parmesan is made in a limited area, and over a limited season, Grana Padano is a cheese for all seasons and is made throughout the Lombardy Plain. In the manufacture of Grana Padano, pasteurized milk has now almost entirely replaced raw milk. It is processed in much larger vats than Parmesan, and the evening and morning milk are processed separately, while the milk for Parmesan is always mixed. There are other minor differences in the two recipes, although they follow the same basic pattern. Grana Padano matures more quickly and becomes flaky. The longer the cheese matures, the more clearly can the tiny, hard grains be felt on the tongue; *grana*, of course, refers to the granular structure, while *padano* means "of the Po." The color is usually lighter than that of its great rival, being almost white in some cases. As a table cheese Grana Padano is much less common than in its grated form. It is preferred in cooking and in soups since it doesn't tend to form threads.

There are other varieties of grana, including one from the neighborhood of Lodi, the low-fat, sharper and sometimes slightly bitter *Grana Lodigiano*, which has small eyes and weighs up to 50 kg (110 lbs). Another type is the *Grana Lombardo* from the province of Milan. The production and inspection of grana cheeses is controlled by the Consorzio per la Tutela del Grana Padano.

LEFT: Everywhere in Italy you can find small, well-stocked groceries with a fine display of cheeses from many parts of the world. Centrally placed in the group are the hard, grating cheeses such as Parmesan and Pecorino, so important in the Italian kitchen.

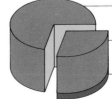

total production Italian cheese 512,200 tons p.a. (100%)

production Parmigiano Reg. and Grana Padano 158,600 tons p.a. (31%)

of which exported 5,900 tons p.a. (3.7%)

Centuries ago, the cattle that grazed on the lush summer pastures of the Italian Alps were herded south at the approach of winter. One of the several resting places along the route was the small town that gave its name to a great and famous bluish-green-veined cheese – *Gorgonzola*. The milk from these cows was made into cheese, a rather poor quality milk to be sure, for the cattle were tired from their long journey, and it was for this reason that the cheese was originally called *Stracchino Gorgonzola* (from *stracco* meaning "tired"). There are several legends that describe the genesis of this blue cheese; all are fanciful and probably apocryphal, and suggest that the blue mold came about as the result of a happy accident.

Gorgonzola is known to have been made for at least a thousand years, and was initially matured in the caves of the valley of Valassina, which were no doubt ideal for the formation of *Penicillium* mold. Later, maturing rooms were constructed all over the region. Until the nineteenth century Gorgonzola remained a typical regional product of small cheese-makers. The curd of the evening milk, which had been curdled immediately and had ripened overnight, was transferred the next morning into a mold of wooden rings lined with a cheese cloth, and covered afterwards with the warm, new curd of fresh morning milk. These two curds were considered essential in the manufacture of Gorgonzola. After being pierced to allow the invasion of air, the cheese was left to develop its mold for several months; the entire maturing procedure took over a year to complete.

A cheese of unusual mildness

In today's modern cheese factories, Gorgonzola is made according to a less time-consuming process – it would seem that the world is impatient for each consignment of Gorgonzola cheese. The quality, however, is by no means impaired by the urgency. This is how the cheese is made: *Penicillium gorgonzola* is added to fresh, pasteurized milk, together with an acidifying agent. The curd particles are cut and stirred until they are the size of hazel nuts, and are then packed in portions into cloths, placed in aluminum molds and are turned regularly and salted in a humid but warm room. After two weeks of maturing, this time in a cold,

ABOVE: A wedge of genuine Italian Gorgonzola. It is no longer merely a region cheese: as one of the world's most famous cheese types, Gorgonzola is much in demand wherever cheese is appreciated.

LEFT: Dolcelatte, meaning "sweet milk," is the trade name of a well-known factory-made Gorgonzola.

BELOW: One of the many attractive little towns of northern Italy, Como on the Lago di Como.

LEFT: Paglierini is a delicious, soft cheese with a subtle aroma. Its name derives from the straw mats (*paglia*) on which it is sold. The cheese is a regional speciality of Piedmont.

moist environment, one side of the cheese is pricked for mold development. Ten days later the other side is given identical treatment. The total maturation period is a mere three months. The taste and aroma are possibly less pronounced when compared to those cheeses made by the old method, and the body of the cheese is somewhat softer. It is elastic in consistency and possesses small holes. In color it is white to straw yellow, with blue-green veins and a wrinkled, reddish crust. Gorgonzola is packed either whole or in segments, usually in aluminum foil. It is unusually mild for a blue cheese, and thus is excellent as a dessert cheese, especially when accompanied by a glass of, say, Valpolicella or Barolo.

Gorgonzola can be used in cooking to make a number of attractive dishes. Try it in Mousse au Fromage (recipe section) or in place of Roquefort in salad dressings. The Milanese like to stuff ripe pears with Gorgonzola; in the north they mix it with the fresh cream cheese Mascarpone.

The *Gorgonzola Bianca*, or *Pannarone*, is only lightly salted and does not form a mold, except on the crust where it is washed away. After maturing for about a month it acquires a piquant, slightly bitter taste. White Gorgonzola is made only in some parts of Lombardy, mainly around Lodi, and has attained considerable popularity in Venice.

Many years ago, the traditional cheese of northeastern Italy, *Asiago*, was made on the southern slopes of the Dolomites. Through the improved breeding of their cattle, the farmers increased the milk yield, and cheese production shifted from the primitive dairies to cooperative factories in the foothills. The factories were founded by cattle owners and cheesemakers together, and by 1910 there were 176 in existence. The home of Asiago cheese is the province of Vicenza, west of Venice. Asiago is a hard cheese, which comes in two varieties: the semifat *Asiago d'Allievo*, made from skimmed evening milk and fresh morning milk, a cheese which is rather piquant and popular as a grating cheese; and the full-fat mountain cheese *Asiago grasso di monte*, with its much smoother texture. The latter is sufficiently ripe after about six weeks.

A descendant of the Asiago, called *Pressato*, is found locally in Lombardy and Basso Veneto. The fat content is inclined to be somewhat variable, depending on the basic ingredient – either skimmed or whole fresh morning milk, or raw and skimmed evening milk mixed with fresh morning milk. It may be enjoyed after a mere one or two months, but can be allowed to mature for longer periods. Pressato is a flat, round cheese with a brown-painted crust. Its texture is elastic, its color white to straw yellow, and its flavor mild to piquant. The body of the cheese contains many pea-size holes.

The delicious gift of Piedmont
From the Valle d'Aosta, north of Turin in the province of Piedmont, comes the wonderful *Fontina* cheese, which many connoisseurs would unhesitatingly place among the first

ABOVE: Cheeses galore displayed in a specialist food store in Venice.

ABOVE: Records show that Taleggio has been made since the eleventh century, and possibly well before. It is a semihard, mountain cheese, also made in the valleys, with a lovely, mellow taste.

LEFT: Indisputably one of the world's great cheeses, in perfect combination with a flask of wine – Fontina from the Valle d'Aosta, Piedmont.

half dozen great cheeses of the world. Originally a sheep's milk cheese, Fontina has become the most important source of income for the cattle owners of the area. Nowadays the summer milk of cows is processed directly in the cooperative mountain chalets, the milk being contained in small copper kettles heated over a wood fire. The maturing period lasts for three months, and takes place in cooperative curing rooms in the valleys. In winter and early spring, when the cattle are stabled, Fontina is made in the village factories; a few of the larger concerns, however, operate throughout the year. They boast big, double-walled, steam-heated vats that can accommodate hundreds of gallons of milk – a far cry from the traditional copper kettles still being used in the mountain chalets.

The semihard Fontina varies in weight from between 10 and 20 kgs (22 to 44 lbs). It has a flat, round form and a thin, smooth, brownish rind. The paste has only a few holes and is white to yellow in color. The flavor is faintly nutty, faintly sweet, and the texture creamy smooth.

Fontina takes its name from Mount Fontin near Aosta. It lends itself to the elegant dish *fonduta*, a Piedmontese speciality related to Swiss fondue. Fonduta is made with fresh, white truffles, Fontina cheese, eggs and milk, Fontina made entirely from the raw milk from the Valle d'Aosta bears the stamp of the Consorzi della Fontina Tipica. *Fontal* is the name accorded to Fontina-type cheeses made from pasteurized milk, regardless of whether they come from Aosta or other regions.

The fresh and delicate Stracchini
The trouble with *Taleggio* cheese, like certain others of the Stracchino group, is that it matures and loses its fresh flavor rather too quickly to travel any distance. With modern, refrigerated transport, Taleggio can be found outside the valley near Milan, after which it was named. The cheese was probably made there as early as the eleventh century, but is now made elsewhere in the Alps and on the Lombardy Plain. It has always been made during the cool months from a raw mixture of preripened evening milk and fresh morning milk. On the plains, in the large creameries, it is produced throughout the year from

large quantities of pasteurized milk. The curd is not pressed but is turned regularly in the vat. Rubbing with brine during the curing period allows the formation of the flaky, reddish, soft rind. The consistency of the cheese is compact and sometimes rather brittle; the color is white to pale yellow; and the taste mild yet fruity, as the cheese melts on the tongue. The traditional method of preparation undoubtedly results in a fuller and more characteristic aroma.

Lombardy and Piedmont together produce *Stracchino Crescenza*, and the best quality cheese is said to come from Milan and neighboring Pavia, to the south. It is a delicious dessert cheese which matures so quickly that an unexpected rise in temperature can spoil the entire production. For this reason, Stracchino Crescenza used to be made only in winter, but today it is made throughout the year in factories with air-conditioned rooms. The texture can be soft and melting (*pasta cremosa*) or more solid (*pasta sostenuta*).

Theme and variations

Although not strictly a Stracchino cheese, *Robiola* is a Stracchino type – soft, delicate and quick to mature. A square-shaped cheese of between 250 and 500 g (.5 to 1.1 lbs), it was previously made from a mixture of cow's, sheep's and goat's milk, usually partly skimmed. Nowadays it is made entirely from cow's milk. The curd is hardly cut at all, and the cheeses ripen in straw or linen-lined wooden boxes. The temperature in the curing room is kept low, and the cheesemakers rub the cheeses regularly with a brine cloth as soon as mold begins to form. The *tipo dolce* with its delicate, mild taste matures in 8 to 10 days; the fully mature, full-bodied *tipo piccante* develops its light truffle aroma in 30 to 40 days.

Originally, Robiola came from the Alpine foothills of Lombardy, but is now made over a much larger area of northern Italy. A smaller version, called *Robiolino*, has a lovely, smooth and creamy exterior. The curd is extensively worked until very soft and smooth. With the aid of molds, the cheeses are shaped into bars or rolls. The fresh type tastes a little sourish; the more mature type is fuller and creamier.

From the same area comes a number

LEFT: Sentinel haystacks near a small and primitive farmstead at Soltera.

LEFT: Bel Paese, a modern factory cheese that has attained international status. Its mildness forms a good contrast to the stronger flavored cheeses on the table.

BELOW: The label of a mixed cheese, and a regional speciality. It tells us that the cheese is made from the pure milk of goats *(capra)* and sheep *(pecora)*.

BELOW: Sheep grazing in an almond orchard near Catania, Sicily. Many Italian cheeses are Pecorinos, made from the milk of ewes, and large flocks of healthy sheep are among the country's main assets.

of descendants of the Robiola, bearing the collective title of *Italico*, as well as all kinds of fancy names. These are soft cheeses with or without surface flora, and among them is the famous cheese *Bel Paese*, which means "beautiful country." Invented in 1929, Bel Paese is a flat, round cheese from Lombardy, weighing .5 to 1 kg (1.1 to 2.2 lbs). It matures for only a short time, and with its soft, mild taste is a worthy member of this selection of dessert cheeses.

Finally, Mascarpone deserves a mention, although it hardly rates the title of "cheese" as it is made from fresh cream and doesn't ripen at all. It was originally made only during the autumn and winter in Lombardy, but is now made throughout Italy. Mascarpone is strictly a desert cheese, although one recipe from around Trieste advises that it be mixed with Gorgonzola, mustard and anchovies. The product is made from whole cow's milk and is sold in muslin bags. It is globe-shaped like certain versions of Mozzarella, and the creamy yellow paste is very soft, having the consistency of thick cream. Mascarpone is usually served with fruit and sugar, and may be flavored with liqueurs such as Strega or Chartreuse. Some types are sold with a candied fruit inside the cheese.

Following the route of the sun, southwards down the Apennine peninsula, the traveler will notice how the cattle pastures gradually give way to the more arid, burnt-umber territories of sheep, goats and buffalo. Interesting cheeses are made everywhere. The sheep of the Sopravissina breed yield great quantities of lovely, fat milk during their lactation period, which all goes to make fine *Pecorino* cheese. Pecorino is the name given to all Italian cheeses made from ewe's milk, and there are, of course, many varieties. Pecorino was made in the time of Pliny, and in the first century A.D., Columella recorded a recipe for *Pecorino Romano*, the oldest and best of the type. It is made in both central and southern Italy, while on the island of Sardinia, which supports 2.5 million sheep, *Pecorino Sardo* is a major industry.

Until the end of the last century, Pecorino was a true shepherd's cheese. Salt makers then began to take over the salting and curing of the fresh curds, and started simple dairies themselves. These progressed to become large, modern cheese factories which made Pecorino (together with the cheese Provolone) the most important export cheese after grana, especially to the United States with its considerable Italian population. Pecorino matures in about eight months, and the weight varies. The smooth crust of the cylindrical cheese was previously treated with oil mixed with earth, but

ABOVE: Both a milk-producing and a draught animal, the water buffalo is found in southern Europe and Asia, where it survives the hot climate more easily than do cattle. True Mozzarella is made from buffalo milk.

today this is done with a red-brown synthetic material. The texture of the straw-yellow cheese is hard and compact. It is made of fresh ewe's milk, first heated, then curdled by lamb's rennet; in Sicily they add peppercorns to the curd, to make the piquant *Pecorino Pepato*. Although Pecorino may be used as a table cheese, it is used principally for grating and in cooking.

As the rapidly rising Pecorino industry demanded more and more of the Sardinian sheep's milk, it seemed as if the shepherd's cheese *Fiore Sardo* would become extinct. But with new methods of preparation, factories began to improve the quality, and the cheese survived. Fiore, made from raw milk, can either be eaten fresh after salting, or after several months of maturation in a cool, dry environment, which allows it to develop a full, piquant flavor.

Whey and albumen cheeses
Although it is generally referred to as a cheese, strictly speaking, *Ricotta* isn't a cheese at all, since it is not made from the pressed curds of milk but from the whey, the by-product. It is prepared either from sheep's milk whey, *Ricotta pecora*, or from cow's milk whey, *Ricotta vaccina*. More specifically, the Ricottas are named after the region of origin: thus we have *Ricotta Romana, Ricotta Sarda* and *Ricotta Siciliano*, all made from the whey of sheep; and *Ricotta Piedmontese* made from cow's

ABOVE: A cheese with an unusual method of preparation is the kneaded or plastic-curd cheese. The cheesemaker adds hot whey to the curd. After a pause the whey is run off, and fresh, hot whey is added. Immersed in the whey, the curd rests for 20-30 minutes at a temperature of about 45° C (113° F).

ABOVE: This treatment makes the curd tough but elastic. Cut into pieces, and then into smaller strips, it is again immersed in hot water and whey. The cheesemaker now starts to knead the curd, pulling it into long threads. This accounts for the generic Italian name for the cheese: *Formaggio di pasta filata* – "... paste that threads." The curd is intensively worked until ready for the next stage.

ABOVE: He molds it into ball shapes, and these are also immersed in the hot whey mixture.

ABOVE: The curd is now so elastic and malleable that it can be modeled into a variety of shapes, whatever may suit the cheesemaker's fancy: melons, sausages, piglets, lambs, people.

LEFT: The most typical shape of these plastic curd cheeses (Provolone, Caciocavallo, Ragusano, etc.,) is the pear shape. They are suspended on strings, perhaps because some types were once smoked.

whey, which usually has a softer texture.

Whey contains no casein protein (this has been left in the curd), but does contain the protein albumen, as well as part of the milk fat, minerals and vitamins. The albumen sets at a high temperature, incorporating the other constituents. Ricotta was once a product of expedience through poverty, but these days milk is added.

There are three varieties of Ricotta: the unmatured, unsalted *tipo dolce*; the salted, dried and somewhat firmer *tipo moliterno*, and – solely around Bari on Italy's heel – the *tipo forte*, which matures in long, wooden containers. All types are round in shape; weight 1 to 1.5 kg (2.2 to 3.3 lbs); and are fresh, white, and softly crumbling in texture, with a pleasant mildness and a touch of sweetness in the taste. On Malta, *Rkotta* is made in practically the same way, except that it is not a whey product, but a curious combination of three parts cow's milk to one part filtered sea water; it is sold by weight from eathenware bowls.

The sculpted cheeses
Some types of curd, when treated in a certain way, become very pliant and malleable. Such cheeses are known as kneaded cheeses, or plastic-curd cheeses, and their Italian name is *Formaggio di pasta filata*, which denotes that the curd can be drawn out in stringy lengths. The milk is usually raw cow's milk, and to obtain the desired whiteness, winter milk is preferred, summer milk being considered too yellow. The curd is first heated in warm whey to about 45°C (113°F), when it will stretch into tough, elastic fibers. It is then cut into long, thin slices and immersed in hot water and whey, at which point the cheesemaker kneads it vigorously by hand, in much the same fashion as a baker might knead his dough. At a certain point his experience will tell him that the curd is ready to be shaped. He molds it into balls of a specified weight, which are again placed into hot water and modeled into a variety of shapes. Next the cheeses are transferred to cold water in order to make them firm, and then to a brine bath where they remain for several days, before being taken out and dried. Unless the cheese is to be matured for any length of time, it is then dipped in

paraffin wax. The intensive treatment of the hot curd produces a very compact paste with a smooth finish.

One of the most famous varieties of *pasta filata* is *Provolone*. In times gone by, people preferred it well matured and smoked, a tradition since Roman times. Today, the milder Provolone with its firm, close, occasionally crumbly texture, and its delicate, light taste is more popular. Provolone, a name which originally meant "large oval," or "large sphere," is molded in a wide variety of fanciful shapes, then tied round with a cord by which it is suspended, and which leaves its impression in the crust. Other types of kneaded cheese are the Sardinian *Casigiolo* and the loaf-shaped *Ragusana* from Sicily, which at six months is a delicious table cheese, but when older is best for grating. There is also *Caciocavallo*, an ancient variety whose name means "horse cheese," or "cheese on horseback," and which might refer to the fact that the Romans – who made this cheese – fashioned it in the shape of a horse head. There is another explanation: Caciocavallo cheeses were often hung in pairs over a pole, as one might straddle a horse, and were also made of mare's milk.

Cheese where the buffalo roam
Mozzarella cheese has achieved world fame due to its being a main ingredient in the ubiquitous pizza. True Mozzarella is made from buffalo milk, but since there are too few buffalo to meet the demand, cow's milk is used, sometimes mixed with buffalo milk for the sake of authenticity. True Mozzarella should be very moist, delicate of flavor, and slightly giving as you bite into it. The cheese is eaten fresh, often with sliced tomatoes and a few anchovies. The shape varies from the usual oval ball to a wide range of forms, including those known as "buffalo eyes" *(occhi di bufala)* and "buffalo eggs" *(uova di bufala)*. A very special kind of Mozzarella called *Manteca* contains a piece of whey butter in its center.

Finally, *Caprino* is a cheese made from goat's milk, and has existed since recorded history. The aroma of the white paste, and the distinctive, fresh but sourish taste clearly denote the origin of the milk. Caprino is a soft cheese, sold fresh from the wooden containers in which it is packed.

Name	Milk	Type	Rind	Form	Weight	% Fat content
Asiago		■	□	low cylinder	9-13 kg	36-52
Bel Paese		●	❖	flat disc	0.5-2 kg	50
Caprino		○	—	container	varying	40-45
Fiore Sardo		◓	□	low cylinder	1.5-4 kg	45
Fontina		◓	□	low cylinder	10-20 kg	45
Gorgonzola		◓	✂	low cylinder	6-12 kg	48
Grana Padano		■	□	low cylinder	24-40 kg	32
Mascarpone		○	—	container	100-125 g	70
Mozzarella	*	●	□	ball	0.5-1 kg	44
Pannarone		●	□	low cylinder	6-9 kg	52
Parmigiano Reggiano		■	□	low cylinder	22-36 kg	32
Pecorino Romano		■	□	low cylinder	6-22 kg	36
- Siciliano		■	□	low cylinder	4-12 kg	40
Pressato		●	□	low cylinder	9-14 kg	30
Provolone		■	□	varying	1-6 kg	44
Ricotta		○	—	flat disc	1-1.5 kg	20-30
Robiola		●	❖	loaf	250-500 g	48-50
Robiolino		●	❖	bar.	50-100 g	30-45
Stracchino Crescenza		●	—	loaf	0.05-4 kg	50
Taleggio		●	❖	loaf	1.7-2.2 kg	48

✳ Buffalo
Key to symbols on page 34. 453 g = 1 lb; 1 kg = 2.2 lbs.

The foundation of Italian cuisine

LEFT: Pizza as pizza should be – large as a cartwheel, and made from fresh Italian vegetables, Mozzarella cheese and perhaps a few slices of of garlic-scented salami.

LEFT: Reblochon is a French Alpine cheese, made under almost identical conditions in Italy. It was perhaps originally a monk's cheese, and has been made for hundreds of years.

BELOW: Traveling in Tuscany, you can buy your lunch from a roadside food stall: salami, bread, wine and, of course, cheese.

Without cheese, Italian cooking would be missing one, perhaps even two dimensions. Nowhere in the world does cheese play a more important role in the kitchen than in Italy. This is true for everyday cooking as much as for refined cuisine. The most diverse dishes are prepared with cheese, or embellished with it – soups, pasta (what is pasta without cheese?), meats, sauces, desserts and pastry. In an attempt to praise Italian cooking, it is often favorably compared to French cooking, yet they are as different and individual as chalk and cheese. Italian cooking is boldly and everlastingly *Italian* – it is not French, and stands supremely in its own right. The historical influence of French cooking is of no consequence when it comes to evaluating the quality of Italian cuisine, with its deep foundations and traditions harkening all the way back to Roman civilization. What has really stood the test of time is the matchless, satisfying combination of pasta, wine and cheese.

The cheesecake of history

Roman gastronomy has had both a famous and infamous reputation, partly due to the fanciful writings of contemporary historians, and partly to our belief that despotic rulers are inevitably prey to every vice including gluttony. Roman emperors, then, feasted on incredible amounts of food, and were notorious for regurgitating halfway through their meal (perhaps we should say "orgy"), in order to make room for the next course. Less well documented is the daily diet of the average citizen. Cato's *De Agricultura*, which we have already mentioned, informs us that the average Roman enjoyed bread, *puls* (a kind of porridge), meat, wine and

cheese. He also includes a recipe for a cake called Libum, which might well have been his favorite cheesecake: "Wash hands and the utensils carefully. Grind down two pounds of cheese [this would probably have been either Ricotta or salted, fresh cheese] in a mortar; add one pound of meal or, for a softer cake, half a pound of fine flour, and mix thoroughly. Form the mass into a loaf, place it on leaves, and bake slowly on a hot fire under a heat-proof earthenware dish." The recipe does work, and it makes a very good and nourishing cake.

Pass the cheese, *per favore*

Each region of Italy has its own culinary traditions, its own staple preferences and its own methods of preparation, which have always depended on the climate and what the soil can be coaxed to provide. On Sardinia, for example, the barbecue has been commonplace since well before Roman times, and the habit of passing home-made sheep's cheese from person to person, as a group sits around the open fire, still remains.

Italy produces her own special type of rice for risotto; corn is grown for polenta, or corn meal; and durum wheat for the pasta. Pasta has more variety than the whole range of sounds capable of being produced by a symphony orchestra and its names are sweet music to the Italian ear: spaghetti, fusilli, macaroni, tagliatelli, lasagne, tortellini, ravioli, rigatoni. The home of pasta is Naples – but the Neapolitans are too generous to keep it to themselves. The north of Italy demands the flat, ribbon-shaped *pasta all'uova*, made from eggs and flour, which is so good with butter and parmesan cheese, or the *salsa Bolognese*; but there are also pastas in the form of butterflies, little hats (Cappelletti), little wheels (Ruote), shells (Conchiglie); some to toss into soup, some to boil or fry or fill – and almost always they are sprinkled with a generous handful of grated cheese, or cooked with cheese, or covered by a cheese sauce. Italy enriched the world with its fonduta and gnocchi, its cheese pastry, its pizzas and above all its cheeses for the table, to be eaten on their own, or with fruit, and washed down with Italian wine. It is for this reason, as much as any other, that Both Petrarch and Dante called Italy the *"Bel Paese"*!

Portugal

It has been established that from the sixteenth century the Portuguese were great consumers of cheese, and have continued to be so, in spite of the fact that back in 1661 King Alfonso VI had a huge consignment of Dutch cheese thrown into Lisbon harbor. No doubt, the king's act was a gesture of contempt for a people against whom his country had been at war. Nevertheless, the Dutch trade was so dependent on the Portuguese market that when an earthquake hit Lisbon a century later, in 1755, cheese prices instantly fell.

Agrarian problems

Portugal's own cheese production is hampered by slow agrarian development and economic problems. Nowhere in the country can cattle raising guarantee the farmer a proper existence. The north of Portugal, a continuation of the Spanish mountain ridges, descends to the mainly flat coast and the Douro River Valley. This region has the city of Porto as an agricultural center, and although it is the most suitable area for farming, the farmers themselves lack knowledge of modern methods. Their plots of land are small, and there are few resources for development. In the south there are large landowners, but they are hindered by a shortage of labor.

With a taste for cheese, and within the limits of the situation, the Portuguese have long relied on home production, making cheese for consumption on the farm itself, or for sale in the local market. The cheeses produced are unusual and individual; while prepared by the same basic principle, they differ in shape, color, consistency and taste from farm to farm. In recent years, however, in the large towns, modern cheese factories have been established; these are now provided with regular milk supplies and have achieved good sales in the populated areas.

To protect and encourage the individuality of Portugal's unique cheeses, and to raise production standards, dairy product testing stations have been set up. Suggestions and improved techniques are sought after, for most of the farmhouse cheeses are in need of improvement: 10% are very bad and 80% are of not more than acceptable quality – the remaining 10%, though, are of a very high standard.

ABOVE: A shepherd and his flock in the Serra de Estrela. The ewe's milk is the base of Portugal's principal cheese, Queijo de Serra.

Name	Milk	Type	Rind	Form	Weight	% Fat content
Alcobaca	◩	■	—	flat disc	200 g	55
Alvorca	◩	■	—	flat disc	200-300 g	48-52
Castelo Branco	✳	■	—	loaf	1 kg	52
Queijo da Ilha	◿	■	▢	cylinder	2 kg	43
Queijo de Evora	◩	■	—	flat disc	100-150 g	42-45
Queijo de Serra	◿◩	●■	❖	varying	0.8-1.5 kg	40-55
Queijo Fresco	◿◩	○	—	flat disc	50-100 g	44-52
Queijo Seco	◿◩	■	—	flat disc	50 g	35-55

✳ ◿◩◿

Key to symbols on page 34. 453 g = 1 lb; 1 kg = 2.2 lbs.

ABOVE: Goat's milk is also used in cheese-making, often in combination with ewe's milk. These goats are being tended by their owner, a farmer from Nazaré on the Atlantic coast.

Cheese from flowers and thistles

In the mountains of southern Portugal, sheep and goats supply the milk that makes the country's most important cheese, *Queijo de Serra*, or "mountain cheese." It is a cheese type with many variants: flat, round, semihard to hard cheeses of 800 to 1,500 g (1.8 to 3.3 lbs). They are usually made on the farms from raw milk, although there are a few small factories that will take the entire milk yield of a flock. Most farmers do not use rennet cultures, but prefer to make their own from the flowers and leaves of a thistle species that grows wild; the plant is also cultivated for the purpose and can be bought on the market.

The milk is first sieved through a cloth containing the vegetable rennet. Some farmers now acknowledge the more reliable animal rennet, and use a combination of this and the thistle rennet, which continues to be employed because it influences the pliancy and taste of the cheese. The curdling strength and time varies considerably. The farmer works the curd with his hands, rather than cutting it. The red rind flora that develops during ripening is regularly removed, and after five to seven weeks olive oil is rubbed on the rind, making it shiny and a little greasy. The paste is light yellow, quite supple and soft while young, but harder and often crumbly after an extended ripening period. The fat content varies between 40 and 55%. With the help of standardized

LEFT: A tile painting from the marketplace at Santarém, Estremadura. Cattle are mostly found in the north, and along the flat coastal areas.

cultures and uniform methods, efforts are being made to simplify production techniques and to make a cheese of an even, regular quality. Unfortunately, this can only be achieved at the expense of some loss of flavor.

Other cheeses of the Queijo de Serra type are *Alcobaca*, a small, flat, rindless disc with an almost chalk-white paste; *Niza*; *Azeitas*; *Serpa*; *Toman*; *Castelo de Vide* and many other regional varieties.

Salty cheese and green wine

The rindless *Alvorca* is a hard, cylindrical cheese showing a reddish tinge on the outside. It has a fat content of 48 to 52% and weighs between 200 and 300 g (.4 to .7 lbs). *Queijo de Evora*, from Evora, east of Lisbon, is a goat cheese, hard, rindless, flat and round, with a dry, salty-tasting paste that develops a mold; it weighs from 100 to 150 g (.2 to .3 lbs). The cheese is often laid in olive oil and sold unwrapped. *Castelo Branco* is made from a mixture of cow's, goat's and sheep's milk. No rind is allowed to form and the crust flora is carefully scraped away. When flora ceases to form, after about 80-90 days, the cheese is considered ripe; wrapped in tin foil, it finds its way to the consumer. The heavy, cylindrical *Queijo da Ilha*, "island cheese," is another hard type, exclusively made on the Azores, but also eaten on the mainland. Inside its dry rind you will find a

RIGHT: Farmhouse cheese is produced individually on a small scale, but in considerable variety. Peasants have been selling it from baskets like this for hundreds of years.

cheese of crumbly consistency with many small cracks. It tastes quite piquant and sharp, and is supposed to have a fat content of 43%, but this can vary, depending on the quality of the workmanship.

Queijo Fresco is, as its name suggests, a fresh cheese type. Small, slim and round, the cheese is by no means a standardized product, because techniques and recipes vary from farm to farm, as does the type and quality of the milk used. The rennet and renneting temperature are inconsistent, for example, as are the salt and moisture content. Most cheesemakers remove the whey by manually kneading the curd, which is wrapped in a cloth. The cheese takes its shape from the hoop from which it is sold unripened. If Queijo Fresco is left lying for too long, it dries out and shrinks considerably. The cheese is also made in factories, from pasteurized milk.

A more durable version of Queijo Fresco is the *Queijo Seco*, which might seem a contradiction in terms, since *seco* means "dry." The cheese is treated with brine, becomes light yellow in color, is rather hard or even crumbly, and has no rind. The flat discs of cheese each weigh about 50 g (.1 lb); the fat content in the dry matter – again different from maker to maker – varies between 35 and 55%; and the taste is sharp and salty. Finally, also worth mentioning are *Cabreiro* (ripened for three months in brine) and *Requeijao*, a Ricotta type. Foreign varieties are also manufactured: *Edam*, also called *Bola*; and, on a smaller scale, *Camembert*, *Emmental* and various processed cheeses.

Portuguese cooking is simple, substantial and more strongly spiced than Spanish cuisine. Cheese is seldom used in dishes, but often served as a snack after the main course. As characteristic as the sharp-tasting sheep's milk cheese is the wine that should accompany it, the *vinho verde* unique to Portugal. The name means "green wine," not because of its color, which is rarely green, but because of its extreme youth and sparkling freshness.

It also frequently accompanies the popular Iberian dish of salt cod, known as *Bacalho* in Portugal. *Bacalho* and *vinho verde* are good companions, as one quenches the thirst provoked by the other.

Spain

Spain has sharply contrasting areas of climate and vegetation. In the north-west, along the Cantabrian mountain range and into the far corner of Galicia, there are verdant hills, valleys and good grazing land. In the south it is hot, arid and subtropical. Cotton, sugar cane, apricots and oranges are grown. Like most of Spain, it is sheep country, and only quite recently have cow's milk cheeses gained ground at the cost of Spain's many and varied ewe cheeses. The former are primarily produced in the rainy northwest and on the islands, while the sheep cheeses come from all over the country. It is true that cattle are also kept in the south, in Andalusia, but they are bred mainly for their meat.

By far the most well-known and popular Spanish cheese is *Manchego*, a sheep's milk type with the highest production record of all – some 2.5 million kg (5.5 million lbs) a year. It is made from the herb-scented milk of the Manchego breed of sheep, and comes from the hills and plateaus of La Mancha, the home of Don Quixote, south of Madrid. A Manchego cheese is a flat cylinder of 2.5-3 kg (5.5-6.6 lbs), is full fat, and has a creamy white, firm interior with just a few little eyes. The rind is straw yellow in color and is sometimes paraffined. At one time the impressions it bore were made by the beautifully woven rush baskets in which the shepherds had pressed the curd by hand; now cheese factories mold the cheese in forms which imitate the decorative pattern. You can choose between *Manchego Fresco* (fresh), *Curado* (ripened from three to thirteen weeks), *Viejo* (older than three months), and *Manchego en Aceite*, which is immersed in olive oil, developing a gray to black rind in the process, and can be kept for a year.

Other sheep's milk cheeses of the Manchego type are: *Grazelema* from Cadiz; the hard *Oropesa*, or *Queso de la Estrella*, from the region of Toledo; *Queso de los Pedroches* from Cordoba; and *Queso de la Serena*, another hard cheese, which can be kept for two years. Pedroches is traditionally curdled with vegetable rather than animal rennet, as are the Portuguese mountain cheeses; shepherds prepare the cheese in molds of woven broom twigs, from the milk of their Merino sheep, world famous for their wool.

In the Basque country farmers make quantities of *Idiazabal*, a long-keeping

LEFT: A scene typical of the Spanish countryside, both arid and often beautiful, where the dry soil and hot climate is more suitable for sheep than for cattle.

LEFT: Manchego is made from ewe's milk, and is Spain's biggest seller. When ripened, it is a delicacy, with its characteristic flavor of a sheep cheese.

BELOW: Compared with Spain's 23 million sheep and goats, there are hardly any cattle at all – a mere 3 million – but they are gaining ground.

white cheese. They smoke it above a fire in the kitchen and sell it directly to their customers. *Gorbea* and *Prensado de Orduna* are similar types; the latter is ripened in mountain caves. *Queso de los Bellos*, or *Queso Bellusco*, is a hard cheese from Asturias in the north, made from sheep's milk or a mixture of sheep's and goat's milk. It has a rough crust with yellow and brown spots, and a white paste having a pleasant, nicely sharp flavor.

Fresh sheep's milk cheeses are also made. *Burgos* is named after the fine old town in the center of the produc-

RIGHT: Traditional costume matches the products she sells – a cheese seller in Tenerife, one of the Canary Isles.

tion region, a white, round-shaped cheese of 1-2 kg (2.2-4.4 lbs), with no rind, a fresh, light taste, and the characteristic aroma of a sheep's milk cheese. *Villalón* is an identical product, pressed by hand, steeped in brine for a few hours before being packed in chipwood boxes. It has a fresh, sourish taste, sometimes riper than Burgos, but sharing the same character.

Aragón is a soft to semihard type that is cured for one week and can be kept for a further few weeks. The cheese is usually made from a mixture of sheep's and goat's milk, and takes the form of an irregular ball with an indented top. This is another cheese that is still made mainly on the farms.

All these cheeses have a high fat content, due to the richness of the milk. The harder types contain at least 46%, the soft to semihard varieties usually have between 50 and 56%.

Sour and salty, sweet and mild
There is one Spanish cheese made from cow's milk whose production surpasses all others: the *Queso de Mahón* from the Balearic Islands, and especially Minorca. Even though it is usually made exclusively from whole cow's milk, the Spanish sometimes forget themselves and add 4 to 8% sheep's milk. It is an attractive cheese with a mellow taste. The paste is light to dark yellow with small holes, firm to hard in consistency; the rind is dry and compact, and usually yellowish-brown in color with irregular, dark

RIGHT: A farmer from Palafrugell on the Mediterranean Costa Brava, hand milking one of his herd. In this part of Spain the land conditions are favorable for cattle, but still far from ideal. Only the northwest has really good grazing.

spots. It is a good type from which to make processed cheese.

Quite a different cheese is *Quesucos* from the region of Santander, a soft type which only ripens for about six days. *Queso Pasiego sin Prensar* is related; it is a small cheese of irregular shape with a fat content of 58%. There is also a pressed and ripened *Pasiego Prensado*, which has less fat and a very mild, neutral taste. *Armada* is unique, the only cheese to be made from colostrum or "beestings," the first milk given by a cow after calving. Armada is a long-keeping semihard cheese, piquant and slightly bitter.

The northwest offers a wealth of cheeses, and included with those mentioned above are *Tetilla*, with its fresh, sourish flavor and salty overtones; *Cebrero*, a mushroom-shaped cheese (the molds are filled to overflowing, and a broad "cap" results), which is either eaten when fresh or ripened for a few months; and *San Simon*, a semihard, smoked farmhouse cheese, pear-shaped, with a hard, shiny rind and a taste that is fine, creamy and just a little sourish. Finally, *Ulloa* is a semihard, flat cylinder, white to light yellow in color, with a mild taste. It is ripened outside the farm in an open shed, protected by the sun but dried by the wind.

Fresh, white goat's milk cheeses are common everywhere. Typical is the *Cabra de Alicante*, sold directly after it is made, a cheese with a lovely aroma of fresh milk. The *Cabra de Cadíz* is another fresh type, ready after a few days; it has a yellowish rind, a firm consistency and a sharp but agreeable flavor. Sometimes these cheeses are treated with olive oil to increase their keeping properties.

Fresh, unpressed cheeses, that still contain a quantity of whey, are very popular in Spain. They are made from unpasteurized milk which is only very lightly acidified, and therefore the cheeses are prone to harbor germs. A "safe" factory cheese has been developed from pasteurized cow's milk, the *Queso Fresco Rosell*, named after its inventor, a Professor Rosell, and this has become very successful.

Along with the Spanish cheeses, well-known international cheese types are widely produced, among them Edam and Gouda.

Name	Milk	Type	Rind	Form	Weight	% Fat content
Aragón	🄐🄖	●	☐	ball	0.6-1.5 kg	54
Burgos	🄖	○	—	flat disc	1-2 kg	58
Cabra de Alicante	🄐	○	—	flat disc	150-500 g	40
Cabra de Cadíz	🄐	●	☐	flat disc	1.5 kg	50
Cebrero	🄒	■	☐	mushroom	2-5 kg	50
Idiazabal	🄖	■	☐	cylinder	1-2 kg	53
Manchego	🄖	■	☐	low cylinder	2.5-3 kg	50-62
Queso de Mahón	🄒	●	☐	rectangular	2-4 kg	45
Queso Fresco Rosell	🄒	○		container	250 g	50
Queso Pasiego	🄒	●	☐	varying	varying	48-58
Quesucos	✳	●	☐	flat disc	0.1-3 kg	45
San Simon	🄒	●	☐	pear	1-2 kg	40
Tetilla	🄒	●	—	pear	1-1.5 kg	40
Ulloa	🄒	●	☐	flat disc	0.75-1.25 kg	45
Villalón	🄖	○	—	bar	0.5-2.5 kg	54

✳ 🄒 🄐 🄖

Key to symbols on page 34. 453 g = 1 lb; 1 kg = 2.2 lbs.

131

Yugoslavia and Albania

The eastern end of the crescent formed by the European Alps joins a bleak, arid mountain range that stretches almost the entire length of Yugoslavia. These are the Dinaric Alps, traversed by fertile river valleys with a Mediterranean climate. The richly wooded western slopes of this alpine range descend into Macedonia and Serbia where there are harsh winters, while to the north of the country the climate is more temperate. Here are the plains of Vojvodina, the granary of Slavonia. In spite of the great contrast, Yugoslavia is predominantly agricultural, and 80 % of the land is drained by the tributaries of the river Danube.

There are plenty of cows, but over the entire country, including the islands, there are twice as many sheep. The once-numerous goats have now gone, because they destroyed the newly planted, virgin forests. Collective farming in Yugoslavia is not so far advanced as in other parts of eastern Europe; farming families continue to live in isolation, especially in the mountains, and still make cheese according to recipes handed down from generation to generation. Production has always been on a limited scale, yet as early as the Middle Ages certain hard cheese types were sent to Dubrovnik and Constantinople. Even the Roman colonists knew of them – "pressed by hand," wrote the historian Columella in the first century A.D., a technique still used today in Bosnia and Hercegovina to make the plastic curd cheese *Presukača*. In fact, the cheese was probably introduced by the Romans, since it so closely resembles Provolone and Caciocavallo, cheeses where the curd is heated with hot water and kneaded to a variety of shapes. The Italian cheese Caciocavallo does, in fact, have a Yugoslav counterpart: *Kačkavalj*.

In common with certain other cheesemaking countries, where the whey is utilized, Yugoslavia makes albumen cheese. Heating the whey causes the albumen protein to flocculate, and it is then used to make a type of cheese. In preparing *Manur*, milk is often added to increase the output, and so the fat content varies. This also applies to *Urda* or *Skuta* whey cheeses. They are eaten fresh and unsalted, unless the cheeses need to be kept: then they are salted and pressed into wooden molds. In Slovenia they are made into balls, while in Macedonia

they are stuffed into paprika peppers, which gives the cheeses a sharp taste.

Many cheese types are ripened in brined whey, like the Macedonian *Bijeni Sir*, a semihard to hard cheese made from sheep's milk, cow's milk, or both. The cheesemaker beats the curd with a wooden stick, until it has the consistency of yogurt. The drained curd is then cut into strips and ripened for three to four weeks in a tub filled with salted whey. The cheese develops no rind; it possesses a solid consistency with many small holes and has a sharp taste. Unlike Bijeni Sir, the *Tucani Sir* is made exclusively on farms, and the method of preparation has remained fairly primitive. The farmer crumbles the curd, previously salted, into a barrel, packs it in tightly, and places a heavy stone on top in order to press the cheese and expel the whey, which is then replaced by fresh, brined whey.

From the mainly mountainous region of Bosnia comes the cheese *Beli Sir u Kriškama*, mild and slightly sour in taste. It is ripened in brine, often with parchment between the curd layers, and it acquires a soft and supple consistency after about four weeks of

LEFT: On the slopes of the bleak, desolate Dinaric Alps are small areas of fertile land. Sheep roam the foothills, and their milk is used to make the countless varieties of Yugoslavian cheeses.

BELOW: A street market where cheeses are sold, in Kotor, Montenegro.

ripening. The farmers make it with raw milk that has spontaneously soured, while factories use acidified, pasteurized milk. Another brine-ripened type, *Feta*, is originally Greek, and is a sheep's milk cheese. In Macedonia a cheese is made from buffalo's milk, sometimes mixed with cow's milk: *Sir iz Bivoljegmleka*. Its buffalo origins are easily recognizable from the aroma; the cheese is made only for home use.

A wealth of recipes

Somborski Sir is an interesting, soft cheese, originally made by the Serbians in Vojvodina in the sixteenth century. Raw sheep's milk, cow's milk, or a mixture of the two is used, mixed with 20 to 30% water. The layers of curd are stacked in a vat with a high rim, which is later removed, so that about a quarter of the cheese sticks out of the vat like a soufflé. Active bacteria, feasting on the soft curd, create a lot of gas, and the cheese acquires a bitter taste. *Mješinski Sir* is made on the mountain farms of Bosnia, Hercegovina, Dalmatia and Montenegro, from boiled and skimmed milk; the curd is pressed and put into sacks to mature

Name	Milk	Type	Rind	Form	Weight	% Fat content
Beli Sir u Kriškama	🐄🐑	●	—	rectangular	1 kg	45-50
Bijeni Sir	🐄🐑	■	—	rectangular	varying	35-40
Grobnički Sir	🐑	■	□	cylinder	10-20 kg	45-52
Kefalotir	🐑	■	□	cylinder	9-10 kg	45-50
Manur	🐑	■	□	ball	3 kg	40
Mješinski Sir	🐑	●	—	container	varying	15-35
Njeguški Sir	🐑	■	❖	cylinder	2.5 kg	50
Presukača	🐑	■	□	varying	varying	45
Somborski Sir	🐄🐑	●	—	container	2-10 kg	50
Tucani Sir	🐄🐑	●		container	varying	60-70

Key to symbols on page 34. 1 kg = 2.2 lbs.

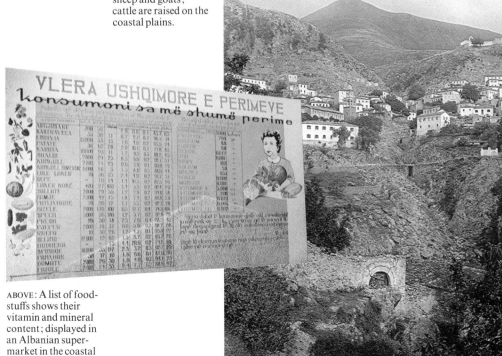

for a year, in the manner of the Rumanian Brindza cheeses.

Among the hard, grating cheeses is the big, cylindrical *Kefalotir* (originally a product of the Greek-Macedonian mountain dwellers), made from raw sheep's milk. The even heavier *Grobnički Sir* from Croatia is aromatic and piquant, with lots of holes in the paste. From the Lovčengebergte in Montenegro comes the hard, cylindrical, sheep's milk cheese *Njeguški Sir*, which after three or four months' ripening develops a dark yellow color and a piquant taste. In Croatia, *Lički Sir* is dried and smoked above an open fire. It, too, is a hard cheese made of sheep's milk, but cow's milk is sometimes used, mixed with the former or on its own. Care must be taken with the drying of this cheese: if dried too quickly, the rind becomes too hard and the paste too soft.

Over the centuries an incalculable number of cheese recipes have been handed down through farming families. Although these have the place of honor on the farms, the range of Yugoslavia's cheeses has recently been increased by the addition of foreign types made in factories, including *Gouda* and *Trappist* (Port-Salut type).

A very popular product is *Kajmak*, although whether or not it is strictly a cheese is open to question. Kajmak is cream skimmed from whole milk, which is salted and packed in wooden barrels. It is sold by weight from its wooden container, either fresh or briefly ripened, and is often used to make cheese pastry. As might be expected in a country where cheese is made on every farm, cheese is an important part of the daily diet. In Slovenia and Croatia cheese completes the meal; in Serbia it precedes the main dish.

Albania

Albanian cheeses are similar to those of neighboring countries. In the north, milk comes from Illyrian cows and water buffalo, and in some places from sheep and goats. These are due to be replaced by cattle, for the goats – although important to the rural economy – are damaging the newly planted forest trees.

133

Greece

It is reasonable to suppose that ancient Arcadian Greece, a land of gods and shepherds, flowing with milk and honey, would be skilled in the art of making cheese. Heroes would have enjoyed small white cheeses made of sheep's milk or goat's milk, accompanied by resin-scented wine and the peppery milk-bread called *arto-laganus*. Sheep and goats were at home in the mountainous, inland landscape, but the Greeks also had cattle. In fact, Homer once described the beautiful goddess Pallas Athene as "cow-eyed," and the nymph Galatea as "whiter than curd." Today these hardly seem to us like romantic descriptions of classical beauty, but Homer's intent was obviously complimentary. What still rings true, however, is his account in the *Odyssey* of the cyclops Polyphemus, son of the sea god Poseidon, and a sheep farmer who prepared cheese in the traditional manner. Here is Homer describing how the hero Odysseus entered the cyclops' cave, accompanied by his companions: "We did not find him at home, for he was herding fat sheep in the field. With great astonishment we looked at everything. There were racks, heavily laden with cheeses. In the stables the lambs and rams were pushed against each other, separated by age: the oldest, the middle group, and the very young. The casks were overflowing with whey, [and there were] the sturdy pails and trays into which he milked." One of Polyphemus's main characteristics was his perpetual hunger, hence the vast and continuous supply of cheese. Modern Greeks are hardly less demanding, for they head the list of the world's cheese fanciers, consuming a yearly – and classic – average of 15 kg (33 lbs) per person. To achieve this average, Greek farms and factories need to make a lot of cheese, and practically all of it is made from the milk of sheep, still the most useful animal in this mountainous country.

Cheese and myth

The Greek landscape is dominated by the Pindus range in the north and the mountains of Morea in the south, and most of the rock strata is limestone, interspersed with marble. Olive groves are sparse and there are few other tree varieties, for it is said that Greece was almost entirely denuded of trees in ancient times, mainly by shipbuilders when Greece realized her

LEFT: The classic scene that inspired pastoral poetry – the essence of Greek country life as it has existed, virtually unchanged, for over thirty centuries.

LEFT: The colorful national dress is still worn by the Greeks on special, festive occasions.

future as a maritime nation.

According to the ancient Greek historian Herodotus, the glory that was Greece had been nourished on unpromising soil. "Poverty," he wrote, "has lived in Greece from olden times; but the Greeks are industrious and resist poverty." The land that remains is still fit only for primitive agriculture, and farmers spend their entire lives trying to cultivate small areas of fertile land in the mountains, tending vines, growing tobacco, gathering olives for the press. The shepherd has one of the most time-honored occupations, since the sheep has always been the most important animal, providing wool, meat and milk for cheeses. In fact, there is hardly a Greek myth in which a shepherd fails to appear in the plot, one of the most famous being Daphnis, a son of Hermes. Which brings us back, briefly, to the story of Odysseus and the cyclops Polyphemus, who returned home to his cave of cheeses. Homer continues: "He sat down and he milked the sheep and the bleating goats, everything according to the rules of the art; and under each mother he pushed a young

RIGHT: In this small dairy, the cheesemaker produces sheep cheese every day. In the background is his primitive press, which uses rocks as counterweights.

ABOVE: The cheese that every visitor to Greece comes to know and love: white Feta. Sold everywhere, it is a main constituent of the Greek daily diet.

The only animals that seemed to thrive on the stony hillsides were sheep and goats, and their milk was the sole source of protein in the daily diet. Even this became further impoverished, so that cheese was regarded as a luxury following the Peloponnesian wars of the fifth century B.C., when orchards, farms and livestock were destroyed. Yet the importance of cheese has survived throughout history, largely because the hardy mountain sheep were productive while other nourishing food sources had failed. Cheese, like bread, was a staple food, and was often combined with bread in Greek recipes, probably in order to give the common, coarse-grained loaf extra flavor and moistness. The cheese made by Polyphemus, and by most ancient Greeks, was undoubtedly the ancestor of the modern *Feta*, the whey being retained to make albumen cheese.

In the mountains and the plains of Greece, even under the smoke of modern Athens, the shepherds still prepare their Feta cheese in exactly the same way. They keep the milk in leather sacks during the day, and it quickly curdles due to the flora of lactic acid bacteria present in the sacks. When heated over a fire, the proteins in the milk – casein and albumen – flocculate, enclosing the milk-fat particles. The curd floats to the top and is then skimmed off with little baskets. It can be eaten immediately as fresh cheese, but it is often dried in the air and kept.

Feta as a modern cheese

In the cheese factories, for the preparation of Feta, cow's milk is sometimes used instead of sheep's milk. Feta cheese made exclusively from cow's milk loses some of its familiar character: it is not as smooth and fragrant, and takes on a yellow color which does not normally appeal to the Greeks. This means that the cow's milk must either be mixed with sheep's milk and/or goat's milk, or that the cow's milk must be decolored before the processing begins. By mixing, the cheesemaker can vary the fat content: sheep's milk is very high in fat, goat's milk much less so.

In order to give the cheese better keeping qualities, the cheese factories generally start with pasteurized milk, which is soured and preripened. As soon as the milk curdles, the curd is

one. After that he curdled half of the white milk and stacked it in plaited baskets; the other part he put away in barrels to drink from."

From this story one might conclude that Polyphemus the cheesemaker was an object of Greek envy – a person, albeit one-eyed, who was never in want of a good meal of cheese and milk. Although the Athenians were said to live in considerable luxury, and were able to afford meat, wine and good bread, most average Greeks were vegetarians by force of circumstances, as many still are today. Meat was a rare treat, and the peasants of classical Greece lived mainly on a diet of barley porridge, wild fruit, olives, cultivated figs, wild birds, cheese, goat's milk or watered wine. Sometimes a meal might be supplemented by fish. Olive oil was one of the major exports, along with Greek wine, and thus olive groves and vines became important crops, at the expense of cereals. Good grazing was scarce, and the cattle, such as they were, pulled the primitive plow; if their milk was used for the manufacture of cheese, it couldn't compare with the popular ewe's milk types, quickly made and even more quickly eaten.

ABOVE: A farmyard on the island of Corfu, off the western coast of Greece, one of the most fertile and progressive Greek islands.

BELOW: Sheep are the ideal domestic animals for a peasant community living in isolation in a barren country. Not only do they supply wool, but meat too, and milk to make the vast quantity of cheese demanded by the population.

cut into blocks, which after a short rest period are scooped into molds or hung in cloths. The molds are turned regularly, and the curd in the cloth is pressed. The curd is then divided into rectangular pieces; these are salted by hand or placed in a brine bath, dried for a short time in molds, and finally ripened in sealed molds; after each turning they are hermetically sealed. A characteristic of Feta is that it ripens in its own whey, mixed with brine; it may thus be called "brine cheese." The cheeses made by this process do not develop a rind. The paste is very white, a bit sourish, piquant and quite salty to the taste, but not bitter. In northern Greece, Feta cheese is made under the name *Telemes*.

Kefalotyri and Kasseri

Kefalotyri is a hard cheese, used in certain Greek dishes, and is produced during the lactation period of the sheep and the goat in cheese factories across the entire country. The name is said to come from the cheese's resemblance to the Greek hat called a *Kefalo*, but it also often carries its regional name: Pindus, for example, is named after the Pindus mountain range, while Skyros is named after a small island in the Aegean.

The milk is always processed raw. After curdling, stirring, heating and a day's pressing in molds, the cheese is rubbed with salt before being returned to the molds for three days for a good rind to form. The cheeses are then ready, but they usually remain during the warm months in cooled storage rooms; thus the ripening time can never be exactly determined. Long-ripened cheeses have a low moisture content and are insensitive to high outside temperatures. These dry cheeses are mostly used for grating.

A great deal of fresh Kefalotyri is kept by the factories for the preparation of *Kasseri*, a kneaded, plastic curd cheese with good keeping qualities. The Kefalotyri is cut into bars, which are preripened close together and, like Italian Provolone, made supple and plastic in hot water.

Mitzithra and Galotiri

The whey that remains after the preparation of Feta and Kefalotyri cheese is not always thrown away, but used as raw material for the manufacture of *Mitzithra*, an albumen cheese similar

ABOVE: Odysseus escaping from the cave of the cyclops Polyphemus, an illustration from a Hellenic vase. Polyphemus was a cheesemaker, and Homer's description of his techniques is perhaps the earliest on record.

to Ricotta. The flocculated curd is put into little baskets and is eaten fresh, preferably when still warm. As an alternative, balls are formed from the curd, which are stored for use as a grating cheese in the summer. This sort of cheese is made by the Macedonians under the name of *Monuri*; *Urda* comes from Epiros; and *Anthotiros* from the island of Crete.

One of the oldest of Greek cheese types, a sheep's milk cheese that is made at home in many parts of Greece, is *Galotiri*, a relative of the above cheeses, coming somewhere between Feta and Mitzithra. The freshly yielded milk is left to ripen for an hour, so that it becomes a little sour. It is then boiled, causing the proteins to flocculate. The curd is mixed with salt and for the next few days is occasionally stirred, after which it is put in a sack of animal skin and filled up with the curd from the next milk yield. After three months the cheese is ready for eating.

A salty, island cheese

Some of the islands in the Aegean Sea produce a veined cheese called *Kopanisti*, made by cutting the

Name	Milk	Type	Rind	Form	Weight	% Fat content
Feta	✳	●	—	rectangular	varies	45-60
Galotiri	◿	●	—	container	varies	varies
Kasseri	◿◿	■	☐	flat disc, bar	varies	40
Kefalotyri	◿◿	■	☐	low cylinder	5-10 kg	40-45
Kopanisti	◿	✕	—	container	varies	varies
Mitzithra	✳	○	—	basket	1 kg	varies

✳ ◿◿◿

Key to symbols on page 34. 1 kg = 2.2 lbs.

prepared curd, putting it into cloths, kneading it by hand and forming it into balls the size of an orange. These are placed on racks to dry and soon develop a mold flora. With the kneading treatment that follows, the cheese-maker works this flora, together with a quantity of salt, well through the curd. Covered with a clean cloth, the cheese ripens for one or two months in earthenware pots. It is called "pot cheese," a type made in other warm countries too. The high salt content gives the product good keeping qualities.

The Greeks also produce foreign imitations. Greek cheese factories that use cow's milk often manufacture a Gruyère-type cheese called *Graviera*; *Parmesan* and *Fontina* are also made in modest quantities.

Cheese – food for the gods

Herodotus's comments on the proverbial poverty of the Greeks still applies: for the greater part of the rural population, little has changed since antiquity. Even the working-class city dwellers enjoy scant prosperity. Nevertheless, the people are extremely hospitable, a national trait that was also established in classical times, as the following legend shows. The great god Zeus and his son Hermes, the helper of travelers, decided to visit the aged couple Philemon and Baucis. The old people had no idea of their guests' identities, but with their natural generosity, and in spite of their poverty, they managed to produce a tempting spread, including cheese, olives, cherries, endive salad, radishes, boiled eggs and, as a dessert, figs, dates, grapes and a slice of honeycomb – a royal menu for a Greek at that time, and even today it would be far from ordinary.

For the average family, the day starts with fresh, warm bread, Feta cheese and perhaps an egg: a combination born of simplicity, but tasting good just the same, especially with the sweet, strong coffee that follows. Slices of cheese also constitute the main part of the midday meal, with olives, tomatoes, cucumber and peppers. On special occasions this might be preceded by watermelon and very small pieces of charcoal-grilled mutton, but, generally, meat is a luxury. For the low-income groups, cheese is the only good source of protein other than bread, and, as we

have seen, the Greek cheese consumption is the world's highest.

The influence of tourism has, in recent years, brought many changes to Greek eating habits. The popularity of home cheese types is decreasing as foreign imitations gain more and more ground.

While the main meat dish of Greece is undoubtedly the kebab, other more sophisticated dishes are found in the cities, and particularly in the hotels that cater to tourists. As one might expect, cheese features in several of these specialities, among them the well-known Moussaka, where grated Kefalotyri cheese is sprinkled between layers of an aubergine and meat mixture. A more simple version is Papoutsakia, aubergines stuffed with meat and sprinkled with Kefalotyri cheese. Pastitsio is another layered concoction, with macaroni and meat sauce and grated Kefalotyri. The other important cooking cheese is, of course, the versatile Feta, which is added to a beef casserole called Stifado, to dishes with chicken, or with shrimp and tomatoes, and to the delicious spinach and cheese pie made with *filo* pastry, called Spanakopita.

East Germany (D.D.R.)

Most of the landscape of East Germany is flat and green, especially to the north of Berlin and along the Baltic coast. Because of the fairly high annual rainfall, it is rich pastureland, admirably suited to raising cattle and making dairy products. Cheesemaking here was considerably influenced by the Dutch during the eighteenth century, and pioneered by the Prussian King Friederich II, who founded a model cattle farm near Berlin in 1730. He gave the farmer's daughters a wedding present of 24 talers, silver coins, if within two years they learned to make cheese of the same quality as their Dutch teachers.

The present economy of East Germany is not geared to large-scale production of cheese, and a shortage of good cattle fodder has somewhat reduced the milk yield. Nevertheless, many well-established types are produced, both traditional German and foreign ones.

Few hard cheeses are made. *Tiefländer* is a sort of Emmental cheese, and there is some *Chester* (or Cheshire) and *Cheddar*, production being confined mainly to the area once known as Mecklenburg, and used for the manufacture of processed cheese. In the range of semihard cheeses, all of which have rind flora, there is more of a variety. *Tollenser (Tilsiter)* is sold everywhere; there is also *Steppenkäse*, and the rather more interesting *Steinbusch*, which is scooped out onto a long draining table, like the Belgian Herve cheese. This cheese is made in a cube shape, weighing a maximum of 700 g (1.5 lbs), with a smooth, light-yellow, solid but not crumbly paste; a mild, rather than piquant, flavor; and a reddish, rather dry rind with a coryne flora. There are varieties with fat contents of 30, 45 and 50 %.

LEFT: In the large collective farms of East Germany, cattle are treated and milked by modern, highly mechanized methods.

LEFT: Stamp with a dairy subject. Note the two rows of cows under a roof in the meadow. A milkmaid supervises the milking process, done by machine.

Name	Milk	Type	Rind	Form	Weight	% Fat content
Altenburger Milbenkäse	🐄	◖	–	bar	25 g	?
- Ziegenkäse	🐄🐐	●	✤✤	flat disc	250 g	20-45
Steinbusch	🐄	◖	✤	cube	200-700 g	30-50

Key to symbols on page 34. 453 g = 1 lb.

From the Thüringerwald comes *Altenburger Ziegenkäse*, a soft cheese made from raw cow's and goat's milk. When factory-produced, it is made from pasteurized milk and with varying fat contents. Kummel is always mixed in it, and a combination of Camembert and coryne molds is introduced to produce a white and red flora, a combination that demands special ripening conditions, its development being activated with whey. The Ziegenkäse looks like a thick pancake; it weighs 250 g (.6 lb), has a strong taste and aroma, and a soft creamy-yellow paste with hardly any holes. If the curdling temperature is too low, the cheese remains too soft; but if the temperature is too high, it becomes chalky and hard. Another speciality from the same region, and one that has now almost vanished, is the *Altenburger Milbenkäse*, crumbly, sharp and piquant bars of cheese, made from cow's milk Quark, to which kummel is often added. The Quark is left in the Milbentopf to become riddled with cheese mites, which are later brushed off. The sharp-tasting cheese is eaten with bread, and sometimes softened with coffee or beer.

More than half of East Germany's cheese production consists of fresh cheese, 90 % being skimmed-milk Quark. *Sauermilchkäse* is also produced in the central part of the country. East Germany does not, at present, export cheese.

BELOW: An attractive old farmhouse in the region formerly known as Mecklenburg, now divided into separate districts.

Poland

ABOVE: Wooden, roofed sheep pens built high up in the isolated Tatra Mountains.

As a cattle-breeding country, Poland is divided into two main areas. The Carpathian Mountains, where shepherds first introduced recipes for mountain cheese, is a grazing area favored by a breed of red-colored cattle, while the black-and-white patched cows prefer the lowland area of the country, with its moderate climate. By the tenth century, Cracow and Warsaw were important trading centers where cheese, among other goods, was brought and sold to Scandinavia, Russia and western Europe. The Polish seaports played their part in the Baltic sea trade, which was dominated by the Hanseatic League of merchants.

In the nineteenth century, along the northern side of the Carpathian Mountains, the preparation of *Grojer* (Gruyère) cheese started, and later on the production of *Ser Trapistaw* (Trappist cheese).

One of the first cheese factories was started by a farmer named Daniel Jonasz in 1879. The large landowners on their own farms handled 300 liters (330 quarts) of milk daily, and cooperatively produced no less than 2-2.5 million liters (2.2-2.8 million

Name	Milk	Type	Rind	Form	Weight	% Fat content
Podhalanski	◿◿	▮	▢	brick	500 g	?
Ser Trapistaw	◿	▮	▢	loaf	1.2 kg	45
Ser Twarogowy	◿◿	○	—	varying	varying	30-42
Ser Tylzycki	◿	▮	❖	loaf	4 kg	45-50

Key to symbols on page 34. 453 g = 1 lb; 1 kg = 2.2 lbs.

BELOW: Cattle being milked by means of a mobile machine, in a meadow near Gdansk, once known as Danzig, the seaport on the Baltic Sea.

quarts) yearly, supplying cheese factories like the one founded in Wilczyce in 1901. About the same time, cooperative factories arose, offering a good price for farmer's milk. After the Second World War, during which almost half of Poland's cattle was lost, the development of collectivized agriculture lagged far behind heavy industry. In recent years, however, government efforts to make Poland into a real dairy country are having some success.

The unprofitable large estates were forced to make room for government undertakings, each with an average of fifty men, and large collective farms, comprising an average of twenty-three families. As far as modern livestock is concerned, the black-and-white cattle have remained the most important; there are also some three million sheep.

The choice of cheeses in Poland is rather limited, and cannot be compared to a country like Yugoslavia, where cheese recipes were handed down as part of the family heritage. Polish cheeses, though, are of good quality. The semihard versions of *Edam* and *Gouda* are the most common, but there are also some hard cheeses like Grojer, *Emmentalski* (Emmental), and *Cheddar*, plus a number of soft ones – *Limburski* (Limburger), *Ser Harcenski* (Harzer), *Ser Tylzycki* (Tilsiter), *Camembert*, *Brie*, and *Rokpol* (Roquefort). The shape of the semihard cheeses is sometimes different from the original.

A real Polish cheese, from the lower Carpathian Mountains, is prepared from a mixture of cow's and sheep's milk – the *Podhalanski*. It has a brick shape, moderately large holes in the paste and a solid rind. It is usually sold slightly smoked. *Ser Olsztynski* is a skimmed-milk cheese, ripened in barrels, and produced mainly for the processed cheese industry. For *Ser Solankowy*, a brine cheese, only sheep's milk is used. Kneaded cheeses are also made in Poland, as well as *Ser Twarogowy*, a fresh curd cheese with a fat content that can vary between 30 and 42 %. *Ser Turystycny*, "tourist cheese," is a well-known product, but not officially registered, and therefore the preparation differs from place to place. It is a remarkable exception, especially since the government's dairy department now centralizes cheesemaking in modern factories.

Czechoslovakia

The first mention of cheese in the area that is now Czechoslovakia was found on bills from the Brevnov monastery in Bohemia during the tenth century. The oldest known cheese was the *Homolsky*, a sour-milk type with a cone shape. In Slovakia, to the east, there is even a town called "cheese market" – Kežmarok – which had marketing rights for cheese as early as 1269. In days gone by, the cheeses were mainly made from sheep's milk by mountain shepherds, then on country estates, and toward the end of the last century by cooperative factories.

Shepherds still make mountain cheeses in Czechoslovakia. Toward the end of the lactation period in the hot summer, the *baca* (head shepherd) prepares his *Oŝtêpek*, a sheep's milk cheese with good keeping qualities, weighing between 300 and 500 g (.7 to 1.1 lbs). Made in an egg shape, the cheese has a solid to hard paste and the characteristic sheep flavor. The curd is formed while covered with the whey, and is afterwards immersed in hot water to give it a smooth surface. Finally, the cheese is put in a decorative mold, brined, then smoked above a wood fire in the shepherd's mountain hut; in three to six days the cheese becomes dark-yellow to brown. During the same period a quantity of *Parecina* is also made: a sheep's milk cheese with kneaded curd, similar to the Italian Caciocavallo – two smoked ball-shaped cheeses tied together – having an elastic consistency and a piquant, sourish taste.

Bishop's breakfast
On the high mountain pastures of Slovakia *Hrudkovy Syr* is made. The curd is loosely cut and kneaded in whey into a ball or egg shape of about 3 to 5 kg (6.6 to 11 lbs); it is then suspended in a cheese cloth to drain. After a maximum of seven days' ripening on racks built on the mountain slopes, the cheeses are sold either to passing trade or to cheese factories. The factories process the product to make a cheese called *Bryndza*. The Hrudkovy is first washed and the rind removed. It is then crumbled, salted, ground and molded, a process that makes a spreadable, slightly sour and sometimes rather salty cheese. In central and eastern Slovakia, certain microorganisms invade the paste, greatly to its advantage – the Liptauer-type *Liptovská Bryndza* cheese is

famous. Bryndza is also made of mixed sheep's and cow's milk. It is very popular spread on sandwiches, accompanied by pickled onions and beer.

Nine centuries ago Bishop John of Moravia used to breakfast on *Olmützer Quargel*, still popular today. Quargel is a short-ripened Quark mixed with a long-ripened Quark, dried for a few days at room temperature while the surface develops a mold and ferments. The flora is washed off and the Quargel ripens further in boxes, or nowadays in silos, until the rind surface has become orange-colored and a very remarkable taste has developed. The cheese is related to the German Handkäse, and is sold in bricks, discs, or in slices.

The Czechoslovakian cheese industry has progressed very rapidly in recent years and now makes about one hundred different types. Today Oŝtêpek and Parecina are produced in cheese factories as well as by shepherds, but cow's milk is used instead of sheep's milk. The reason is that sheep breeding is spread over too wide an area, and their milk production is only geared to summer months.

ABOVE: Landscape in the Riesen Gebirge near the frontiers of Poland and East Germany.

BELOW: Haymaking, a vital part of the farm economy for the coming year. Hay is a precious cattle food for the winter months ahead. A bad harvest followed by a long, severe winter, when cattle need more hay than usual, can be disastrous for the small farmer.

Name	Milk	Type	Rind	Form	Weight	% Fat content
Liptovská Bryndza	△◿	●	—	container	varies	50
Olmützer Quargel	△◿	●	—	flat disc	0.9-2 kg	varies
Oŝtêpek	△◿	◧	☐	ball	300-500 g	42-47
Parecina	△◿	■	☐	bar	varies	48

Key to symbols on page 34. 453 g = 1 lb; 1 kg = 2.2 lbs.

Hungary

With the exception of the Alps and the spurs of the Carpathians, the Hungarian republic consists of vast plains, such as the Alfold. There are fertile pastures in the wet regions, and the dry areas are covered by the treeless *puszta*, where nomads used to herd their cattle.

In the early days of the Magyars, and even later in the reign of Stephen, cattle were considered of value only as draught animals or for slaughtering; milk was not to the Hungarians' taste, and very little was made into cheese. Yet by the thirteenth century, some advance had been made toward a dairy industry. Hungarian sheep's milk cheese was being sold in the little town of Késmárk – "cheese market" – founded by German colonists. Although cheeses from cow's milk, notably *Emmental* and *Gruyère*, were made by Swiss immigrants in modern times, Hungarian cheese production only gained recognition between the two world wars.

Production continued after 1945. The farmer's standard of living considerably improved when the Hungarian Milk Industry Trust began to buy milk from the collective and government farms and to regulate cheese preparation. In Szombathely there is now a government farm with no less than 1,200 Frisian cows. All Hungarian cheese is made from pasteurized milk, and small farms have stopped production. In the meantime, the government is working toward extending cattle-breeding areas, partly by irrigating the *puszta* region. Cheese production, some of which was exported, almost doubled to 28,000 tons during the decade leading up to 1973.

The Hungarian Dairy Institute has developed a new sort of cheese, the *Teasajt* ("tea cheese"), a loaf-shaped, full-fat cheese weighing .5 kg (1.1 lb), with an ivory-colored paste, an agreeable sourish flavor and a spicy aroma. The Tilsiter-type *Ovari* is made by the same institute. *Balaton*, named after the Hungarian lake southwest of Budapest, is a large, rectangular, heavily pressed cheese, with a rather rancid but fascinating taste, due to the butter acid bacteria; it ripens (sometimes in foil, without a rind) in four weeks to become a light-yellow, firm product that melts on the tongue. *Lajta* is also a new cheese: bar-shaped, full-fat, with a semihard, smooth paste, and a white to straw-yellow

color and an orange rind. The taste is fresh, but slightly piquant.

The Caciocavallo-type *Kaskaval* is one of the traditional sheep's milk cheeses, as is a brine cheese resembling the Greek Feta. The well-known *Liptauer*, like its Czechoslovakian counterpart Liptovska Bryndza, is made from both sheep's and cow's milk. The best type of Liptauer is based on a cheese called *Gomolya*, brought in by the shepherds, to which factories add paprika. Liptauer is packed in bottles or boxes. Gomolya – also called *Tarkó* or *Turo* – is made from milk thickened over a fire, then allowed to curdle spontaneously, or with rennet, as it hangs in a cloth in the sun. This cheese is the major ingredient of the *túróscsusza* – eaten practically every day – a sort of macaroni covered with Turo, sour cream and pieces of fried bacon.

ABOVE: A shepherd of the plains, dressed in traditional costume. With him are two sheepdogs.

RIGHT: Racks of cheeses in the ripening room. These are a Hungarian version of Port-du-Salut, one of France's most widely imitated types.

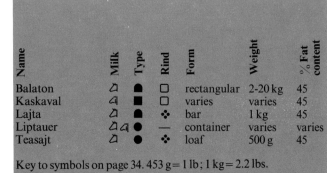

Name	Milk	Type	Rind	Form	Weight	% Fat content
Balaton	⌂	■	□	rectangular	2-20 kg	45
Kaskaval	⌂⊿	■	□	varies	varies	45
Lajta	⌂	■	❖	bar	1 kg	45
Liptauer	⌂⊿	●	—	container	varies	varies
Teasajt	⌂	●	❖	loaf	500 g	45

Key to symbols on page 34. 453 g = 1 lb; 1 kg = 2.2 lbs.

Rumania

The river Danube's course to the Black Sea shapes the border of southern Rumania, where the foothills of the Transylvanian Alps descend to the lowlands of Walachia. To the northeast is Moldavia, another fertile area; the remaining part of Rumania is mostly mountainous. Agriculture is very important, although postwar industrialization has pushed it into second place. The government farms have as much pasture as arable land. Cattle breeding has increased considerably, and large herds of milking breeds roam the great plains. Rumania has the fourth largest sheep population in Europe, after the Soviet Union, Spain and Yugoslavia.

One of Rumania's oldest cheeses is made of sheep's milk, the *Brinzâ de Burduf*, which weighs an impressive 60 kg (132 lbs). The well-pressed, ripened and ground curd is put in a specially-made sheepskin or goatskin sack called a *burduf* – hence the name of the cheese. It is sown together with raffia after being filled with the curd, which then ripens as the temperature is gradually lowered. The final product resembles a firm, somewhat crumbly, but easy-to-spread Quark. The paste is light yellow in color and strongly aromatic; the surface is gray-brown with small, green and white mold spots. *Brinzâ in Coajâ de Brad* is packed in a container of fir bark, which lends a special flavor to the cheese; it weighs from .5 to 10 kg (1.1 to 22 lbs).

Rumania also makes a plastic-curd cheese rather similar to the Italian Caciocavallo, and has been doing so since Roman times. These cheeses are each called after their district of origin, the most well-known types being *Cascaval Dobrogea* (from the steppes) and *Cascaval Penteleu* (from the Penteleu range in the Carpathians).

Rumania's most popular cheese, which used to be called after the town of Braila on the Danube, is now known as *Telemea*. Previously it was made from raw milk by small cheese factories, but the modern factories now use pasteurized sheep's milk, cow's milk or a mixture of cow's and buffalo's milk. First it ripens in containers of salted, sour whey for a month; then in a much cooler atmosphere for a year. It is sold while still in its whey. The cheese is soft, rather sour, and with a salty taste, often spiced with kummel.

Name	Milk	Type	Rind	Form	Weight	% Fat content
Brinzâ de Burduf	⌂	●	–	container	2-60 kg	45
Brinzâ in Coajâ de Brad	⌂	●	–	container	varying	45
Cascaval Penteleu	⌂	●	–	container	2-8 kg	45
Harghita	⌂	■	□	rectangular	1.5-3 kg	50
Nasal	⌂⌂	●	□	loaf	1-1.5 kg	45
Telemea	✳	●	–	cube	1 kg	42
Urdâ	⌂⌂	○	–	varying	1-3 kg	50

✳ ⌂⌂ and Buffalo

Key to symbols on page 34. 1 kg = 2.2 lbs.

Nasal ripens in cool, moist rock cellars. The cheese is washed with brine, and its thin, pliant, grayish-yellow rind is sprinkled with gypsum powder before the cheese is packed. Made from cow's and/or sheep's milk, the paste is very lightly colored and deliciously spicy, with a soft to solid consistency. *Harghita* sheep cheese, named after the mountain range, has only been made since 1960. It is a rectangular-shaped cheese with a cream-white paste and a brownish-yellow rind; a pure culture of butter acid bacteria gives it a strong aroma. *Urdâ* is a sort of Ricotta, unsalted, and eaten fresh with dill. It is made from the whey that remains after preparation of Brinzâ and Telemea cheeses.

The state cheese industry also produces some foreign types, and Rumanian cheese consumption increases in pace with rising exports.

ABOVE: Although cattle breeding is done on a large scale, and collective farms have been established, many isolated small holdings remain.

BELOW: Protection against the extreme cold of a Carpathian winter: a shepherd tending his flock.

ABOVE: A beautiful example of folk art from the churchyard in the small village of Maramures.

Bulgaria

In ancient times Bulgaria was peopled by the Thracians, then by the Romans, who maintained trade routes across the Black Sea. Among the many commodities exchanged was cheese, and it has remained an important product. The country has two cheese regions, separated by the Balkan Mountains – the fertile plateau of the north and the well-irrigated plains of the Marica in the south. In former times both regions produced mainly sheep's milk cheeses. *Kâskaval*, probably introduced by the Romans, was the most important; before the sixteenth century it was prepared in mountain huts and exported to Turkey, Egypt and Palestine. It had to be a hard cheese with good keeping qualities. There are now two types: *Balkanski Kâskaval* from the highlands, and the smaller *Polubalkanski Kâskaval*, or *Demi-Balkan*, from the lowlands. In the 1930s the mountain cheesemakers modernized their technique considerably, but they still begin with raw sheep's milk. After the curdling, the curd is turned with a sort of hoe and cut with the *lira*, a lyre-shaped cutter. It is then thoroughly stirred, for the whey must have a chance to drain in order to produce a dry cheese. After a prepressing in the cheese vat, the curd receives a "cheddaring" treatment and is kneaded to form a round ball, which is then rubbed with dry salt and ripened in a damp place for 50 to 60 days. For the first few weeks it is turned daily and cleaned with brine; it is turned for a final time just before paraffining or packing in transparent foil. Preferably, the cheese should not become older than ten months, as the gradual decomposition of the milk fat can cause a burning taste. It has a flat, cylindrical shape with a nice, smooth, amber-colored rind and a yellow paste with very few holes. The taste is just sourish and somewhat salty, the aroma piquant. The Demi-Balkan is 8 cm (about 3 in) high compared to the 11-13 cm (about 4-5 in) of the Balkanski Kâskaval. The most important difference is that the Demi-Balkan has a higher moisture content and a slightly lower fat content. *Kâskaval Vitoscha* is related to the previous types, but has a much less pronounced taste and aroma. It is made of cow's milk, and has a striking amber color and a tough consistency.

LEFT: A cow grazes by a field of maize and its peasant owner spins wool, provided by her flock of sheep. The people of the farming communities in these remote regions are almost entirely self-supporting.

Name	Milk	Type	Rind	Form	Weight	% Fat content
Balkanski Kâskaval	◿	■	▢	low cylinder	9 kg	50
Demi-Balkan	◿	◣	▢	low cylinder	7 kg	48
Sirene	◿◿	◣	—	container	0.5-100 kg	46

Key to symbols on page 34. 1 kg = 2.2 lbs.

A salty preference

By far the most popular, or most produced, of Bulgarian cheese types is *Bjalo Salamureno Sirene*. Commonly known as *Sirene* cheese, it represents 75% of total production. There are two types, distinguished not by size but by national character. The Bulgarians themselves prefer the Sirene made of pasteurized sheep's milk, a semihard cheese, kept in brine in the wooden or tin containers in which it ripens. Farmers, as well as cheese factories, produce it. The cheese has no rind, and the paste is white, without holes, often rather crumbly, lightly sour and somewhat salty, with the characteristic sheep's milk flavor. Most visitors to Bulgaria seem to prefer the cow's milk Sirene, which has a blander taste and a more solid consistency.

BELOW: Flocks of sheep are an inevitable part of any Balkan landscape, as here in the vicinity of a small church near Samokov, in the Rhodope Mountains.

LEFT: A familiar postage-stamp subject in predominantly agricultural communities – a milking scene.

Soviet Union

The Union of Soviet Socialist Republics is a seemingly endless series of lowlands, much of it infertile tundra, surrounded by mountain ranges like the Caucasus, the Crimea and the Carpathians. The south and the southwest of the European part are especially fertile, and cheese has been made there since prehistoric times, both in the lowlands and on the mountain slopes. Archeological excavations in Trans-Caucasia have unearthed primitive cheese molds, and near Jerewan an ancient cheese dairy has been dug up, complete with basalt barrels for souring the milk. About 700 B.C., prehistoric Russia was conquered by the Scythians, who were already trading with the Greeks. Scenes including Scythians appear on Hellenic vases. Herodotus, the Greek historian, tells about their love for horses, and indicates that they made cheese from the milk of their mares, drying it on spear points. The beginning of the ninth century A.D. brought the Swedish Vikings from the north, who also brought with them a Scandinavian speciality – cheese.

Though the Soviet Union is now probably the biggest agricultural

ABOVE: Tadjikstan shepherd in the mountain area near the Afghanistan border.

BELOW: A rare picture of a Soviet cheese shop. This one is in Armenia, and features the very popular Jerevansky cheese.

producer and the third largest cattle land in the world, cattle breeding was for a long time subordinated to the growing of crops, and the preparation of cheese remained primitive. In recent years, however, the country's official food policy has switched intentionally, and swiftly, from emphasizing starchy foods to promoting foods rich in animal proteins, including cheese.

How Gouda became Tilsit

The country's most famous cheese, and the most imitated, is the *Tilsiter*, or *Tilsit*, which originated in East Prussia. It was created accidentally by a Dutch woman in the city of Tilsit in the nineteenth century. Like many Dutch cheesemakers, she made Gouda cheeses, but in this particular case the cellar in which they were stored was too damp. Her cheeses turned soft and sharp, and cracked. A new cheese was born. At that time it was made from raw milk, usually of a low fat content, and spiced with kummel – perhaps the most popular flavoring in the whole of Europe, other than caraway seeds. Under an orange rind flora caused by brine washings, there developed a

BELOW: A version of Jerevansky is Chanakh cheese, here floating in a brine bath. It has a really sharp flavor.

ABOVE: Chanakh cheeses being carefully tested before leaving the factory.

piquant paste, which took some five months to mature. The modern Tilsit is considerably milder; pasteurized milk is used in the mechanized preparation, and the ripening time is usually shorter. It is a firm but smooth cheese, ranging from 30 to 50% fat, and made in the form of a loaf or a cartwheel, still possessing the familiar cracks in the paste, a few round holes here and there, and a full, savory flavor with a slightly sourish aftertaste.

The eastern Baltic Sea areas produce more good cheeses. The Latvian whole-milk *Latvysky Syr*, for example, is treated with a strong brine, and after two months of moist ripening it shows the correct flora on its sticky rind. Similar to this cheese are the Volga cheeses: *Volzky Syr*, in block form, and the much sharper-tasting *Pikantnyj Syr*.

Desertny Syr has a very light-colored paste, completely free from holes, and a rind with only a trace of orange-red flora. During its eight to ten days' ripening, it is sprayed with *Penicillium candidum*. Other washed cheeses include the lean, rather crumbly *Salduskyj Syr* with its irregular little holes and the more solid *Syr Rambinas*, a bitter-piquant type from which, after ripening, the flora is scraped away. The cheeses are packed in drums, where they can be kept for about three months.

The Soviet Union also makes Camembert-like cheeses with a white rind flora, such as *Zakusocnyj Syr*

and *Desertny Bely*, but hard cheese types are much more general. They often resemble Emmental, and their names indicate the mountain regions of their origin: *Moskoyskyj Syr, Kubansky Syr, Karpatsky Syr, Altajsky Syr* or *Sovjetsky*. The rindless *Gollandsky Syr* (Edam type) and *Stepnoj Syr* (Gouda type) enjoy a traditional, centuries-old popularity.

Kneaded or plastic curd cheeses include *Kav Kazsky Syr* and *Južny i Syr*; brine cheeses are *Sulguni* and *Cecil*. The last is an odd Armenian cheese made from cow's or sheep's milk with a very low fat content – at most 10% – acidified with sour whey, sour milk or yogurt. After curdling, the large flakes that arise from heating are kneaded by hand, until the curd can be plaited into thick threads and then into spirals, balls or rolls.

Motal is a cheese seldom made in the factory, being a typical kolkhoz (collective farm) cheese. It ripens for three or four months in a tube of sewn-up goatskin. A related type is the Armenian *Daralagjazsky Syr* with its crumbly curd, made of sheep's or goat's milk, or often both. It shares with Motal the addition of salt and herbs – garlic and thyme – worked into the curd. The ripening takes place in leather bags or in stone bottles covered with earth.

A very well-known, semihard, Armenian brine cheese is *Jerevansky Syr*. It ripens in tins which, during the first two months, are sealed with a rubber plug in the lid, which is removed to allow regular topping off with brine. Another semihard cheese, also from Armenia, is *Telpanir*, comparable to the Turkish *Tel Peynir*. *Gornoaltajsky Syr* is a really hard cheese from the Altai Mountains. Made from raw sheep's milk, its orange-red smear is regularly washed off, and the rind is finally dried. Sometimes the cheese is smoked, when it becomes almost as hard as its mountain home, but it is excellent for grating and has a piquant, nutty, smoky flavor.

The Russians enjoy their fresh cheese, often mixing it with sugar, nuts, jelly or chocolate. The Armenians are connoisseurs of cheeses, and are fond of their sharp Jerevansky, a cheese that regularly provides farmers and shepherds with their midday snacks in the fields.

Name	Milk	Type	Rind	Form	Weight	% Fat content
Cecîl	⌂⌲	■	—	varying	varying	10
Daralagjazsky Syr	⌲⌲	■	—	container	varying	25
Desertny Syr	⌂	●	❖	cylinder	varying	50
Gornoaltajsky Syr	⌲	■	❖□	cylinder	8-10 kg	45
Jerevansky Syr	✳	■	—	rectangular, cylinder	4-6 kg	50
Kavkazsky syr	⌂	■	□	cylinder	8-10 kg	45
Latvysky Syr	⌂	■	❖	cube	2-2.5 kg	45
Sovjetsky Syr	⌂	■	□	rectangular	12-16 kg	50
Syr Rambinas	⌂	●	❖	hexagonal	0.8-1.2 kg	30
Tilsit	⌂	■	❖	loaf, cartwheel	2.5-5 kg	45

✳ ⌂⌲⌲

Key to symbols on page 34. 1 kg = 2.2 lbs.

Intensive dairy farming

ABOVE: The map shows the distribution of intensive dairy farming over the American continents and illustrates the relatively low importance of this type of economic activity, especially in Latin America. Cheese production is concentrated in the Dairy Belt along the Great Lakes (notably in Wisconsin and New York State) and along the St. Lawrence River in Canada.

CANADA

Ottawa Montreal
New York
Washington

San Francisco

Los Angeles

UNITED STATES

ATLANTIC OCEAN

MEXICO

La Habana

Ciudad de Mexico

CUBA

JAMAICA   HAITI

PUERTO RICO

GUATEMALA
EL SALVADOR

HONDURAS

NICARAGUA

COSTA RICA   Panama

PANAMA   Bogotá

Caracas
VENEZUELA

GUYANA
SURINAM
FRENCH GUYANA

COLOMBIA

Quito

ECUADOR

BRAZIL

PERU
Lima

BOLIVIA
La Paz

Brasilia

PACIFIC OCEAN

PARAGUAY

Rio de Janeiro

São Paulo
Asunción

CHILE
Santiago

URUGUAY
Montevideo

Buenos Aires
ARGENTINA

THE AMERICAS

ABOVE: Both American continents have a vast wealth of cattle and sheep, both meat and dairy breeds, that are vital to their economy. Cow's milk cheeses are popular in Canada and the USA, where Cheddar types are well established, while South American countries prefer varieties of fresh cheese, known collectively as *Queso fresco*.

Canada

Ignore Canada's climate for a moment, to consider the vast area of fertile acres occupying the northern half of the American continent. There are great opportunities for agriculture and cattle breeding, especially in those areas between the Rocky Mountains, along the Pacific Ocean, and the spurs of the Appalachians in the southeast. Now add the harsh, almost Arctic climate that affects practically the entire country during the winter months. In the east, where the warm Gulf Stream brings a mild, wet climate, conditions are more favorable than in the west. Along the southern border the cattle can remain outside the whole year round, but elsewhere in the country the grazing season runs from May to the end of October at the latest.

From the early days of French colonization in the sixteenth century, Old World cattle were imported, not always with great success. Today, however, the Canadian milk herds are the result of successful breeding with Norman-British cows, shipped to New France in 1669 by the statesman Colbert. In 1783 the English arrived, along with numerous other European immigrants who dispersed northwards. By 1851 Quebec had almost 300,000 cows, and Ontario a similar number. *Cheddar*, under English influence, became the most important type of cheese, and remained so. It was originally made on the settlers' farms for their own use or for sale in the surrounding districts.

Cheese factories only appeared in the second half of the last century. In 1864 the farmhouse cheesemaker Harvey Farrington founded the first cheese factory in Ontario; three years later there were two hundred.

The biggest cheese in the world
It became increasingly clear that the economic condition of the frequently impoverished dairy farmer could be improved by stimulating the demand for milk, and with it the sale of cheese. When plans for the Chicago World's Fair of 1893 were being made, Canadian authorities decided to give Ontario international fame as a cheese area by making a monster ten-ton Cheddar, using 103,000 liters (113,300 quarts) of milk. Mighty Cheddars were not exactly unknown – one was made for the wedding of Queen Victoria – but this was the

ABOVE: Lake O'Hara in the Cathedral Mountains. Vast areas are unspoiled, natural landscapes of breath-taking beauty, where only a relatively small proportion of the land is suitable for human settlement.

ABOVE: Portrait of a prize dairy cow, painted perhaps by a cheesemaker as skilled with the brush as with the milking pail.

largest, and of record size until the Wisconsin cheesemakers produced one of seventeen tons for the 1964 New York World's Fair. The Ontario cheese was made in the Government Dairy Produce Testing Station at Perth, and the curd was supplied by fifteen different factories. A gigantic steel cheese mold was designed; a method for reaching the required pressure of 200 tons was carefully calculated; and a solution was found for turning the huge cheese.

After ripening through the winter, the Cheddar, led by the local band, was ready to begin its procession to Chicago. The first part of the journey saw the cheese conveyed on a reinforced wagon pulled by trained horses, and then the journey was continued by special train, applauded by a great crowd all the way. When it was unloaded at the exhibition site, it fell straight through the floor!

For six months, during the summer, the awesome cheese stood in a glass-roofed hall, in anything but an ideal temperature – truly an object of wonder to the fair's visitors. It was eventually bought by an English tea importer, Thomas Lipton, who

LEFT: Cheese is one of the protein body-builders, and a sensible part of the daily diet.

shipped it to Liverpool, where it was found to have deteriorated. Yet when the cheese factor Arthur Rowson inspected it later, he found – to everyone's surprise – that it had recovered completely, all but a top layer of 30 cm (about 12 in), in the fresh English air. A London restaurateur then took it over, and the gigantic cheese made yet another triumphal procession behind eight horses, and was finally cut into pieces with garden spades. Part of the cheese was sent back to Canada, with the compliments of the restaurateur. The two-year-old cheese still tasted delicious for all its adventures.

Variety cheese

Canadian Cheddar is made from non-pasteurized milk, which gives it a strong, full flavor in addition to the pithy aroma of English farmhouse Cheddar. Most of the export cheese is made from raw milk, but pasteurized milk is also widely used.

The Canadian government promoted the high quality of the product by giving premiums to good manufacturers and dairy farmers, and by subsidizing the improvement of cheese factories. Even during the Second World War, in spite of the U-boat menace, Canada provided England with large quantities of Cheddar. At present, however, export is much lower. The active immigration policy of the government has brought emigrants from many European countries; a population that has

Name	Milk	Type	Rind	Form	Weight	% Fat content
Cheddar	⟁	■	□	cylinder, rectangular	18-41 kg	48
Oka	⟁	◖	□	flat disc	0.5-2 kg	45
Richelieu	⟁	◖	❖	brick	1.82 kg	50

Key to symbols on page 34. 1 kg = 2.2 lbs.

BELOW: With a cheese iron, a core of cheese is removed and subjected to various tests. Texture, elasticity, smell and taste are among the qualities examined by the grader.

grown from five to twenty million people since 1900 can easily consume all its own cheese.

The immigrant farmers tried to make the same cheese as that of their original homeland, usually without complete success because of the different soil conditions, climate and milk. Neither could they learn from each other's experience, due to the isolation of each homestead. However, they did manage to make good cheeses, which in some ways resembled the originals, while others being made became new Canadian cheese types. Their number has now risen to forty-nine, under the collective name of *Variety Cheese*. One of these, *Oka*, rather like Port-du-Salut, is made at the Trappist monastery of the same name near Montreal. The cheese has a very mild aroma and a softly piquant flavor; it is made, they say, from a secret recipe smuggled out of France! In Canada and the United States the demand for this cheese far exceeds the supply, but the monks refuse to increase production, and nobody has yet succeeded in making a passable imitation.

The Italian Bel Paese cheese is a different story. In Canada it is called *Richelieu*, an exclusive product of very fresh, sweet milk, with a fat content of 3.8-4%. Twenty-four years of research and experiments were needed to find the ideal recipe. The body is Brie-like, soft, melting and creamy, the rind washed but hardly reddish.

Most of the Variety Cheeses have poor keeping qualities; consequently, factories must be located close to the large population centers, where milk is relatively expensive. Furthermore, supplies of winter milk are limited. Another factor adversely affecting production is that most immigrants prefer the genuine cheeses from their homeland, which are imported at prices below that of their Canadian descendants. The result is that many Variety Cheese makers have ceased production. Half of the sixty remaining factories, however, have begun to profit from the sudden popularity of pizza, for which a lot of *Mozzarella* is needed. Variety Cheese consumption is increasing again, with the annual per capita average jumping from 4.3 to 7.5 kg (9.5 to 16.5 lbs) in the last ten years. This includes *Cottage Cheese* and the processed cheeses that are also made in Canada.

United States

The discoverers of the New World found no familiar livestock – neither sheep, cows nor goats – to supply their milk, meat and cheese, and later settlers were obliged to import their own animals. They did, however, find tobacco, potatoes, tomatoes, maize and turkeys, so there were some compensations. The imported cattle became of vital importance as draught animals, and providers of the necessary commodities. From 1611, the English established cattle at Jamestown; the Dutch in New Netherlands brought their own cattle, probably Frisians; while the Scandinavians brought their large, yellow-colored animals to their American settlements. These various breeds were crossed as a matter of necessity, and after a while little could be traced of their original characteristics. Careful breeding was impossible during the early pioneering days, when man and beast had to fight for survival under the most primitive conditions. Many animals failed to live through the harsh winters, when not enough food was available and the cattle were generally in poor condition.

In spite of the difficulties, the settlers made several varieties of cheese, mainly Cheddar, according to the methods of their home country. In 1650, New England could meet its own requirements in butter and cheese and traded with the surplus. But it was not until long after the War of Independence that radical improvements in agriculture, stock breeding and dairying were made. Improvements were essential, for in the nineteenth century cities expanded at such a rate that the demand for meat and dairy products rose steeply.

The pioneer cheesemakers
Although cheese was made by methods long established in Europe, the colonists' equipment was fairly primitive. The limited milk yield was an additional problem. Milk had to be kept for a few days until there was enough to make one cheese. The farmer's wife warmed the milk above a fire and suspended in it a strip of calf's stomach which, being impregnated with rennet, curdled the milk. The whey was then drained off, and the curd cut and divided with a knife, before being pressed under stone weights. When gas began to form in the paste, due to the action of bacteria,

ABOVE: A herd of dairy cattle grazing in a Vermont meadow. Vermont is in the Dairy Belt which stretches across part of New England and includes the Great Lakes region. Milk and milk products readily find consumer markets in the nearby big cities on the Eastern Seaboard, and other towns as well.

LEFT: Dairy farm in Virginia. Cows are usually kept in open stables where they can move about. The doors may remain open overnight, to give the cattle freedom of movement. This appears to increase the milk yield.

LEFT: Originally, all cattle were imported from Europe, from which today's American breeds have descended.

the cheese became inflated and had to be pricked to allow the gas to escape. If inflation continued, the cheese was thrown away or given to the pigs. Cheese which did not rise during or after the first months could be kept for a year or more, and be transported as well.

Cowboys and cooperatives

In the nineteenth century, two entirely different types of establishments developed in American cattle farming. Around the large population centers lived farmers who endeavored to produce a large milk yield and who carefully selected, fed and tended their cows, sometimes keeping them in stables throughout the year. But in the endless prairies were the ranches with their enormous herds bred for meat production, semiwild longhorn cows, driven by cowboys over great distances to the slaughterhouses or railway stations. The rough prairie grass was good enough for this kind of cattle; they were barely looked after and were of no importance for dairy production. With a view to increasing the value and character of the herds, breeders formed cooperatives, scientifically concentrating on the improvement of stock. The same development occurred in dairy cattle farming, stimulated by the activities of the dairy industry. Danish, Guernsey, Ayrshire, New Hampshire, Frisian and brown Swiss cows were ordered from Europe, and were no longer crossbred, except if it proved beneficial to the milk yield. Goat's cheese was made in Colorado and California, for which Swiss Saanen and Toggenburg goats were imported.

Founding the factories

Initially, farmhouse cheesemaking had a fundamental, hit-or-miss approach. All this was to change with the establishment of the first cheese factories in the nineteenth century. The first were in New York State, where enterprising, professionally knowledgeable farmers processed the milk from many farms. An enterprising farmer named Jesse Williams of Rome, N.Y., who had a reputation for making high-quality cheese, began the trend when he decided to process the milk from the farm of one of his sons, in addition to that from his own farm. Gradually, more and more farmers supplied him with their milk, which Williams made into cheeses of the usual high standard. His business expanded, and the "American way of dairying" spread along the East Coast and elsewhere. By 1882, when most European countries were installing their first cheese factories, America already had 3,000 units.

Another nineteenth-century development, which was to encourage the changeover from traditional farmhouse methods to large-scale factory production, was the revolutionary improvement in transport facilities. Better roads, new waterways and the first railways linked the countryside with the large population centers. Milk products were among the goods that could now travel longer distances, to reach the growing towns where, due to the influx of immigrants, there was great demand. Farms which made cheese for local consumption were thus supplemented by cheese factories producing large quantities for the growing markets. New York remained the biggest dairy-producing state until well into the twentieth century, but from the 1860s Wisconsin, with its ideal climate for keeping cattle and growing fodder, was proving strong competition.

In 1845 Swiss colonists founded the Wisconsin village of New Glarus. Various types of cheese were made in the traditional way from the milk of their brown cows, but exclusively for their own consumption. Later, they overcame their prejudice against large-scale factory-made cheeses, which by then were of a better and more stable quality. The Italians, too, made their traditional cheeses; the French produced dessert cheeses; and the Scandinavians and the Dutch followed suit, making versions of their national cheese types. Indeed, so much cheese was produced in Wisconsin that the market could not cope. Worse, the cheese factors in the large cities did not have sufficient storage space to keep the increasing stock. Cheese prices tumbled, but with the establishing of the Dairy Board of Trade in 1873, steps were taken to ensure that distribution would be properly channeled.

In the early 1890s some American cheesemakers had tried to increase their profits by skimming the milk before making the cheese, reconstituting the fat content by adding cheaper fat. The quality deterioration did not

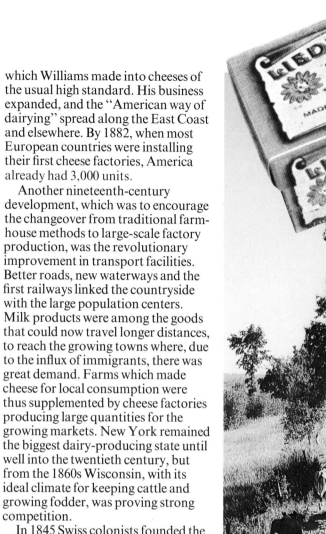

LEFT: One of America's finest cheeses is Liederkranz, the trade name of a soft cheese with a red smear on the rind. It is closely related to the German Limburger types, but the taste is much milder. When it is allowed to ripen fully – the condition preferred by most connoisseurs – the taste is finely piquant and the aroma full.

CENTER: American cattle have been declining in numbers over recent years, but the yield per animal is increasing.

ABOVE: A box of American Camembert, the famous cheese that originated in Normandy.

escape the attention of foreign buyers, and exports collapsed. In 1895 an act was passed that forbade the making of cheese with alien fat (or "filled cheese," as it was known), and determined an easily recognizable shape for a skimmed milk cheese, but the damage had been done. Canada had already taken over the export markets opened by the United States, and has remained the larger cheese exporter.

American cheese production gradually recovered, helped by the first American Dairy School at the University of Wisconsin, where future cheesemakers received a scientific training, and where an extensive network of contacts both at home and abroad was built up.

Despite setbacks, the American dairy industry developed into an important branch of the economy. The number of cheese factories is declining, but those remaining process larger quantities of milk and, with the aid of refrigerated transport, the supply can be gathered from far afield. Additionally, production can be adjusted to fluctuations in public taste and demand by the so-called "flexible plants," which can produce a variety of cheese types. Although the numbers of dairy cattle have been declining for many years, total milk production is steadily increasing. This is because the milk yield per animal is still rising – as it should in view of the fact that the average yield per cow in the United States is well below the milk yield in many countries.

This discrepancy might seem odd in a country famous for having introduced the milk shake, and for having championed ice cream. Less surprising is the fact that America has pioneered several new cheese types, the most original being a space-age variety with the appropriate name of *Nuworld*, a veined cheese where the marbling is white instead of the usual greenish-blue. This effect was achieved by subjecting the cheese to ultraviolet radiation during processing, producing a white cheese with a blue-cheese taste. In spite of a promising start, it was found that the anaemic Nuworld was both expensive to make and, therefore, difficult to market. Cheesemakers are undoubtedly still on the threshold of discoveries, and when the next new cheese appears it will probably have been developed in America.

All cheeses designated by the collective name *American Cheese* belong to the Cheddar family. Herkimer County in New York was the cradle, but today Wisconsin is the Cheddar state. The descendants of the old British aristocrat with its severe cylinder shape have diversified into any number of types or "styles," as the saying goes: large wheels, small wheels, tall cylinders or flat discs, bars and barrels, bricks and cubes, sausage and pineapple shapes. There is unpackaged cheese, or cheese packed in transparent plastic, in cartons; or in glazed or earthenware pots. One can choose from cheese without a rind or with a rind; from colors ranging from white or ivory to yellow or orange. There are hard and soft American cheeses, mild and sharp, neutral and spiced, not to mention those flavored with cumin, pimento, sage or port.

In principle, the old English recipe is still followed, characterized by the cheddaring process which makes the warm curd particles stick together. This takes place either in the modern cheddar tower, or in the cheesemaking vat during the preparation of the curd, which is raked to the sides of the vat and packed together to form a fibrous mass there. Subsequently the curd is milled, slated and pressed.

Long-hold, short-hold

There is long-hold or so-called export Cheddar, a cheese with a low moisture content which becomes nicely sharp in taste after one year's maturation. Because of its closed body it is very good for packing in portions. In addition there is a domestic or home-trade Cheddar with a slightly more moist and softer body, which is ready for consumption after six months. The traditional cylinder-shaped Cheddar weighs 30 to 40 kg (66 to 88 lbs); the *Mammoth* weighs at least 50 kg (110 lbs) and is the largest version apart from the uncontested champion called the *Barrel*, which comes in a round metal vat or rectangular carton. Barrel can weigh up to 300 kg (660 lbs), but it is sold in pieces to avoid your having to carry it home! Smaller cheeses, all with cylindrical shapes, are: the *Daisy*, 10-11 kg (22-24.2 lbs); the *Longhorn*, 6 kg (13.2 lbs); the *Flat* or *Twins*, two cheeses of 15-16 kg (33-35 lbs) in one box; the *Young American*, 5 kg (11 lbs), sometimes packed in quartets;

the *Picnic*, 5 kg (11 lbs); the block-shaped *Rindless Cheddar*, 20 kg (44 lbs). There are also a number of loaf cheeses.

The method of preparation is, of course, more important than the shape. The pronounced taste of *Washed Curd Cheese* is due to a procedure discovered in New York. By thoroughly washing the curd with cold water, the moisture content of the cheese increases, and it therefore matures more quickly. It develops the character of a mature Cheddar, but does not have the long-keeping quality

BELOW: The largest milking stations are found in the United States. Hundreds of cows stand in stables and are milked mechanically, in keeping with the modern systems of automation. Cleaning the stables, preparing the silage, feeding the cows, everything is mechanized. Such techniques are necessary to meet the increasing demand for American cheeses.

ABOVE: An isolated dairy farm in Virginia. The first English cattle were imported to Jamestown, Virginia, in 1611.

LEFT: The constant supply of food for cattle, especially during the winter, is a major concern of dairy farmers. These cows are being fed with corn silage, a cattle food equal to hay.

BELOW: An attractive display of American cheeses. From left to right: Cream Cheese (foreground), Port-Salut, and a domestic Parmesan sitting on top of a Cheddar. In front is a round, processed Cheddar and some grated Parmesan, and an American Cheese (with knife) sitting on top of another domestic Parmesan.

one might expect. This is another variety that is being made in long-hold and short-hold types.

Colby Cheese, first made in 1882 in Colby Township, Wisconsin, is washed in exactly the same way as Washed Curd Cheese, but it is not cheddared. Because of its higher moisture content it is ready after three or four weeks, and isn't a cheese for keeping. It has a granular, soft and somewhat porous consistency with a creamy to deep-yellow color; it is very popular because of its mildness, and is often used in snacks and salads. A closely related cheese is *Stirred Curd* or *Granular Cheese*, neither of which has a cheddared curd.

The Californian *Monterey* or *Jack* is similar to Colby but is creamy white and softer, with more holes, or eyes. The cheese was copied from an old monks' recipe, and marketed by David Jacks since 1916. Today the designation "Jack" only refers to Monterey with an extra-high moisture content, also known as *High Moisture Jack*, an excellent basis for Mexican dishes. In addition, there is a very dry, easily grated variety, the *Grating-Type Monterey*.

BELOW: A dessert special – Cottage Cheese fills a canta-loupe melon, and is decorated with other fruits.

Endless variety
The list of Cheddar derivations is virtually endless, but here are a few more: *Smoked Cheese* is smoked over smoldering wood, or flavored artificially with smoke salts or liquids. *Spiced Cheese* is Cheddar with herbs or spices added. *Pineapple* is a pine-apple-shaped cheese from Litchfield County, Connecticut, which matures in nets for several months and is rubbed with oil, shellacked or waxed so that it acquires a hard, shiny exterior. *Herkimer* is the New York Cheddar variety which today is made only in limited quantities; unlike most related cheeses it is pure white with a sharp taste.

Unusual Cheddars are thus plentiful in America. The original type has probably remained the most popular – the ordinary orange-yellow slice, grilled between two slices of bread, or melted on a hamburger. But American Cheddar is more affectionately wedded to that homely companion, apple pie.

Cottage Cheese

The average American eats 8.5 kg (18.7 lbs) of cheese per year, of which 3.6 is Cheddar; the central place of American Cheese in culinary practice is indicated by these facts. The next favorite is the famous American *Cottage Cheese*, of which each American consumes no less than 2.4 kg (5.3 lbs) per year.

There are several highly popular types of Cottage Cheese in the United States. *Acid Curd Cottage Cheese*, made without rennet, has a fresh, butter acid aroma and a smooth texture. In the Eastern states it used to be very well known as *New York* or *Country Style*, but it has now largely been displaced by *Sweet Curd Cottage Cheese*. This is prepared with rennet and has a very mild smell and taste. It is marketed under names like *California, Frisco, Popcorn* or *Flake Cheese*. *Creamed Cottage Cheese* carefully excludes undesirable bacteria and is mixed with 4% salted cream before packing; it is often enriched with vegetables or fruit. *Whipped Cream Cottage Cheese*, with a fat content of 8% due to the addition of whipped cream, is tenable for only a short time because of the bacteria present in the air. If stored for too long, whey sometimes separates off. In the matured type of *Pennsylvania Dutch*, white mold spores are added on purpose.

The factor that has made these fresh granular cheeses so popular – apart from their many uses in the kitchen – is undoubtedly their high protein content and low calory count. They have an established place in most slimming diets. Cottage Cheese keeps well in the refrigerator and can also be frozen. Thawing should be done slowly and carefully.

A cheese which bears a close resemblance to Cottage Cheese is *Bakers' Cheese*, a low-fat variety with finer granules, more moisture and a sourer taste. It is generally used in cheese pastry.

A. The first stage of Creamed Cottage Cheese production is pasteurization of the low-fat germ-free milk. The milk must also be free of any smell of stable or fodder. To be pasteurized, it is passed through thin pipes or between thin plates which are encased in a water jacket. Every particle of milk must be heated to 72°C (162°F) for at least 15 seconds.

B. 5-6% starter (lactic acid or other acids) is added, and if desired some rennet and clot-promoting calcium chloride. The temperature of the milk should be 32°C (90°F). At this point – which determines the final quality of the grains – the curd is cut into small cubes (upper vat in the illustration). Heated to about 52°C (126°F), it reaches its proper firmness while the whey is being drained off. The curd is then washed a few times in cold water (middle vat) to reduce the acid flavor. Finally, salted cream is mixed with the soft, granular curd (lower vat).

C. The cheese is ready and is transferred to the filling apparatus. It may be non-creamed, in which case only dry salt is mixed in. In the slightly different long-set or modified method, coagulation time is longer because it takes place at a lower temperature, and less starter is used.

D. Plastic cups and lids are stacked to pass automatically under the funnel-shaped end of the machine.

E. The packaged cheese is immediately taken to a cold storage room, from where it is distributed.

total production U.S. cheese 1,410,000 tons p.a. (100%)

production Creamed Cottage Cheese 43,400 tons p.a. (3.1%) of which exported virtually nothing

RIGHT: In contrast to the large automated milk stations, there are still many farms that stick to the old, traditional ways.

Among the remaining varieties of cheeses consumed in America, accounting for almost 30 % of the total consumption, the mild, fresh, rich *Cream Cheese* is one of the most popular.

When, after 1880, Cream Cheese factories spread out from New York all over the country, the production underwent a revolutionary change due to the invention of the separator. This device made it possible to separate the whey immediately from the hot "Cream Cheese mix" (a mixture of cream and milk) and to pack the curd hot. The maximum storage time of the end product was doubled by this "hot-pack" method to 60 days. There are nevertheless some factories which retain the earlier "cold-pack" method, because the aroma of the cheese is fuller and its consistency less cohesive. Quite often spices or other flavorings

ABOVE: In the south, extensive cattle farming for meat is much more common than dairying. Vast herds graze the prairies; the cowboy and his horse have yet to be supplanted by a more efficient method of herding; so far, none has been found.

are added to Cream Cheese.

Neufchatel Cheese, which is made according to the French example, resembles Cream Cheese but contains more moisture and less fat. This causes it to taste more sour, although there is no difference in acidity. Unlike the French, Americans usually employ the "hot-pack" method for this cheese too. Another difference is that the Americans like it fresh, while the French prefer it ripened, with white surface molds – like Camembert.

Cold Pack Cheese, or *Potted Cheese,* is a fine, smooth mixture of one or more cheese types ground together. The components, principally well-aged high-quality Cheddar, are stated on the plastic or earthenware pot. It may be prepared with vinegar or some other acid, salt, spices, herbs or other flavorings such as wine or port.

Name	Milk	Type	Rind	Form	Weight	% Fat content
American Cheese (Cheddar)	◿	■	□	varying	varying	50
Brick	◿	●	❖	brick	2.5 kg	50
Colby	◿	■	□	varying	varying	50
Cottage Cheese	◿	○	—	container	220-900 g	0.4
Cream Cheese	◿	○	—	varying	100 g	73
Liederkranz	◿	●	❖	rectangular	175 g	50
Monterey	◿	■	□	rectangular; cartwheel	200-500 g; 3-4 kg	50

Key to symbols on page 34. 453 g = 1 lb; 1 kg = 2.2 lbs.

Cheeses with character

The growing demand for soft cheeses which have undergone surface ripening is striking. The statement that America's cheese preferences are determined more by size or package than by taste is denied by the popularity of their *Camembert, Brie, Bel Paese, Munster, Port-Salut, Limburger, Brick* and *Liederkranz.* The latter two are considered American originals. Brick was made in Wisconsin as early as 1875. It has a reddish-brown, somewhat dried-out crust, and an ivory-colored paste which is softer and easier to cut than Cheddar, but firmer than Limburger. Brick has a mellow, stimulating aroma and a rather sweet taste which is easy to distinguish from both Cheddar and Limburger – being less sharp than the first, less strong than the second. It has numerous irregularly spread holes. After a few months' curing, and if the flavor is sufficiently well developed, the cheese is cut into pieces of varying size or packed in slices.

The robust Liederkranz (the trade name for a very mild, Limburger-type cheese) with its golden-yellow, creamy, almost melting paste was developed in 1892 after years of experiment. It was an imitation of the Bismarck Schlosskäse which could not be imported in any real quantity, and many connoisseurs praise it more highly than the original.

Finally there are many versions of foreign cheeses, including the blue-veined types *(Blue, Gorgonzola, Stilton),* Italian cheeses *(Parmesan, Romano, Provolone, Mozzarella, Pizza cheese),* Dutch cheeses *(Edam, Gouda),* Swiss specialities *(Emmental, Gruyère)* and various whey cheeses *(Gjetost, Sapsago* and *Ricotta).*

No country has a better market for processed cheese than the United States, but this kind of cheese (as opposed to "natural" cheese), will be dealt with in a separate section (see pp. 227-228).

American cheeses are rarely sold whole as "bulk cheese," but are usually packaged by the producer and sold in small sacks, boxes, cartons, tins, etc. This could give rise to considerable confusion were the package not provided with a label bearing all the relevant information about the nature of the cheese: *type:* "natural" or "pasteurized process cheese"; *composition:* "low moisture," "part

ABOVE: The bakery kitchen of Sardi's restaurant in New York City. Note the large slab of Cream Cheese next to the cook. Also on the table are cheese cake and strawberry cheese cake, specialities of the city.

LEFT: A fine 18 kg (39.6 lb) wheel of Cheddar cheese, coated with black wax.

RIGHT: Brick is one of the few cheeses of exclusively American origin. The cheese has an open texture with many irregular holes. The picture was taken at Zabar's gourmet shop in New York City.

skim"; *taste:* "sharp," "smoke"; *additives:* "olive," "pimento"; *presentation:* "shredded," "chopped cheese crumbles," "slices, individually wrapped"; *weight:* "net weight 4 ozs," "contains 1 cup"; *instructions for preservation:* "keep refrigerated." Sometimes, as with Liederkranz, it is indicated on what date the cheese is expected to reach full maturation.

Strict controls are exercised on the quality of the cheeses themselves, and of all products derived from them, by the individual states as well as by the Food and Drug Administration and the Federal Standard of Identity. The United States exports little cheese. Imports are expected to increase in the future, and the consumption of cheese per capita is growing steadily.

Research has shown that cheese consumption per capita is highest on the West Coast; that Italian cheeses are becoming more and more popular; and that foreign-born Americans have the highest purchase ratio of natural cheeses to process types. It follows that a country as vast in area, diversified in tastes, and as progressive as America is in offering selection and convenience, would have a wide variety of appetizing cheeses. Compared with Europe, the American cheese industry is in its infancy. Americans of the future can expect to develop a taste for their own natural, national cheeses and an ever-increasing appreciation of imported types.

Central America

From Mexico's narrow, pinched-in waistline at the Isthmus of Tehuantepec, the twin ranges of the Sierra Madre extend northwards. One range runs parallel to the Pacific Ocean, the other along the Gulf of Mexico. Between them, at an average height of 1,820 meters (about 6,000 feet), stretches the vast plateau of Anahuac. On this plateau, on the site of Mexico City, there once stood the capital of the Aztec empire – Tenochtitlán. Here was the imperial court of Montezuma, emperor of the Aztecs. Nearby was another great culture, that of the Mayas, which reached its peak between 300 and 900 A.D. The Mayas occupied the Yucatan peninsula, most of Honduras, Guatemala and El Salvador.

Although a highly advanced civilization, the Mayas lacked some of the essential elements for survival. They had no pack animals, no ploughs or wagons. These facts cast doubt on the supposition that they were ever in contact with Oriental cultures, where these aids were used so extensively. Although their culture disintegrated, there are still about one million Mayas who live in almost the same way as their ancestors did 1,400 years ago.

The Aztec culture, by way of contrast, came to a sudden and violent end in 1519. In that year Hernando Cortez landed with six hundred Spanish adventurers and deposed the mighty emperor of the Aztecs who ruled all Mexico. Two years after Cortez had first set eyes on Tenochtitlán, Montezuma was dead, his precious treasures plundered, and the great culture died with him.

A Spanish priest soon after the conquest recorded his impressions of many local foods and drinks. Cheese was not among the items listed. Domestic animals were first brought to the New World by the Spanish. The cattle were probably longhorns, but they were unable to adapt to the climate, the food and the altitude. Later, they were supplemented by brown Swiss and Hereford cows, and from these various breeds the hybrid Mexican cows were developed.

Close by where Cortez had landed, the conquistadors founded the seaport Veracruz, which became a flourishing trading center. They attempted, as conquerors will, to introduce the natives to Spanish customs and religion, and to establish some of the

ABOVE: An old label from a goat's milk cheese called, strangely enough, Queso de Holanda – "Dutch Cheese." Since the Dutch are not renowned for their goat cheeses, one might conclude that "Holanda" was synonymous with all that is good in terms of cheese.

ABOVE: Cuba promoted its dairy produce by issuing this postage stamp in 1968. The cow is a Frisian, and with it is a bottle of milk, a pot of yogurt and some ice cream, but – no cheese.

comforts of home, which may have included the making of cheese. As far as the Mexicans were concerned, though, the value of cattle lay in their ability to provide meat or leather, and in their attractiveness as an exportable commodity; cheese had a low priority.

Cattle have been kept mainly in the highlands of northern Mexico, where they were bred for export to the USA. Before the First World War there were only a few small cheese factories near Mexico City. On farms in the rest of the country, some cow's and goat's milk was made into cheese, the curd being pressed by hand and dried in the shade.

Between the First and Second World Wars, land was taken from the large estates and given to the Indian peasants. After 1945, economic growth began to expand in Mexico, but there is still very little dairy

production. Most farmers keep only a few cows to suit their limited needs. On the large estates things are different: the herds of cattle give excellent milk yields, but even here progressive farming is hampered by the scarcity and cost of fodder.

Mexican cheeses

Asadero, or *Oaxaca*, is a fresh and easily melted cheese that was made in the early days on the farms of Oaxaca in southern Mexico, but now mostly in cheese factories. It is a plastic curd cheese like Provolone, for which the kneaded curd is pulled in threads. They are wrapped together in a ball, put in brine for ten minutes, then packed in a plastic bag for immediate sale. This cheese is eaten with beer and bread or tortillas.

Anejo is a white, dry cheese with a crumbly texture, usually made from

ABOVE: The Mexican countryside near Popocatepetl, an active volcano about forty miles south of Mexico City.

skimmed goat's milk. The cheeses each weigh 5 to 10 kg (11 to 22 lbs) and are usually packed in jute, in groups of six. *Enchilado* is the name given to Anejo when covered with a thick coat of chili powder, giving the cheese a red rind. It has a strong taste and is best used, mixed with more chili powder, to fill pancakes. One of the few types with a foreign influence is *Queso de bola*, similar to Edam.

There is a lot of *Queso Fresco*, fresh cheese, to be found in all Latin American countries, under different names. Tamales and tortillas, which were enjoyed at the court of Montezuma, can be filled with it, accompanied by pulque, an alcoholic drink made from the sap of an agave species.

Other Central American countries

Guatemala, bordering on Mexico and Honduras, is predominantly mountainous. Only a small part of the country is given over to pastureland for cattle and sheep. In the 1920s good quality livestock were imported, but more for meat than for milking. Cheesemaking is of little or no importance, being only for home consumption.

Honduras has greater areas of pastureland, about 35% of its territory, and cattle breeding is of great value to the economy. The country is largely mountainous, though, which creates transportation difficulties. Practically every farm makes its own cheese, which it supplies to the cities, and a quantity is imported.

El Salvador is the smallest and yet the most densely populated country of Central America. El Salvador is divided into three widely differing parts by two mountain chains: the Sierra Maestra del Norte along the Honduras border and the Cadena Costera running parallel to the coast. The plateau in between enjoys a moderate climate and is very fertile, with ample pastures for cattle breeding. A considerable quantity of cheese is made, and in particular the fresh types, which are usually appreciated in hot countries for their keen taste. *Queso Enredo* is a fresh cheese, also made in Honduras. *Enredo* means "twisted together," for this is a *pasta filata* type of cheese, like the Italian Provolone. The curd/whey mixture is heated in an earthenware pot on an open fire, and salt is added. The

LEFT: Cheese vendor in Mexico. White, fresh cheese is by far the most popular type in most Latin American countries.

LEFT: Mexico City, a modern metropolis that still contains some sixteenth-century buildings and stands some 7,500 ft above sea level.

Mexico has a typically Latin American, spicy culture, which is why Mexicans enjoy Enchilado, a cheese covered with chili powder.

ABOVE: Sheep grazing on the green pastures of Acaxotchitlán. Domestic animals are relative newcomers, introduced by the Spanish conquistadors.

cheesemaker next pulls the curd into threads, which are then molded together to form flat cheeses of 60 to 80 g (2 to 3 oz), ready for sale.

Queso Coyolito is a semihard cheese made in the southeast. When the milk yield of one farm is insufficient, it is combined with milk from other farms. The whole milk is curdled, and the curd is cut into pieces, each the size of a nut. After a rest period of 30 to 45 minutes, the whey is drained off, and the curd is left to increase its acidity before it is formed. After a six-hour stay in the brine bath it is taken out and washed with coconut milk. The curd is again divided into pieces and pressed for ten days, followed by a twenty-day ripening period, during which time it is periodically rubbed with salt. The cheese is given a loaf shape before marketing, and is sold in the immediate neighborhood. It has a tough but elastic texture and a piquant taste.

Nicaragua also makes cheese, probably just sufficient for its own needs. Costa Rica has cattle, and makes quite a lot of cheese; cheese factories had already been established there by the beginning of this century.

Cuba, pearl of the Antilles and largest of the West Indian Islands, is situated at the entrance to the Gulf of Mexico. Its coastline is flat, with sandbanks and coral reefs. Inland the plains are fertile and the climate healthy. Cortez took part in the conquest of Cuba, under the command of Diego Velasquez. He settled on an estate and it was there, for the first time, that European horned cattle were imported. Yet in spite of the advantage, Cuba has not become a dairy country. Cattle herds are a luxury, kept for meat rather than for milk. There is a native cattle breed, and there are even pure-bred Jersey and Holstein cows. Quite a bit of *Pategrás* is made, a hard cheese similar to Gouda, made from whole or partly skimmed milk. The cheese, one of Cuba's best, has a Gouda shape, weighs 4 to 5 kg (8.8 to 11 lbs), is covered with red wax and wrapped in red cellophane paper.

Jamaica, with its beautiful grassland and good cattle, has, nevertheless, an underdeveloped dairy industry. Haiti imports much cheese from the USA. The Dominican Republic has ranches on which cattle are bred, and its farmers keep a few cattle for home use, but, like Jamaica and Haiti, has little to offer in the way of indigenous cheeses.

Puerto Rico, smallest of the West Indian islands, does possess a few cheeses worthy of mention. The greater part of the island is fertile, hilly country with good grazing land. The cattle are raised to be used as draught animals, as well as for their meat and milk. The Zebu breed, imported from Senegal, were crossbred with island cattle, and the resulting hybrids became more adaptable, and more valuable than the parent breeds.

Queso del Pais, or *Queso de la Tierra*, is a white cheese that is eaten fresh, when it is as soft as Cottage Cheese. It is made on the farms and in cheese factories; the farm cheeses are mostly smaller in size and weigh 1.5 kg (3.3 lbs). A ripened variety of the cheese is also sold, which is hard and bitter. The *Queso de Prensa* is a hard cheese of whole milk. *Queso de Puna* is like Cottage Cheese, but is given a firm shape by using a cheese mold. In addition to these home types, much of the cheese in Puerto Rico is imported.

Name	Milk	Type	Rind	Form	Weight	% Fat content
Anejo	⚬	○	—	varying	5-10 kg	?
Asadero	⚬	■	—	varying	0.1-3 kg	26
Pategrás	⚬	■	□	cartwheel	4-5 kg	40
Queso Coyolito	⚬	◑	□	loaf	20-22 kg	?
- Enredo	⚬	■	—	flat disc	60-80 g	?
- Fresco	⚬	○	—	varying	0.5-1 kg	15-40
- de Pais	⚬	○	—	flat disc	1.5 kg	?
Queso de Cabra	⚬	○	—	pear	varying	?
- de Cincho	⚬	○	—	container	varying	55

Key to symbols on page 34.

Venezuela and the Guyanas

A nineteenth-century American consul in Venezuela was surprised into commenting on the fact that a nation with less than three million inhabitants – that is, less people than cows – should have to import great quantities of butter and cheese.

These dairy products were consumed almost entirely in the big cities. Venezuelans living in remote country areas were thought to prefer the fresh fruit at their disposal – despite its lesser food value – as being more refreshing in the extreme heat. But even if country people had hankered after the expensive foreign cheeses, they would not have been able to afford them. There were, however, their own fresh cheeses for them to choose, which were made locally.

Queso de Cincho is a popular cheese which is still made on farms. The preparation is simple. Fresh milk, with starter and salt, is left in the cheese vat for twenty-four hours until it has coagulated. Then it is hung in sacks so that the whey can flow out. It is a very soft cheese with many small holes, and is always eaten fresh.

Queso Llanero is made in the same way but the curd is placed in molds and becomes hard and crumbly. It has a strong taste and is used in baking or is grated over a finished dish.

Queso de Mano takes its name from the fact that the curd is worked by hand until the right consistency is achieved; then it is put in layers in wooden molds where it remains for twenty-four hours. As Venezuela is a banana and maize country, naturally the leaves from these two foodstuffs are put to good use: both to keep cheeses moist and to give the cheeses their own special aroma. The young Queso de Mano is packed in banana leaves which are prepared by cutting away the tough middle ribs, pulling the leaves into small rectangles in the direction of the grain, and then rubbing them in cold water.

Maize leaves are used to pack *Cuajada*, a cheese from the Andes which resembles Queso de Cincho, except that extra cream is used in its making. *Queso de Cabra*, a very popular cheese molded by hand into a pear shape, has a real goat taste.

In Venezuela, cheese is used to flavor sauces, especially the cheese and tomato sauce called *chorreada*, which accompanies boiled potatoes or meat dishes. *Quesco Blanco* features

ABOVE: The Caroni River valley. Venezuela's grasslands along the wide river valleys afford good grazing for cattle.

RIGHT: Milk shop in Paramaribo, the capital of Surinam.

in a kind of cheese and banana cake, also served with meat, to form a slightly sweet, spicy contrast. (For data on Queso de Cabra and Queso de Cincho, see p. 160.)

Cheese was introduced into the colony of Surinam by the Dutch West India Company in 1620 and in the flourishing trade during the next two centuries, imports rose. Surinam's hot moist climate, like that of former British and French Guyana, makes the raising of cattle and therefore cheesemaking very difficult.

BOTTOM RIGHT: A modern road is quite useful for moving cattle particularly in areas that are not densely populated. Traffic is not much of a problem here.

Colombia

The greater part of the population of Colombia lives on the slopes of the Andes Mountains, on the treeless plateaus and in the *llanos*, the river valleys through which the tributaries of the Amazon and Orinoco flow. Colombia has an almost complete range of climatic variations. There are intensely hot forest regions in the lowlands, the plateaus are temperate and the high peaks of the Andes are perpetually covered with snow. Cattle breeding is confined to the temperate zones, but as the cattle are of mediocre quality, so is the milk.

Most cheese is produced by cheese factories from pasteurized milk. One of the most important concerns is situated on the mountain slopes at Sopo, a small village north of Bogotá. The factory is old and by modern standards unhygienic, but the number of people employed there is relatively high: the conflict of labor versus automation is not yet an economic problem in Colombia.

Queso de Pera is the most typical of the farmhouse cheese types, a Provolone-like product made exclusively by women from a recipe that has been handed down through generations, usually by word of mouth. A few years ago the director of the Sopo cheese factory was visiting a small village, where he was given a piece of Pera cheese to eat. He found it so delicious that he offered $40,000 for the recipe. Unfortunately, the woman who made it was unable to describe exactly how she did it. The director invited her to come to the factory for a month to show the workers how to produce good Queso de Pera. To make this plastic curd cheese, partly skimmed milk is heated to 30°-32°C (86°-90°F) in a large cheese vat and slowly stirred until the milk becomes sour and coagulates. It is then drained, and the curd heated in hot water. The cheesemaker works the mass with a ladle until it acquires the right degree of elasticity. Small portions are then cut off and flattened to form a 10 cm (4 in) square, in the center of which is placed a piece of *bocadilla*, a sweet made from guayaba fruit. This is enclosed by the curd, rolled up to form a sort of long rissole, and finally wrapped in plastic.

Gruyère and *Emmental* are made according to the Swiss recipe. The milk for these cheeses is standardized at 2.3% fat, and they are sold young, because the piquant flavor of ripe

LEFT: Cattle being herded along an old track in the countryside near Bogotá, capital of Colombia.

cheese is not very popular. This is why only very briefly ripened cheeses are sold, such as *Queso Sabana, Queso Glaris* and *Queso Holandés*. For these types, salt is added to the curd, which is then drained and cut into pieces of different weights. After pressing in molds of varying shapes, the cheeses are ripened for 5 to 12 days, dipped in yellow or red paraffin wax, then wrapped in cellophane paper. *Queso Bernina* ripens for 8 days at room temperature, which gives it a slightly piquant flavor. It has a fat content of 50% and is packed in weights of 220 or 260 g (8 or 9 oz), in aluminum foil. *Queso Azul* is a blue-veined type. There are several imitations of foreign cheeses as well, including a cream cheese, *Queso Filadelfia*.

Around the city of Bogotá, in the high mountain valleys, grow fine, white potatoes. The people are fond of them served in a piquant sauce, in which cheese, onions, shallots, tomatoes, cumin, oregano and black pepper are mixed. In the hotter regions, sweet cassavas and bananas replace the potatoes, used in dishes invented by the Indians, and are made even more tasty by adding fresh cheese.

Name	Milk	Type	Rind	Form	Weight	% Fat content
Queso Bernina	◁	○	—	varying	220-260 g	50
- de Pera	◁	■	—	varying	500 g	?

Key to symbols on page 34. 453 g = 1 lb.

LEFT: This farmstead is between Cartagena and Baranquilla, coastal towns on the Caribbean Sea. Only the irrigated plateaus and the river valleys are really suitable for cattle breeding.

Peru

In common with most countries of South America, Peru has tremendous potential in terms of agricultural and mineral wealth. A large proportion of these resources remain undeveloped, and there are areas of the country that have yet to be thoroughly explored.

Spanish colonists were the first to introduce cattle to Peru, but owing to the lack of organized farming, the cattle ran wild, and only a few were tended for their milk and meat. It is estimated that at the end of the sixteenth century there were at least 100,000 cows in Peru, but by the beginning of the twentieth century there had been no obvious improvement in the dairy situation. Butter was made by hand for home use, and the Indians made some cheese from a mixture of 90% cow's milk and 10% goat's milk. This cheese was sold in Lima and eaten fresh, and is still popular today. By 1926 two modern dairy factories had been established in Lima, but they only supplied pasteurized milk. Today the question of whether Peru can develop a successful dairy industry is still largely ignored.

The taste for *Queso Blanco* is shared by most, if not all, Latin American countries, and Peru is no exception. To make this "white cheese," the milk is brought to a temperature of 82°C (180°F), and as a starter either citric or acetic acid is added, rather than sour milk. After a few minutes' stirring, the coagulating milk is left for 15 minutes, after which the whey is run off. The curd is salted, then stirred for a further 20 minutes. At room temperature it is ladled into molds and pressed. The next day it can be packed and sold.

This kind of cheese is ideal for hot countries, as it can be prepared in a few hours. It has a sourish taste and a consistency very like Mozzarella, but although the cheese is easy to cut, it is not a good melter.

Queso Blanco is used in several traditional Peruvian recipes, notably in dishes containing the staple potato. The *papas* are boiled whole and served with a cheese and chili sauce, or they may be mashed and seasoned with chili and lemon juice, then garnished with shrimp, Queso Blanco, corn and eggs.

Modest rewards
Peru has a great shortage of dairy produce, and although a Swiss-Peruvian organization gives help and

ABOVE: Food stalls at the station, where trains will stop for the lunch break. Local fruits, fresh cheese, bread and drinks can be had very cheaply.

BELOW: The ubiquitous pack animals of South America, the llamas. There are two wild species and two domesticated breeds.

Name	Milk	Type	Rind	Form	Weight	% Fat content
Queso Blanco	🐄🐐	O	—	varying	varying	?

Key to symbols on page 34.

advice to many small cheesemaking concerns, far too little cheese is produced. The government works continually to correct this situation by improving the pastures, importing good-quality milking cattle and encouraging the growing of cattle fodder; but due to the permanent shortage of fodder, the milk yield is still low.

Another problem is that the farmer finds it impossible to fix a price for his milk that competes with the imported milk powder – usually subsidized by the exporting country. The home-produced milk is mostly mixed with between 25-50% "recombined milk" made up of milk powder, butter oil, stabilizers and water.

Dairy experts visit the farms to give information about cattle care, which includes hygiene, vaccination and correct feeding. They are only rewarded by a modest rise in production. Realistically, when one considers that a milk tanker must negotiate some very primitive roads and cover great distances to pick up a load, and that canoes and mules are still the most common means of transportation, it is clear that Peru is a long way from becoming a major cheese producer.

Argentina

Both sides of the Rio de la Plata estuary – Argentina to the south, Uruguay to the north – are covered with pampas, the world's biggest grasslands, partly dry and partly blessed with an ideal rainfall and moderate climate. From 1580, when the Spaniards under Juan de Garay were establishing permanent settlements, they embarked upon an agrarian policy to replace the coarse grass of the pampas with a softer variety. One of the aims was to provide good grazing land for cattle, since the soil was fertile and the climate favorable.

Today the whole of Argentina is agricultural, and cattle breeding is extensive. Sheep and cows graze on the pampas, and the enormous numbers of sheep make Argentina one of the largest wool-producing countries in the world. Also, vast quantities of meat are salted, deep-frozen and exported. Although the meat industry is more profitable than dairying, Argentina has developed into an important dairy-produce country. Following the foundation of a national herd book of pedigree cattle in 1886, specially selected milk breeds have been imported, including such breeds as Holstein and Jersey cows, renowned for their quality milk and high yields. These types were crossbred with the native Crillos, to create a breed that had the hardness and adaptability of the Argentine stock plus the yields of the European cattle.

The cheese industry got off to a slow and inauspicious start. In 1855 a certain Josef Magnasco opened a cheese dairy, with the aid of five employees; he developed two home cheeses, *Chubut* and *Goya*, which even today have no real status. Yet by 1903 there were 324 dairy factories in Argentina, and production increased regularly, particularly during the First World War, when export prices were favorable. In 1973, cheese production was 219,000 tons. Exports accounted for 6,902 tons, which went mainly to other South American countries. The range of Argentina's cheeses covers a lot of European types, in addition to home varieties.

Queso Blanco is a typical country cheese, just like fresh cheeses everywhere. Characterized by simplicity of preparation, it is one of the oldest kinds. From time immemorial, the milk that was left over, the day's surplus, was hung up in a cloth to become

ABOVE: A small ranch in the province of Catamarca, on the lower slopes of the Andes. Although Argentina is more a country of cattle breeding than dairy farming, cheese production is regularly increasing.

thick and dry. The product has a fresh sour flavor and is often used in Argentinian cookery in accordance with family tastes, which transcend rules and recipes.

Quartirolo is also a fresh cheese, used in salads and sandwiches, and in a special dish mixed with calf's tongue and ham. Such is the demand for this cheese that manufacturers cannot maintain consistent standards; it is often sold too fresh, when the paste is hard and white and lacking in flavor.

A smaller Quartirolo with a weight 2.5 kg (5.5 lbs) is known as *Mantecoso*; *Cremoso* is closely related, having the same basic elements, but it is prepared by a different method. It is sweeter and less fruity than the Quartirolo.

Crema is similar to the French Petit Suisse and Neufchatel. Argentinian *Mendicrim* is particularly successful, and since 1957 has been the most popular cheese of the *Queso de Crema* type. Some manufacturers, in the hope of producing a more competitive product, add excessive cream. Unfortunately, the keeping qualities of Queso de Crema are limited: the cheese must be eaten within one week;

LEFT: Argentinian cattle drivers are called *gauchos*, the equivalent of the North American cowboys. The cattle roam wide areas, and the *gauchos* guard the herds, check the fences and drive the animals together when they are moved to other destinations.

and it should be well wrapped to avoid contaminating smells.

Mozzarella is very popular in Argentina, where the cuisine has undergone a heavy Italian influence. In pizzas and as a filling for pasta, Mozzarella is the outstanding cheese. It has a rather rough texture, similar to the *pasta filata*, or plastic curd, type. Ripening time is a minimum of 24 hours, and the Mozzarella must be eaten fresh. The color is white or creamy, the body firm with some elasticity. A favorite local way of preparing this cheese is to cut it into slices and marinate it in olive oil and spices such as paprika, ginger, cayenne pepper or coriander. A good quality pizza cheese called *Mendirela* comes from Mendizabel.

Cheddar is one of the most popular cheeses, particularly the one produced in Santa Rosa, near where most of Argentina's wine is produced. Cheddar, too, is marinated by some connoisseurs: slices are placed in sherry, whisky or cognac, and left for 24 hours covered by a cloth; the final product is eaten with a spoon.

Gouda is one of the semihard cheeses sold in Argentina. It is often used in hors d'oeuvres, for the flavor is not too dominating and it mixes nicely with spices and a little olive oil.

Saint-Paulin, with its soft, mild flavor, is specially recommended as a dessert cheese. The Saint-Paulin from the Magnasco factory has a very good reputation – so good, in fact, that it is considered one of the best descendants of the original French cheese. It is sold under the name of *Crescenza*.

Many other foreign cheeses have been copied, including *Romano*, *Sardo, Gruyère* and several blue-veined types. It is interesting to note that the millions of sheep are hardly ever milked for cheese production, in spite of their great numbers and obvious potential.

In Argentina, two large meals are prepared every day, between which the Argentinians have managed to sandwich – so to speak – an extra meal, lest anyone should go hungry. A greatly esteemed snack is Provolone alla patta: a thick slice of Provolone, covered with fresh, peeled and sliced tomatoes and lots of oregano, garlic and parsley, which is heated in the oven or under the grill, until the cheese melts.

BELOW: Label of an Argentinian cheese. Magnasco is the trademark of the factory founded by Josef Magnasco in 1855.

Name	Milk	Type	Rind	Form	Weight	% Fat content
Crema		O	—	loaf	3.8 kg	55
Quartirolo		O	—	loaf	3.8 kg	50

Key to symbols on page 34. 1 kg = 2.2 lbs.

RIGHT: Independence Day in Buenos Aires is celebrated with typical enthusiasm. One of the day's highlights is the procession of decorated carts and wagons, pulled by powerful Argentinian cattle.

Brazil

Brazil sprawls across the larger part of the South American continent, with a reputation largely built on coffee, nuts and footballers. The northern part of Brazil is watered by the Amazon and its tributaries. Across the plateau are dense forests which are, for the most part, impenetrable, and even today there are areas which have not been explored; this is hardly surprising when you consider that the Brazilian jungle is an area equal in size to the whole of central Europe.

In spite of its vastness, the climate is not as varied as you might expect: north of the Amazon there is a tropical rain climate; the southeast has an agreeable, moderate climate with sufficient rainfall to have extensive pastures where enormous herds of cattle are kept. In between are large, arid patches, which explains why only a small part of Brazil is cultivated.

Land of contradictions

The present Brazil is a land of contradictions, with a wide gap between the rich and the poor. More than half the population are farm laborers, working under the most primitive conditions for extremely low wages. Yet, on the other hand – and in contrast to Brazil's other South American neighbors – Brazil is an elegant showplace for modern architecture.

Culturally, Brazil has marked differences with other Latin American countries. Prominent are the Portuguese and West African influences which go back several centuries, but there are also the traditional Indian ones. The Indian heritage is poor, and never grew into great civilizations such as those of pre-Columbian Peru, Mexico and Guatamala. The Inca and Aztec empires were wealthy and progressive; their staple foods included the superior sweetcorn and the potato (not to mention the tomato), while the staple of the Brazilian Indian was the starchy manioc root, some varieties of which are poisonous. Beans have largely overtaken manioc as the great staple, and was probably introduced to Brazil about the same time as cheese. The Portuguese colonists of the sixteenth century were the first cheesemakers, producing a simple fresh type from imported cattle.

The country has roughly 80 million cattle, but there is no indication that dairy breeds are the most important. There could be a variety of reasons for

ABOVE: Local markets are always characteristic of the particular region, with the foodstuffs being as abundant and as varied as they need to be. The Brazilian is a hearty eater who can pack away two or three large meals a day.

RIGHT: An old label from a Batavo cheese pack. Batavo is the trade name of an Edam type.

BELOW: A cowboy supervising corraled cattle at the Feira de Santana.

this. One is that the Brazilian people are a mixture of many races, none of them with a rich dairy tradition, and consequently they are relatively indifferent to dairy products. The national cattle, mainly the Zebu breed, are meat stocks; Brazilian farmers found that importing milking cattle was an unpractical proposition, because of the animals' need for intensive care, plus the problems of acclimatization. In the south, however, traditions have changed over the past fifty years. Around the two most heavily populated areas – Rio de Janeiro and São Paulo – 80% of Brazilian milk is now produced by Dutch, German and Polish settlers.

An improving situation
Of the seven million dairy cows, 6% are pedigree animals, mainly Frisians and Jerseys; the remainder are interbred with Zebu types, resulting in animals with high disease resistance, good climate adaptation and relatively good milk production.

A few million fatting cows are milked – how often depends on their calving date, their milk production and the price of milk. Some of the big cattle breeders prefer this type, importing them from the United States and Canada. The breeding animals are well cared for, unlike those on the ordinary dairy farms, and they produce accordingly: the former 5,000-6,000 liters (5,500-6,600 quarts) yearly, the others only 4,300 liters (4,730 quarts). When an animal has to cover 5 kilometers (3 miles) of ground daily to find food and drinking water its production drops. Generally though, Brazil's milk production is increasing annually by 10%.

Cheese production has also increased slowly to a mark of about 50,000 tons yearly. The typically Brazilian Minas and Prato cheeses represent 70% of the total production. There are six different Minas cheeses, made on farms or in small cheese factories.

The national range
Minas Frescal has been made in Minas Gerais since the seventeenth century. In today's cheese factories the pasteurized cow's milk is soured, curdled and stirred now and then. After 20 minutes the milk reaches the appropriate thickness and salt is added. The wet mass is scooped into

BELOW: A *mestizo* cowboy enjoying a strong *cigarro* at the end of his arduous day.

Name	Milk	Type	Rind	Form	Weight	% Fat content
Minas Frescal	🐄	●	—	flat disc	900 g	42
Minas Prensado	🐄	●	▫	flat disc	500 g	42
Requeijão	🐄	■	▫	flat disc, cube	250-500 g, 2-12 kg	varies

Key to symbols on page 34. 453 g = 1 lb; 1 kg = 2.2 lbs.

QUEIJO TIPO BATAVO
CASTROLANDA
INDÚSTRIA BRASILEIRA
MARCA REGISTRADA
BRASIL INSPECIONADO 2128 S.I.F.
DEVE SER PESADO A VISTA DO COMPRADOR
FÁBRICA: CARAMBEÍ CASTRO - PARANÁ
CONSERVADOR: P.VII
CORANTE: C.I
ALÍNEA I POSIÇÃO 0404
USINA DE BENEFICIAMENTO DA COOPERATIVA CENTRAL DE LATICÍNIOS DO PARANÁ LTDA.
C. G. C. K.º 76.107.762/001
RÓTULO REGISTRADO NA DIPOA SOB N.º 6165

ABOVE: A more recent label of a Batavo cheese pack, depicting a Frisian cow. The text on the right reads: "Must be weighed in the buyer's presence." Very often, cheese is not labeled, but sold loose, by weight. Note the inspection number and mention of preservatives and coloring matter.

perforated molds and turned after 5 minutes. Some 40 minutes later the curd is sprinkled with a fine layer of salt and after 2 hours it is turned and salted for a third time. Then it goes to a cool storage room where after 2 days it is ready to be packed in foil.

Minas Prensado has a much firmer consistency and regular holes. The soured milk is left for preripening; after it curdles it is cut, warmed with hot water and stirred. After a short time the cheesemaker pushes it to one side of the vat, scoops it up in a sieve-like device, spreads it on a table and presses it into small molds with his hands. As soon as the cheese has taken shape, it is kneaded, put into a cloth and pressed for 10 minutes. A second pressing follows without a cloth, after which the cheese is brined for 6 hours. It is drained, left to stand in a cool room for a day and is then ready for consumption.

Requeijão is a kind of cooked cheese, the result of melting Sauermilchquark with cream. *Requeijão de Sertão* refers to a cheese that is not factory-made, but prepared in the traditional way. In the northeast it is baked with bread and often eaten for breakfast. The cheese has a thin yellow-white skin, a close firm body, and a sweet to lightly sour flavor. Also popular as a dessert, it is served with the hardened Brazilian marmalade, solid enough to cut.

Many foreign types are made, including *Prato* (Gouda type), *Mozzarella* and *Quartirollo*.

The quality of Brazilian cheese itself is slowly improving. Much technological help has been gained from France, Italy and West Germany, in particular, and a specialized institute provides education and research in the dairy field. A final boost to the national cheese industry? Because of import duties, cheeses from abroad have become very expensive.

The Brazilians have developed a liking for cheese. Breakfast in Brazil might consist of cheese sandwiches and as lunch and supper are both hot meals, there is plenty of opportunity to incorporate cheese in the day's menu. A typical luncheon dish is an omelette, covered with white cheese, then rolled. Baked rice is also served with cheese, as is a casserole of brown beans, onions, garlic and tomatoes.

Chile

Nearly three thousand miles long, and in places less than sixty miles wide, Chile must be the world's narrowest country. Between the Pacific and the volcanic Andes, a fertile valley extends southwards, where vineyards mingle with orchards, and crops of alfalfa are grown for cattle fodder. In the south, and on Tierra del Fuego, where sea and ice have shattered the coastline into a thousand islands, great herds of sheep graze. Throughout Chile, cattle have been established since the sixteenth century, and their milk was made into cheese on the haciendas. After 1945, pure-bred milking cattle were imported, and the cheese factories obtained modern equipment from Europe – mostly from Denmark.

Chile's *Tipo Chanco*
The cheese industry of modern Chile consists of fifty dairy plants. They produce about 20 million kg (44 million lbs) of cheese annually, accounting for some 90% of the total production. 60% of this is factory-made *Tipo Chanco*, a traditional cheese type which is still made on the old farmsteads in the countryside, but in much smaller quantities.

The freshly yielded milk that goes to make Chanco is first curdled, and the curd is cut with the *lira*. After a rest, the whey is partly removed and salt is added. After having stirred the mass for ten minutes, the cheesemaker proceeds to work the curd by hand. He wraps it in a cheese cloth and puts

LEFT: The horse is still the best way of getting about one-eighth of haciendas. But cars and trucks are gaining ground.

ABOVE: The wide, mountain pastures of Portillo, in Central Chile. Although only about one-eighth of Chile's surface area is grassland, the country supports millions of sheep and cattle.

it into perforated molds. The mass is thoroughly kneaded and pummeled, after which it is pressed for 24 hours. A well-ripened cheese is whitish-yellow in color with an ochre rind. It has a mild flavor, and the paste has few holes. Most Chanco is made around Santiago.

Other varieties
Quesillos is a small, flat, round, fresh cheese, and very popular as a first course on Sundays with a little garnish of lettuce, celery, a couple of slices of avocado, and a slice of tomato, with the occasional addition of ham. A lot of *Queso Fresco* is also made, in common with most South American countries, and goes under the name of *Fresco*, *Queso Blanco* and a variety of other fancy names. Although Chile prefers meat rather than cheese, the former often being cheaper, a range of good imitations of popular European cheese types has a well-established home market.

Name	Milk	Type	Rind	Form	Weight	% Fat content
Quesillos	◿	○	—	flat disc	varies	varies
Tipo Chanco	◿	■	❖	cube	6-10 kg	50

Key to symbols on page 34. 1 kg = 2.2 lbs.

AFRICA

ABOVE: Cattle and egrets have long been a part of the African scene, although dairy farming is either primitive or nonexistent. Dairying is now being encouraged by economic aid and training schemes from wealthier countries. Increased consumption of milk and cheese would begin to combat the protein deficiencies often evident in African diet patterns.

Africa

When David Livingstone was exploring the Upper Zambesi River in northwest Angola, he met the chief of the Balonda tribe, who showed him his herd of thirty beautiful cows, which had been bred for meat. Chief Katema was delighted to learn from Livingstone that the cows could be milked as well, and that their milk was a sort of food. In common with many other African tribes, it had never occurred to the Balondas to milk their cattle. Since milk was not part of the African diet, it follows that cheese was unknown.

ABOVE: A Berber woman milks her sheep. In Algeria, a large proportion of the population consists of Berbers, a nomadic people who roam the deserts and steppes with their cattle.

Cheeses of North Africa
The majority of Africa's indigenous cheeses are to be found above the Sahara. Tunisia is one of the few countries with a profitable cheese production. *Sicille* is a semihard, cylindrical cheese of 3 to 15 kg (6.6 to 33 lbs) with a solid, white, elastic body and many small holes. The taste is sharpened by the paprika grains that are added, and the cheese is often rather rancid. It is made of sheep's milk, mixed with a little cow's and goat's milk. The curd is pressed in high, cylindrical baskets, then covered with salt and cured in damp cellars. Sicille can be eaten after a month, or can be left to ripen for three months, at which point it is a semihard cheese, or for more than a year if a hard cheese is desired.

Testouri is a ball-shaped, fresh cheese, for which the curd is beaten to obtain a fine, smooth texture. After a period of rest, the curd is formed by hand into balls, which are placed in a brine bath for 24 hours and then eaten fresh. *Oriental* is a brine cheese like Feta. *Numidia*, made from sheep's or goat's milk, is a sharp-tasting, blue-veined cheese, while *Sarde*, a sheep's milk cheese made near Beja in the north, is rather like Spanish Manchego.

Egyptian water buffalo cheeses
We know that the ancient Egyptians were among the earliest peoples who learned the technique of cheese-making, just as they had learned to make bread and wine. Cheese was included among the provisions interred with the dead – traveling rations for the journey to the next world. Cheese, as well as wheat, also served as a means of payment in wages, rent or taxes, a system that was maintained in Europe until the nineteenth century.

ABOVE: Algeria has a great deal of mineral wealth, as yet largely unexploited. Industrial and living standards have improved considerably over the past few decades, and modern milking stations such as this handle good daily yields of milk.

Most Egyptian cheeses are made from the milk of the water buffalo, often supplemented by cow's milk. Like the cow, the water buffalo is used as both a draught and a milking animal. Sheep and goats are found on the farms, but their milk yield is generally low.

Egyptian farmers make a cheese called *Kariesch*. They leave the milk to sour spontaneously, and after one to three days the cream floats on top of the milk. It is then skimmed off and churned into butter. The thick mass of milk is scooped out and put into cloths to allow the whey to drain off. The lean curd is then cut into rectangular pieces and sprinkled with salt. These are left for a few days to enable the salt to penetrate, at which point the cheese is ready for consumption. It can also be ripened in brine.

Beda is made on the farms and also in cheese factories from raw skimmed milk or pasteurized milk, either from cows or buffalo. The curd is put into molds, turned a few times, put into a cloth and pressed between two planks. This fresh cheese may then be cured in the boiled and cooled whey, which has been retained from the pressing process.

Misch, like Beda, is made from skimmed milk. Instead of using whey, however, the cheeses are cured in salted milk, or a mixture of salted milk and water. Spices are often added, and the cheeses ripen in pots for more than a year, developing a very strong, Roquefort-like taste.

Rumi is a cylindrical cheese from buffalo and cow's milk, and is made in cheese factories. Left to ripen for three months at room temperature, the cheese develops a dry rind, a semihard body with many small holes and a strong salty flavor, not unlike that of a

LEFT: Touaregs in the
Tamanrasset oasis at
Ahaggar in the central
Sahara. The Touaregs,
although nomadic,
keep large herds of
cattle and flocks of
sheep and goats.

mature Gouda. *Rahs* is related to
Rumi; it is a factory-made cheese,
whose production is confined to the
season from January to June, because
the high prices of summer milk would
affect profits.

There are eight medium-sized
cheese factories in Egypt, but they
suffer from a shortage of skilled per-
sonnel. Several foreign types of cheese
are produced, in part to accommodate
the considerable number of Europeans
living in the country; and the cheeses
manufactured are *Kaschkaval, Cheddar, Emmental* and *Roquefort*.

South of the Sahara
In the dry Sahel, south of the Sahara
Desert, attempts are being made to
teach the population to keep their
goats in fenced areas and to use the
milk for human consumption. Niger
has large herds of cattle, around 6
million goats, 4 million cows and 2.5
million sheep. The Touaregs in the
north maintain some 15% of the cattle
population, but the greater proportion
belongs to the nomad Peulh, a shepherd people who move with their herds
to the steppes and daily accommodate
the cattle from village farms. In
periods of drought, large numbers of
cattle die, and great efforts are being
made to improve matters by introduc-
ing a better water supply, more
efficient working methods, animal
care and regular vaccination.

Kenya and Tanzania
Of all African countries, Kenya is the
most advanced in agriculture and
cattle breeding, due to the influence of
European colonists. There is a training school in Naivasha which teaches
dairy production. Fresh cheese is made
there by filtering skimmed milk
through a cloth suspended from a tri-
pod of branches. Naivasha also has a
large dairy factory, which exports its
cheeses to Uganda, Tanzania, Zanzi-
bar, India, Pakistan, the countries
around the Persian Gulf, and even to
Germany and England.

In Tanzania a few small cheese factories make cheeses from raw milk,
but they are not of a very high quality.
There is a move to combine these
widely dispersed cheese factories in
order to increase production and improve distribution. Traditional eating
habits and tastes will have to change,
however, before cheese finds a ready
market in these areas.

BELOW: A cheese
warehouse in Kenya,
where substantial
quantities of cheese
are produced and are
widely exported.
European influences
have made for a con-
sistently high quality
of dairy products here.

Name	Milk	Type	Rind	Form	Weight	% Fat content
Beda	⌂	○	—	varying	varying	40-45
Sicille	✳	■	▢	cylinder	3-15 kg	?
Testouri	⌂⊿	○	—	ball	varying	?

Key to symbols on page 34. 1 kg = 2.2 lbs.

ABOVE: Famous for
their diet of fresh
blood and milk, the
Masai of Kenya are at
one with their cattle.
They used to be no-
madic cattle raisers,
but many are now
sedentary farmers.

South Africa

In 1652, Jan van Riebeeck was not only the first Dutch colonist in South Africa, but he was also the first person to attempt cheesemaking there. It was not a very successful attempt, but he at least established a precedent. Five years later the first real colony was founded by nine Dutchmen, ex-soldiers and sailors, who chose farming as their new profession. From the Hottentots they bought cattle – animals that soon acquired the name Afrikander. The livestock had all the desired qualities for the climate in which the colonists lived and worked. Later settlers arrived, bringing Frisian cattle with them, and when the British turned up, they were accompanied by Ayrshires and Jerseys. Crossbreeding these different stocks with the Afrikanders produced an exceptional dairy cow, but development was slow.

It was not until the end of the last century that the government decided to stimulate the dairy industry. Experts trained in the United States, Canada and Australia were engaged to visit farms with cheesemaking installations, and to demonstrate the process for making Cheddar. Their efforts were very successful and can be considered the foundation of South Africa's modern dairy industry.

As always, cattle fodder was of prime importance. The country was fortunate in that there was plenty of it available. Long before the arrival of the colonists, the Bantu tribe was cultivating sorghum for their cattle. The

ABOVE: In the Kalahari Desert, not strictly a desert but an area of scrubland, deep wells provide the water for ranches and cattle-breeding stations.

BELOW: Cheesemaking in South Africa is now a well-developed industry. Here slabs of curd are piled up in the vat.

Name	Milk	Type	Rind	Form	Weight	% Fat content
Bloukrans	◿	◖	✂	cylinder	varying	50
Cheddar	◿◿	◼	□	rectangular	10 kg	45-55
Drakensberg	◿	●	□	loaf	varying	62

Key to symbols on page 34. 1 kg = 2.2 lbs.

British planted maize, originally to provide it as a food for the natives, but it soon proved excellent for the livestock. Certainly the most useful and prolific fodder is the cloverlike alfalfa.

Getting organized
A certain Joseph Blayne, sometimes called the father of South Africa's dairy industry, established the country's first cheese-processing plant. Its success encouraged others, and after the Boer War more cheesemakers established themselves, mainly in the eastern and central areas of the country, where the best conditions were to be found. In those days, transportation from the inland areas was slow and difficult. In 1914, less than 500,000 kg (1.1 million lbs) of cheese were made, and 2.5 million kg (5.5 million lbs) had to be imported. The First World War sent up the prices, and as a result dairy produce became a more interesting economic proposition. It soon became apparent that price controls were needed, and a Dairy Industry Control Board was founded in 1930. The smaller cheesemakers went out of business and large centrally placed cheese factories with good supply facilities sprang up, causing the cost of production to fall sharply.

There are now 33 factories producing about 20 million tons of cheese a year. The Dutch and English taste for cheese is definitely noticeable. *Cheddar* is the most popular; it is often rectangular in shape, rindless and prepacked. *Gouda*, in its original cartwheel form, and *Baby Gouda*, weighing .5 kg (1.1 lbs), are also top sellers. Some more originally foreign cheeses are also produced, including *Brie*, *Camembert*, some Italian types, the Greek *Feta* and *Bloukrans* (a blue-veined cheese). A cheese called *Drakensberg* is also gaining popularity. This is a cream cheese of South African origin, a quick ripener with a lovely, creamy taste. In addition, a lot of fresh cheese and *Cottage Cheese* is eaten.

Cheese is divided into five groups, according to fat content: high fat, whole milk, medium fat, low fat, skimmed-milk cheese. Processed cheese is always made from Cheddar. Most cheeses are made from cow's milk, although there is a growing interest for fresh cheese from goat's milk.

THE MIDDLE EAST

ABOVE: Most varieties of cheese in the Middle East are made from the milk of sheep or goats, animals that are well adapted to arid regions with poor vegetation. Cheeses have been produced in these regions for thousands of years, very simple types and generally rather salty.

Turkey

Turkey is the connecting link between the European and the Asiatic world. On the European side lies Istanbul, the former Byzantium, capital of the Byzantine imperium – an extravagantly beautiful pearl, set in the fertile, rolling landscape of Thracia. On the Asiatic side is a totally different picture. It is dominated by the high central plain of Anatolia, a disconsolate, barren, treeless steppe region of sheep and goats. The irregular fringe of the Mediterranean coast used to be part of the Levant and Roman seafarers and traders bought and sold many goods, including cheese, in the market places of its commercial towns.

It is possible, but by no means certain, that cheese was made in Turkey during neolithic times, well before the Romans, but we do know for sure that the area has been producing cheese for centuries in more modern times.

Agriculture remains the most important means of existence, although the farms are generally very small and often primitive. In recent years, modern farming and cattle-breeding methods have been introduced, and Turkey's stocks, kept for both meat and milk, number some 15 million

ABOVE: The large flocks of sheep cover great distances in search of fresh grazing – wherever the sheep go, the shepherds and their families go too. Part of the fresh sheep's milk is made into such cheeses as Erimis Peynir, an ancient nomad cheese.

BELOW: Although sheep predominate, Turkey has more cattle than many countries in Europe, including the United Kingdom. It has a similar number of goats, including 6 million Mohair goats, used primarily for their fine wool.

cows; a similar number of goats; and about 35 million sheep, whose milk goes to make the favorite national cheese. One of the problems facing the dairy industry is a lack of good cattle fodder: not enough acres are under cultivation with the result that the animals are only of moderate quality, and the milk yields are low. This is unfortunate, since cheese is one of the most important food items on the Turkish table; the farms that provide milk, however, are numerous and widespread. Sheep's milk is the type generally preferred for cheesemaking, either alone or mixed with cow's or goat's milk.

Cheesemakers pay a deposit to the farms in the autumn, which enables them to collect the milk from the farms the following spring, for as long as the lactation period of the animals lasts. If the distance from farm to cheese dairy is too far to be practicable, the milk may be processed into curd in a small regional dairy before being sent to the larger dairy or factory to finish the process. Although communications have greatly improved of late, most of the cheese factories, or *mandira*, as they are called, are located

BELOW: Primitive techniques are used to make the most characteristic and traditional cheeses. If modern methods were applied, certain natural qualities might well be lost. Both yogurt and cheese are thus prepared by the wives of nomad shepherds; these milk products form an important part of their daily diet.

near the big cities, where they have a large market and can obtain good prices.

Turkey's salty favorite

The soft, fresh *Beynaz Peynir* accounts for 95% of the total production of sheep's milk cheese. Because it is traditionally made of sheep's milk, the cheese is to be found throughout Turkey, and particularly in Thracia. The milk used must be very fresh and free from impurities. On the farm, raw milk is filtered through a cloth; in the factory the milk is pasteurized and passed through a cleaning centrifuge. Rennet is then added, and the milk curdles in 1.5 to 2.5 hours. The curd is then cut into pieces, wrapped in a piece of cloth and put under the press which may, in the simple farm dairies, be but a few heavy stones. Three hours after pressing, the curd is unpacked and cut into little cubes. To give the cubes greater consistency they are often immersed in brine. As soon as they have dried out, they are carefully laid in tins. Between each layer of cheese a layer of salt is added, and as soon as the container is full, any remaining whey is poured off and replaced by clean brine. The lid is then soldered on, and the cheese is left to ripen in the brine for anywhere up to six or seven months. Sometimes the cheese is sold fresh, but when cured it has a much better and more individual taste. Not surprisingly the cheese is rather salty (salt may account for up to 15% of the total dry matter); it can be soaked in fresh water to dispel some of the salt before use.

Some other favorites

Kasar Peynir takes second place in the list of Turkey's cheeses. It, too, is generally a sheep's milk cheese, but it may also be a mixed-milk, or even solely a cow's milk cheese, depending on the availability. It is a hard plastic-curd cheese of the Kaschkaval type.

There are quite a few varieties of the plastic-curd type. *Abaza Peynir* is a small, flat round cheese made in the north and northeast of Turkey; it is produced from different types of milk or a combination of milks. Some of the cheeses are smoked, and are known as *Cerkez Peynir*: the smoking increases the keeping properties. *Erimis Peynir* is produced by nomads in southeast Anatolia; it is sold unripe on the local market and bought by merchants who

Name	Milk	Type	Rind	Form	Weight	% Fat content
Abaza Peynir	✳	■	—	flat disc	500 g	50
Beyaz Peynir	◿	●	—	cube	500 g	45
Kasar Peynir	◿◿	■	□	cartwheel	10-12 kg	42
Mihalic Peynir	◿	◣	□	container	varying	46
Tulum Peynir	◿	◣	—	container	varying	6-56

✳ ◿/◿/◿/

Key to symbols on page 34. 453 g = 1 lb; 1 kg = 2.2 lbs.

LEFT: A Turkish village woman carrying a milk churn probably containing sheep's milk, the preferred type for Turkish tastes.

ripen it further, in the manner of the French *affineurs*. *Tel Peynir* is a lean kneaded cheese made from skimmed milk left over from buttermaking.

Tulum Peynir is another interesting cheese reminiscent of Rumanian Brinzâ; it is older than Kasar Peynir and becoming rather rare. To milk of an unspecified type, olive oil or yogurt may be added. The curd is put into large sacks, suspended from the ceiling for an hour or more and vigorously pressed by hand in order to expel the whey. The rather dry curd is then taken out, crumbled and salted, and packed into the *tulum*, a bag made of the cleaned and dried skin of a sheep or goat. The cheesemaker presses the cheese into the bag, using a stout wooden club to compress the curd; he then adds a few handfuls of salt and ties up the sack. The cheese is left to ripen for 3 to 4 months in a cool place until it becomes quite firm.

Around Bursa, opposite Istanbul across the Sea of Marmara, a hard, brine cheese is made, known as *Mihalic Peynir*. Two cheesemakers are needed to process this cheese. The first step is for them to half fill an oak barrel with first-grade sheep's milk. After curdling, the cheesemakers begin to crumble the curd, slowly creating a well in the center of the mass. While one continues to work the curd, the other pours hot water into the hollow, bringing the temperature of the curd to between 40° and 45°C (104° and 113°F). After a rest of 1.5 hours, the curd has sunk to the bottom of the barrel and is scooped out into a cheese cloth. The curd contained in the cloth is suspended from the ceiling and beaten to get rid of the whey. The cheesemakers then remove the curd and cut it into large pieces before immersing it in brine baths of the correct salt content. After 15 days the cheese is transferred to wooden vats, where it is allowed to ripen for about three months. More salt is added as necessary, and the vat is hermetically sealed. A good Mihalic has a rather salty taste. Its rind is thick and light in color; the paste is firm and characterized by a number of small eyes.

Recently, some foreign cheeses have been introduced into the national selection. Processed cheese is now made, and a Swiss factory has started to produce a Gruyère-like cheese known as *Gravyer Peynir*.

Syria

Wherever there is a supply of milk, cheese can be made, and it is invariably made wherever there is a surplus. In a temperate climate we would expect to find cheeses of both quantity and variety, but in a desert country like Syria a product such as cheese has little economic importance, and there are but a few small factories. Most of Syria's cheese is made by farmers and the wandering groups of Bedouin. Agriculturally speaking, Syria's prosperity comes from wheat, barley, cotton, sheep breeding and the cultivation of fruit and vines. Not much cheese is sold on the market; it is mostly produced for the cheesemaker's own consumption and that of his family.

Lebnye is a Bedouin cheese which is made by boiling sour milk with rice or barley until it thickens into a homogeneous mass. This is left for three days and then mixed with thyme and other herbs; it is then packed in small, stone pots and topped up with olive oil.

A type of Sauermilchkäse is made from skimmed milk (mostly the milk from sheep or goats, but cow's milk might be added when and where available). Whole milk is first put aside in leather bags for 12 to 24 hours to become sour. After curdling, the mass in the bag is kneaded and shaken until the butter fat has separated. The butter is then removed, and the remaining skimmed-milk curd is mixed with salt and hung up in cotton bags. As soon as sufficient whey has drained from the curd, it is formed into small balls the size of apricots, put into a glass jar and then covered in olive oil as a preservative measure. These cheeses, when over a year old, are known as *Lebenen Be-zet*.

Other domestic cheeses made from sheep's and goat's milk are *Akavi*, *Ifravi* and *Stambuli*. The Ifravi is a globe-shaped cheese; the remaining two are rectangular with rounded edges.

There are also some semihard types that have good keeping properties, mainly due to their salt content. *Hullon* and *Shulal* are made all over Syria, and particularly in the eastern steppe areas. The curd is cut into strips, immersed for a while in salt and then dried in the air. The salt spreads through the cheese when it is boiled in fresh water. *Kashkawan* is a Kashkaval type that is finished in small cheese factories from ready-made curd supplied by cheesemakers.

LEFT: Damascus is one of the oldest cities in the world, and dates back to 7000 B.C. It is built on the site of a vast oasis in the middle of desert country. Although the markets offer a wide variety of produce, very little cheese is sold. What little is made is used for home consumption.

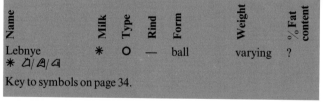

Name	Milk	Type	Rind	Form	Weight	% Fat content
Lebnye * 🔲/🔲/🔲	*	O	—	ball	varying	?

Key to symbols on page 34.

LEFT: The lake of Homs was created by building a dam and diverting the river Orones. It is a precious reservoir in this desert country. In the irrigated plain that surrounds it, fruit and cereals are grown.

Lebanon

RIGHT: In Lebanon, milk for making cheese is supplied by Bedouins and small farmers like this one, posing with his animals on a mountain track.

Lebanon is situated on the east coast of the Mediterranean, with Israel to the south and Syria encircling the east and north. Its position gives rise to its great seasonal contrasts – hot, often scorching summers and mild, wet winters. A chain of mountains runs parallel to the coast, where winter snows provide reservoirs of water for the summer supply.

Lebanon, one of the old Levant states, was a prosperous trading center for the seafaring Phoenicians a thousand years before Christ, with its bustling towns such as Byblos, Sidon and Tyre. Because of its central position it has remained a great trading area, with Beirut as its principal city. The country is undoubtedly one of the most developed of all the Middle East states. Educational standards are high, and there are three different universities in the capital. Favorable trade and social advantages have done little, however, to prevent the intermittent periods of internal strife in recent years. The political situation has greatly disturbed the economy, persuading many important companies to move, at least temporarily, to quieter countries. There is little in-

dustry owing to the shortage of raw materials. Apart from the oil refineries, most of the economic activity is in arable farming and, to a lesser extent, in cattle.

The people's cheeses

As in other Middle Eastern countries, it is the Bedouin, as well as the farmer, who supplies most of the milk and makes cheese. A typical Bedouin cheese is *Halloum*, a durable, sheep's milk variety that is light yellow in color and tough and salty to the taste. It is found in most Lebanese markets and is often skewered and grilled over charcoal. Because of its adaptability as a cooking cheese, Halloum is found all over the Middle East, and even as far west as Greece, where it is known as Halloumi, and as far south as Australia, where it is called Haloumy. Serving this cheese as a kind of kebab probably originated in Turkey. In general, though, cheeses are not much used in Middle Eastern cooking, most people preferring to eat it in its fresh form.

The most popular cheese in Lebanon is *Baladi* (the Arabic word for "native"). This is a white cheese with a crumbly texture. Originally it was made only from sheep's milk, but today cow's milk is also used. The finished product is made both salted and unsalted. *Akkawi* is made exclusively from cow's milk, which is in rather short supply; this results in the cheese's being more expensive than the standard range of sheep's milk cheeses.

Labneh, which has many local variations, is popular throughout the Middle East. It is made by draining soured milk which has attained a yogurt-like consistency. Labneh is one of the most simple kinds of cheese, as after the thickening and draining process it needs no further processing. The cheese varies according to the type of milk used and the fat content of the milk.

In Lebanon there is a cheesemaking unit in an institution controlled by a Catholic monastery, and also a few cheese factories in Chtaura and Chyah, but for the most part cattle breeding is a greater priority than dairying. Cheese manufacturing does not take place on any notable scale.

RIGHT: The town of Byblos, an important Mediterranean trading center since the days of the Phoenicians, where cheeses were probably imported.

Name	Milk	Type	Rind	Form	Weight	% Fat content
Akkawi	◁	○	—	varying	varying	?
Baladi	◲	○○	—	varying	varying	?
Halloum	◲	◼	☐	varying	varying	?
Labneh	✳	○	—	varying	varying	?

✳ ◁/◲/◲

Key to symbols on page 34.

Israel

ABOVE: Not surprisingly, Israel produces a kosher cheese, which is manufactured in many styles and flavors and is exported to four continents. A koshered product is one that complies with the strict Jewish dietary laws.

ABOVE: The city of Jerusalem viewed from the Mount of Olives, with the dome of the Khubat as-Sachra mosque in the center of the picture. Determination and hard work have completely revitalized Israel's dairy industry, and cheese is now an important product.

RIGHT: In the old part of Jerusalem a flock of animals is being herded up these stone steps, as has been done for centuries.

Apart from a narrow strip along the coast and the Jordan valley in the north, Israel is dominated by the Negev Desert, which is partly irrigated to provide arable land for mixed farming. Cheese may have been introduced into Israel from Mesopotamia. According to the Old Testament, Abraham and his shepherd people, who migrated from Haran to settle in Canaan, knew about cheese; their cheeses would certainly have been those small, white, sheep's milk types so popular in the Middle East.

Industrial genesis

Because of Israel's tremendous progressive development, brought about by employing Western techniques and standards to industrial and agricultural productivity, Israel now has the most advanced cattle-breeding and dairy industry in the Middle East. By

applying the results of scientific research, production has increased 25% over the past five years. To produce a fairly wide range of European cheeses, a supply of good-quality dairy milk is necessary. With this in mind, Israel's cattle breeders crossbred native cattle with imported Frisians, establishing an Israeli-Frisian type that has perfectly adapted to climatic conditions and can hardly be distinguished from the pure Frisian breed.

By judicious breeding and the provision of the right roughage, extra fodder and good care, the cows now have a milk yield of between 5,300 to 6,500 liters (7,150 quarts) yearly, they thus are among the world's greatest milk producers and, as such, are bred for export. On the collective farms – the kibbutzim – herds of some 200 or 250 cows are maintained, while on ordinary farms the herds number about 15 to 20; the size of the herd is dependent on the availability of roughage and imported concentrates.

Israel's sheep have also benefited from the introduction of progressive farming techniques; the Awassi breed is the favorite. With careful selection and good breeding each sheep pro-

Name	Milk	Type	Rind	Form	Weight	% Fat content
Brinzâ	✳	●■⌒	—	cube	300 g	45
Duberki	✳	■	—	ball	varying	?
Gewina Zfatit	✳	○	—	flat disc	0.2-3 kg	28-45
Lebbene	✳	○	—	varying	varying	?

✳ ◿/◿/◿

Key to symbols on page 34. 453 g = 1 lb.

BELOW: A pastoral procession on the Nahal Sinai kibbutz near Al Arish in the Gaza Strip. Kibbutzim are collective farms, and were founded in 1909. They have played a very impor-tant part in the colonization of Israel, especially in the cultivation of desert areas.

duces some 250 liters (275 quarts) of milk per lactation period (December to July) with a fat content of 7.4% and 11% of fat-free dry matter. Sheep's milk is used for both cheese and yogurt.

A land of milk and cheeses

In 1920, *Brinzâ* cheeses were brought from the Balkans, Turkey and Russia to Palestine. Shortly thereafter a few kibbutzim began to make Brinzâ from sheep's milk, although conditions in those days were rather primitive. Today modern cheese factories specialize in the manufacture of sheep's milk cheese, and a fine quality Brinzâ is produced. These little cheeses are rectangular in shape, and weigh about 300 grams (10.5 oz); 25% cow's or goat's milk may be added.

Gewina Zfatit, a cheese containing a high percentage of salt, has been made for centuries in North Galilee. Originally it was a rather large-sized, sheep's milk cheese, but factories now make a smaller version with a lower fat content. The cheeses are eaten fresh for the most part and are easily recognizable by their flat, round shape and by the impression left by the basket in which they are prepared. To make these cheeses, pasteurized milk is curdled at a rather high temperature. The curd is regularly turned in the baskets, but it is not pressed, and the surface is salted dry. The product can be eaten immediately, provided that it is stored in a cool place. Gewina Zfatit has a white paste, both inside and outside, and it is pliant when fresh. As the cheeses mature they become very hard. They are made with varying fat contents: the full-fat cheese is 45%, for which 25% cow's milk might be used; the half-fat cheese is 28%, for which a mixture of cow's, goat's and sheep's milk is allowed.

The Bedouin usually makes *Djibne* cheese from such a mixture, cutting and pressing the curd into rectangular pieces. Djibne can be eaten after a day, but can also be kept for months in brine. Then there is *Lebbene*, a sort of drained yogurt that is found in other Middle Eastern countries under different names. It can be eaten fresh or may be formed into little balls which are either preserved in olive oil or dried in the sun to make *Duberki*, a real delicacy. The whole cheese can also be sun-dried; it is then known as *Kislik*. As the drying process makes the cheese

LEFT: The construction of an irrigation pipeline, which will take water from the Sea of Galilee to the Negev Desert. It is part of an extensive system of pipelines and canals that has worked miracles in the country's desert areas.

BELOW: The market at Beersheba in the Negev Desert, where sheep and goats are bought and sold. The market attracts the nomadic Bedouins, who are considered the livestock experts throughout the Middle East.

very hard, Kislik must be softened in water before eating.

As might be expected in a hot climate, great care must be exercised by cheesemakers who produce European types. For a long time European cheeses were made from imported skimmed-milk powder and margarine. Now margarine is no longer used, and milk powder is used only during the months of low milk production; at this time only the best low-fat milk powder is used in combination with fresh milk. Such good quality is achieved that the cheeses are indistinguishable from those prepared with fresh milk alone.

Cheese goes kosher

The government provides subsidies to keep the price of fresh cheese in line with other foodstuffs. The industry contributes its share by making available a great assortment of attractive packagings. The ripened cheeses are mainly standard types marketed under fancy trade names, including *Romadur, Limburg, Camembert, Bel Paese, Brie, Edam, Gouda, Danbo, Cheddar* and *Emmental* types, as well as *Kashkaval, Roquefort* and *Provolone* types, the latter three being made from sheep's milk. One of Israel's specialties is kosher cheese which is widely exported, along with types of processed cheese. The annual consumption of processed cheese and natural cheese together is 12.5 kg (27.5 lbs) per head. Today the most modern manufacturing methods are applied to cheesemaking, a completely closed and controlled cooling chain is utilized, from animal to consumer. Automation will shortly be taken further with the introduction of aseptic pre-packing, the programing of production and the planning of delivery.

Jordan

Only the narrow, mountainous western strip of Jordan is fertile. It is here and in the capital Amman that the major part of the population, numbering around two million, has settled. Agriculture is practically the sole natural source of prosperity in this region, but as irrigation has only been carried out on a small scale, crops are still greatly dependent on weather conditions.

The remaining part of the country consists of basalt deserts and sandstone mountains. This is the land of the Bedouins, the nomadic tribes who live in tents made of goatskin and have inherited the job of administering livestock and dairy produce throughout most of the Middle East. The Bedouin herds number some 75,000 sheep, 600,000 goats, 20,000 camels and 60,000 cattle. As of old, most cheese is made of goat's and sheep's milk. A most surprising phenomenon is the existence of prosperous Dutch cows on this barren, gravelly soil, animals which in their own country are used to green and lush meadows. Development aid has made this miracle possible, even though for the rest of their lives the animals have to exist on a diet

BELOW: Fresh water is rare. Only limited areas have been developed so far, but irrigation has greatly improved the prospects of agriculture.

Name	Milk	Type	Rind	Form	Weight	% Fat content
Labaneh	⌂	○	—	container	250 g	10

Key to symbols on page 34. 453 g = 1 lb.

TOP: Donkeys carry the milk to the new dairy center at Russeifeh, near Amman. In addition to fresh cheese, the dairy manufactures Laban, a product resembling yogurt, and Labaneh, which is like Quark.

LEFT: The label from a carton of Labaneh, a thicker version of Laban, and made from skimmed cow's milk.

of chopped straw, alfalfa and concentrated fodder.

Bearing in mind the importance of good grazing to cheesemaking, it is obvious that this restricted diet is a major influence on the type and quality of cheese produced. Perhaps it was hoped that the milk of Dutch cows might be able to provide something approaching a European variety of cheese. Given time for the cattle to adapt to the climate and fodder, such cheeses may be possible in the future, as a result of greater properity, the influence of Western culture, and the continued development of irrigation. It is likely, though, that cow's milk cheeses will have a hard time competing against the traditional nomad favorites.

Labaneh and fresh cheese

In Russeifeh near Amman is a brand new cheese factory. Evidence of the primitiveness of the industry is that cow's milk is transported there by donkey. The factory produces the yogurt-like *Laban*, the thicker *Labaneh* and also some fresh cheese.

Labaneh is produced by heating fresh milk with a small quantity of fatless milk powder to approximately 85°C (153°F); it is kept at this temperature for five minutes and then cooled to 47°C (65°F). The milk is then soured, poured into churns and placed in the incubation room until it reaches the correct degree of acidity. After a period of two days in the cooling cell, the contents are poured into bags and left to drain for fourteen hours. The drainage is hastened by placing churns filled with water on top of the bags. Finally, the Labaneh maker adds salt to the mass (1.5% of the mixture), then packs the cheese in plastic beakers.

For the production of fresh cheese, a mixture of 97% milk and 3% fatless milk powder is used. This is heated to 74°C (133°F) and then cooled to 36°C (65°F), the correct temperature for adding the rennet. After thirty minutes hot water is added, and the curd is poured out onto a cloth mounted on a wooden screen, so that it may drain. The curd is then formed by hand into rectangular pieces which are wrapped in small squares of cloth and are pressed for about ten minutes. The cloth is then removed, and the small cheeses are transported in camel-drawn vehicles to the various markets.

Saudi Arabia

Saudi Arabia comprises the greater part of the Arabian peninsula, a vast plateau gradually descending eastwards from a rocky ridge that rises steeply and inaccessibly from the Red Sea. The country has a dry climate; it seldom rains and most of the land is desert, inhabited by Bedouin Muslims, the majority of whom are of the Wahabite sect that forbids the use of tobacco and alcohol.

Life in the desert depends on the prosperity of the oases. As in all countries with extensive desert and steppe regions, particularly in Saudi Arabia, there are two main groups of people: farmers with permanent homes in the oases and the nomad tribes. The farmers cultivate corn, vegetables and fruits, and in particular the fine-quality dates which are widely exported. The nomads are mostly Bedouin, who wander with their families searching for areas of grazing in the arid desert. They are continually on the move, taking with them their camels, sheep and goats and leading a meager, hard life.

The mother of camels
The Bedouins' food consists mainly of camel's and goat's milk, cheese, dates and sometimes coffee. Bread is rather scarce, and meat is a rare treat which often occasions a party. Sometimes an old senile camel dies, providing an unexpected feast, or perhaps a lizard or desert rat is caught and finds its way into the pot. There are few peoples living in a more inhospitable land and in greater poverty – yet their pride and hospitality is legendary.

As far as the Bedouins are concerned, life without the camel – in Saudi Arabia the dromedary – would be insupportable. It is the faithful helper and milk source. On one of the plateaus of the Arabian peninsula, or so the legend goes, the first camel was tamed. This happened thousands of years ago, but the plateau is remembered and revered by the Arabs, who call it Om El Bel – "the mother of camels." The Arabs recognize in the constellation of Orion the shape of a camel, and in the Pleiades a small herd of camels.

After the birth of a calf, the mother yields for two years a white, sweet milk that is rather fatty. This goes to the camel calf for the first year, and to the camel's owner for the second year for human consumption.

Name	Milk	Type	Rind	Form	Weight	% Fat content
Jupneh	🐑🐐	O	—	flat disc	varying	?

Key to symbols on page 34.

BELOW: Camels, donkeys, sheep and goats are the mainstay of the Bedouin tribes, but all depend on the supplies of water from the precious wells in the desert. The staple diet of the Bedouin consists mainly of cheese, milk and dates. Meat is a rare luxury.

LEFT: Milking a goat in a street in Aden, on the southern coast of the Arabian peninsula. From sheep's and goat's milk, small and simple cheeses are made.

The nomad cheeses
The Bedouins generally call their cheese *Gibne*, for which they normally use sheep's or goat's milk. The milk is curdled with the aid of animal rennet, or with the sap of fig leaves and other vegetable juices. *Jupneh* is prepared by boiling the milk and then cooling it to 25°C (77°F); the curd is formed by immersing a strip of salted lamb's stomach in the milk. After about an hour, the curd is found floating on top of the whey. It is then skimmed off and laid on a cloth, the ends of which are folded over to enclose the curd, which is pressed between two planks. A heavy object on the upper plank gives the Jupneh cheese its flat, round shape. The product is either eaten immediately, or boiled for fifteen minutes in brine. An alternative method of preserving the cheese is to store it in weak, cold brine in a tightly closed barrel. The salt is washed off before use.

What the nomads produce in excess of their own needs is usually sold in small shops that sell dairy produce. In addition to these cheeses, Saudi Arabia imports quantities of white cheese types, principally from Rumania and Czechoslovakia.

Iraq

Six thousand years ago, in that area of Iraq known as the Fertile Crescent, the Sumerians laid the foundation of one of the world's oldest civilizations. The area is fertile because it lies between the two great rivers, the Euphrates and the Tigris, where for centuries agriculture and cattle breeding have been the most important means of existence. So rich were the grazing lands, that milk and cheese production far exceeded domestic requirements, and the surplus was brought to the markets to be purchased by town dwellers, among them the priests, writers and craftsmen who made cities like Ur and Nineveh into cultural centers.

It is unlikely that the Sumerians were the first to learn the skill of cheesemaking. Ancient though their civilization proves to have been, primitive neolithic farmers cultivated the Fertile Crescent long before them. It was they who were the first to discover the wild, indigenous wheat from which they made bread, and they probably knew how to make cheese as well. Compared with these farmers, the Sumerian and Babylonion cultures were highly civilized, as archeological discoveries have shown.

We also know from the Old Testament that these pastoral people included cheese in their daily diet, as was confirmed by the discoveries at Ur. One of the panels of the so-called "royal standard" depicts cows, sheep and dairy utensils. On a Sumerian frieze found at El-Obeid, the milking

ABOVE: Lambing time in the foothills of Kurdistan, where Iraq borders on Turkey and Iran.

BELOW: Many irrigation projects have been carried out and more are under construction. This reservoir at Dokan is situated in the northern hills, where arable farming and cattle raising are being developed.

and curdling of the milk is pictured with artistic detail. Sir Leonard Wooley, who was in charge of the excavations at Ur between 1922 and 1934, writes that cheese was made from the milk of cows and goats. From this cradle of civilization, the art of cheesemaking spread slowly westward to ancient Greece and Rome.

Iraqi specialities

In Iraq today cheese is still made, but on a modest scale and without much care. Most cheeses are generally made of sheep's milk during the months of April, May and June. To make *Meira* curdled milk is heated until the curd separates from the whey. It is then put into linen bags and pressed with a heavy stone to expel the remaining whey. After salting, the curd is cut into strips and put in a sheepskin in which it can be stored for 6 to 12 months. It eventually becomes quite hard, and is sold at the market in Baghdad.

Lour is made of whey to which milk is added. The curd is salted but not pressed, and the cheese must be eaten fresh. So must *Fajy*, a lean cheese flavored with garlic or onion for which no rennet is used. Fajy is not marketed, but made entirely for home use.

Iraq also makes some *Mozzarella* and *Cottage Cheese*, and there is a substantial production of processed cheese: Iraq has the largest processed cheese factory in the Middle East. For its preparation, considerable quantities of Cheddar are imported.

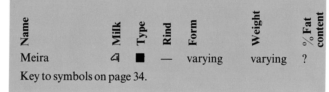

Name	Milk	Type	Rind	Form	Weight	% Fat content
Meira	◿	■	—	varying	varying	?

Key to symbols on page 34.

CENTRAL AND EAST ASIA

ABOVE: Although water buffalo are the principal milk-producing and draught animals of Central Asia and the Far East, theirs is by no means the only milk to be made into cheese. In addition to the milk provided by sheep and goats, cheeses are made from the milk of camels, horses, donkeys and – in Nepal and Tibet – the yak.

Iran

Iran has an extensive central plateau or tableland ringed by mountains, an area that experiences a continental climate. Its valleys and mountain slopes, however, receive sufficient rainfall, and the vegetation in these areas is subtropical. Iran's traditional large estates are being divided up into smaller lots for individual farmers; 35% of the population earns its living by agriculture and the breeding of livestock. Many sheep and goats are kept, and this is reflected in the nature of many Iranian cheeses.

For *Seret Penir*, however, the milk of the camel, horse or donkey is said to be used. This is a genuine nomad cheese, where the fresh milk is put immediately in the sun, in flat earthenware dishes, and left for five days. When the milk becomes sour, the thickened mass is ladled out with a skimmer, then wrapped in linen cloth and smoke-dried. From this cheese small balls are formed, and they too are sun-dried until cracks begin to appear in the surface. The cheeses are then immersed in brine and the cracks closed by hand. The surface of each cheese ball is rubbed with beeswax, and after ten weeks of ripening they are ready for consumption. Their keeping quality is excellent, however, and they may be kept for several years.

Kaschgaii, also a cheese with good keeping qualities, originated in the Zagros Mountains. Milk of any milking animal is used – whatever happens to be around. It is boiled together with

a type of yogurt, and stirred every morning for ten days. The curd is then heated and poured into wooden molds, then heated again a few days later, before being stored in stone huts for ripening. Kaschgaii is a very hard cheese with a cylindrical shape.

Lighvan is a brine cheese made from sheep's, goat's or cow's milk. The curd is left for three to four months in progressively weaker solutions of brine. Cheese from sheep or goat's milk is preferred because the animals live and are milked outdoors, whereas cow's milk cheese may take on stable odors or other foreign flavors due to the fodder concentrates which are fed to the animals.

For *Panir Kusei*, the dairy farmer molds the curd by hand and kneads it vigorously. He then puts it in an earthenware pot and rams it down hard. The pot is sealed with paper or cloth, and may be covered with a layer of loam. It is stored for three to four months, either in natural cellars or placed upside down in sand, with the bottom of the pot just sticking out above the surface. The percentage of moisture decreases slowly during ripening, and any bacteria present are destroyed during the process.

The inventiveness that many cheesemakers show in the process of making durable cheeses, especially in hot countries, deserves admiration. To give milk a keeping quality in very adverse or primitive conditions is almost an art.

Name	Milk	Type	Rind	Form	Weight	% Fat content
Kaschgaii	✳	■	☐	cylinder	4-7 kg	?
Lighvan	✳	◖	—	cylinder	500 g	?
✳ Any milking animal						

Key to symbols on page 34. 453 g = 1 lb; 1 kg = 2.2 lbs.

Afghanistan and Pakistan

By a carefully planned system of irrigation, the northern mountain valleys of Afghanistan have been made suitable for agriculture. In these watered valleys there is also excellent grazing for camels, sheep and goats, animals that are of great economic value because of their supply of wool and hair. These commodities are both exported and used within the country for making Afghan carpets. In fact, the entire economy rests primarily on the regular supply of the wool from 22 million sheep.

Improverished tribes form the majority of the population, 75% of whom are still illiterate. They wander with their herds as they have done for thousands of years, living in tents under the most primitive conditions. In the summer their flocks of sheep graze the mountain pastures; during the winter they trek through the valleys, an inevitable migration since the natural vegetation is too sparse to tolerate very intensive grazing. The nomadic tribes make their cheese from buttermilk, for the milk fat is too precious and is made into *ghee* (butter oil) for export to India.

Cheeses by the people

Krut or *Qurut* is a cheese of the buttermilk type. The buttermilk is boiled to make the protein flocculate, and the curd is then hung in a cloth or special basket. What remains after draining is kneaded with salt. By drying in the sun – perhaps on the roof of the tent –

ABOVE AND LEFT: Two portraits of the water buffalo. These specimens come from an area near Karachi in Pakistan. Note the long, curling horns and the powerful build.

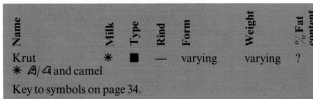

Name	Milk	Type	Rind	Form	Weight	% Fat content
Krut	*	■	—	varying	varying	?

* 🐄/🐄 and camel

Key to symbols on page 34.

LEFT: A small Gilgit village near Rawalpindi, in the foothills of the Himalayas. In these primitive areas, animals are still used for virtually any task – grinding corn, drawing water, carrying loads – for which the West has found mechanical solutions.

the curd becomes a dry mass that can be kept for years. Before consumption it is crumbled and soaked in water.

When the drained curd is cut into rectangles after being pressed between stones, it is known as *Pasteikrut*. The cheesemakers often curdle the milk by adding the rennet from the stomach of a new-born lamb. After five minutes or so, the milk thickens. They drain it in small cotton sacks and take the finished product to market, where dealers improve the cheese's keeping qualities by cutting the surface with a knife and sprinkling it with salt. This cheese is called *Shûr panir*; it is prepared in the same fashion in Tibet, Iran and Saudi Arabia.

Afghanistan's industrial development is still in its initial stage, and it may well be a long time before a dairy industry is established. Cheeses are made by the people for the people, simple types that are to be found here and there in the markets, especially the market center at Mazar-i-Sharif.

Pakistan

Pakistan is for the greater part a dry and steppe-like region. The best area for agriculture is the Punjab, with the town of Lahore at its center. In the Punjab it is the buffalo, along with the goat and sheep, that produces most of the supply of milk. Of the different wild buffalo types, only the Arni breed could be tamed, big brown animals almost twice as heavy as cows, with beautiful broad horns that incline slightly backwards.

The Pakistanis are trying to make a quick-ripening *Cheddar* from buffalo milk; but problems have arisen for which solutions have yet to be found, mainly because the composition of buffalo milk is substantially different from that of cow's milk. It must be acknowledged as a brave try, however, particularly in view of the fact that Mozzarella might have seemed the obvious choice. It is indeed paradoxical that in countries where cheesemaking began at such an early period, technological progress finds acceptance so late and so laboriously.

China and Tibet

LEFT: Water pump in the yard of an old farm, part of a people's commune near Peking. The commune is named after Marco Polo, who traveled to China in the thirteenth century.

ABOVE: Postage stamp showing a Chinese dairy farm. Contrary to the picture's theme, the Chinese are not fond of milk.

An age-old culture, the most ancient civilization in the history of mankind, now living within a relatively new political system, China still remains an enigma to most of the Western world. Its cultural traditions are unparalleled and unprecedented. From China came some of the really fundamental inventions; art and philosophy were highly advanced at a time when the rest of the known world was still chipping flints.

Although they have made equally great advances in early agricultural techniques and in farming, the Chinese have never considered milk as being fit for human consumption, and this attitude still persists.

The Chinese have had cattle since time immemorial, but like the water buffalo, they were used mainly as work animals. It is surprising that a people living so close to Tibet and Mongolia, where the milk of yaks, cows and goats is drunk and processed, should continue to reject so valuable a food. But tradition is tradition, and since the Great Wall was built, the Chinese have consistently protected themselves from outside influence.

Grain, vegetables, soya beans and

BELOW: An enlargement of a Mongolian postage stamp, issued in 1969 to commemorate the tenth anniversary of the cooperative movement. The painting, by the Mongolian artist Tsewegdjaw, shows how mares are milked. Mare's milk is used for some rare local cheeses, about which little is generally known.

the so-called "soya cheese" are the basic foods, yet the product derived from the soya plant can hardly earn the name cheese. In the big towns there are a few dairy farming plants, with very good quality milking cows, where cheese is made for the resident Europeans and for the more progressive Chinese.

Enter the yak

A large proportion of Tibet is mountainous country, over 16,000 feet high. To the south are the great river valleys of the Upper Indus and the Tsangpo, while to the east there are fertile plains with good grazing. Unlike the Chinese, the Tibetans appreciate the value of milk, although the farmers of the valleys keep cows of an indeterminate breed and poor quality. But the low quality is not surprising in an area devoid of useful vegetation. Mountain sheep are much more suited to the terrain, and so is the yak, the only bovine animal that has really adapted to Tibet's harsh climate and high altitudes. Yaks have been bred for centuries, not only as work animals but as milking animals, and they are very particular about their diet. As they only eat grass, it means they must conduct a constant migratory search for new pastures.

The nomads are completely dependent on their animals as a source of food. Milk, butter and cheese are therefore of paramount importance. As they move on, their motion churns the milk into butter, and when they stop to camp, the butter fat is heated and made into a sort of butter oil, known as *ghee*. This is used as a food and in the tea that they drink from morning to night. It is also used for lighting and is an important trading commodity.

The Tibetans know nothing about coagulants. The sour buttermilk left over from making *ghee* is heated and drained, and becomes a sort of fatless sour cheese, which they call *Chura*. This is mixed with tea and flour, and shaped to form rolls. A yogurt type of sour milk, *Zho*, may be turned into fresh cheese by pouring off the whey.

As in China, drastic agricultural and social changes are taking place in Tibet. What development can be expected as far as dairy farming is concerned is hard to forecast. But at least the Tibetans believe wholeheartedly in milk, and its end products, as food.

Name	Milk	Type	Rind	Form	Weight	% Fat content
Chura ✳ ◁ and yak	✳	■	—	varying	varying	–

Key to symbols on page 34.

Japan

It is probable that the first dairy products to enter Japan came from India via China, along with a more abstract influence – the Buddhist religion. In the seventh century A.D., the Japanese emperor was ceremonially presented with *so* ("dairy produce") each year. Since those days, there was no record of cheese production taking place until the appearance of Portuguese traders in the 1500s and 1600s.

Cheese in quantity was made for the first time in 1875, on the island of Hokkaido. A second cheesemaking plant was established on the same island in 1900 by Trappist monks. Hokkaido, as far as soil and climate are concerned, is by far the most suitable terrain for cattle. There are many productive farms with stocks of fine-quality cattle, although by modern standards the herds are small in size. Various types have been imported for breeding purposes, but the Frisians appear to be the best milkers, and these are now very much in evidence throughout the country. Few of the farms have meadows, however, and the cattle are largely dependent on roughage and concentrates.

Before the First World War, milk was already being processed to make cheese and milk powder. It was not until the 1960s, with the proper stabilization of prices and the changing market for cheese, that the situation began to improve radically.

Cheese instead of rice

There are few, if any, countries like Japan: steeped in ancient traditions, yet so totally accepting of Western styles. Western eating habits are becoming more and more popular. The use of rice is rapidly declining, while cheese production has risen from 12,000 tons in 1963 to 41,000 tons in

ABOVE: Japanese cheese, probably of the Gouda type, being removed from the brine bath. Although Japan has no dairy tradition, cheese is gaining in popularity.

Processed cheese is most popular, but Gouda, Cheddar and Camembert types are now being produced in increasing quantities.

LEFT: Domestic cheeses stacked in a warehouse.

BELOW: The wrapper from a portion of processed cheese. Most of the milk used to make cheese in Japan comes from herds of black and white Frisians.

1973 (this includes the production of processed cheese). The importation of foreign cheeses has also greatly increased: 6,500 tons in 1965, to 34,000 tons in 1973. To supplement the foreign types, Japan makes its own *Cheddar*, *Gouda* and *Camembert*.

Processed cheese is still the most popular, and a large part of the imported cheese goes directly to the processing plants. Its mild flavor is more to the Japanese taste than that of natural cheese. To give it an even more acceptable taste, and to adapt it to the average eating habits, processed cheese is often wrapped in seaweed or bamboo leaves, or mixed with sesame seed.

In spite of their liking for processed cheese, the Japanese are beginning to develop a palate for natural cheese types. Western-style, self-service restaurants and snack bars are found alongside the traditional eating houses. The familiar, international cheese sandwich that has become a worldwide snack for travelers can be found almost everywhere. Catching up with the cheese sandwich is pizza: although its Italian origins are somewhat obscured by the use of Dutch Gouda cheese, and it is probably served with tea or *sake*.

In all the large supermarkets, cheeses are widely displayed. Public demonstrations are given on how to use cheese in the traditional dishes, there are cookery lessons on television, and recipes are offered in newspapers and magazines.

RIGHT: Because only about one-sixth of Japan's land area is suitable for agriculture, there is a lack of good grazing. Nevertheless, Japan has many fine farms, like this one with its Dutch-style architecture and cattle.

India and Nepal

LEFT: A cow passing a shrine, perhaps dedicated to the monkey god Hanuman, in the sacred city of Banaras. Cows and the milkmaids called *gopis* feature prominently in Indian lore and religion: *gopis* are the maidens that attend the god Krishna.

India's contribution in terms of varied dairy produce is minimal, which might seem paradoxical in view of the fact that its cattle population is by far the largest in the world. Recent estimates put it at something like 170 million cows, but an accurate census is impossible. The cow, of course, is sacred to the Hindus. Cows wander through the streets of Delhi, India's capital city, and are found sitting in the middle of main streets or blocking the sidewalks – they are only very gently nudged out of the way to make room for passing cars and buses.

Another paradox is that sacred though they may be, cows are beasts of burden, and the burden is considerable on the primitive acres owned by the peasant farmers. Their power is used to draw the plow, to thresh corn or pull loads. Their milk, deprived and of low yield, is a source of food, while their dung is used for fertilizer or fuel, or even to repair the roof. In return, cows receive veneration, but precious little green grass or nourishing fodder, and no veterinary attention.

The Indian ox, or Zebu, and the water buffalo are both more adap-

LEFT: In a Nepalese cheese dairy, a worker cleans the cheeses in the ripening room. This picture, and the one below, was made by the United Nations Food and Agriculture Organization.

LEFT: Packing the cheeses for export in attractive baskets made of woven reeds. Nepal has built a small but flourishing export trade in cheese. The product compares well with Indian and imported cheese types.

table. The Zebu is particularly indifferent to extremes of heat and is resistant to tuberculosis. The buffalo, on the other hand, produces over twice as much milk as the Zebu, and the milk has a higher protein and fat content.

Because of the reverence for the sanctity of life – *ahimsa* – which is fully realized in the religious observances of the Jain sect, the majority of Hindus are vegetarians. Milk is an important food, due to its protein content and the fact that it is the product of a living animal; products from dead animals are strictly proscribed, which is why rennet is often avoided as a curdling agent, except in the more progressive areas of the dairy industry. It is curious that cheese, except in the form of yogurt and the soft curds known as *pannir*, or *panir*, has not succeeded in replacing meat. It must be due to the Indians' refusal to accept rennet and their failure to find a vegetable substitute apart from lemon juice.

A better future?
In spite of the restrictions imposed by religious practices, the Indian five-year-plan has allocated a large sum of money for cattle breeding and improv-

ing the dairy industry. By cross-breeding with European cattle types, the nation hopes to achieve a better milk yield and earlier maturity. Around the larger cities the Indian Dairy Corporation has made considerable efforts to combat the problems of climate, disease, public indifference and poor economy. In the Aarey Milk Colony, near Bombay, there is a superb modern farm with 15,000 buffalo, producing 70,000 liters (77,000 quarts) of milk daily; in the countryside, however, little has changed, and the outlook seems unpromising.

The best known Indian cheese is *Surati Panir*. It is now in some demand because in its concentrated form it has a high nutritional value and curative effects are attributed to it. Surati Panir is made of buffalo milk, acidified by a sour milk starter; rennet is added and the curd is arranged in layers with salt in between and is contained in baskets. After draining, the curd is left in its whey.

To make *Dacca* the curdled milk is also put into baskets, after being crumbled by hand. A plank is laid on top of them, and after 10 to 14 days the cheeses are sufficiently dry to be smoked over an open fire of cow dung or wood.

Bandal is another smoked cheese type, while *Chauna* often serves as a base for sweets. It is acidified with sour whey, or with lemon juice, giving it a smoother curd. *Srikand*, a genuine farmhouse product made without rennet, is also eaten with fruits such as bananas, mangoes and papaya. Yogurt, as a milk derivative, is an important part of the Indian diet. It is served in various forms as *raita*, where it is mixed with either cooked or marinated vegetables such as cucumbers, aubergines, onions and tomatoes, or sometimes with fruits. When mixed with milk and curdled with lemon juice, yogurt becomes the cheese known simply as *panir*; it may be mixed with peas to make the popular vegetarian dish *mattar panir*.

Cheese consumption in India is still very limited. The Muslims are fond of dairy produce, as are the Europeans, but throughout the country it remains difficult to obtain good cheese.

Nepal

Butter and cheese have always been made in Nepal, for they are of essential

Name	Milk	Type	Rind	Form	Weight	% Fat content
Bandal	⌂✳	○	—	basket	varying	35-65
Dacca	⌂✳	●	—	basket	varying	35-45
Surati Panir	✳	○	—	basket	varying	50

✳ Buffalo

Key to symbols on page 34.

BELOW: In the marketplace of a small village in north Nepal. Cheese is offered for sale, made from sour buttermilk remaining from the preparation of *ghee*, a butter oil and important export commodity.

importance to the mountain people. Cattle-breeding areas are found in the north and in the subtropical valleys where buffalo, zebus and cows are kept. But on the high mountain slopes close to the Tibetan border it is the yak that gives the milk. On the lower slopes the *sherpas* breed chowries – a cross between a yak and a zebu – and move them from pasture to pasture. From their milk, which is first soured with a sort of yogurt called *Dahi*, butter is churned on the spot. It is made more durable by boiling, so that the moisture evaporates. This *ghee*, as it is called, is sold after the pasture season is over, and it is one of Nepal's most important export articles. The buttermilk remaining from the butter preparation is boiled in a copper vat, and the resulting curd put into a bamboo basket, from which it can drain. The product, which is similar to that made in Tibet, is a cone-shaped cheese sold in the local markets; it is usually eaten in soup. Alternatively, the cheese may be cut into strips, dried on the roof of the hut and smoked by the smoke that arises from cracks in the roof.

Swiss dairy experts have been sent to Nepal by aid programs, and have built the nation's first cheese factory in the mountains. The aim was to give farmers a better income by founding such factories and by improving pastures and promoting sales. In a single week a cheese kettle weighing 70 kg (154 lbs) was carried along narrow mountain paths from Katmandu to Longtrang, and in 1953 the world's highest cheese factory began production. In spite of many difficulties, a Gruyère-like cheese was made, one that could fetch good prices and that eventually found a ready market in India.

With the help of foreign aid, more factories have been constructed and the local inhabitants have been trained in cheesemaking; the Nepalese have successfully managed their own factories since 1964, when the last foreign expert left. The income of the farmers has considerably increased thanks to regular supplies of milk, and hard cheese made in Nepal can now be bought for half the price of tinned cheese from India.

Other Asian countries

Cheese production in Southeast Asia is sparse and limited, owing to climate, terrain, poor economy and lack of demand. In Laos a certain amount of goat's milk and cow's milk is produced, but not enough to make any appreciable difference in cheese production. Here and there a few families may have a surplus of milk to make cheese, and in Vientiane on the Thailand border a small cheesemaking plant proposed to make *Cottage Cheese*, but there is little or no information available.

In Thailand, Danish and German immigrants have increased milk production, with the result that excellent fresh cream, milk and yogurt, as well as *Quark* and *Cottage Cheese* are now on the market. The Germans opened a milk shop in Chiang Mai, but it was unsuccessful as there is little sales potential in the north of Thailand. In scattered areas one might find supplies of cheese; a few state agricultural research stations experiment with certain products, including milk, butter and cheese.

Singapore, the biggest seaport and trade center of Southeast Asia, maintains a fairly good selection of imported cheeses in the shops and markets, and although no milk is produced locally, regular supplies arrive in refrigeration ships from Australia.

The Chinese in Hong Kong are still closely attached to their traditional eating patterns, which means that not much cheese is consumed. However, quite a lot of imported cheese is stocked for the European and American community.

The Philippines

The most interesting cheese in the entire area is made in the Philippines; it is known as *Kesong Puti*. The cheese is prepared from buffalo milk, and the homemade variety is manufactured as follows: sieved, raw buffalo milk is heated in an open pan to a temperature of 80°-90°C (176°-194°F). Immediately after heating, six or seven spoonfuls of vinegar per quart of milk are added. The vinegar is not the acetic acid variety familiar in the West, but one obtained by fermenting the sap of the water palm in an earthenware jar. The milk curdles at once, the curds are put in a cloth and transferred to a mold. After one or two hours, when the whey has drained sufficiently, the cheese is immersed in brine, the tem-

ABOVE: Water buffalo foraging for food on the island of Ceylon, now Sri Lanka.

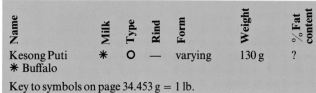

Name	Milk	Type	Rind	Form	Weight	% Fat content
Kesong Puti * Buffalo	*	O	—	varying	130 g	?

Key to symbols on page 34.453 g = 1 lb.

RIGHT: Roadside cheese stall in the Philippines. The cheese, Kesong Puti, is wrapped in banana leaves, which protect it from the heat of the sun and consequent loss of moisture.

perature of the cheese being 25°-30°C (77°-86°F). After two hours of brining the cheese is tasted to judge whether it is salty enough. It is then packed in banana leaves, an ideal packing material because it costs nothing and retains the moisture of the cheese. Two small cheeses of 130 grams (about 4 oz) each are obtained from one liter (1.1 quarts) of milk.

Kesong Puti is also made using rennet extracted from the stomach of the buffalo calf. The rennet is stirred in raw milk at 25°C (77°F). After an hour the curd is cut and placed in a strainer; next it is salted and packaged, again with the use of banana leaves. This time, the leaves are folded to form cylinders and curd is poured into them. A banana leaf placed on the bottom of the cylinder keeps the curd in but allows more whey to drain off, the quantity of curd being replaced as the moisture is dispelled. The bottom leaf is then folded around the cylinder and sewn up with raffia. After a few hours, when the whey has drained away, the cheese is sold.

There is also a Kesong Puti cheese made professionally from larger amounts of milk – 50 to 100 liters (55 to 110 quarts) a time, and to which starter and rennet are added. These cheeses are packed in aluminium foil, in portions weighing 100 grams (3½ oz). Kesong Puti cheese may be cut into slices and baked in vegetable oil, then served with baked or boiled rice – a popular dish in the Philippines.

Australia and New Zealand

ABOVE: Calves drinking from a milk dispenser on a farm in Halcombe, New Zealand. Together Australia and New Zealand have almost 250 million sheep, a figure that far exceeds the human population. The sheep are not milked; cheese is made solely from cow's milk.

Australia

Two-thirds of Australia is desert, with a tropical climate in the north and a subtropical climate in the south. Along the northern and eastern coasts there is a profusion of vegetation; Queensland and New South Wales in particular are suitable for cattle breeding and dairy farming.

There was no beef in Australia until the British established their penal colonies in Botany Bay. It was Governor Phillip, in 1788, no doubt missing his traditional Sunday lunch, who ordered the import of seven horses, six cattle (including a bull and a calf), twenty-nine sheep, twelve pigs and a couple of goats.

In the early years the cows were mainly bred for slaughter, but thirty years after the arrival of the first cow, milking started in Illaware, south of Sydney. Milk products and cheese followed – the beginnings of a dairy industry. A greater variety of cattle breeds were needed, and so Ayrshires and Frisians, Shorthorns and Jerseys were imported. Cattle were able to remain outside throughout the year, and this meant a great saving, as no money was spent for sheds or stable feeding. During the winter there was more than enough maize, rye, barley, lucerne (alfalfa) and sugar cane.

Towards the end of the nineteenth century, the very first dairy plant was established in New South Wales. This was quickly followed by cooperatives financed by the farmers themselves. British farmers and cheesemakers who emigrated to Australia brought a sound knowledge of cheesemaking with them. *Cheddar* is made in exactly the same way as in Britain, and it is still the most important type. Australian cheese is made almost exclusively from cow's milk, in spite of Australia's millions of sheep. As immigration increased and became more varied, a demand grew for other cheese types. The French and Swiss wanted their *Gruyère* and *Camembert,* the Germans their *Tilsit* and *Limburger*, the Italians their *Parmesan* and *Gorgonzola*, the Greeks their *Feta*, the Dutch their *Gouda* and *Edam*.

The Australian blue cheese named *Maczola* is a Gorgonzola type: it is of a smaller size than Gorgonzola, with a lower fat content, and it is produced by the Macleay River Dairying Society. Hence the name "Maczola": a combination of Macleay and Gorgonzola.

LEFT: A stage in the preparation of Australian Cheddar. The thick slabs of curd are put through the curd mill.

RIGHT: The milled and salted curd is poured into the molds.

Name	Milk	Type	Rind	Form	Weight	% Fat content
Cheddar	△	■	☐	cylinder, rectangular	4.5-36 kg, 18.2 kg	50
Cheedam	△	◗	☐	rectangular	18.2 kg	45

Key to symbols on page 34. 1 kg = 2.2 lbs.

Haloumy is like Feta cheese with a lower fat content, but with the addition of certain herbs, and mint in particular. Because of the large-scale production of Cheddar, a lot of processed cheese is made in Australia, and production will no doubt increase, since many highly modernized factories have recently been constructed.

Cheeses that are endowed with the "Kangaroo" trademark are those which have been given at least 92 points, having passed an official valuation. One of these cheeses is *Cheedam*, a cheese developed by the Australian scientific institute, CSIRO. It is prepared in much the same way as Cheddar; but as its name suggests, it has certain affinities with Edam, although it possesses a character all its own. Cheedam is a pleasant, bland cheese that has found a ready market in Japan.

Mersey Valley is a smoked cheese with a fat content of 45%. *Romiliano* is similar to Caciocavallo. The CSIRO has also developed a process for making fresh cheese from skimmed milk. Starting with soured full-cream milk, or skimmed milk with skimmed-milk powder added to increase the content of dry matter to 35%, this strengthened milk is then pasturized, cooled to a certain level and grafted with a lactic acid culture. After reaching the desired acidity, the milk is homogenized and, after further fermentation, is finally cooled. The fresh cheese can then have fruit or other flavors added.

ABOVE: A herd of Jersey cows. Jerseys are the most typical dairy cows – as opposed to meat types – and were first introduced in the 1860s.

The animals have a relatively small build, and weigh about 400-450 kg (800-990 lbs). Their milk is particularly rich in butterfat.

New Zealand

Famous for its natural beauty, a mountainous country of immense glaciers in the alpine valleys, volcanic hot springs, lakes and rivers, New Zealand is predominantly agricultural. In the fertile areas the soil is rich and varied. Crops of tropical fruits are grown, cereal crops are harvested, and the lush grazing provides food for the countless millions of sheep which constitute one of New Zealand's principal commodities; the export of frozen meat, wool, and dairy products from cattle are the mainstay of the country's economy.

Apart from the Maoris, the first settlers in New Zealand were the British, their arrival spearheaded by the missionary Samuel Marsden, who preached his first sermon there in 1814. Marsden, with considerable foresight, brought with him a bull and two cows and must have been proud to donate, nine years later, a flourishing herd of fifty cattle to the Missionary Society "for the comfort and support of their missionaries."

A new wave of settlers arrived after the British had firmly established a colonial governor, and the town of Auckland became the seat of government in 1841. A demand for cheese brought about the establishment of a cheese factory close to Wellington harbor. 1862 was an historic year for the New Zealand cheesemakers when a certain Thomas Syers imported some livestock – a bull named "The Old Marquis" and two cows called "Duchess" and "Lucy." These were Jerseys, specially bred for a high milk yield and therefore completely different from the New Zealand meat stock.

Keeping it cool

With the introduction of British refrigeration ships in the 1880s, the door opened for a flourishing export trade. These ships were part of the framework of English colonial trade policy, which was designed to obtain a cheap source and supply of food for the home market. But this was only possible if the food reached British ports in good condition. An early pioneer cheesemaker had already discovered a method of transporting his cheese to England. He packed it in the usual deal packing cases, but with a thick layer of wood shavings around them to act as an insulating material. The cheese arrived in extremely good condition, and proved to be equal to

ABOVE: About half of New Zealand's land area is fertile pasture, favored with an agreeable marine climate and sufficient rainfall to encourage abundant vegetation.

RIGHT: These so-called cream stands are becoming obsolete. The milk and cream churns used to await collection when the farmers did their own separating, but the task is now carried out mainly in the factories.

BELOW: Cheesemaking in Waihi, on the North Island of New Zealand. Large open vats are filled with preripened milk, and the right amount of rennet added.

BELOW RIGHT: The curd is gathered into slabs and stacked against the sides of the vat. The pieces are turned to rid them of excess moisture, and to attain the correct degree of firmness.

the best English Cheddar. In 1886 he shipped his cheese in a refrigerator ship, and won the first prize at the Colonial and Indian Exhibition in London.

New Zealand Dairy Board

With the expansion of overseas trade, and the subsequent growth of the dairy industry, it became necessary to establish an official board of control. In 1936 the New Zealand Dairy Board was founded. It had eleven members, chosen by the cooperative dairy federations, and two delegates from the government. The board now buys all the butter and cheese designed for export, and has final responsibility for the end price obtained. Although it cannot make decisions on the actual cheesemaking techniques, the board exercises strong checks on quality and can influence the extension of the

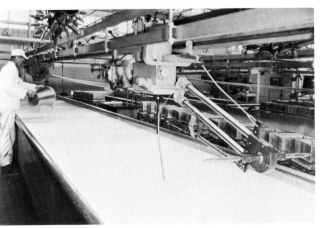

national cheese range if this is considered necessary for marketing reasons. The board has no doubt helped to make New Zealand dairy farming and cheesemaking the efficient, modern and quality-conscious business that it is today.

An assortment of cheeses
Because the origin of the New Zealand people is predominantly British, *Cheddar* has always been the most important cheese. It is prepared in well-equipped factories, with a technology mainly developed in New Zealand. In fact, New Zealand is the world's largest producer and exporter of Cheddar cheese (Cheddar occupies 90 % of the total cheese production), and the largest exporter of dairy products in general, including milk powder, butter and casein. The main market for Cheddar has always been Britain, and the New Zealanders themselves rarely chose any cheese other than Cheddar until about twenty years ago. The influx of immigrants to New Zealand brought about the development of foreign cheese types, and these were subsequently adopted by the export trade.

Current market trends have also engendered the export of cow's milk *Feta* cheese to the Middle East, where they are suggesting that the New Zealand farmers look into the possibility of manufacturing cheese from the milk of their vast sheep population; goat farming has also increased

ABOVE: Dairy cows waiting to be milked on a large New Zealand farm. Mechanization has had a marked effect on farming, partly because of the shortage of labor and the high wages. Much of the milk yield is churned into butter; New Zealand is the world's biggest exporter of butter.

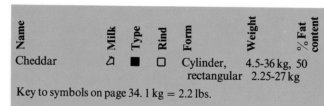

Name	Milk	Type	Rind	Form	Weight	% Fat content
Cheddar	🐄	■	□	Cylinder, rectangular	4.5-36 kg, 2.25-27 kg	50

Key to symbols on page 34. 1 kg = 2.2 lbs.

BELOW: Export cheeses are loaded aboard ship. In 1973, 90,000 tons of cheese were exported, 90 % of the year's production.

following interest from Middle East markets. Japan is another big customer, especially for processed Cheddar, and a variety of Gouda cheese known as *Egmont*, one which is particularly suitable for processing.

Colby cheese, a close relation to Cheddar, is also an important addition to the cheese range, and is widely exported to the United States.

In terms of production, Colby ranks next to Cheddar, and the method of manufacture is similar. A mixed strain of lactic acid bacteria is used as a starter, which gives Colby a nuttier flavor and a more open texture than that of Cheddar. Also, the curd has to be kept in a loose, more granular state than in the cheddaring process; it is mixed for about two hours before salt is added, in roughly the same quantity as that in Cheddar.

Many familiar European types are made as well: *Danbo, Havarti, Romano, Gouda, Gruyère, Parmesan* (in grated form), *Blue Vein,* all mostly prepacked, and processed cheese which for the greater part is exported.

New Zealand is mainly committed to export. The home market consumes a relatively low proportion of cheese – 4.8 kg (10.6 lbs) per capita per annum. The New Zealander is a meat eater and the price of meat is only half the price of cheese.

Cheese is used in cooking to about the same extent as in Britain, and with the same traditional recipes such as macaroni and cheese, Welsh rarebit, sauces and sandwiches. It is also very popular as an addition to salads.

In 1974, 73 million kg (160 million lbs) of cheese were exported, 47 % of which went to the United States, 22 % to England, 19 % to Japan (where it is turned into processed cheese) and the remainder to Southeast Asia, the Caribbean and Central America.

Fortunately, the New Zealand Dairy Board has done good business in the past few years. Britain's entry into the European Economic Community in 1973 was achieved with special arrangements for provisional protection of New Zealand's dairy exports. The future – of cheese anyway – seems assured.

LIVING WITH CHEESE

ABOVE: Connoisseurs used to buy cheese, sent from remote French villages, at the old market in Les Halles, Paris. Les Halles, alas, is gone forever, but cheese is finding newer, bigger and more distant markets. You can buy cheese in every city, every village, from factories, farms and street markets, in almost every country in the world. Shops can now rely on refrigeration and air freight to supply a remarkable selection of rare and wonderful cheeses.

Storage and treatment of cheese

In the descriptions of individual cheeses we have already touched upon the subject of storing them correctly and keeping them in good condition. Although no one single rule can be laid down, we can distinguish between some groups, each with a different set of requirements. Storage and treatment cannot be separated from the ripening process: every cheese ripens with time and one of the aims of correct storing is to let this process continue as regularly as possible and under optimum conditions.

Fresh cheeses
Fresh cheeses, like Speisequark, Cottage Cheese and Fromage Frais, could be considered an exception to this rule. With these cheeses the aim is to prevent further ripening as much as possible, since they must be fresh when they reach the consumer. This explains why a closed chain of refrigerated storage and transportation is essential, starting with the manufacturer, via wholesaler, exporter, importer, sales organization and so on down to the cheese shop. During its journey the cheese must stay cool all the time.

Soft, semihard and hard cheeses
Soft, semihard and hard cheeses need specific conditions, calculated to let the ripening process continue. The warehouses must be hygienic and the cheeses should be laid side by side on clean planks of good wood. Cheeses stacked on each other cannot breathe properly. The atmosphere should be adapted to the type, temperature and relative humidity being regulated within narrow limits. Air circulation is also important. Regular quality tests should be carried out, in the first place by inspection and tasting, perhaps supported by bacteriological and chemical tests in a laboratory.

Cheeses with dry rinds
In the storage room the cheese rind starts to form and thicken. The rind protects the cheese, in the same way as our skin protects us, preventing the penetration of microorganisms and regulating the moisture retention of the body. The rind is very important and deserves every care and attention during storage. Mold tracks, if they are not meant to develop on the cheese type, must be removed by brushing, rubbing with a dry cloth, salting,

BELOW: Imported Swiss Emmental cheeses arriving at the central market in Paris. Fast transportation insures a steady supply of cheese from the manufacturer to the cheese shops in most parts of the world.

ABOVE: Young Swiss cheeses are stored in the warehouses of wholesalers, where they are left to ripen. Experts from the Swiss Cheese Union examine random samples and judge their qualities: texture and color, formation of holes, taste, aroma, shape and storage condition.

washing or scraping. These actions are usually performed when the cheese is turned. It is laborious work and to lighten it the cheese is often treated with a rind-covering substance. The most well-known are paraffin and plastic wax. Both can be applied as soon as the cheese is stored and later on the process may be repeated.

To apply a layer of paraffin, the cheese must be immersed in a hot paraffin bath. The advantage of paraffin wax is that any gas escaping from the body of the cheese is let through. Plastic is more flexible. It is applied with a sponge, by hand or mechanically. It gives slightly less protection against the build-up of mold and its gas transmission capacity is less.

Cheeses with surface molds
With many cheese types, the rind is the carrier of a microflora that gives the cheese its enchanting smell and flavor. The white mold of the Camembert type must be allowed to develop as fully as possible for it helps to ripen the cheese. Cheeses of the Limburger type, with an orange-red smear of coryne bacteria on the rind, need a damp atmosphere for correct de-

LEFT: Camembert cheeses are packed at the cheese factory at Authou in Normandy, the original birthplace of this famous white-mold cheese. Here the cheeses are being fed into the packing apparatus.

velopment. The growth of the bacteria is encouraged by regularly "washing" the rind with a damp cloth. This can also be done mechanically.

Packing

Packing plays an important role with all cheeses, and there are a wide range of materials in which cheese can be wrapped or packed. Various systems have been developed for soft or hard, bulk or cut cheeses as a result of the rich gradation of cheese types and a general demand for attractive-looking, but very reliable packing materials.

This goes particularly for the sensitive soft cheeses. Brie on a small rush mat, for example, looks delicious when it is at its peak, but when it is not . . . forget it! A good piece of pre-packed Brie would be a much better choice in such a situation.

It is usual to wrap soft cheese types in paraffined paper or lacquered aluminum foil. Parchment may also be used sometimes (e.g., with Munster and Romadur). The parchment absorbs some moisture, which is necessary with this type of cheese, and can be easily removed. After wrapping, the soft cheese types are usually packed in boxes. In the past it was normally in a chip box, but today a folding carton is often used, which can easily be manufactured in all the desired forms (for example, for a single portion of Brie). Banderoles – small bands, sometimes made of straw – are often used as well, particularly for goat cheese.

The pre-packing of semihard and hard cheese, is a more recent procedure than the pre-packing of soft cheese. It made its appearance with the self-service shops and supermarkets and is now part of everyday life. For these cheese types, several possible methods may be used. Ripened cheese is cut into pieces and these wrapped in a translucent foil. The thin foil tightly encloses the cheese, giving it an attractive appearance. Hermetic sealing, however, is not possible with this material: the cheese can only be kept in its wrapping for a few days.

Alternatively, pieces of cheese (or complete cheeses of small dimensions) can be vacuum-packed in shrinkage bags. After the cheese is put in, the air is sucked out. The transparent bag is either closed with a clip or sealed, and then exposed to heat. The material

LEFT: The cheeses are machine-wrapped in paper and automatically boxed.

LEFT: The now-packed Camemberts are placed in boxes for export.

shrinks and fits the cheese like a glove. An excellent method for cheeses of irregular shapes, such as Provolone, for example, this air-tight packing prevents mold growth. Slices of cheese are vacuum-packed in the same way. Some nitrogen gas may be inserted to prevent the slices sticking together. Vacuum-packed cheese can be kept for about five weeks, preferably below $10°-12°C$ ($50°-54°F$). This type of packing is recognizable by the much thicker material and the prominent clip or seal seam.

Rindless cheese

A third possibility is not to allow the cheese to undergo its normal ripening; instead, it is immediately vacuum-packed as soon as it is removed from its brine bath and dried. Ripening then takes place in the packing, and no rind is formed because of the absence of air.

Cheddar is particularly suitable for rindless ripening in foil. The preparation of the cheese must be adapted in some respects, among other things in the starter used. Ripening should also take place at lower temperatures than normal; consequently, the process is slower.

LEFT: Although soft and delicate, Camembert cheeses are swiftly transported to markets throughout the world.

Cheese in the shops

With fast trucks, ships and planes – properly refrigerated all the way – the cheese retailer has supplies of cheese delivered to his door at least once every week; even the most perishable cheeses can arrive in perfect condition. The cheese shop, the most important link between producer and consumer, usually has refrigerated rooms and cooled display units where the cheese is on view so that the consumer can choose from a wide variety of cheeses. Not so long ago this was quite impossible.

Apart from the obvious seasonal cheeses (for example, the first "grass cheese" in spring, and some sheep cheeses) there is little *"arrivage de fromages"* nowadays. This used to be the cry of the Paris messenger boys when they delivered fresh cheeses to the shops, warning the buyers to hurry before the supply was sold out. Today, via the different sales channels and possible intermediate stations, there is a steady flow of cheese to the final sales outlets.

There are many different places where one can buy cheese. The market trader, from his attractive stall, knows just how to present his wares, and generally does it with style. His knowledge and expertise is important to the trade. The range, as in the shops, is constantly increasing, and the buyer who knows the market has all the advantages.

The specialized cheese shop
A well-equipped cheese speciality shop instills confidence in prospective buyers. A great variety in cheese types, some tastefully arranged in a cooled showcase, some carefully tended and displayed on scrupulously clean planks, a great range of cheese giving pleasure to the customer. Most likely, he never realizes the problems such an assortment can cause the trader, but to him it is also a demonstration of the trader's professional skill. He must be an expert buyer, always taking into account his customers' taste and his own storage facilities.

The stability of cheese cannot be taken for granted. Soft cheeses, for example, require a temperature of 5°–8°C (40°–46°F). The cooled showcase will be the only place for them in the shop. Semihard cheeses can be stored at a somewhat higher temperature; 6°–12°C (43°–53°F) is usually suitable. Low temperatures cannot do

ABOVE: An old-fashioned cheese cellar. Neatly arranged and carefully cleaned, the bulk cheeses are waiting to be sold by weight.

any harm, but could cause problems when the cheese is suddenly exposed to a much higher temperature, resulting in the moisture in the air condensing on the cheese surface. If this happens, the plastic layer more or less dissolves and the cheese may lose its protective jacket. If the storage temperature is higher than 12°C (53°F), the process of ripening will be accelerated, often resulting in an undesirable bacteria development and a strange smell and flavor.

Cheese needs space. For 1,000 kg (2,200 lbs) of cheese about 30 meters (100 feet) of shelving is needed, through which air can properly circulate. An additional 30 meters (100 feet) will be necessary for presentation and sale.

The maxim "first in, first out" usually applies. Otherwise cheeses could remain in stock for too long and deteriorate. The good cheese shop, if only for its own interests, must avoid this.

As far as presentation is concerned, the cheese trader should not only be a good buyer, but also a real window dresser, who knows how to arrange his cheeses – with their attractive labels – in such a way that every sort appears to full advantage and invites purchase. This can be achieved by attractive combinations and contrasts: putting a few cheeses in red cellophane between the yellow and white ones, and varying the display with other richly colored wrappings and cartons,

LEFT: A great variety of processed cheese is very much in evidence in this Japanese supermarket. Note the colorful wrappings bearing Japanese characters or English lettering.

LEFT: A new building has replaced the old, attractive Victorian market in Shrewsbury, Shropshire. In this English market, Cheddar and Cheshire are predominant.

ABOVE: A specialized gourmet shop: "Cheese Village" in New York City. It boasts over 325 varieties of cheese.

with cheeses on straw, cheeses on leaves and with articles that can be combined with cheese, such as nuts, olives or several bottles of wine.

The shopkeeper must also create and maintain the highest hygienic conditions, in the shop as well as in his own personal appearance. He must be a cheese expert, giving the customer not only the cheese he wants, but his attention and advice as well. Most of his clients will be looking for individual service and advice about the specific qualities of various cheeses, about differences in flavor, about their possible use in cooking, or perhaps their value in certain diets. They will also want information on suitable combinations for a cheese plate, or which wines go well with the cheeses, or perhaps about storage conditions. One of the most common questions is: "Can the rind of a washed cheese be eaten?" In theory, the answer is: "Yes, if the cheese is not plastic coated." But in practice this is not entirely true: in some cases the plastic layer cannot be torn off and can hardly be seen. So the safest advice is to cut off the rind.

Opinions vary on the white rind of

BELOW: A street market in Besançon, France. Every provincial town has regular markets offering a remarkable variety of French and foreign cheeses, and in particular those regional specialities which are not commercially produced on a large scale.

Camembert-type cheeses. Some people find the rind the best part, others remove the rind or scrape its surface.

It is always worthwhile to find a good cheese shop. Make friends with the shopkeeper, ask his advice and discuss his cheeses with him. A sympathetic cheese specialist is the best teacher you can find.

The supermarket

In the supermarkets and shopping centers there is usually no source of expert information available. Here the cheeses have been divided into portions, pre-packed and provided with their names, weights and prices, and possibly with additional information. You will not find the real specialities here. In general, the emphasis will be on semihard or hard cheeses, which have more resistance to handling than the softer varieties. These earlier types can be found in the cooled showcases, pre-packed in small units.

Pre-packed cheese has its advantages. You choose the piece you like best, its weight and price have already been determined, no waiting is necessary and if it is vacuum-packed, the cheese can be stored in its packing for quite a long period.

Practical hints

We have noted the essential difference between the cheese boutique, where information may be given to the cheese connoisseur, and the supermarket, where the customer has to find his own way around the different cheeses, qualities and packings. Without the necessary basic knowledge, it is questionable whether the customer will ever really get what he or she was after. It is usually impossible to handle the cheeses in the supermarket and to assess their quality by means of the simple tests described on p. 26. However, you are not left completely in the dark. The pieces or boxes of cheese usually lie conveniently arranged on the shelves, provided with a label showing the name, type, the price per kg or lb, the weight and the price per item. Sometimes also the fat content, the age and the latest date of sale are indicated. From this brief you can learn a lot about the cheese. In addition to all the information found in previous sections, we give a few hints, specifically to help you find the cheeses you want in the shops.

Names like Emmental Switzerland, Parmigiano Reggiano and V.C.N. (Véritable Camembert Normandie) indicate guaranteed quality cheese from a famous cheese area (see also p. 29.)

Farmhouse cheese (*Fromage fermier*) is made from raw milk and usually has a fuller flavor and aroma than factory cheese.

Sheep cheese and goat cheese have a special aroma. *Pur chèvre* is a guarantee that the cheese is from goat's milk only, not mixed with cow's milk.

Fat content: the more fat in the cheese, the more creamy its aftertaste. Note that a high fat content does not necessarily mean that the cheese has a softer consistency: this is rather a matter of the proportion of dry matter to moisture.

Age: the older the cheese the more dominating the flavor. Sometimes age

differences are indicated on the labels.

Latest date of sale: after this date the optimum period of ripening is exceeded and the quality begins to deteriorate.

Apart from studying the label, it is possible by a closer look to get additional information.

Washed cheese should have an evenly colored rind. If you are unsure about the rind formation of a given cheese, consult the various descriptions of the cheese in the country-by-country portion of the text.

Cheese that has begun to sweat in the packing has been stored at too warm a temperature or has been exposed to light for too long. The flavor of the cheese has deteriorated.

Cheese that appears dented has been under pressure too long.

Damaged foil can cause mold build-up.

Cheeses meant to have holes *should* have them, as the cheese type dictates. If there are no holes at all the cheese will probably have a less pleasant and less full flavor than is usual, due to the lack of bacteria action during ripening.

Blue-veined cheese should have wide-spread, evenly distributed veins. The paste should have an even, whitish color and not be too crumbly.

Soft cheeses should be soft from outside to inside. If the center is firm and chalk-white, it is not yet ripe. A Camembert or Brie that looks too dry with a rind that is hard to the touch, was stored too long, or kept under

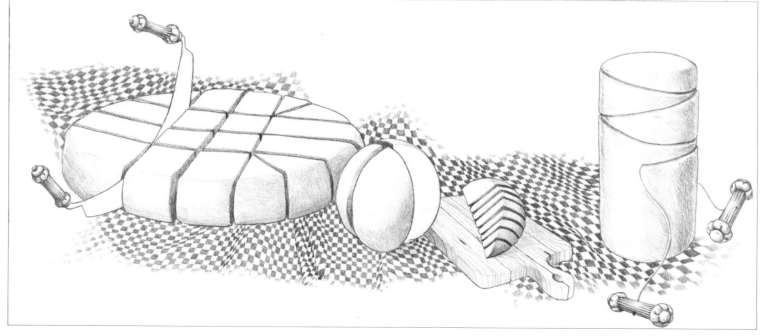

conditions too dry or too cold – again, factors that negatively influence the final flavor.

Goat cheese should be soft. It tends to become hard rapidly, becoming less tasty in the process.

A cheese having a white-colored body when it should be yellow usually has an acidic flavor.

Fresh cheese is generally most tasty if it is prepared in the proper season. This varies of course from type to type and from country to country.

When studying the price, remember that large units are cheaper than small pieces; older cheese is more expensive than young cheese; fat cheese more expensive than lean cheese; grated cheese and cheese cut into slices more expensive than non-cut cheese (one pays for the convenience).

Fancy additions like fruits, spices, nuts and brandy flavoring increase the cost. Good cheese does not need these trimmings anyway.

Gift packing is usually very expensive.

In many countries there is a tendency away from pre-packed factory cheese and toward fresh cheese sold by weight in specialized cheese shops. If this trend continues, factories will have to adapt their production and marmeting methods if they do not want to lose an important part of their cheese turnover.

Cutting the cheese

In the shop you can see how the big

and not-so-big cheeses are cut by expert hand, using a knife (possibly heated) or – for soft and creamy or old and hard types – a wire cutter. It is very useful to know how to cut cheese in handy portions with a minimum of loss.

Semihard cheese in the shape of a cartwheel can be cut in various patterns. See the illustration for an example. Globe-shaped cheese is best divided into four sections and then into smaller portions. From cylindrical-shaped cheeses, horizontal slices are cut which are further divided into portions. Rectangular cheeses are less of a problem. The central part is easily cut into slices. Cheeses with a soft body, usually smaller, are cut into triangular portions. Pyramids can be cut vertically into fours.

LEFT: Cheese display at Zabar's, a famous gourmet shop in New York City.

BELOW: Further examples of cheese cutting: A flat, round cheese can be cut into wedges, like a cake. Rectangular cheeses should be cut into slices, the middle pieces to be consumed first, the end pieces can be put face to face, to prevent their drying out. Pyramid or cone-shaped cheeses should be divided as shown.

OPPOSITE PAGE, TOP: An attractive bouquet of cheeses in the window of a French cheese shop. Saint-Marcellin is a soft cheese from the Isère Valley in the French Alps. It was evidently a royal favorite, for mention of it may be found in the account books of Louis XI in 1461.

OPPOSITE PAGE, LEFT: Cutting cheese correctly improves its appearance and helps to keep it in good condition; some even claim that it enhances the flavor. Cartwheel shapes, such as Gruyère and Gouda, are best cut according to the method shown. Only cut what you think you can use more or less immediately. Ball-shaped cheeses like Edam can be divided into four sections, and manageable portions cut from these. Cylinders, such as Cheddar and Stilton, can be divided into horizontal slices. Always cover cut surfaces with clean plastic wrap or metal foil to prevent their drying out.

Cheese in your home

There is no doubt that the majority of cheeses have a beauty and attractiveness entirely their own. After all, some cheeses have taken hundreds of years to perfect, it is right that they should be uniquely appealing. A fine wedge of farmhouse Brie on a straw mat; a yielding Camembert in its chipwood box; a fresh goat's milk cheese wrapped in bright green or autumn-tinted leaves; a noble piece of blue-veined cheese next to a bunch of grapes; a mellow, honey-colored slice of old Gouda on a simple, wooden cheeseboard – all of these promise delight and are the ambassadors of good taste.

Cheese is both cosmopolitan and democratic, for it is eaten almost throughout the entire world. Cheese is most frequently enjoyed just as it comes, in generous portions accompanied by crusty, fresh bread or crackers, and washed down with beer or wine. It is equally important in the kitchen, as an ingredient to simple, wholesome dishes and in highly refined cuisine. Cheese has a traditional place on the table, is taken in sandwiches to work, and is indispensable in the good restaurant. The increasing, worldwide popularity of cheese is due not only to its remarkable variety, but also because modern transportation and storage techniques have made the selection available to most areas, and thus more easily available to the average consumer than ever before. This new emphasis on cheese follows the current trend in the interest in food generally, encouraged by food manufacturers, by advertising, and by shops everywhere.

Cheese has its own, individual nature. It should be carefully treated both by those who make it and by those of us who eat it, if we are to gain the maximum enjoyment from each particular aroma and flavor.

Room temperature
In the first place, cheese must be eaten at the right temperature. Soft, semi-hard and hard varieties are best enjoyed at about 20°C (68°F), and fresh cheeses a little cooler. If a cheese is stored in a cold cellar or in the refrigerator, it should be allowed to reach room temperature to unfold its taste and aroma to the full; this may be a matter of one hour, but sometimes much longer, depending on the difference in temperature between the storage place and the room, and also,

ABOVE: Cheese and wine – two of life's pleasures to be enjoyed in a relaxed, and preferably sunny, atmosphere.

of course, on the type of cheese. A hard cheese requires more time than a soft one. In the final analysis, however, it is largely a matter of personal preference. Only experience will tell you exactly how long is needed for each cheese to reach the temperature where it treats your nose and tongue to the perfection that it promises.

Storage

Where should you keep your cheeses between purchase and consumption? The spot you choose must not be at too low a temperature, as the cutting surface of the cheese and also the rind are inclined to dehydrate, impairing taste and smell.

Granted, in these days of modern houses with central heating it is no easy task to find a cool, not cold place. If you have a cool cellar you are lucky, because nothing is better. Preferably, the cheeses should be placed on clean, unpainted and unvarnished wooden boards. The cut surface of a cheese can be smeared with butter before being covered with aluminum foil or shrink foil, or wrapped in a damp cloth. But do this only with semihard or hard cheeses. Soft cheeses are never put in

ABOVE: An evening at home with a few friends, some well-chosen cheeses and a good glass of wine.

BELOW: A communal dish that has been made for centuries in the Swiss Alps – the famous fondue. There are various recipes employing different cheeses; two classic recipes can be found on p. 219: Fondue Neufchâteloise and Fondue Fribourg.

a damp cloth; they can best be kept in their own wrapping, if this is not of cardboard only. If it is in cardboard, remove the cheese and wrap it in aluminum foil or transparent film.

Refrigerators can, of course, be used; yet the temperature there – 3°-4°C (37°-40°F) – is really too low for cheese. Protect the cheese by placing it in a plastic bag, which should be tightly closed; then wrap the entire piece in aluminum foil or transparent film, or place it inside a plastic box. The crisper, or vegetable bin, at the bottom of the unit and the space inside the door are the least cold. Never wrap small pieces of cheese together: their flavors would mingle and they would lose their individuality.

Cheeses should never be placed in the freezer, where the temperature is – 20°C (– 4°F), as most cheeses will be destroyed or at least their quality hopelessly impaired. For example, cheese spreads lose their creamy structure and become unpleasantly crumbly. Yet, there are some varieties better capable of withstanding the freezer climate, such as Quark types. These should be thawed slowly, and afterwards must not be refrozen.

How long can cheeses keep?

The semihard and hard cheese varieties can be kept for weeks; they may be bought in fairly large quantities, which is sometimes cheaper than buying small pieces. Store them carefully and cut each time a piece large enough to be eaten within a few days. A full-size cheese certainly looks attractive on a cheese board, but to bring it repeatedly to room temperature does not improve the cheese, even though doing so once will not harm it.

Much more sensitive are the soft cheeses, due to their higher moisture content and the fact that their surface ripening or mold development continues. There are three groups. Soft cheeses with a tendency to become runny – such as Brie, Camembert and Liederkranz – have a very short life. When you buy them, they should be newly or almost ripe. Eat them at once or the next day: if you need to keep them longer, wrap them in aluminum foil at room temperature. Remember that once a cheese turns liquid, it will not solidify in the refrigerator but only dry out. Cheeses with a firmer paste, such as Pont-l'Evêque and Reblochon, can be kept in the refrigerator for some days. These cheeses continue to ripen, however, and once they are past their peak, the quality quickly deteriorates. Speedy consumption is thus recommended. Fresh cheeses and thick cream cheeses (Cottage Cheese, Speisequark, Crème Chantilly and Petit Suisse, for example) are less sensitive and can be kept in the refrigerator for some weeks, even if they have been opened or cut into.

Finally, there are foil-ripened and vacuum-packed cheeses. They may be stored for long periods as long as their wrapping is not opened.

Do not discard

Soft cheeses cannot be stored too long at room temperature without becoming runny and overripe. In comparable circumstances harder cheeses start to "sweat" their fat. However, wrongly treated cheese need not be totally discarded. The fat drops can be wiped off with a dry cloth. Should the cheese become too dry, it can still be ground or grated and then sprinkled on sandwiches or used in casseroles, soups, or other hot dishes. Next time look for a better storage place! Molds may also

ABOVE: A fine assortment of British cheeses, with special crackers known as "Bath Olivers."

BELOW: An attractive buffet of cheeses and other snacks, for a party held in an old farmhouse.

be wiped off without causing any health risk. If the mold has penetrated into the cheese then a layer can be cut away. Even dried blue-veined cheese need not be thrown away: a lovely cheese cream can be made of it by adding it to butter or cream.

Selecting and serving cheese

The intriguing variety of the world's cheeses – fresh, soft, semihard, hard, mild, strong and sharp-tasting, with either bland, spicy, pithy or fruity aromas – guarantees that there is surely something for everybody. And how exciting it is to find new cheeses, experimenting and trying to gather from the packaging what the contents promise. On the other hand, the wide choice can be very difficult too.

What is needed is some method of deciding how and when to use which cheeses. Perhaps some guidance can be given here.

With bread, the semihard to hard cheeses are preferable and everybody knows best what he or she likes. A mild or perhaps a more pronounced type? Members of a family can have diverging tastes in cheese as well as other things. Satisfy everybody by putting both a mild young cheese and an older or more pithy cheese on the table.

On the cheese plate following the main meal there should be at least three types of cheeses, widely differing in character. The food and drinks being served are among the things that influence the cheese selection. This is discussed at greater length in the section on cheese and wine (see p. 220).

For cooking, flavor is not the only point to be concerned about; the texture and melting qualities are also important. Sometimes you need a good melting variety which does not pull into threads (e.g., for Raclette or hot cheese canapés). The thready varieties have their place too (e.g. in fondue). And sometimes – as for cheese schnitzels – you need a cheese that becomes soft but does not melt completely. For soups and sauces you can choose among the piquant and hard types which are so suitable for grating. Consult the recipe section beginning on p. 206 for further information.

Another important thing to take into account is the best time to enjoy each particular cheese, breakfast, for example, is hardly the time to have a

ABOVE: French cheeses, selected and carefully arranged on a cheese board. This variety covers a wide range of flavors and aromas.

piece of Roquefort with a glass of Burgundy. Nor should a cheese dessert be served after a Japanese sukiyaki or Chinese meal. But few Italian spaghetti dishes are complete without cheese. Your own good taste, backed up by some knowledge and experience, is your best guide in the world of cheese.

Nutritive value

Cheese has an important place in the diet. Not only is it good to eat, and a pleasant additive to the enjoyment of life, it is a complete food in itself. Cheese contains almost all the nutrients the human body needs, and in a concentrated form. It contains the proteins casein, albumen and globulin, of which casein is the most important. Casein is found in milk and milk products only. These cheese proteins are particularly valuable since they are built up from amino acids from which humans can synthesize their own body protein.

Moreover, most cheeses are rich in milk fat. During preparation and ripening, the fat has been partly broken down, like the proteins, making it easily digestible.

Average composition of cheese per 100 g (3½ oz)

Name	% Fat Content	Fat in grams	Proteins in grams	Carbohydrates in grams	% Moisture	Calories
Blue	45	30.5	21.5	2.0	40	368
Camembert	45	22.1	20.9	1.0	53	286
Cheddar	48	32.2	25.0	2.1	38	398
Cottage Cheese	4.2	4.2	13.6	2.9	78	106
Danbo (10% fat)	10	5.5	34.5	1.0	56	191
- (30% fat)	30	15.4	28.6	1.0	52	257
Emmental	45	31.0	29.0	1.0	36	399
Gouda	48	29.0	25.0	1.0	42	365
Parmesan	40	26.0	36.0	2.9	33	390
Speisequark						
- (5% fat)			13.5	3.4	81	72
- (45% fat)	45	11.3	8.7	3.4	75	150

Cheese contains several vitamins: the water-soluble vitamin B as well as the fat-soluble vitamins A and D. It also has an impressive list of minerals. Indispensable for the human body are calcium and phosphorus, both of which can be obtained, for the greater part, from milk and cheese.

Cheese lacks those fattening carbohydrates – such as milk sugar – which have largely been converted into milk acid during the production process.

Along with the protein, fat and carbohydrate values, we have indicated the caloric value of some cheese varieties in the list on this page. The calories have been calculated according to the "energy value" of the various cheeses. The caloric value per weight unit fluctuates with the fat and moisture content of the cheese. The lower the caloric value, the higher the moisture content of the cheese; the higher the caloric value, the fatter the cheese. The moisture content can only be indicated approximately as it decreases as the cheese gets older.

Recipes with cheese

The history of food and cooking is an integral part of the fascinating story of human culture and civilization. When we try to imagine what the daily life of other peoples in other times must have been like, we should discover what food they ate, how they cooked, which utensils they used and invented, and how they managed to provide themselves with the necessary ingredients for the daily meal. It is also true the other way around: when we get to know a foreign cuisine, we not only discover new dishes and new flavors, but we are also invited to taste and to experience something of the character and the way of life of the people who created the dishes.

It is particularly true in the twentieth century that cookery has become truly international. Refrigerated transport has made it possible to enjoy fresh Italian vegetables, British lamb, and soft French cheeses in virtually every corner of the world.

Cheese has its own place in the culinary world. Of course, it classifies first of all as a complete and nourishing food. It is also a lovely snack, to be enjoyed with a glass of wine in the company of good friends. It is part of any French dinner. And it can be used in the kitchen, as the chief ingredient of many a dish, or as a refined flavoring.

In the selection of recipes that follow, you can find many suggestions. Use your imagination to develop, change or vary them to your own

ABOVE: An arrangement of British products on a traditional pub table: a York ham, a Stilton and some Cheddar, a pint of beer and a pie. Only the wine in non-British.

tastes and preferences. Herbs and spices, for instance, may be adapted to your taste. The cheese types prescribed (we have often indicated them in general terms) can be interchanged. You can find substitutes easily enough in this book.

The recipes are loosely divided according to their nature, from breakfast dishes through lunch snacks to hot dinners and desserts. The recipes will serve four persons (of average appetite), unless otherwise stated.

Standard American measurements have been used throughout. Please consult the "Conversion Tables" on p. 240 for British and metric equivalents.

Breakfast

What a curious experience – eating a food that you positively know was prepared in exactly the same fashion two thousand years ago. The experience is yours when you try one of the Roman recipes which have been preserved in writing. Marcus Porcius Cato (234-149 BC) recorded the recipe for Savillum. This is likely to have been an everyday food in ancient Rome. It is a compact cake of corn grits with a mixture of cheese and honey. The Romans baked it in an earthenware pot in the glowing embers. It can be prepared in advance and served cold at breakfast. Cut a thick slice, spread some more honey on it – delicious!

Savillum
Oil, 8 oz corn grits,
1 lb Ricotta, 8 oz
honey, 1 egg, poppy
seed

Grease a heatproof dish with oil. Mix the grits, cheese, honey (save a little of this) and beaten egg together. Place the mixture in the dish, cover, and bake in an oven preheated to 400°F for 50 minutes until done. Then cover the top with the rest of the honey, scatter poppy seeds over it and put the Savillum, still uncovered, back into the oven for a few minutes. It can also be fried on top of the stove in a frying pan and the honey may also be mixed through the dough all at once.

The Romans also had a recipe for Pulmentum, the predecessor of to-day's Polenta, the corn porridge that is such an important part of the menu in central and southern Italy. The Romans, by the way, did not have maize yet (this came from America many centuries later); they used millet or spelt as the chief ingredient of this dish. There were many variations on the theme, prepared with milk, fresh cheese, honey, etc.; and the parallel with today's breakfast cereals can not be denied. Another version of the

Polenta is the Rumanian Mamaliga, so thick that it hardens when cooled. The Rumanians break it into bits and eat it with eggs, sour cream and cheese.

Polenta
2⅓ cups water, 1 tsp salt, 4 oz corn grits, butter, 4 oz Parmesan cheese

Bring the salted water to a boil in a pan with a thick bottom. Sprinkle in the corn grits while stirring continuously, making sure that the water continues to boil. Cook over a low flame for about 30 minutes, stirring occasionally, until the Polenta is done.

The mush must be thick enough for a spoon to stand up in. It is eaten topped or mixed with butter and grated cheese. Once it has become cold it can also be fried in oil and eaten with tomatoes and grated cheese.

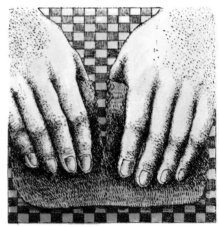

In most countries the cooked breakfast is unknown, and if it does exist (e.g., the famous British breakfast), eggs, bacon or even fish are preferred rather than cheese. In a gastronomical country like France, the *petit déjeuner* is nothing but a cup of coffee and an un-buttered roll. Sandwiches with cheese are a more nourishing start of the day, and they are the mainstay of the Dutch breakfast. The thriftiness of the Dutch is exemplified by the use of the cheese slicer which produces impossibly thin slices: the careless big chunk of cheese is taboo at breakfast.

Lunch
At lunchtime, there is more time and perhaps more appetite to take some trouble over the preparation of an appetizing snack. Nothing is more simple than hot cheese canapés in their many variations. The great thing is that you can prepare them a few hours in advance and keep them in the refrigerator; they need only a few minutes in the oven, preheated to 450°F, or under the grill, and they are ready. Welsh Rarebit is a bit more complicated to prepare, but well worth the trouble.

Quick Pizza
4 slices of white bread, butter, 2 tomatoes, salt, pepper, 4 oz Cheddar or Gouda cheese, anchovy fillets, black olives

Toast the slices of bread and butter them. Peel the tomatoes, cut them in slices and place them on the slices of toast. Sprinkle salt and pepper and the grated cheese on top. Decorate each slice with a latticework of anchovy fillets cut lengthwise, and halved black olives in between. Place the slices underneath a hot grill until the cheese has melted.

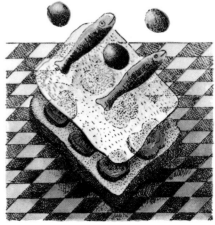

Welsh Rarebit
4 slices of bread, 3 Tbs butter, 7 oz grated Cheddar, 8 oz beer (pale or stout), 2 egg yolks, 2 tsp mustard, cayenne pepper, paprika

Cut the crusts off the bread, toast the slices and keep them warm. Melt the butter on a low heat, stir well and add the grated cheese and the beer gradually. Continue stirring until the mixture is smooth. Mix in the loosened egg yolks, mustard and pepper, pour the sauce over the slices. They can then be put under the grill and sprinkled with paprika, but this is not essential.

Croustades Montagnardes
Bread, sliced cheese, chives

This is the simplest form of cheese canapé, the bottom of which is a slice of toasted bread and the top melted cheese. Real farmer's bread with a slice of not overmature cheese on it, sprinkled with fresh chives needs no additions at all.

BELOW: Croustades Montagnardes, a simple and very tasty snack at any hour of the day.

Gouda and Asparagus Canapés
4 slices white bread, 2 Tbs butter, 3½ oz ham, 1 can of asparagus spears (about 12), 4 slices semimature Gouda cheese, parsley, paprika

Toast the slices of bread and butter them. Place one slice of ham with 3 strained asparagus spears on it on top of each slice. Cover the slices with a slice of cheese and put them under the grill or in the oven until the cheese has melted. Garnish with chopped parsley or ground paprika.

Sauerkraut Toast
4 slices white bread, 2 Tbs butter, 3½ oz sauerkraut (preferably the sort made with wine vinegar), 4 thick slices of smoked bacon, 4 slices semimature cheese or processed cheese, paprika

Toast the slices of bread and butter them. Boil the sauerkraut for 10 minutes in a little water, drain and divide between the toast slices. Fry the slices of smoked bacon and lay them on the sauerkraut. Cover the slices with cheese and place under the grill or in the oven until the cheese has melted. Sprinkle them with paprika before serving.

LEFT: Gouda and asparagus canapés are a delicious combination of ham, cheese and asparagus spears.

The Italian Pizza has conquered the world. It can be served as a complete meal, is fun to make and fun to eat. It is a good example of typical Italian cooking: simple, resourceful but filling. It is composed from the inexpensive ingredients of the region: tomatoes, often planted between olive trees and ripening quickly in the hot southern sun; anchovies, caught in the Mediterranean since time immemorial; and Mozzarella, produced from the milk of buffalo and cows. This cheese is really indispensable when making a genuine Italian pizza; additionally, Parmesan cheese may be grated on top.

But the ingredients vary; every pizzeria offers a selection of pizzas, each with a different flavor and taste. The dough is kneaded with vigor and skill; it is rolled, tossed and formed with a rapid spinning motion into a wafer-thin, round of dough. It is topped with the selected ingredients and put into the oven on a long, wooden shovel.

These days you can buy ready-made pizzas which only need warming in the oven. There are also cartons with all the ingredients, enabling you to make quite a good pizza with a minimum of fuss. But nothing is better than an entirely home-made pizza, starting from a rising yeast dough and prepared with fresh ingredients. As far as the cheese is concerned, apart from Mozzarella there are many other suitable kinds; the cheese should melt well and not draw into threads. Try Gorgonzola or another blue-veined cheese (with tomato, bacon and herbs), or Cheddar (with snips of onion, garlic and parsley), or Emmental (with diced ham, beaten egg and capers), or Parmesan (grated over mushrooms, paprika and black olives). But let us not forget the original recipe: Pizza Napolitana.

Pizza Napolitana
For the dough:
2⅛ cups flour, 1 tsp salt, 1 oz yeast, 1 tsp sugar, approximately ⅔ cup water, 2 Tbs olive oil

For the topping:
2 onions, 2 Tbs olive oil, 2 cloves of garlic, 8 oz fresh tomato puree, 12-13 oz Mozzarella cheese mixed with 1½-2 oz Parmesan, thyme, basil, oregano, salt, pepper, sugar

Sift flour and salt in a bowl. Stir the yeast and sugar with some tepid water until the yeast becomes liquid. Make a hollow in the flour, pour in the yeast, cover it with a thin layer of flour and place the bowl covered with a clean cloth in a warm place, away from drafts.

As soon as the yeast forms bubbles, gradually add the remaining tepid water and olive oil. Start stirring from the hollow. Work liquid and flour in the bowl with a fork until the dough forms into a ball. Place the dough on a board dusted with flour and knead till it looks shiny and elastic and comes away from the hand easily. Put the dough back in the bowl, replace the cloth and leave the dough rising in a warm place for about 1 hour. Divide the quantity into four portions and knead each portion again on the flour dusted board. If the dough is still slightly sticky, use a little more flour. Shape each ball into a thin round shape, bend the edges up a little and place them onto a baking tray dusted with flour.

For the topping: fry the finely chopped onions on a low heat in the olive oil until they are soft; add the chopped garlic, tomato puree and herbs and let it simmer for a few minutes. Season with salt, pepper and sugar to taste and divide the filling equally over the 4 bases. Grate the cheese, put it on top of the pizzas and add a few drops of olive oil. Place the baking tray on the bottom shelf of the oven, preheated to 450-500°F and bake the pizzas for approximately 10 minutes until they are golden brown.

While British dishes may look less festive than the exuberant Italian foods, Cheese Pie is still a very good and statisfying dish. It is savory and nourishing, and goes well with a good glass of beer.

Cheese Pie
For the pastry:
4 Tbs butter, ⅔ cup flour, 1½ tsp salt, 2-3 Tbs water

For the filling:
3½ oz bacon, 9 oz Cheddar, ¼ cup milk, 2 eggs, parsley, paprika

Using two knives, cut the butter into the flour to which the salt has been added. When the butter has been cut fine, gradually add water and make a ball of the paste, still using the knives. Roll the pastry lightly on a board dusted with flour. Turn the pastry, dust flour on the top and repeat the rolling several times. Leave the pastry folded for about 1 hour in a cool place and then roll it out thinly. Line a thinly buttered pie dish with the pastry. Place the fried bacon in it, followed by the sliced cheese and pour the eggs, beaten loose with milk, on

BELOW: Pie crust filled with thick slices of aubergine – but you can choose any filling you like.

top. Place the pie on the bottom shelf of an oven preheated to 450°F and bake for about 20 minutes until golden brown. Sprinkle with paprika or chopped parsley.

Aubergine Pie

This is a tasty variation of the Cheese Pie. Cut an aubergine in finger-thick slices. Lay these on the filling of the cheese pie and scatter grated cheese over them. In this way, by choosing other fillings, one can embroider endlessly on the theme of cheese pie.

There are almost as many omelette recipes as there are ingredients. The basic ideas is simplicity itself: beat eggs with milk, mix in some savory or sweet extras, and let set over a fire. As so often, it is the many possible variations that make the dish so interesting, and among the recipes there are quite a few where cheese plays an important part. For the basic Cheese Omelette and the tasty Soufflé Omelette, any sort of cheese that melts well and draws no threads can be used. An omelette with a fresh salad is a complete meal and, many would say, one of the best!

BELOW: There are almost as many recipes for omelettes as there are ingredients. The version shown here is the light, soufflé omelette.

Cheese Omelette
4 eggs, 4 Tbs milk, $2\frac{1}{2}$-3 oz well-matured grated cheese, salt, pepper, 1 Tbs butter.

Beat the eggs and milk together and mix $1\frac{1}{2}$-2 oz of the grated cheese and some salt and pepper through it. Brown the butter in a frying pan, pour in the batter and allow it to set over a low flame. From time to time draw the congealed portions from the sides of the pan to the center allowing the rest to run out over the bottom of the pan and set. This also makes the omelette somewhat less compact. As soon as the top is no longer liquid scatter it with the rest of the cheese and fold the omelette in two.

Instead of mixing the cheese through the batter, one can also lay slices of semimature cheese on top of the omelette.

An omelette can also be made successfully with fresh cheese. Cover the omelette with fresh cheese as soon as it is no longer liquid, scatter chopped herbs on it, and roll the omelette up.

Soufflé Omelette
4 eggs, 4 Tbs milk, $2\frac{1}{2}$-3 oz Parmesan cheese, salt, pepper, 2 Tbs butter

Separate the eggs. Beat up the egg yolks with the milk and some pepper until foamy. Whip the egg whites with a little salt until very stiff and fold the egg yolks carefully into the egg whites. Allow the omelette to set without stirring. Scatter the cheese over one half and fold the other half over it.

Quite a different recipe, and an unusual one, is Moules au Fromage: the combination of sea food and cheese is a very good one (as is fish in cheese sauce). When mussels are in season this dish can be served as the main course of a light meal, accompanied by lots of fresh French bread, and followed perhaps by a mellow piece of dessert cheese.

Moules au Fromage
1 leek, 1 onion, 1 winter carrot, thyme, 3 Tbs butter, salt, pepper, 8-9 oz cooked and shelled mussels, 8-9 oz Mornay sauce, some cream, 1 oz grated cheese, paprika

Sauté the leek, which has been cut into rings, the chopped onion and slices of winter carrot with the thyme in the butter until tender. Salt and pepper to taste. Place the mussels in a buttered heatproof dish, distribute the vegetables over them and pour the sauce, which has been finished off with some cream, over it. Scatter the grated cheese and paprika over it and put the pan in the middle of an oven preheated to 375-400°F for about 20 minutes until the dish is warmed through and has formed a brown crust.

Latin America has contributed a few successful cheese recipes to the international world of gastronomy. While a good piece of meat is an important element in the following recipes, it is the cheese that gives them a special, refined accent; the Latin Americans are meat eaters and think nothing of consuming an extra steak or two (as long as they can pay for them, of course). Two hot meals a day are usually consumed, and grated cheese is a standard ingredient. The secret of Churascos – a combination of steak, cheese and avocados – is the blending

of hearty and fresh flavors: a satisfying meal, served on toast. Tortilla de Papas is a potato dish with sausage and grated cheese. Here again, many variations are possible.

Chorizo may be unknown to you: it is a piquant sausage with oregano and garlic, often for sale in markets and delicatessen shops nowadays. You may settle for an ordinary sausage and add the spices yourself.

Churascos
1-1¼ lbs fillet steak, pepper, 2 Tbs butter, 3½ oz mild semihard cheese, 8 slices of toasted bread, 1 avocado, salt

Salt the meat, beat it flat, sprinkle pepper over it and sauté on both sides in butter for a few minutes until it is golden brown. Cover the steak with the sliced cheese and allow this to melt in a covered pan or under the grill. Cut the meat into 4 pieces the size of the toasted bread and place them on the 4 slices of toast. Lay a slice of fresh avocado and finally another slice of toasted bread on top. Press well and serve.

Tortilla de Papas
1-1¼ lbs potatoes, cooking oil, 3 eggs, salt, black pepper, chili powder, 3½ oz chorizo, butter or oil, grated cheese

Peel the potatoes and cut them into very thin slices. Dry them with a clean cloth and deep-fry them in the cooking oil until brown and crisp. Beat up the eggs with the herbs and mix the slices of potato and the finely chopped chorizo through them. Fry

the mixture in butter or oil in a frying pan, making a 2-inch-thick pancake. Cover with a generous layer of grated cheese.

211

In the Arabian and Latin American world, pulses – beans, peas, lentils – occupy a more important place in the daily diet than they do in Europe and North America. Pulses are great sources of protein. This makes them a very suitable food for those countries where meat consumption is low, either because of religious scruples or simply because people are too poor to afford it. Although beans and lentils are quite a cheap food, they are available in considerable variety, and can be combined with meat, cheese, sauces and herbs to provide dishes that are both nourishing and tasty. Here are two famous Latin American dishes – one with lentils and the other with beans.

Frijoes de Queso
1 chili pepper (dried or fresh), 4 onions, 1 clove garlic, oil or lard, 16-18 oz beans (frijoles), 16-18 oz tomatoes (skinned and diced), salt, oregano, $3\frac{1}{2}$ oz Cheddar or Gouda cheese

Pour boiling water over a dried chili pepper and soak for $\frac{1}{2}$ hour. (Put fresh chili pepper into salt water for 1 hour.) Cut it in two, remove the seeds and chop into small pieces. Sauté three of the four coarsely chopped onions with the chili and the crushed clove of garlic in some fat in a frying pan.
   To the soaked beans add some salt and enough water to just cover them. Cook for about 30 minutes over a low flame until done and drain through a colander. Sauté the remaining onion in a frying pan, add the drained beans and cook them for about 5 minutes over a high flame. Turn down the

The Italian kitchen is the birthplace of many types of pasta, that mainstay of virtually every Italian meal. They need grated cheese (e.g., Parmesan) to bring out their flavor and can be made into many simple but satisfying lunch dishes. In Italy, pasta is served as a hot starter before the main course. Many Italians make their own pasta, but even that from the factory has the individual flavor that is often missing in the products of other countries. An important thing to remember is to rinse the boiled pasta with lots of cold water, to prevent sticking.

Rissotto Milanese
1 onion, 1 paprika, 3 Tbs butter, 9 oz chopped meat, 2 cups rice, 3 cups water, 1 bouillon cube, pinch of saffron, 2 tomatoes, $3\frac{1}{2}$ oz mushrooms, season salt, rosemary, $3\frac{1}{2}$ oz Gruyère cheese

Cut the onion and the sweet pepper (from which the core and seeds have been removed) into pieces. Sauté these in butter and cook the minced meat with them. Add the dry, unwashed rice and fry until golden brown. Add the bouillon made from the cube and boil for 20 minutes until the rice (with

Sopa de Lentegas
(8 servings)
16-18 oz lentils, salt, $3\frac{1}{2}$ oz lean smoked bacon, 7 oz stale bread, $1\frac{1}{4}$ cups milk, 2 onions, 2 cloves garlic, 1 sweet red pepper, oil, pepper, curry powder, ground paprika, $3\frac{1}{2}$ oz grated cheese

flame and add the skinned, diced tomatoes, bring to the boil again, and finish off the dish to taste with salt, oregano and half of the cheese (which is cut into small pieces). Put the beans in an ovenproof dish. Divide the rest of the cheese over it and put the dish in the middle of the oven, preheated to 425°F, for 20 minutes.

Lasagne
16-18 oz lasagne noodles, salt, oil, 2 large onions, 2 cloves garlic, 16-18 oz chopped meat, pepper, oregano, nutmeg, 9 oz tomatoes, 2 oz Mozzarella, 2 oz Parmesan cheese, chives

the saffron in it) is done.
   Add the sectioned tomatoes and mushrooms for the last 5 minutes. Finish off the risotto with herbs and salt as necessary. Stir the grated cheese through when the mixture has been removed from the flame.

Boil the lentils in salted water with the chopped bacon until done. Soak the bread in the milk. Sauté the finely chopped onion, garlic and sweet red pepper (cut into strips, having removed the core and seeds) in oil until golden brown; add herbs to taste. Mix these with the lentils. Add the bits of bread. Put the mixture in a dish, sprinkle thickly with grated cheese and scatter drops of paprika dissolved in oil over it.

Boil the lasagne noodles in plenty of salted water for about 20 minutes, or until done. Stir once while boiling to prevent their sticking to the bottom of the pan. Rinse in a colander with cold water.
   Sauté the finely chopped onion and finely chopped garlic with the chopped meat in oil until golden brown and season the mixture with herbs to taste. Place half of the noodles in the bottom of a buttered ovenproof dish, and distribute half the meat mixture over it. Then place the sliced tomato on top, and on this the rest of the meat and lasagne noodles. Top the whole lot off with slices of Mozzarella. Sprinkle the Parmesan cheese over it and put the dish in the bottom of an oven preheated to 375-400°F for about 30 minutes until it is heated through and has formed a brown crust. Sprinkle with chopped chives. Green lasagne, colored by the addition of spinach during manufacture, can also be used instead of ordinary lasagne.

Appetizers

At the end of a busy day, sit back and relax with a glass of your favorite drink and some snacks. Cheese is somehow a perfect companion to any drink, and can be enjoyed in many forms. Of course, you can just cut a solid piece of semihard cheese into small squares, decorated if you wish with little bits of onion, ginger, olive, pineapple, gherkin, etc. Just eat them from your hand – delicious! Cheese scones and cheese biscuits need a bit more preparation, as does the satisfying Cheese Pastry, which can be kept in the refrigerator and served cold. The cheese cream described under Chester Biscuits can be used in many other snacks: fill celery stalks with it, or shape it into little balls and dust these with grated cheese; serve with a cocktail pick and chopped garden herbs.

OPPOSITE PAGE: Lasagne, an Italian pasta dish of meat with a cheese sauce gets a nice brown crust in the oven.

Chester Biscuits

For the biscuits:
1¼ cups flour, ¼ cup butter, 2 oz grated Cheshire cheese, ¼ cup finely chopped almonds, 3 egg yolks, salt, pepper

For the cream:
⅓ cup butter, 1 oz grated Cheshire cheese, 1 oz grated Parmesan cheese, salt, pepper, paprika

FOR THE BISCUITS: Knead all the ingredients together until a ball forms that sticks together. Set apart in a cool place. Later, roll the dough into a thin sheet, cut out rounds, lay them on a buttered baking tray and bake them in the middle of an oven preheated to 375)F for 15 minutes until golden brown.

FOR THE CREAM: Mix the ingredients thoroughly and put the cream on half the cooled biscuits, then lay another biscuit on top and press it down firmly.

Dinner

Cheese works wonders in many dishes. Theoretically, you could devise a complete menu where every course would be a cheese dish, and the whole still a reasonably varied and tasty meal. But don't put this into practice – imagination and variation are two of the most important aspects of the art of cooking. Still, cheese is the finishing touch to many dishes and gives them a refined taste that might otherwise be difficult to achieve.

A salad of fresh fruits and vegetables with cheese and a few other surprise elements is an original entrée: fresh, light and appetizing. These salads can be prepared well in advance and be served straight from the refrigerator. They look especially nice in a high glass bowl, sprinkled with some paprika or finely chopped parsley, and perhaps decorated with a slice of lemon.

Cheese Pastry

½ sweet red and ½ green pepper, 1 onion, 3½ oz butter, 3 eggs, 1 cup self-raising flour, 7 oz grated cheese, pepper, salt, paprika

BELOW: Cheese pastry, a savory loaf, baked in the oven but served cold. It is excellent as a satisfying snack, and can be given additional flavor and nutritional value by the addition of bacon to the recipe.

White Celery Salad

2 stalks white celery, 1½-2 oz blue cheese, 1½-2 oz semimature Brick or Gouda cheese, 1½-2 oz cashew nuts, 3½ oz peeled shrimp, 1 lemon, 1 Tbs oil, salt and pepper, 1 sour apple

Wash the peppers, remove the seeds and core, and cut into small pieces. Chop the onion until fine. Beat the butter and eggs until frothy, add the flour and then mix in the red and green pepper, onion, grated cheese and pepper, salt and paprika to taste. Place the dough in a buttered cake tin and place the pie in the center of the oven, preheated to 375°F for about 50 minutes until golden brown. Allow it to cool, cut into slices and serve.

Clean the celery and cut into thin rings. Crumble the blue cheese and dice the Brick or Gouda. Chop the nuts until fine. Shred most of the shrimp, reserving a few for decoration, and mix everything together.

Blend 1 Tbs lemon juice with the oil, add salt and pepper to taste, and dress the salad with this. Add the small pieces of apple only at the last moment to avoid discoloration. Decorate with the remaining shrimp.

Greek Salad
1 small green cucumber, 8-9 oz tomatoes, 3½ oz Feta or other sheep cheese, 2 Tbs tarragon vinegar, 2 Tbs olive oil, freshly ground pepper, paprika, thyme, basil

Wash the cucumber and dice it unpeeled. Mix in the peeled tomatoes and broken up cheese. Make a salad dressing of the tarragon vinegar, olive oil and herbs and mix it lightly with the rest of the ingredients.

Feta is fairly salty, so the salad probably does not need any additional salt.

Pear Cocktail
6-8 oz cheese (Fontal or some other crumbly cheese), 2 pears, 1 pint sour cream, the juice of 1 lemon, sugar, sweet red pepper

Cut the cheese and pears into fine strips. Blend the sour cream with the lemon juice and a little sugar and fold in the cheese and pear strips. Garnish the cocktail with strips of sweet red pepper.

Soup is an invitation to use your imagination and show your daring. When diced, cheese forms the body of the soup; when cut into fine slivers, it is a spicy flavoring; grated cheese sprinkled on top enhances the flavor and aroma of almost any soup. As a rule, soups should not be allowed to boil for any length of time after the cheese has been added; it may draw threads and become bitter in taste. It is

better to add it at the last moment, or at the table. Remember that cheese contains salt, so do not salt your soup too heavily when you are going to add cheese.

The soups are followed by a few hot entrées, which you should probably prepare only for people with an exceptionally hearty appetite! For modest eaters, these dishes are a complete meal.

Leek and Cheese Soup
2 large or 4 small leeks, 1 onion, 1 clove garlic, 2 Tbs butter, 4 cups bouillon, thyme, basil, 2 oz short macaroni, salt, 3½ oz Gruyère cheese, 3 Tbs white wine

Cut the washed leeks into rings, chop the onion and the clove of garlic until fine and sauté them in butter until brown. Add the bouillon, thyme and basil and boil the soup gently for 15 minutes.

Boil the macaroni separately in plenty of salted water for 15 minutes

until done and rinse in a colander with cold water. Stir it into the soup. Melt the cheese in the heated wine and continue to stir until a smoothly bound sauce has been achieved. Pour the soup into individual portions and pour the melted cheese over it.

Soupe à l'oignon
1-1¼ lb onions, 1 Tbs oil, 2 Tbs butter, 4 tsp flour, 4 cups strong beef bouillon, salt, pepper

For the croutons:
4 slices bread, 1½-2 oz grated Gruyère or Parmesan cheese

Slice the onion and sauté in oil and butter until the slices are glazed and golden brown. Turn them over occasionally. Sprinkle the flour over the onion and fry for a few more minutes. Then pour the bouillon over little by little. Allow the soup to simmer for 20 minutes, remove the excess fat and finish off with salt and pepper to taste.

The croutons are either placed in the bowls and the soup poured over them, or sit on the soup in the bowls and are liberally covered with grated cheese.

Dutch Cheese Soup
3 eggs, 2 Tbs cream, 2½ oz extra-mature Gouda, 1½-2 oz ham (finely chopped), chives, 3 cups bouillon, some Dutch gin, bread croutons

Beat the eggs with the cream and mix in the grated cheese, the finely chopped ham and finely cut chives. Bring the bouillon to the boil and pour into the egg mixture while beating continuously. Serve in bowls, accompanied by a glass of gin which may be added to the soup. The croutons are served separately.

RIGHT: Tartelettes au Roquefort, prepared with the famous sheep's milk cheese, and decorated with walnuts.

Tartelettes au Roquefort
3½ oz Roquefort, 1 oz walnuts, cognac, 1 egg yolk, about 1 Tbs cream, tartelettes (tart shells), parsley

Rub the Roquefort through a sieve. Reserve 2 walnuts and chop up the rest into small pieces. Blend the Roquefort with the chopped nuts, a dash of cognac, the egg yolk and enough cream so that a creamy cheese mixture is formed. Fill the tartelettes with this and bake them for 50 minutes in an oven preheated to 375°F until they are golden. Garnish with pieces of walnut and parsley. They can also be served unbaked (with an aperitif as a cold starter). The tartelettes must then be much smaller and the egg yolk may be omitted.

The tartelettes can be bought ready-made.

Provolone alla patte
7 oz Provolone, 16-18 oz tomatoes, salt, pepper, 1 clove of garlic or garlic powder, oregano, chopped parsley

Lay ¾-inch-thick slices of Provolone on aluminum foil on a baking tray. Peel the tomatoes, remove the core and cut the pulp into very small pieces. Blend with salt and herbs to taste. Put some of this mixture on the slices of cheese and place under the grill or in the top of an oven preheated to 375-400°F until the cheese begins to melt a little. Cut into small pieces, this is a delicious snack to have with an aperitif.

The *pièce de résistance* of most dinners is a good piece of meat, and many meats are very happily combined with cheese: steak grilled with a slice of cheese, veal with a creamy spread of butter and Roquefort mixed, cutlets filled with ham and cheese, ragout sprinkled with grated cheese, tongue of veal with a rich Sauce Mornay, etc. There are endless possibilities. We give the recipes of a few of the more famous dishes, followed by a cheese soufflé, some vegetables prepared with cheese, and a few interesting ways to prepare the faithful potato, so often neglected in cooking.

Kalbsrücken Kempinski
Salt, 4 veal steaks, 4 Tbs butter, 1½-2 oz mushrooms, 2 onions, 4 tsp flour, 1 cup bouillon, ½ cup cream, pepper, celery salt, basil, 1½-2 oz extra mature cheese, sweet red pepper or tomato

Salt the steaks, fry them in 1/3 of the butter on both sides until golden brown and place them in a flat heat-proof dish. Wash the mushrooms and cut them in slices. Chop the onions until fine and sauté them with the mushrooms for 5 minutes in half of the remaining butter. Salt and pepper to taste and divide the mixture over the steaks. Melt the rest of the butter in the same pan, add the dry flour and the bouillon little by little, stirring continuously until a smoothly bound sauce is formed. Add the cream and herbs. Pour the sauce over the mushroom-onion mixture, sprinkle the grated cheese over it, and place the dish in the middle of an oven preheated to 370°F for 30 minutes. Garnish with strips of red pepper or tomato.

Carré de Porc au Fromage (6 servings)
Salt, pepper, 2-2¼ lbs carré of pork (with ribs), 6 Tbs butter, 10-11 oz mature cheese

Fry the salted and peppered meat in butter for about 40 minutes until golden brown and done. Cut the meat between the ribs almost to the end. Place a thick slice of cheese in each groove and allow it to stick out about ¼-½ in above the meat. Then place the meat in the center of an oven preheated to 400-425°F until the cheese has melted (after about 15 minutes). Before serving place a paper cuff around each rib.

Cheese Soufflé

4 tsp butter, 4 tsp flour, 1¼ cups milk, salt, pepper, paprika, Worcestershire sauce, tabasco, thyme, 3 eggs (separated), 1½-2 oz extra-mature cheese, 1½-2 oz ham, 2 Tbs madeira, butter

Melt the butter, add the flour and very slowly add the milk, stirring gently until a smooth sauce is obtained. Mix in the herbs and spices. Stir the warm sauce through the beaten egg yolks, put everything back in the pan and mix in the grated cheese and diced ham. Finally stir in the madeira and finish off to taste.

Beat the egg whites until very stiff and fold them quickly and carefully into the sauce. Transfer the mixture to a buttered ovenproof dish (capacity 1 quart). Fill the dish no more than two-thirds and place in the bottom of an oven preheated to 375°F for about 30 minutes until done and golden brown. Place the lid next to the dish in the oven. When ready, cover it with the hot lid and serve immediately.

Fonds d'Artichauts au Gratin

3½ oz bacon, 7 oz mushrooms, 2 tsp butter, 4 artichoke bottoms, 1 cup Mornay sauce, salt, pepper, rosemary, 1½-2 oz Gruyère, paprika

Fry the bacon until crisp and golden brown. Pour off the excess fat. Wash the mushrooms and sauté them in butter for a few minutes only. Cut the bacon and the mushrooms into small pieces and stir them into the Mornay sauce. Add salt, pepper and rosemary to taste. Place the artichoke bottoms in an ovenproof dish, pour the sauce over them, sprinkle on the grated cheese and put the dish in the middle of an oven preheated to 350-375°F for about 20 minutes. Scatter paprika over it before serving.

Polpettine di Spinaci alla Ricotta

16-18 oz spinach, 8-9 oz Ricotta, 4 Tbs flour, salt, pepper, 3 egg yolks, 3½ oz grated Parmesan cheese, ¼ cup butter

Boil the washed spinach for 5 minutes, allow to drain thoroughly and chop until fine. Mix in the Ricotta, flour, salt, pepper, egg yolks and half the grated cheese and form into small balls. Slide them one by one carefully into a pan of almost boiling water and simmer for 3-4 minutes. Remove them from the pan with a slotted spoon, place them on a heated dish, dab with melted butter and sprinkle on the rest of the cheese thickly.

BELOW: Stuffed potatoes, baked in their jackets, and covered with a generous layer of cheese.

Emmentaler Rösti

2 onions, 3 Tbs butter, 1½-1¾ lb potatoes, salt, pepper, 1½-2 oz Emmental

Sauté the finely chopped onions in half the butter until golden brown. Peel the potatoes, grate them coarsely and scatter salt and pepper over them. Add the grated potato to the onion in the frying pan, press them down with the center of a spoon and fry them over a medium flame for about 20 minutes. Turn the cake as soon as the underside is golden brown and the top is glazed. To do this allow it to glide onto a board, put the rest of the butter in the frying pan and fry the other side of the Rösti until golden brown. Place the slices of cheese on top and put under the grill until the cheese melts and is golden brown.

Stuffed Potatoes

6 large potatoes, ½ cup milk, 2½ oz Cheddar, Cheshire or Stilton, salt, pepper, season salt, 1½-2 oz grated cheese, ¼ cup butter, parsley

Brush the potatoes until clean, wrap them in aluminum foil and bake them in the center of an oven preheated to 375°F for about 1 hour until done. Cut off one end of each potato and hollow them out carefully. Mash the contents and blend with milk, diced cheese, salt and herbs. Fill the potatoes with the mixture, scatter grated cheese over them, dab with butter and put them next to each other in an ovenproof dish in the oven for another 20 minutes approximately until a golden-brown crust has formed. Garnish with a sprig of parsley before serving.

Steak Sauce
1½-2 oz Quark, 5 tablespoons milk, 1 tsp mustard, 1 tsp grated horseradish or horseradish paste, 1 Tbs orange marmalade, salt, pepper

Stir the Quark with the milk and carefully mix in the horseradish, rum and orange marmalade. Season with salt and pepper to taste.

Mornay Sauce
1 Tbs butter, 1 Tbs flour, 1 cup bouillon, 1 egg yolk, ½ cup cream, 1½-2 oz grated hard cheese, salt, pepper

Melt the butter, sprinkle in the flour and add the bouillon little by little, stirring continuously. Beat up the egg yolk with the cream and mix through the sauce. Then add the grated cheese and finish off with salt and pepper to taste.

Desserts

To conclude the meal, nothing better than cheese. Just one well-chosen cheese may be all you need. Think of a fresh, white, sourish little goat cheese, accompanied by unsweetened whipped cream. A rare delight to follow a perhaps rather heavy dish of venison or a mighty steak. Cheese and fruit are an appropriate, if seldom tried combination: Cheddar with apple, cherries, melon, pears; Emmental with grapes, apple, peach or pineapple; blue cheese with apple, pear or blue grapes; and many more combinations are possible.

But we will not go into the cheese board as such at this point; there is a separate section on cheese and wine later in this book. We will now take a look at some other cheese desserts with which to round off the meal. First of all there is the Fromage Cardinal, a mixture of four famous cheeses, which to the purist may sound a bit profane, but is very good to eat. And it saves you the trouble of making up your mind which cheese you like best!

Fromage Cardinal
2½ oz Gruyère, 3½ oz Camembert, 3½ oz Bleu de Bresse, 7 oz Petit Suisse, paprika

Grate the Gruyère. Beat with an electric mixer the Gruyère, Camembert, and Bleu de Bresse into a smooth mass, add the Petit Suisse (reserving a little of this) and beat again for 3 minutes. Place the mass in a smaller bowl so it sticks out over the top, cover with foil and put it in the refrigerator for a few hours. Smooth the top with the remaining Petit Suisse, sprinkle some paprika on top and serve with hard rolls or French bread.

A similar recipe is the following, Mousse au Fromage. It should not be followed by a sweet dessert, unless ice cream or fruits. In fact, the Mousse combines very well with fruits, as the recipe shows. It can also be served as a cold entrée. A tomato or green pepper filled with the mixture and sliced when ice cold, looks most appealing and tastes very, very good.

ABOVE: Fromage Cardinal is a blend of four famous cheeses: Gruyère, Camembert, Bleu de Bresse and Petit Suisse.

Mousse au Fromage
7 oz blue cheese, 3½ oz Cream Cheese, 1 Tbs Worcestershire sauce, 1½ tsp powdered gelatine, 2 Tbs water, 1 cup whipping cream

Sieve the blue cheese and blend with the Cream Cheese and Worcestershire sauce with a mixer. Blend the gelatine with the water, dissolve over a double boiler and stir through the cheese mixture. Whip the cream until stiff and fold carefully through the cheese. Transfer the mousse to a buttered ring mold and put in a cold place to set. Turn out of the mold and garnish with blue grapes. Alternatively, you may fill the center of the ring with fresh fruit salad.

There are more delicacies to end your meal with: pancakes, or Pasha, a Russian speciality for Easter. And try the delicious, sweet Cream Cheese Tart or the Quark Tart, made with fresh cheese, for which you do not need an oven at all. Not only are these recipes great for desserts, they are delicious with a cup of coffee or tea at any hour of the day.

Pasha (8 servings)
4 oz extra-fat fresh cheese, ¼ cup butter, ¼ cup sugar, ¼ cup almonds, 3½ oz seedless raisins, ¼ cup candied orange peel, ¼ cup sour cream, fruit sauce or cream

Sieve the cheese, which must be as dry as possible. Cream the butter with the sugar until soft, mix in the ground almonds, raisins, chopped candied orange peel, sour cream and cheese. Cover a tall mold (a very well-cleaned flower pot will do) with a muslin cloth, place the mixture in it and fold over the corners of the cloth. Put something heavy on top and put the Pasha in a cool place for 12 hours. Then turn it out and serve with fruit sauce or cream.

Cream Cheese Tart
For the pastry:
⅓ cup butter, ⅔ cup flour, ½ tsp salt, 2-3 Tbs water

For the filling:
½ cup sugar, juice of one lemon, salt, ¼ cup flour, 8 oz Cream Cheese, 2 eggs, ¼ cup milk

For the topping:
1 egg, 2 tsp sugar

Make the pie dough (see Cheese Pie) and line a buttered pie tin with it. Mix the sugar, lemon, salt and flour with the Cream Cheese using an electric mixer. When the mass is smooth, mix in the eggs one by one and then the milk, whipping well. Fill the tin two-thirds with the mixture. Bake for 40 minutes in the center of an oven pre-heated to 425°F. Brush with the egg which has been beaten up with the sugar and then place the tart in the oven for a little longer.

Cream Cheese Pancakes
8-9 oz Cream Cheese, Cottage Cheese or Fromage Frais, 2 Tbs flour, 3 eggs, some salt, 2 tsp sugar, butter

If you use Cottage Cheese, push it through a sieve first. Mix the cheese with the remaining ingredients, model the mass into flat cakes and fry them in the frying pan. Sprinkle them with confectioner's sugar and serve with strawberry jam or fruit compote.

Quark Tart
For the pastry:
7 oz dry cookies or graham crackers, 2 Tbs rum, 3 Tbs red jam

For the filling:
3 eggs (separated), 7 oz castor sugar, 16-18 oz Quark, 2 lemons, 8 tablets gelatine, 1 32-oz can of peaches

Line a 9-inch spring mold with transparent foil. Break the crackers into small pieces, mix these with the jam (thinned with rum) and place this mixture on the bottom of the spring mold. Beat the egg yolks with the sugar until white and foamy. Stir the cheese and the grated rind of both lemons into the mixture, little by little.

Warm the juice from both lemons until it steams; remove from the heat; dissolve the gelatine (which has been soaked in plenty of cold water and well wrung out) in it and add the warm juice to the Quark mixture. Cut half of the drained fruit into small pieces and fold these and the cheese mixture into the very stiffly whipped egg whites.

Fill the spring mold with this, garnish the top with the rest of the fruit and allow the cake to set in a cold place for about 24 hours.

LEFT: The fresh Quark Tart can be made without using an oven. It is particularly good as a light dessert.

We have kept until last what is no doubt the most famous cheese meal of all: the fondue. Invented by the Swiss Sennen, living high up in the Alpine meadows and in the solitude of the mountains, this dish was originally eaten in a primitive fashion from one communal pan. Modern Fondue has inherited these ancient traditions, for in Switzerland it is not a daily meal, but a festive one, to be enjoyed with old friends. The hostess prepares the fondue at the table and she takes care that everybody happily gathers round to enjoy this age-old cheese dish.

There must be an ample quantity of cut French loaves on the table, so that every one can dip pieces of bread in the fondue using long fondue forks. The fork is slowly twisted to cut the cheese thread and is slowly lifted to the mouth. Don't be in a hurry, you will enjoy the glorious flavor better . . . and you will not burn your tongue.

Herdsmen and farmers practice the fundamental skills of humanity. They represent all that is lacking in cultured man, especially the city dweller. Perhaps this hankering after lost things is the reason why many people like the sense of friendship and joy of life that is present in fondue.

Fondue Neuchâteloise
1 clove of garlic, 1 cup dry white wine, 10-11 oz Emmental, 10-11 oz Gruyère, 1 tsp corn flour, kirsch, nutmeg, pepper

Rub the fondue pan with a clove of garlic. Pour in the white wine and stir in the grated cheese. Continue stirring until the cheese has melted and the sauce is smooth. As soon as the mixture starts to boil, thicken with the cornflour mixed with a bit of wine. Add kirsch, nutmeg and pepper to taste. Leave the fondue to simmer gently on the fondue stand. Serve white wine or tea. As a break, a glass of kirsch can be served, which in French is neatly called *coup de milieu.*

Fondue Fribourg
2 cups milk or water, 28 oz Vacherin à fondue, black pepper

Place the milk or water in the fondue pan (rubbing with garlic is not necessary). Cut the cheese in pieces, place them in a pan and press them fine with a fork. Continue stirring. When the mixture is smooth, do not let it come to boil. If it becomes too thick, add a few spoonfuls of warm water. Season well with freshly ground pepper. The mixture can take quite a lot without becoming sharp. Serve with tea. In Fribourg the fondue is often spooned onto boiled potatoes.

Raclette

A typical dish of Valais, Raclette has the same function as fondue. The semisoft, full-cream Raclette cheese is halved, the rinds at the cutting surface are removed and the cutting surface is exposed to a brightly burning wood or charcoal fire – or to the heat of an electric Raclette device.

In the meantime the guests are kept busy. They peel the potatoes that have been cooked in their jackets, and put gherkins and silver onions on their plates. As soon as the cutting surface of the cheese liquefies, and the edges become golden, the host or hostess scrapes the half-melted cheese and the crisp edge onto one of the plates. The guests, therefore, do not all eat together, because Raclette must be eaten hot and each takes his or her turn. The pleasant fire, the smell of melting cheese, the contrast between hot Raclette and cool Fendant wine create a very special atmosphere.

Cheese and wine

We may wonder why it is that wine has long been considered the true and perfect partner to cheese. One reason is that cheese on the palate seems to require a foil, and by choosing wine we provide a contrast which is at the same time complementary; we can prove this to ourselves by judicious comparison, and by tasting.

The harmony of cheese and wine cannot be easily achieved with other beverages. The taste of cheese is not generally improved by coffee, neither is it enhanced by tea, although the Swiss prefer to serve tea instead of wine with their favorite fondue. Beer is a better choice as a partner to cheese, and is often preferred in countries that do not produce wine: beer and Cheddar cheese is an established tradition in England, while in Norway the pungent Gammelost is well tempered by the local brews.

ABOVE: A simple, well-prepared meal is enjoyed in the romantic atmosphere of an Italian wine cellar.

LEFT: Stilton cheese with a glass of port, a classic combination shown here with a piece of Cheddar.

Since they are so closely allied in origin, it might seem logical to partner cheese with a glass of milk, but the assertive flavor and clinging texture of many cheeses are neither resolved nor enhanced by milk, for milk is too similar. We might be forced to conclude that alcohol is at the heart of the matter, were it not for the fact that whiskey and gin are decidedly unsympathetic to cheese. So we are left with wine, with its fruity, earthy, aromatic, benign and often heady qualities – these are the ideal companions to the special qualities of cheese.

Yet even here we must exercise a certain amount of selection and judgment, for there are almost as many varieties of cheese as there are wine. Although some eccentric tastes might suggest combining a peppery cheese with a sweet wine, we might begin with

Some successful cheese trays
The key to success is: Combine different types with interesting flavors. Include at least one soft cheese with white mold or red rind growth, one semihard or hard type, one blue-veined cheese and possibly a goat cheese or a fresh type. Processed cheese has no place on the cheese board. It is always nice to include a little-known speciality that you may have found. The following combinations include simple and inexpensive, as well as more extravagant suggestions.

Boursin
Camembert
Gouda
Danablu

Brie
Cheddar
Banon
Gorgonzola

Camembert
Gruyère
Munster
Bleu des Causses
Sainte-Maure

Brie
Saint-Paulin
Chabichou
Munster
Roquefort

Bel Paese
Emmental
Camembert
Pont-l'Evêque

Reblochon
Jarlsberg
Vacherin Mont d'Or
Taleggio
Bleu de Bresse

Tomme au Raisin
Gouda
Appenzell
Carré de l'Est
Livarot
Munster
Bleu d'Auvergne
Roquefort

Boursin
Emmental
Havarti
Reblochon
Camembert
Neufchâtel
Banon
Maroilles
Munster
Bleu de Bresse
Stilton

Banon
Vacherin Mont d'Or
Edam
Chaource
Cantal
Emmental
Pont-l'Evêque
Bleu de Bresse

a simple rule: The wine that accompanies most types of cheese should not be sweet. There are one or two exceptions, however. Connoisseurs usually insist that Stilton cheese be served with port wine which, though heady and strong, is decidedly sweet. The reason for the survival of this partnership is because port was the gentleman's after-dinner drink of eighteenth-century England, and since cheese was served at the end of the meal, it naturally found port as its partner: port was the aristocratic wine, Stilton the aristocratic cheese. Others may point out that the ideal partner to Stilton cheese is a fruity Burgundy, such as a Nuits-Saint-Georges, and who is to say that they are wrong?

The rules that govern our selection of wines to accompany cheese should be regarded more as suggestions than strict guidelines, but they have evolved from experience gathered from centuries of careful judgment. It is generally acknowledged that a wine and a cheese of the same general character prove to be the most successful partners. A fresh, slightly

Some successful wine and cheese combinations

Banon (France)
Fruity red wine or dry rosé, such as Côtes de Provence.

Bel Paese (Italy)
Supple, but not too light red wine, like Barbera or Chianti.

Bleu d'Auvergne (France)
Robust, full-bodied red wine such as Châteauneuf-du-Pape or other Rhône wines.

Brie (France)
Fruity red wine of character; or possibly a good white wine, such as a fine white Burgundy.

Camembert (France)
A lively red wine, neither too light nor too heavy; St. Emilion would be a good choice.

Cantal (France)
Ripe, rather luxurious, red wine, perhaps a fine Burgundy or a full-bodied Rhône wine.

Carré de l'Est (France)
A rather full-bodied red, or a light, spicy white wine, such as Alsace.

Chabichou (France)
A bone-dry white wine, such as Sancerre or Pouilly Fumé.

Cheddar (Great Britain)
A reliable claret, a good Burgundy or Rhône wine, or perhaps a strong dry white wine.

Cheshire (Great Britain)
A reliable claret, a good Burgundy or Rhône wine, or perhaps a strong dry white wine.

Danablu (Denmark)
Powerful reds like Rhône or Rioja.

Edam (Netherlands)
A not too overpowering red wine, such as a fine Bordeaux.

Emmental (Switzerland)
Fresh whites (the Swiss Fendant is very suitable), or light reds (perhaps a young Beaujolais).

Gorgonzola (Italy)
Robust, full reds; among Italian wines, a quality Barolo is a good choice.

Gouda (Netherlands)
A not too overpowering red wine, such as a fine Bordeaux.

Gruyère (France, Switzerland)
Fresh whites (the Swiss Fendant is very suitable), or light reds (perhaps a young Beaujolais).

Maroilles (France)
A powerful red wine, like Rhône or Rioja.

Mozzarella (Italy)
Fresh whites, preferably Italian Soave or Verdicchio.

Munster (France, Germany)
The spicy white Gewürztraminer is the local companion in Alsace; a pithy red wine is also very good.

Parmigiano (Italy)
Full-bodied reds, like Sangiovese or the sparkling Lambrusco.

Pont-l'Evêque (France)
Rather full red wines such as one of the better Beaujolais types (Moulin á Vent, etc.).

Port-Salut (France)
Light, agreeable red wine or a not too heavy white.

Provolone (Italy)
A supple and fruity red wine, preferably not too young.

Reblochon (France)
White and red Savoie wines; also rather full reds from the Rhône area.

Roquefort (France)
Cahors, Roussillon; a glowing red wine like Châteauneuf-du-Pape.

Saint-Nectaire (France)
Powerful reds from Rhône, Provence, Languedoc.

Saint-Paulin (France)
Light, agreeable red wine or a not too heavy white.

Stilton (Great Britain)
Vintage port or a full, ripe red wine of high quality.

Tilsiter (Germany)
A fresh white wine or a not too powerful red.

Weinkäse (Germany)
Rhine or Moselle wine.

sourish cheese is well suited to a dry, light, white wine: Chabichou, the goat's milk cheese from Poitou, France, is a good companion to a crisp white wine such as Sancerre, or a Muscadet from the Loire. Strong, aromatic cheeses demand a strong, robust wine: Provolone, for example, a pretty powerful cheese, needs a wine that can look it straight in the eye, a wine like Barolo.

Many combinations of wine and cheese are thus closely related by region of origin. A really earthy and tangy cheese, a blue such as Roquefort, demands a hearty red wine, and we do not have far to look: the vineyards of Châteauneuf-du-Pape, a mere seventy miles to the east of Roquefort village, produce the perfect partner – equally earthy and tangy.

On the cheese farms of Alsace, the strongly aromatic Munster cheese is balanced by serving it with the spicy, white local Gewürztraminer; in the *trattorias* of Piedmont, blue-veined Gorgonzola is best suited to a warm-blooded Barolo or Barbaresco. In the same way, Reblochon goes well with the light white wines of the Savoie, such as Rousette; Emmental with the delicate Fendant wines from the Swiss canton of Valais; and Parmesan with a red San Giovese or a Lambrusco from Emilia.

Combining cheese and wine of the same region is a good first principle, but it is by no means invariable. Bearing in mind what we have said about sweet wines, it would be a pity to serve a fine *Beerenauslese* hock with a piece of Limburger; when in doubt, the rule of "like character" should be applied. This rule is also useful with cheeses produced by countries that do not make wine, countries like Holland, Belgium, England and the Scandinavian nations. English blue Cheshire has a salty tang that might go best with a St. Emilion from Bordeaux. Mature Dutch Gouda is splendid with wines of the Medoc, while many of the Scandinavian cheeses can be partnered with dry white wines, like Chablis.

The quality of the wine must also be considered when choosing the cheese. If you have stumbled across a treasure trove of Richebourg, that ambrosial wine from the Côte de Nuits in Burgundy, or if you have been saving a few bottles of Haut Brion for a special occasion, you are unlikely to serve them with cheeses like Limburger or

LEFT: When you serve a variety of international cheeses, you may want to accompany them with a selection of wines. Cheese and wine should be presented in ascending order of fullness of taste. Match the mild cheeses to the younger, simpler wines – white or red – and the sharp or well-matured and strongly flavored cheeses to the richer and more robust wines, mature Burgundy, the Italian Barolo, or even port wine.

BELOW: The faintly sweet, nutty Emmental is perfect when accompanied by brown, whole-meal bread and a glass of light red wine.

Romadur, cheeses that you can recognize even before you've seen them. Romadur, Belgium's famous "stinking cheese," needs a rough and ready Chianti to keep it in its place.

On the other hand, a cheese and wine party does *not* have to cost a fortune. A good piece of advice is to aim for simplicity, particularly when on unfamiliar ground. A large selection of cheeses and wines is pleasing only to the expert; to the uninitiated it merely leads to confusion.

Serving cheese and wine

Someone once said that the first duty of a wine is that it should be red. To this we might add that its second duty is to accompany food. There are some fruity and very distinctive white wines that can be enjoyed by themselves – those from the Mosel or Rhine for example. But most reds are best drunk with food, for it is food that somehow gives an added dimension to their flavor. As a food cheese is particularly gifted in this task.

One of the most acceptable moments to serve cheese and wine is at the end of a good meal. In most European countries, this is usually before the dessert, when a few different types of cheese are placed on the table to be enjoyed with the remaining red wine. In France, cheese is an inseparable part of the dinner.

In keeping with the simple approach, the cheese board on the dinner table should offer a limited selection of types. For one thing, appetites are somewhat flagging by the time cheese is presented. There should be a sufficient portion of each type (about 3½ oz per person). A list of possible combinations can be found on p. 221.

The popularity of the wine and cheese party as a social occasion has increased with the availability of the staple ingredients. You could, if you felt sufficiently confident, offer just *one* cheese, such as a whole Cheddar, Stilton or a Gruyère, with a variety of wines to choose from.

The combination of wine and cheese should be supported by additional elements: bread, an assortment of salad things, a few condiments. While the French will always choose bread first and foremost, other nationalities might prefer crackers or crispbreads. Scandinavia and Germany have a great selection of rye and black breads and crispbreads, well suited to the kinds of cheese they produce. Some sophisticated Italians claim that it is vulgar to eat *grana* as a table cheese, but you might well discover the joy of a piece of fresh Parmesan accompanied not by bread but by crisp celery, a few radishes and, of course, a glass or two of fruity Lambrusco.

Make an experiment and decide whether Camembert cheese goes best with a crusty French *baguette* or a slice of pumpernickel, and whether Danish Tybo with caraway seeds should be accompanied by sour rye-bread or a slice of challah (the braided loaf found in Jewish cookery). English farmhouse Cheddar seems designed to be a life-long partner to farmhouse bread, yet it goes equally well with "water biscuits" (an early corruption of the word *wafer* biscuit) or the elegant, crisp crackers known as Bath Olivers.

BELOW: A selection of French cheeses, perfectly matched with a full-flavored Burgundy.

BELOW: The Ristorante de Filippo in Valle d'Aosta, Italy, where they know about good food, good wine and good cheese – especially the local and famous Fontina cheese.

With your cheeses and wines there should be an imaginative selection of breads and crackers, including fresh and crusty French bread, brown bread and granary bread, rye and knäck-bröd, toast and an assortment of wafers and crackers. Some people disapprove of butter with bread and cheese, nevertheless it should be included for those – and there are many – who prefer it. There should also be cheese knives, plates and napkins, salt, and fruits such as grapes, apples and pears, for these go extremely well with cheese.

The quantity of wine needed must be calculated in relation to the possible thirst and drinking habits of the party. If you are serving light white and rosé wines during summer, thirsts may be considerable, and for this reason it is a good idea to include beer, iced water and fruit juices in your selection of drinks. But your first consideration is to the wine, and you should count on about three-quarters of a bottle per person, or three bottles shared between four people.

In wine-drinking countries, and with those familiar with wine, it is customary to serve wines in order of importance: light or modest ones first, leading up to a grand climax. A host serving claret from Bordeaux might begin with a few bottles of *Cru Bourgeois* wine, fairly inexpensive, through to something such as Château Talbot, or a more classy Pauillac wine, and terminate (if he can afford it) with something really grand like Château d'Yquem. It is difficult to present wines in some semblance of order at a wine and cheese party, unless you are prepared to guide your guests through the selection. You can put all your wines on the table at once – or perhaps start with some light wines and bring on the big guns later.

When all is said and done, it is the individual taste – your taste – that is the most important guide to choice. Take a piece of mature Pont-l'Evêque and try it with a glass of full-bodied Burgundy. If you don't agree that this is an ideal combination, try the cheese with a glass of claret, or a white Burgundy, or even a hock. You will soon find, in this pleasant and pioneering fashion, the cheese's true companion. It is the individual, and not the cheese nor the wine, that really decides the ideal match.

Make your own cheese

To make cheese we should first realize that every region where cheese is made has something special to offer – something that is not available to us. We do not have the right cultures for the masterly rind flora of Brie or Camembert, nor the mysterious caves that make Roquefort so uniquely itself. We have no cows grazing on herb-scented mountain slopes to provide the milk for Emmental with its "watering" eyes. Nor do we have the expert fingers for modeling the bizarre shapes of a Pasta Filata. And most of us live under completely different conditions from the conditions responsible for making each cheese, region by region, all over the world so remarkably different – conditions of landscape, climate and type of animal, all of which contribute to a cheese's individuality.

Nevertheless, a few hints that take all of this into account can be useful. In the chapter about the principles of cheesemaking, you can see how cheese is made by first curdling the milk. As rennet is often difficult to come by, we will start with simple recipes which are based on soured milk and do not need rennet. (As in the recipe section, standard American measurements have been used. Please consult the conversion table on p. 240 for British and metric equivalents.)

Fresh Cheese (Quark)
Cover 1 quart of raw milk, mixed with 1 cup of sour milk or buttermilk, or 2 tablespoons of yogurt, and put in a warm spot until it becomes thick. This should happen within 2 or 3 days. Put the mass in a thin cloth (e.g., a cheese cloth), tie it up and hang it for about 12 hours. If the curd is still too moist, let it drain for another 6 to 8 hours. It should then be solid, but not too dry and crumbly. Loosen the cloth, scoop the curd out and sieve it into a bowl or whip it smooth. Stir in whipped cream, and finish the Quark with salt to taste. It can be kept, well covered, in a cool place for a couple of days.

Cottage Cheese
Warm up 1 quart of milk with 4-6 tablespoons of lemon juice until it starts to flake. Continue heating on a low flame until the whey is lemon-yellow, but do not allow it to boil. Put the mass in a thin cloth (e.g., a cheese cloth), tie it up and hang it. When the

ABOVE: Cheesemaking as a domestic craft rather than a factory process: this sequence of pictures shows the production of English Wensleydale cheese in a farm kitchen.

ABOVE: After adding rennet and waiting for an hour or more, the milk has curdled and the whey can be drained off.

LEFT: As more whey is removed the thick curd can be worked in the vat. Note the simple equipment used for this phase of the process.

moisture has drained out sufficiently, put the curd in a bowl. Stir a tablespoon of lemon juice in it, $\frac{1}{2}$ teaspoonful of salt and 1 or 2 tablespoons of cream. The cheese should have a granular structure and be firm to the touch.

Kariesch
Put a clean cloth in a strainer, pour in buttermilk, lift the cloth out of the strainer by its four corners, tie it up and hang it to drain out for at least 6 hours (one-fifth to one-sixth of its original volume will stay in the cloth). Put a clean cloth in a sieve or small basket, and press the Kariesch out. Let it drain for a few hours and turn it. This is an Asian nomads' cheese. Its taste is less creamy than that of the preceding types because nonfat milk has been used.

Krut
Warm up buttermilk, carefully stirring with a rod until it starts to flake. With genuine buttermilk, left from butter preparation, this will take place below boiling point. With soured skimmed milk, particularly if it is fresh, curdling will hardly appear; in that case give it a hand by slowly letting drops of vinegar into it, but no more than 1 teaspoonful per quart of buttermilk. Put a strainer or a sieve on a bowl, cover it with a thick layer of cloth, and pour the buttermilk in. Put a cover on the strainer and let the buttermilk drain for about 2 hours. Knead salt, to taste, into it, fold the cloth over the mass and lay the packet on a dry cloth, folded in four, between two planks. Put a stone or other weight on the upper plank and press the cheese for about 6 hours. Now and then, wring out the folded cloth. In South America the Queso Blanco is made in practically the same way from whole milk.

Quark powder
Crumble dry Krut and grind it. Keep the powder in a closed bottle or in the refrigerator or deep-freeze. This powder can be used instead of fresh Quark to make savory pastry. Since the powder keeps well it is very handy to have in the kitchen.

The recipe for this puff pastry is simplicity itself: mix thoroughly $\frac{1}{2}$ cup flour, $\frac{1}{2}$ cup butter and $\frac{1}{2}$ cup Quark powder. Roll out the paste into a thin piece, fold it up a few times like a

napkin, roll out and fold up again.
After an hour's rest in a cool place,
the paste can be shaped into any form
you like and baked.

Griut

Bring buttermilk slowly to the boil,
stirring occasionally. Let it boil until
about one-third to one-quarter of the
original volume remains. (The buttermilk discolors, becoming a yellow
ochre from the caramelization of the
milk sugar.) Sieve the buttermilk in
the same way as described for Krut
and let it drain for 1 hour. Knead
some salt into it, and let it drain for
another 6 hours. Make little ball
shapes and leave to dry in the sun or
in a warm oven. 1 quart of buttermilk
makes about 3 oz.

Beestings Cheese

Mix beestings (the first milk from a
cow after it has calved) with a little
salt, put into a warm oven in an ovenproof dish until the milk is thick. The
beestings cheese is white with a golden
skin.

Renneted cheeses

Now, some recipes for those who can
get rennet. You might be able to
obtain some from a cheesemaker or a
cheese factory, or buy a bottle, a box
of tablets or rennet powder from a
specialist supplier.

Iran Pot Cheese

To make about 3 to $3\frac{1}{2}$ lbs of cheese,
you need 10 quarts of milk; just under
$\frac{1}{2}$ cup of buttermilk or yogurt; $\frac{1}{4}$ teaspoon rennet; about 5 ounces of salt.
Heat the milk to 86°F, stir the buttermilk or yogurt and the rennet (diluted
with water) through it. If possible,
keep the milk at the same temperature
until it has been curdled. Put it in a
clean cloth and hang it up by the four
corners to drain. Sprinkle the salt on it
(10% of the curd weight left in the
cloth). Leave the curd for 24 hours.
Grind and mince it. Put the mass in a
suitable high-sided stone jar, press the
curd well, pour some brine on it
(3-3$\frac{1}{2}$ ounces salt to 1 quart of water),
close the jar carefully with aluminum
foil and leave 3-4 months in a cool
cellar at a maximum of 64°F. Make
sure the cheese remains immersed in
the brine; top off if necessary.

Fresh Goat Cheese

In the evening, warm up goat's milk to

ABOVE: A cheese press
is perhaps the most
difficult tool to ac-
quire. If you can't find
a suitable second-
hand affair you may
have to improvise – as
farmers did in earlier
times.

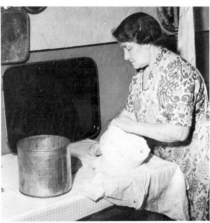

LEFT: The cheese is
taken out of the press,
turned, and wiped
with a dry muslin
cloth once or twice
during pressing.

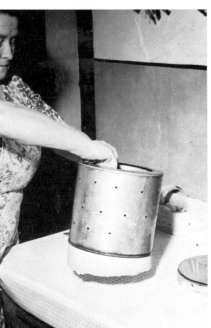

LEFT: The mold may
be made of wood,
metal or plastic. It
must also be perfor-
ated to allow the whey
to escape. The finished
cheese must dry and
ripen to acquire the
desired aroma and
flavor.

75°F. Add 8 ounces of fresh buttermilk per quart, and two drops of
rennet diluted with 8 ounces of water.
Stir well and keep stirring gently for
3 minutes. Put the pan, covered, in a
hay box or in a large basket with
papers between pan and basket to
prevent the milk cooling. Examine the
milk the next morning to see if the
milk has curdled. There should be
some whey on top of the curdled mass.
12 hours after the addition of rennet,
the curd should be put in a cheese cloth
and allowed to drain for 6-12 hours at
a room temperature of about 68°F.
Mix the dry curd with some kitchen
salt and put it in small molds (carefully cleaned flower pots, earthenware
or plastic, are quite suitable). Press the
curd well to remove all the air and
place for 4 hours in a cool spot (60°F).
Take the cheeses out of the molds and
put them in a cool place, on a cheese
cloth, on clean hay or straw. Turn
them regularly, keeping the surface
where they stand as clean as possible.
If they become too dry, wrap them in
thin paper.

Gouda cheese

To make one cheese of approximately
1 lb, you need $4\frac{1}{2}$ quarts milk, $\frac{1}{2}$ cup
buttermilk and $\frac{1}{2}$ tsp rennet, plus salt
for the brine bath.

Warm the fresh whole milk to 95°F,
add the buttermilk and rennet, stir for
3 minutes and wait till coagulation has
taken place. This should happen in
half an hour's time. Cut the curd for
10 minutes into small cubes. The whey
will separate and the curd sink to the
bottom of the vat. Run off as much
whey as possible. Add 2 quarts of hot
water (100°F) to the curd and stir for
15 minutes. Again run off as much
whey and water as possible.

Now you can put the thick packet
of curd in a mold, taking care that it
does not break into many little bits.
Press it with your hands for a few
moments, take it out again, wrap it in
cheese cloth and place it back into the
mold. Put a lid that fits inside the mold
on top of it and apply a weight. After
10 minutes, turn the cheese and wring
the cloth, and apply greater pressure.
Turn the cheese a few more times; after
approximately 1$\frac{1}{2}$ hours it is ready.
During pressing, whey must be
allowed to leave the mold.

Let it rest for a few hours before
putting it in the brine bath for 14-16
hours. You need about 2 lbs salt for

225

BELOW: Mrs. Etty, the cheesemaker, is rightly proud of her cheeses, stored on the shelves in an upstairs room of the farmhouse.

11 quarts water; the cheese should float in the brine. Finally, dry the cheese, store it in a cool place, and turn and dry it daily for 4-5 weeks.

Basic American Cheese
To make approximately 3-3½ lbs curd, you need 11 quarts fresh whole milk, 3 cups buttermilk, 1 rennet tablet (dissolved in some water) and 3½ oz salt.

Warm the milk to 88°F. Stir in the buttermilk. Cover and let stand for one hour; the temperature should remain a constant 88°F. Add the rennet, stir for one minute, cover and wait for another 45-60 minutes. The curd should have coagulated by now. Cut the mass in cubes measuring ⅓ to ½ inch. Stir the curd in the whey for 15-20 minutes; slowly heat over a period of 25-30 minutes to 106°F while stirring constantly. Hold the curd at this temperature for one more hour, all the time stirring for one minute every five minutes.

When this has been done, you can pour the curd-whey mixture into a strainer lined with cheese cloth. When the whey has drained, mix in the salt. Hang the cheese in the cloth to help

LEFT: Another type of cheese – certainly the easiest type to make – is prepared with soured milk, contained in a cloth and suspended to allow the whey to drain off. This cheese is usually salted later, and sometimes flavored with chopped chives.

further draining. After a few hours, transfer the curd into a vat, put a lid that fits inside the mold on top of it, and apply a weight. Some more whey will separate and this should be allowed to run off. After this primitive pressing, you may dry your cheese at room temperature for several hours, apply paraffin and age it in a cool cellar or in the refrigerator.

To the cheesemaker
With all of these recipes, do not expect to create a huge success the very first time. It is good fun, though, to try and try again. Do not hesitate to modify the recipe if need be. Quality of milk, acidifying action of buttermilk, strength of rennet, etc., may vary and you should try to discover the best working method in your personal circumstances.

Processed cheese

In the United States, processed cheese is defined as follows: "Pasteurized processed cheese is a dairy product resulting from the mixing and heating of several lots of natural cheese with suitable emulsifying agents into a homogeneous mass and following this with cooling. It may contain fruits, vegetables, meats."

In principle, the production is as follows:
– the cheese is selected, often a combination of mild to full-flavored sorts, depending on the type of processed cheese to be produced;
– the cheese is slightly heated, up to 21°C (60°F), to facilitate the removal of rind covers like wax, plastic, etc.;
– grinding follows, very carefully, particularly if the cheese has a hard rind;
– the mix ratio should then be determined: the amount of emulsifying agents, water and possibly other additives like butter, whey powder, cream, herbs, spices, bits of ham, sausage, etc.;
– the cheese with the other ingredients is then heated and stirred in a large kettle. The usual type is a steam-jacketed vat, or a cooker which injects live steam directly into the cheese mass. Both vats have mechanical stirring devices.

Three phases
There are three phases in the process. First, a clear layer of fat appears. After addition of the processing salts and with the rise of the temperature this disappears again. Secondly, the hot mass gets a crumbly, granular aspect. With a little more heat it finally becomes smooth, velvety and glossy. In the past, heating took place at lower temperatures than today, when the melting process is carried out under pressure. Minimum heating is to 70°C (168°F) and the cheese is held at this temperature for 1-5 minutes.

The cheese mass is then fed to the packing machine, while checks are made to insure that its composition is up to standard. It is packed and labeled, and finally goes to the cooling tunnels or rooms.

Types of processed cheese
The United Nations Food and Agriculture Organization distinguishes three types: *Processed Cheese* with a type name (e.g., Processed Gruyère); *Processed Cheese* and *Cheese Spread*

ABOVE AND BELOW: A collage of processed cheese labels, arranged as if in a circular container.

(containing more moisture and less fat); and *Process Cheese Products* (containing additions).

Many countries have their own legal standards. In France the indication *Fromage Fondu* is reserved for process cheese with a dry-matter content of at least 50% and a fat content of at least 40%. For *Fromage pour Tartine* the dry matter content must be between 44% and 50% (i.e., it contains more moisture). The terms *Crème de . . .* or *Crème de . . . pour Tartiner* indicate that the product is made exclusively from the cheese type mentioned in the name.

The United States really lays down the law and processed cheesemaking is strictly controlled. *Pasteurized Process Cheese* has a moisture and fat content that should correspond with the statutory limits for the natural cheese from which it is made, or the average in case of a blend. There are a few exceptions to this rule. *Pasteurized Processed Cheese Food* is prepared with additives like cream, milk, lean milk powder, whey powder, fruits, vegetables and meats. At least 51% of the weight must be cheese. The moisture content is 44% maximum, the fat content in the dry matter a minimum of 23%. *Pasteurized Processed Cheese Spread* has a somewhat lower fat content (minimum 20% in dry matter). The moisture content is higher, maximum 60%, making it more spreadable. It may contain fruits, vegetables, meats, etc.

Hi-melt Cheese is something new. A special cheese for kitchen use, it takes high oven temperatures without losing its flavor, and is very suitable for dishes like Welsh Rarebit and Cheese Canapés. There are two types: *Hi-melt Pasteurized Processed American Cheese* and *Hi-melt Pasteurized Processed Cheese Food*. The first has a somewhat higher fat content, lower moisture content and a more pronounced Cheddar flavor. *Imitation Pasteurized Processed Cheese Spread* has a very low fat content and is therefore not up to the requirements set for Cheese Spread. It is suitable for persons with a fat- and calorie-reduced diet.

Pros and cons
Processed cheese has been frowned upon by cheese connoisseurs, and perhaps understandably. In the first place, processed cheese used to be made from

227

BELOW: A collage of
international
processed cheese
labels.

all kinds of cheese leftovers that could not be sold because of certain defects. If at one time the processed cheese factories bought cheese of inferior quality for a low price and a high profit, now that time is definitely over. It is clear today that a market position can only be maintained with a product of the highest quality. Minor defects are acceptable since they are not detectable in the end product.

In the second place, opinions about the flavor of processed cheese can strongly differ. Real cheese connoisseurs look for the individual qualities in flavor and smell of natural cheese, enjoying now a soft, runny Camembert and then a sweet, dry Emmental or a nicely veined Roquefort; they abhor the uniform, neutral flavor and dull consistency of processed cheese. For others, however, processed cheese seems to be all that is wanted. Fortunately, there is a cheese for everybody's taste.

Processed cheese is available practically all over the world in the most simple and the most ludicrous shapes. The packing is often eye-catching, with very vivid colors. American inventiveness has shown the way. A

colored wrapping or an attractive carton is no longer enough. Little dainty baskets, elegant earthenware and glass pots abound; processed cheese will go into almost anything, and the consumer gets something functional or decorative in the bargain.

The big advantage of processed cheese is that it keeps well, much better than natural cheese; it is practically sterile and does not ripen further thanks to the high temperature attained in the production process. Since its invention around the turn of the century, it has been very popular. It is estimated that one-third of the United States' cheese production is marketed as processed cheese.

APPENDICES

Acknowledgments

Grateful acknowledgment is made to the following persons and institutions for their assistance in preparing this book.

Picture sources

Picture research by Ann Horton.

ABC Press (*agency for* Magnum, Pressehusset and Scoop/ *photographers:* E. Erwitt, E. Lessing, G. Nielsen, J. Stacke, D. Stock, B. Uzzle)
O. Abolafia
Allgemeiner Deutscher Nachrichtendienst
Art Directors Photolibrary (*photographer:* B. Fleming)
Australian News and Information Bureau
Barnaby Picture Library (*photographers:* Hedrich-Blessing, E. Manewal, E. Preston)
Bavaria Verlag (*photographers:* T. Fehr-Bechtel, Schmachtenberger, T. Sellhuber)
Kees v.d. Berg
Borden Cheese
British Information Services (British Crown Copyright)
British Tourist Association
R. ter Brerke
Camerateam
Canada House
Dairy Industry Control Board, Pretoria
Danish Agricultural Productsere
Ton Ellemers
English Country Cheese Council
Robert Estall
Mary Evans
FAO
Food from France
Foto-unit
Frans Halsmuseum, Haarlem
Frits Gerritsen
Photographie Giraudon et Lauros-Giraudon
Susan Griggs (*photographers:* M. Boys, S. Galloway, J. Garrett, N. Holland, A. Woolfitt)
Sonia Halliday
Robert Harding (*photographers:* R. Cundy, D. Harney)
Michael Holford
Sherry Kamp
Kimura
Aart Klein
Kon. Bibliotheek Albert I, Brussels
Koninklijke Nederlandse Zuivelbond
Kraft Kitchen
Landbrukets Sentralforbund (*photographer:* A. Svendsen)
Colin Maher
Mansell Collection
Mejeribrugets Hjemmemarkedskontor
ir. P. Meyers
Milk Marketing Board
John Moss
New Zealand Dairy Board

Norske Meieriers Salgssentral
Novosti Press
PAF International (*photographer:* Ch. Délu)
Paul Pet
Pictor (*photographer:* D. Braun)
Picturepoint (*photographer:* J. Baker)
Popperfoto (*photographers:* H. Chapman, M. Duris, J. C. Grelier, J. Mounicq)
Toine Post
Sem Presser
Reflejo
Peter Ruting
Schweizerische Käseunion
Simon Slop
Société Anonyme des Fermiers Réunis
Sopexa
Spectrum Colour Library (*photographers:* H. Douglas-Reid, M. J. Gilson, S. Meredith, E. S. Taylor)
J. W. Stoppelenburg
Svenska Mejeriernas Riksförening
Swiss National Tourist Office (*photographers:* Giegel, Müller)
John Topham Picture Library
Ungarisches Werbestudio
Valio Finnish Co-operative Dairies Association
Peter v.d. Velde
A. A. Verschoor
VVV, Gouda
ZEFA (*photographers:* W. Backhaus, Dr. K. Biedermann, W. Borrenbergen, W. Braun, E. G. Carle, W. Ernest, R. Everts, K. Göbel, H. Grathwohl, Dr. G. Haasch, W. Hasenberg, D. Hecker, B. Julian, G. Kalt, P. Keetman, Dr. H. Kramarz, K. Kurz, Dr. R. Lorenz, H. Mante, G. Marché, M. Nissen, Paul, D. Pittius, Puck-Kornetzki, F. Saller, H. Schlapfer, G. Seider, A. Simonsson, Strachil, Teasy, D. H. Teuffen, H. Wiesner, Dr. H. Wirth).

Special thanks to:
The Delicatessen Shop (John Cavacienti), London
Sardi's Restaurant, New York City
Wells Stores (Patrick Rance), Streatley-on-Thames
Zabar's, New York City

Illustrators
Ritzo Bloem & Partners
Anke Engelse
HBM Design
Eddy Schoonheijt
A. J. Wiskerke

Other sources, consultants and contributors
Robert Collington Ackert, Katonah
Agriculture Development Organisation, Vientane
Alfa-Laval, Amstelveen

American Dairy Association of Wisconsin, Madison
Pierre Androuet, Paris
Angel Arias Alonso, Madrid
Austrialian Dairy Produce Board, Melbourne
Australian Dairy Produce Board, Melbourne
ir. J. C. T. van der Berg, Wageningen
Fa. J. C. N. Boering (F. Sander), Dieman
Borden Food Division, Columbus, Ohio
Mrs. Brown, Tokyo
Leo Burnett L.P.E. (M. R. P. Naylor), Tokyo
Campina, Asten-Someren
Canadian Dairy Commission, Ottawa
Centrale du Vacherin Mont d'Or, Moudon
Centrale Paysanne Luxembourgeoise, Luxembourg
Comité Interprofessionel du Gruyère de Comté, Poligny
Confédération générale des Producteurs de Lait de Brebis
    et des Industriels de Roquefort, Millau
Cooperación Technica Holandesa (Enrique Ortelec),
    Bogotá
Coopérative Laitière de Vicq, Vicq
Dairy Board, Pretoria
Department of Agriculture, Washington
Dutch Embassies in various countries
Hubrecht Duijker, Abcoude
Embassy of the Hungarian People's Republic, The Hague
    (I. Szilasi, dipl. econ.)
English Country Cheese Council (H. R. Cornwell),
    London
Faculty of Fisheries and Animal Science (Dr. Shigeru
    Yoshida), Hiroshima
Françoise Frémy, Matougues
Gerdabel, Amsterdam
Frans Grosfeld, Kortenhoef
J. Hofstra, The Hague
Instituut voor Veeteeltkundig Onderzoek (S. Brandsma),
    Zeist
International Dairy Federation, Brussels
International Neighbor Group (C. Houtman), Eindhoven
Abraham Kef, Amsterdam
Kraft Consumer Services, Chicago
Landbouwhogeschool (Dr. H. Mulder, Dr. J. v.d. Poel),
    Wageningen
Mejeribrugets Hjemmemarkedskontor (L. Rasmussen),
    Århus
ir. P. Meyers, Veenendaal
Milk Marketing Board, Thames Ditton

Ministerie van Landbouw (Mr. Edam, ir. P. Tiersma,
    ir. D. Rozeboom), The Hague
Ministerio de Agricultura, Officina de Planificación
    Agrícola, Santiago
Ministerio de Agricultura, Madrid
National Cheese Institute, Chicago
Nationale Zuiveldienst, Brussels
Nederlands Instituut voor Zuivelonderzoek, Ede
Nederlands Zuivelbureau, Rijswijk
Nestlé Nederland, Amsterdam
New Zealand Dairy Board, Wellington
New Zealand Research Institute, Palmerston North
Norske Meieriers Salgssentral (R. Marcussen), Oslo
Novib, The Hague
Ömig, Vienna
Osta og Smjörsalan (O. H. Gunnarsson), Reykjavik
Österreichische Milchwirtschaft, Vienna
Ostmästaren, Riksost (Mr. Regouw), Stockholm
Produktschap voor Zuivel (P. Wehrmann), The Hague
Sancor Cooperatives Unidas, Argentina
Schweizerische Käseunion, Berne
Dave Smith, Grubbenvorst
Société Anonyme des Fermiers Réunis, Paris
Sopexa, Paris
ir. E. Steinbuch, Wageningen
Sterovita, Dordrecht
Svenska Mejeriernas Riksförening (E. Westerberg),
    Stockholm
Syndicat d'Amélioration du Fromage Saint-Nectaire,
    Besse-en-Chandesse
Syndicat des Fabricants de Pont-l'Evêque et de Livarot,
    Caen
Syndicat des Fabricants du Véritable Camembert, Caen
ir. T. C. Tomson, Heiloo
Unigate, Wiltshire
Union des Industriels Laitiers de Basse-Normandie,
    Rouen
United Dairy Industry Association, Rosemont
Valio Finnish Co-operative Dairies Association (A.
    Artimo), Helsinki
Verband der deutschen Milchwirtschaft (Dr. Malich),
    Bonn
J. S. C. Verschoor, Rijswijk
Voorlichtingsbureau voor de Voeding (Drs. A. J. Bakker,
    A. A. van Vloten), The Hague
Zuivelkwaliteitscontrolebureau (A. Swarte), Amsterdam

Glossary

Albumen cheese: cheese made not from the casein protein in the milk alone, but from the albumen protein or from both albumen and casein proteins, which flocculate when heated.

Blue-veined: a term referring to cheeses with a mold culture spreading through their interior; the veining is usually blue or greenish-blue in color.

Body: the interior of the cheese.

Brine: a solution of salt and water; many cheeses are floated in a brine bath to impregnate them with salt.

Brushed rind: see *Washed rind.*

Butter fat: see *Fat content.*

Casein: one of the milk proteins and the most important one in cheesemaking. Under the influence of rennet (or acid), it turns into an insoluble compound: cheese.

Cheddaring: stacking and turning thick parcels of curd to make the curd particles fuse together and form a thick, fibrous mass.

Coagulation: see *Curdling.*

Consistency: the degree of firmness, thickness or viscosity of a cheese, determined primarily on its moisture and fat contents.

Cooked curd: a term referring to cheeses where the ready curd is after-heated by a process where temperatures do not generally exceed 55-60°C (131°-140°F).

Coryne bacteria: see *Washed rind.*

Curd: the thick, junket-like mass obtained by curdling milk; it contains most of the dry matter in milk and a quantity of whey.

Curdling: the thickening of milk under the influence of rennet. Milk can be curdled without rennet, by souring alone, but this is less common.

Curing: ripening.

Dry matter: all the constituents of a cheese, except moisture (water).

Fat content: the proportion of fat in a cheese, usually given as a percentage of the dry-matter content of the cheese (i.e., without moisture).

Internal mold: see *Blue-veined.*

Kneaded cheese: see *Plastic curd cheese.*

Lactation period: time during which a mammal secretes milk, starting with the birth of its young.

Maturation: ripening.

Milk fat: see *Fat content.*

Moisture content: the proportion of moisture (water) in a cheese.

Natural cheese: cheese in which the normal development

and ageing process occurs, as opposed to processed cheese.

Orange-red smear: see *Washed rind.*

Paste: the interior of the cheese.

Pasteurization: the heating of milk to a specified temperature for a specified length of time; this kills most bacteria in the milk.

Plastic curd cheese: cheese of which the curd is heated in hot whey and kneaded, which makes it easily shaped and molded.

Processed cheese: a cheese product made from natural cheese; the natural development of the cheese has been stopped by the processing, rendering the product more uniform and blander than the natural cheese it was made from.

Protein: body-building substance essential to good health; plentiful in milk and cheese, the most important one being casein.

Raw milk: unpasteurized milk.

Red smear: see *Washed rind.*

Rennet: substance obtained from the stomach sacs of young calves (or other suitable mammals), used to curdle the milk.

Rind flora: molds or bacteria growing on the rind of the cheese, which is desirable in many types.

Rindless cheese: natural cheese ripened in foil so that no rind is formed.

Skimmed milk, skim milk: milk from which (part of) the milk fat has been separated.

Sour milk cheese: cheese curdled by souring, rather than by rennet.

Starter: culture of milk acid bacteria, added to the milk to increase its acidity.

Surface ripening: ripening caused by the rind flora.

Washed rind: a term referring to those cheeses of which the rind is kept moist during ripening, by regularly wiping them with a cloth dipped in brine; this encourages an orange-red growth of coryne bacteria to develop on the rind, which may or may not be scraped off or dried.

Whey: the liquid part of the milk, which is separated from the curd (which contains most of the dry matter) in the cheesemaking process.

Whey cheese: cheese made by boiling down whey; it forms a brown, caramelized paste. The term may also be used for albumen cheese.

White mold: the term refers to cheeses that have rinds covered with a growth of white or whitish molds.

Whole milk: non-skimmed milk.

Bibliography

Among the many books consulted by the author, the following are most informative and may be found useful for further reading.

P. Androuet. *Guide du Fromage*. English edition: New York, 1973.

Annual Bulletin International Dairy Federation (1971, Part IV).

J. de Baere. *Een eeuw Belgische zuivelgeschiedenis*. Brussels, 1973.

P. N. Boekel. *De zuivelexport van Nederland tot 1813*. Utrecht, 1929.

Val Cheke. *Cheesemaking in Britain*. London, 1959.

Cheese Varieties and Descriptions. Washington D.C., 1969.

R. J. Courtine. *Larousse des Fromages*. Paris, 1973.

Fromages de France. Paris, 1953.

Douglas Emmons and Stewart Tuckey. *Cottage Cheese and Other Cultured Milk Products*. New York, 1967.

Kiermeier. *Handbuch der Lebensmittelchemie*. Vol. III/1. Berlin, 1968.

Hartl and Kurt Kretschmer. *Europäische Käsesorten*. Glaubendorf, 1967.

Frank Kosikowsky, *Cheese and Fermented Milk Foods*. Michigan, 1966.

W. Köster, *Käse-Lexikon*. Hildesheim, 1969.

Raymond Lindon. *Le Livre de l'Amateur de Fromages*. Paris, 1961.

Heinrich Mair-Waldburg. *Handbuch der Käse*. Kempten, 1974.

Vivienne Marquis and Patricia Haskell. *The Cheese Book*. London, 1966.

Ulrich Neuhaus. *Des Lebens weisse Quellen*. Berlin, 1954.

T. R. Pirtle. *History of the Dairy Industry*.

Christian Plume. *Le Livre du Fromage*. Paris, 1968.

Henry Pourrat. *The Roquefort Adventure*.

George W. Reinbold. *Italian Cheese Varieties*. New York, 1963.

John T. Schlebecker. *A History of American Dairying*. Chicago, 1967.

Die schweizerische Milchwirtschaft. Thun, 1948.

André L. Simon. *Cheeses of the World*. London, 1956.

U. K. D. White. *Roman Farming*. London, 1970.

Harry Wilson and George W. Reinbold. *American Cheese Varieties*. New York, 1965.

Index of recipes

This index refers to the recipes in the section "Recipes with cheese" on pages 206-219.

Index of cheese names

This index lists the names of the cheeses mentioned in this book. Page numbers prefixed "D" refer to a data panel on that page. When a cheese is made in several countries, there is a separate entry for the most important country or countries where it is made. Another entry refers to the remaining countries.

Abaza Peynir 175, D 175
Acid Curd Cottage Cheese 155
Ädelost 43
Agrini 110
Akavi 176
Akkawi 177, D 177
Alcobaca D 128, 129
Alicante, Cabra de 131, D 131
Aligot, Tomme d' 77, 89, D 93
Allgäuer Gaiskäsle 97, D 101
Allievo, Asiago d' 123
Alpkäse, Tiroler 114, D 115
Altajsky Syr 145
Altenburger Milbenkäse 138, D 138
Altenburger Ziegenkäse 138, D 138
Alvorca D 128, 129
Ambert, Chèvreton d' 77, 91, D 93
Ambrosia 42
American Cheese 153, D 156
Amsterdam 68
Ane, Poivre d' 76, 77, D 93
Anejo 159, D 160
Ansgar 98
Anthotiros 136
Appenzell 103, 109, D 113
Aragón 131, D 131
Armada 131
Asadero 159, D 160
Asiago 29, 117, 123, D 126
Asiago d'Allievo 123
Asiago grasso di monte 123
Augelot 83
Aulus 87
Aunis 77, 87, D 92
Aura 45
Auvergne, Bleu d' 77, 90, D 92
Avesnes, Boulette d' 77, 82, D 92
Aveyron, Bleu d' 77, 90, D 92
Azeitas 129
Azul, Queso 162

Baby Edam 70
Baby Gouda 68, 172
Bagnes 109
Baguette 77, 81, D 92
Bakers' Cheese 155
Baladi 177, D 177
Balaton 141, D 141
Balkan, Demi- 143, D 143
Balkanski Kâskaval 143, D 143
Bandal 189, D 189
Banon 76, 77, D 92, 221, 222
Barrel 153
Beaufort 28–29, 77, 78, D 92
Beaufort (de Montagne) 78
Beaufort d'Hiver 79
Beda 170, D 171
Beli Sir u Kriškama 132, D 133
Bellelay 110
Bellos, Queso de los 131

Bellusco, Queso 131
Bel Paese (Italy) 117, 124, D 126, 221
Bel Paese 157, 179
Belyj, Desertnyj 145
Berykäse (Austria) 29, 114, D 115
Berykäse 110
Bernina, Queso 162, D 162
Bethmale 77, 87, D 92
Beyaz Peynir 175, D 175
Bianca, Gorgonzola 122
Bierkäse, Pinzgauer 115, D 115
Bierkäse, Weisslacker 97, D 101
Biestkäse 100
Bijeni Sir 132, D 133
Billinge 42, 43
Bivoljegmleka, Sir iz 133
Bjalo Salamureno Sirene 143
Blanco, Queso (Peru) 163, D 163
Blanco, Queso 164–165, 168
Blarney 64, D 64
Bleu, Château 37
Bleu d'Auvergne 77, 90, D 92, 221
Bleu d'Aveyron 77, 90, D 92
Bleu de Bresse 77, 80, D 92
Bleu de Corse 77, 87, D 92
Bleu de Gex 77, 80, D 92
Bleu de Laqueuille 77, 90, D 92
Bleu des Causses 29, 77, 90, D 92
Bleu de Septmoncel 77, 80, D 92
Bleu de Thiézac 77, 90, D 92
Bleu du Haut Jura 28, 29, 77, 80–82, D 92
Bloukrans 172, D 172
Blue 64, 157, 205
Blue Vein 194
Blue Vinny 53, 62, D 63
Boerenleidse 71
Bola 129
Bola, Queso de 159
Bossons Macérés 76, 77, D 92
Boulette d'Avesnes 77, 82, D 92
Boulette de Cambrai 77, 82, D 92
Boursin 77, D 92, 93
Boxholms Gräddost 41, 43
Braila (See: *Telemea*.)
Branco, Castelo 129, D 128
Bratkäse, Nidwaldner 110
Bresse, Bleu de 77, 80, D 92
Breton, Petit 87
Brick D 156, 157
Brie (France) 29, 92, D 92–93, 221
Brie 36–39, 42, 51, 64, 75, 112, 115, 139, 157, 172, 179
Brie de Coulommiers 77, 92, D 92
Brie de Meaux 77, 92, D 93
Brie de Melun 77, 93, D 93
Brie de Montereau 77, D 92, 93
Brie, Cendré de 93, D 93
Brie, Petit 92
Brienzer Mutschli 110
Brinzâ D 178, 179
Brinzâ de Burduf 142, D 142
Brinzâ in Coajâ de Brad 142, D 142
Brique de Forez 91
Broodkaas 70
Bruccio 77, 87, D 93
Brusselsekaes 73, 75, D 75
Bryndza 140
Bryndza, Liptovská 140, D 140
Buost 42
Burduf, Brinzâ de 142, D 142

Burgos 131, D 131
Butterkäse (Germany) 97, D 101
Butterkäse (Austria) 115
Buttermilchquark 100

Caboc 63
Cabra de Alicante 131, D 131
Cabra de Cadíz 131, D 131
Cabra, Queso de 161, D 161
Cabreiro 129
Cachat 76, 77, D 93
Caciocavallo 29, 126
Cadíz, Cabra de 131, D 131
Caerphilly 58, D 63
Caerphilly 53, 58, 64
Caithness 63
California 155
Cambrai, Boulette de 77, 82, D 92
Camembert (France) 29, 77, 83, 84–85, D 93, 205, 221, 223
Camembert 37, 42, 51, 52, 64, 75, 112, 115, 129, 139, 152, 157, 172, 179, 187, 192
Cancaillotte 80
Cancoillotte 80
Cantal 28, 29, 77, 89, D 93, 221
Cantal Fermier 89
Cantal, Fourme du 29, 89
Cantal Laitier 89
Caprino 117, 126, D 126
Caramkäse 98, D 101
Carré de l'Est 77, 81, 85, D 93, 221
Carré de Saint-Cyr 77, 87, D 93
Cascaval Dobrogea 142
Cascaval Penteleu 142, D 142
Casigiolo 126
Castelo Branco 129, D 128
Castelo de Vide 129
Castillon 77, 87, D 93
Causses, Bleu des 29, 90, D 92
Cebrero 131, D 131
Cecîl 145, D 145
Cendré de Brie 77, 93, D 93
Cerkez Peynir 175
Chabichou 77, 87, D 93, 221, 222
Chanco, Typo 168, D 168
Chantilly, Crème 43
Chaource 29, 77, 93, D 93
Château Bleu 37
Château, Crème 37, 43
Chauna 189
Cheddar (Great Britain) 54–55, 56–57, D 63
Cheddar (Australia) 192, D 192
Cheddar (Canada) 148, D 149
Cheddar (New Zealand) 194, D 194
Cheddar (South Africa) 172, D 172
Cheddar (United States) 153, 155
Cheddar 53, 54, D 63, 64, 75, 93, 138, 139, 165, 171, 179, 185, 187, 196–197, 205, 220, 221, 222, 223
Cheddar, Rindless 153
Cheedam 192, D 192
Cher, Selles-sur- 77, 93, D 93
Cheshire (Great Britain) 53, 59, D 63, 221, 222
Cheshire 64
Chester 59, 138
Chèvreton d'Ambert 77, 91, D 93
Chevrets 78
Chevrotin 77, 91, D 93
Chubut 164

235

Conversion tables

The recipes in this book are based on American measures. The solid American measures are ounces and pounds, equal to the Imperial measures. Butter, flour and a few other ingredients are given in American cups or tablespoons.

The liquid American measures are less than British Imperial Measures. In the recipes whenever "cup," "tablespoon" or "teaspoon" are quoted they are: American cup = 8 fluid ounces; American tablespoon = British dessert spoon; and American teaspoon = a small British teaspoon.

LIQUID MEASURES

American (Standard Cup)			Metric Equivalent
1 cup	$= \frac{1}{2}$ pint	$= 8$ fl. oz.	2.37 dl.
1 Tbs.	$= \frac{1}{2}$ fl. oz.		1.5 cl.
1 tsp.	$= \frac{1}{6}$ fl. oz.		0.5 cl.
1 pint	$= 16$ fl. oz.		4.73 dl.
1 quart	$= 2$ pints	$= 32$ fl. oz.	9.46 dl.

1.1 quart = 1 liter = 10 deciliters = 100 centiliters

British (Standard Cup)			Metric Equivalent
1 cup	$= \frac{1}{2}$ pint	$= 10$ fl. oz.	2.84 dl.
1 Tbs.	$= 0.55$ fl. oz.		1.7 cl.
1 tsp.	$= \frac{1}{5}$ fl. oz.		0.6 cl.
1 pint	$= 20$ fl. oz.		5.7 dl.
1 quart	$= 2$ pints	$= 40$ fl. oz.	1.1 liter

1 cup	= 16 tablespoons
1 table-spoon	= 3 teaspoons

SOLID MEASURES

American/British		Metric	
1 lb.	$= 16$ oz.	= 453 grams	
2.2 lbs.		= 1000 grams	= 1 kilogram
1 oz.		= 28 grams	
$3\frac{1}{2}$ oz.		= 100 grams	

OVEN TEMPERATURES

Degrees Fahrenheit	Degrees Centigrade	Regulo Gas Mark	
240-280	115-135	$\frac{1}{4}$-$\frac{1}{2}$	Very slow
280-320	135-160	1	Slow
320-340	160-170	3	Warm
340-370	170-185	4	Moderate
370-400	185-205	5-6	Fairly hot
400-440	205-225	7	Hot